Atlas of the Holocaust

Map 1

This map shows the main deportation railways to the most destructive of all the concentration camps, Auschwitz. From each of the towns shown on this map, and from hundreds of other towns and villages, Jews were deported to Auschwitz between March 1942 and November 1944, and gassed.

As the maps in this Atlas record, Jews were killed in many other concentration camps, as well as at Auschwitz; in death camps and slave labour camps elsewhere, or at the hands of mobile killing squads.

The Macmillan
Atlas of the Holocaust

Martin Gilbert

Fellow of Merton College, Oxford

A DA CAPO PAPERBACK

Contents

Library of Congress Cataloging in Publication Data

Gilbert, Martin, 1936–
  The Macmillan atlas of the Holocaust.

(A Da Capo paperback)
  Reprint: Originally published: New York: Macmillan, 1982.
  Bibliography: p.
  Includes index.
  1. Holocaust, Jewish (1939–1945). 2. Holocaust, Jewish (1939–1945)—Maps. I.
Title. II. Title: Atlas of the Holocaust.
G1797.21.E29G54   1984   940.53′15′039240222   83-675995
ISBN 0-306-80218-X

This Da Capo Press reprint edition of *Macmillan Atlas of the Holocaust*
is an unabridged republication of the first edition published in
New York in 1982. It is reprinted by arrangement with
Macmillan Publishing Co., Inc.

Published by Da Capo Press, Inc.
A Subsidiary of Plenum Publishing Corporation
233 Spring Street, New York, N.Y. 10013

List of Maps

Special symbols used in this Atlas

00,000   numbers of Jews in a particular country, town or village before the Holocaust, according to the last peace-time census

11,111   number of Jews seeking refuge elsewhere, deported, or confined to a ghetto

22,222   numbers killed, or deported to their deaths

the borders of Greater Germany at the time of any particular map

the front lines at the time of any particular map

acts of resistance or revolt by Jewish groups or individuals

Introduction

The map below shows the birthplaces, places of work, and places of execution of 17 Jews who were murdered during the war years. The text which follows on this page tells, briefly, something of their personal stories. If a similarly short reference were made to each Jew murdered between 1939 and 1945, 353,000 such maps would be needed. To draw these maps at the author's and cartographer's fastest rate of a map a day, would take more than 967 years.

Among the 17 people whom I have chosen for this map is the historian, Simon Dubnow, who had taught at Vilna, Kovno and Berlin, and who was murdered in Riga on 8 December 1941, at the age of 81. Among other Jewish historians murdered by the Nazis was Emanuel Ringelblum, born in Buczacz, who survived the Warsaw ghetto revolt, but was later caught by the Gestapo and murdered, at the age of 44, together with his wife and children *(page 179)*.

Many thousands of doctors, medical men and scientists were also killed, among them the pharmacologist Emil Starckenstein, born in the Bohemian town of Pobezovice, who had made major contributions to preventive medicine, first as a Professor at Prague, and after 1938, as a refugee in Amsterdam. In 1941, at the age of 58, he was deported to Mauthausen and killed *(page 79)*.

Charlotte Salomon was a painter. Born in Berlin, she had fled to France in 1939, at the age of 22. Later she was deported to Auschwitz and gassed. One of her paintings bore the caption: 'I cannot bear this life, I cannot bear these times.' Rudolf Levy, also a painter, was born in Stettin in 1875, and worked with Matisse. In the First World War, as a German soldier, he won the Iron Cross. Fleeing from Berlin to Paris in 1933, from Paris to Florence in 1940, he was deported from Italy to Auschwitz in 1943. That same year, the Munich-born painter Hermann Lismann, who had studied in Lausanne and Rome, was deported from France to Majdanek *(page 155)*.

Harry Baur, a Marseilles dock worker who became known throughout France as 'the king of character actors', died in Berlin in 1943, after being tortured by the Gestapo. A fellow French Jew, René Blum, successor to Diaghilev as director of the Monte Carlo ballet, perished at Auschwitz in 1944.

Many poets were also murdered, among them Mordechai Gebirtig, killed in Cracow *(page 104)*, Samuel Jacob Imber, deported to Belzec *(page 132)*, Yitzhak Katznelson, killed at Auschwitz with one of his sons *(page 183)*, and Miklos Radnoti, a 35-year-old Hungarian who, after more than three years in different slave labour camps, died in October 1944 on a death march from Bor in Yugoslavia to Györ in Hungary *(page 206)*.

Among the hundreds of thousands of teenagers killed was the 15-year-old Yitskhok Rudashevski, who recorded in his diary the day-to-day life and moods of the Vilna ghetto *(page 156)*, and Judit Sandor, from Budapest, who survived both the death camps and the war itself, but was too weak to survive the peace, and died at Karlstad, in Sweden, in September 1945, shortly after her seventeenth birthday *(page 236)*.

Janusz Korczak, writer of children's stories, educator and social worker, was murdered at Treblinka with all 200 children from his Warsaw orphanage. He had insisted on accompanying them to the death camp. Alice Salomon, director of the children's home at La Rose, near Marseilles, also voluntarily joined her children, when they were deported to Auschwitz *(page 155)*.

In all, more than a million Jewish children

Map 2

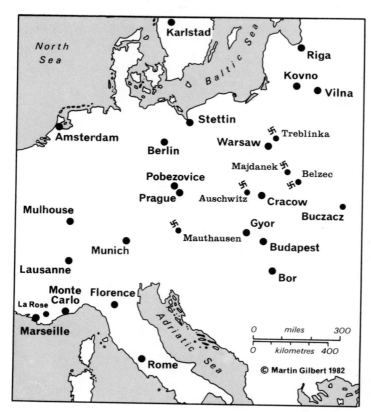

were murdered by the Nazis, among them the three-year-old Pierre Roth, born in Mulhouse *(page 146)*. Thousands of children were shot in the streets, or separated from their parents for the terrible journey to the death camps. Even the tiniest infants were brutally murdered, many wrenched from their mothers' arms, as both were shot, beaten to death, or gassed.

With the death of so many children, future generations were also destroyed, and the natural descent of generation to generation was unnaturally cut off. We shall never know what these million and more children would have made of their lives, had evil men not marked them out to die.

The 314 maps that follow show, in chronological sequence, the destruction of each of the main Jewish communities of Europe, as well as acts of resistance and revolt, avenues of escape and rescue, and the fate of individuals.

The story told in these maps is not complete, nor can the statistics, however carefully researched, be comprehensive. 'With all the resources in the world', as Professor Yehuda Bauer has said, 'it is impossible to show – or even to know – all that was done.'

For each community whose pre-war strength, or war-time destruction, I have been able to plot on one of these maps, two or three other communities existed, particularly smaller ones, for which there is either no room in this Atlas, or for which there is no evidence beyond the knowledge that they were in fact destroyed. The Nazi aim was to blot out these communities and all they represented of life, heritage and culture. Although the Nazis made no specific effort to record every killing, their general efficiency and sense of order was such that much detailed evidence survives of the killings in progress, often as set down at the time by the killers themselves.

The aim of this Atlas is to trace each phase of Hitler's war against the Jewish people: against all those with Jewish blood or of Jewish descent, wherever they could be found. It therefore traces the German conquest of territory in which Jews had lived for centuries, the first random but brutal killings, the enforced expulsions of ancient communities, the setting up of ghettos, the deliberate starvation of tens of thousands – at least 4,000 a month in Warsaw alone – the round-ups and deportations, the creation and

working of the death camps, the slave labour system, the death marches, and the executions up to the very moment of liberation.

The photographs show the places, and some of the people, against whom this enormous organization and effort of murder was directed. Most of them, tragically, are anonymous. Nevertheless, the people in these photographs were real people. Their faces once meant struggle and sorrow, joy and laughter, to those who knew them.

Although this Atlas is one of Jewish suffering, no book or atlas on any aspect of the Second World War can fail to record that in addition to the six million Jewish men, women and children who were murdered at least an equal number of non-Jews was also killed, not in the heat of battle, not by military siege, aerial bombardment or the harsh conditions of modern war, but by deliberate, planned murder. Hence, even in this Atlas, which traces the Jewish story, mention has frequently been made, often as an integral part of the Jewish fate, of the murder of non-Jews. These include Polish civilians killed after Poland's capitulation *(page 38)*, the first, mostly non-Jewish, victims at Auschwitz *(page 46)*, the tens of thousands of victims of the Nazi euthanasia programme *(page 51)*, the non-Jews killed with Jews in the slave labour camps of the Sahara *(page 56)*, the Serbs killed with Jews in April 1941 and January 1942 *(pages 58 and 87)*, the Czech villagers massacred at Lidice *(page 101)*, the Poles expelled and murdered in the Zamosc province *(page 139)*, the Gypsies deported to the death camps *(page 141)*, the non-Jews killed with Jews in the reprisal action in Rome *(page 181)*, Greeks and Italians taken hostage and drowned with Jews in the Aegean *(page 192)*, the French villagers massacred at Oradour-sur-Glane *(page 195)*, and the tens of thousands of Gypsies, Russian prisoners-of-war, Spanish republicans, Jehovah's Witnesses and homosexuals murdered at Mauthausen *(pages 232-3)*.

I have tried in this Atlas to give a chronological presentation of how the Holocaust evolved, and to show how that evolution was bound up with the changing course of the Second World War. The facts set down here will I hope add to our knowledge of what was done to the Jews, with particular reference to where it was done, in what circumstances, and on what massive a scale throughout every territory which came under Nazi domination.

Acknowledgments

The sources for all the facts shown in this Atlas are given in the Bibliography on pages 246-253. In gathering this material, and in preparing the maps themselves, I was particularly inspired by Rabbi Hugo Gryn, a survivor of Auschwitz, whom I first met in the spring of 1974, when work on the Atlas was beginning. His desire to see the story told in as much detail as possible has been a strong influence on my work; as were his personal encouragement and specific suggestions at every stage in drafting the maps and preparing the text.

For Hugo Gryn, as for many of the survivors who have helped me to collect material, or have encouraged me to map particular events, the act of recollection itself is often painful. They feel strongly, however, that unless the full scale and range of the slaughter is set down, many of its episodes will never be recorded, thus blurring the full enormity of the Holocaust, and reducing it to little more than a footnote to the history of the Second World War.

As the work proceeded, I also gained inspiration from the work of the French lawyer and historian, Serge Klarsfeld, whose father was deported from Paris to Auschwitz and perished there, and whose own comprehensive edition of the deportation lists of Jews from France, first published in 1978, is not only a model of scrupulous historical research, but also provided the basic material for thirty-three of the maps in this Atlas.

For the maps themselves, I am indebted to the cartographic work of Terry Bicknell, who transformed my rough and tentative drafts into maps of the highest quality. The Atlas owes much to his skills and patience.

As the maps evolved, I was helped considerably by the kindness and wisdom of Dr Shmuel Krakowski, the Director of Archives at Yad Vashem, Jerusalem, and himself a survivor, who not only provided me with valuable material, but also encouraged me in my researches: his knowledge of the fate of Polish Jewry in the war years, and of events in many other regions, has been an indispensable help, as has been his own pioneering work on Jewish resistance in Poland between 1942 and 1944.

I am also grateful to Professor Yehuda Bauer, of the Institute of Contemporary Jewry at the Hebrew University of Jerusalem, who scrutinized the maps when they were still in draft, and who gave me important guidance as to themes and sources; some of the most important research work on the Holocaust is being done by his pupils, and under his supervision.

When the maps were already at an advanced stage, they were helped by the critical scrutiny of Dr Arthur Cygielman.

Two institutions, Yad Vashem in Jerusalem and the Wiener Library in London, provided me with considerable help from their own substantial holdings, both published and manuscript. I was also helped in my search for materials, and for other reference works, by the late Dr Chaim Pazner, who not only gave me enormous personal encouragement, but also introduced me to the experts at Yad Vashem, whose assistance has been of considerable value.

I am also grateful to Taffy Sassoon, who helped to collate the material once it was assembled, and who translated documents and articles from Hebrew and Yiddish. The typing of the texts was done by Esther Gerber, who came specially from Jerusalem to Oxford for this task, and by Sue Rampton.

In its last phase, the Atlas benefitted from the cartographic corrections of Danuta Trebus, whose work was financed in part by a grant from the Memorial Foundation for Jewish Culture. Work on the original maps was made possible by the generosity of Rex and Deborah Harbour.

My sincere thanks are also due to Frederick A. Praeger, of Westview Press, Boulder, Colorado, for his encouragement of the project in its early stages; to Max J. Holmes, of Holmes and Meier; to Martin Savitt, and the Board of Deputies of British Jews, which published an illustrated 23-map school edition in 1978; to Arthur Wang, of Hill and Wang, who published this school edition in the United States; and to Paul Shaw, then Educational Officer to the Board of Deputies, who gave me good guidance on the presentation and content of many of the maps at this early but important planning stage, and who encouraged me to continue with the present larger work.

I am also grateful to Michael O'Mara, Managing Director of George Rainbird Ltd, whose interest in the project has been a main factor in its fulfilment, as was his appointment of Erica Hunningher as its editor. Her efforts on behalf of the Atlas have been continuous, persistent and substantial.

Many people have written to me with suggestions for specific maps, or have answered my own requests for information. In this regard I should like to thank: Chana Abells; Dr Yitzhak Arad, Chairman of the Directorate, Yad Vashem, Jerusalem; the late Ehud Avriel; Dr Gershon Bacon; Dr Konstantin Bazarov; Professor Shlomo Ben-Ami; Andras Bereznay; Professor Yehuda Blum; John A. Broadwin; Peter Brod; Hyam Corney; Dr Szymon Datner; Professor Dr L. de Jong, Director, Netherlands State Institute for War Documentation; Adina Drechsler; Melvin Durdan; Dr Elizabeth Eppler, Assistant Director, Institute of Jewish Affairs, London; Henning Gehrs, Librarian, Museet For Danmarks Frihedskamp 1940-1945, Copenhagen; Richard Grunberger; Clara Guini, Reference Librarian, Yad Vashem, Jerusalem; Professor Yisrael Gutman; Jerzy Herszberg; Alfred Herzka; Professor Daniel Ivin; Stanislaw Kania, Main Commission for the Investigation of Nazi Crimes in Poland; Hadass Kaufman, Secretary of Archives, Yad Vashem, Jerusalem; Dr Rivka Kauli; Donald Kenrick; Dr J. Kermish, Director of Archives, Yad Vashem; Warren Kimball; Yehudit Kleiman; Erich Kulka; Janet Langmaid; Naomi Laqueur; Curt Leviant; Dr Dov Levin; Karin Levisen, Press and Cultural Department, Royal Danish Embassy, London; Lawrence Litt; Fritz Majer-Leonhard; Hadassa Modlinger; Miriam Novitch; Thomas Orszag-Land; Professor Dr Czeslaw Pilichowski, Director of the Main Commission for the Investigation of Nazi Crimes in Poland; Hayim Pinner; Leon Pommers; Leslie Reggel; Matthew Rinaldi; Dr S. J. Roth, Director, Institute of Jewish Affairs; Dr Livia Rothkirchen, editor of *Yad Vashem Studies,* Jerusalem; Michele Sarfatti, Centro Di Documentazione Ebraica Contemporanea, Milan; Dr Schulz, Landeshauptarchiv, Koblenz; A. E. Scopelitis, Embassy of Greece, London; Mrs M. Segall; Tovia Shahar; Dr Shmuel Spector; Jennie Tarabulus; Michael Tregenza; Harold Werner; and K. Zailinger, Director, Service Social Juif, Brussels.

The photographs in this volume come principally from the archives of Yad Vashem, Jerusalem. Others are from: Serge Klarsfeld (title page, and 145); The Main Commission for the Investigation of Nazi Crimes in Poland, Warsaw (page 209); The Museum of Denmark's Fight for Freedom 1940-1945, Copenhagen (page 167); I am grateful to those who put these photographic archives at my disposal; and to Tomasz Krasowski, who accompanied me on my own journey through Poland during which I took the photographs on pages 16, 82, 103, 148 and 182. The photograph on page 155 was taken by me in 1976.

As with each of my books, the support and advice of my wife Susie has been of inestimable value, both in terms of the structure of the work, and of her scrutiny of its content at every stage in the long process of evolution; to her are due not only my thanks, but also those of every reader who finds the Atlas of service.

I should welcome any corrections, and also any extra material, for future editions, to add to the existing maps, or to help prepare new maps.

Martin Gilbert
Merton College
Oxford

12 March 1982

Map 3

ANTI-JEWISH VIOLENCE BEFORE THE FIRST WORLD WAR

Baltic Sea

Dusyata

TSARIST RUSSIA

Siemiatycze [1]
Minsk
Bialystok [80]
Mogilev
WHITE RUSSIA
Warsaw
Lodz
Brest-
Siedlce [30]
Litovsk
Gomel [12]
Pinsk
Starodub
Czestochowa
Lublin
THE PALE
Konotop
VOLHYNIA
Nyezhin
Zhitomir
Kiev
Pereyaslav
PODOLIA
Smyela
Botosani
UKRAINE
Dorohoi
Elizavetgrad
Burdujeni
Sulita
Ekaterinoslav
Ananayev
Tirgul Frumos
Kishinev [49]
Nikolaiev
Melitopol
Jassy
Odessa [300]
Bacau
Akkerman
Sea of Azov
CRIMEA
RUMANIA
Simferopol
Calarasi [60]
Black Sea

© Martin Gilbert 1982

0 miles 150
0 kilometres 200

Jews had lived throughout Europe for more than a thousand years. But no century had passed without their being attacked, expelled and killed.

Before the First World War, several hundred Jews had been killed in a series of violent attacks, or 'pogroms', in all the towns shown above, throughout western Russia and Rumania. As on each of the maps that follow, the numbers of those killed are shown inside a black box.

The murder of 49 Jews in Kishinev in 1903 led to protests throughout the Christian world; but the pogroms had continued.

Immediately after the First World War, tens of thousands of Jews were murdered in the western Ukraine (*opposite*). In a single town, Proskurov, the numbers killed far exceeded the total deaths in 40 years of pogroms throughout Tsarist Russia.

Further killings took place in Hungary in 1919, with the overthrow of the Communist regime, in which some Jews had played a prominent part. In Germany, at Nuremberg, Munich, Rosenheim, Zwickau, Coburg and Salzburg, Adolf Hitler preached hatred of

Map 4

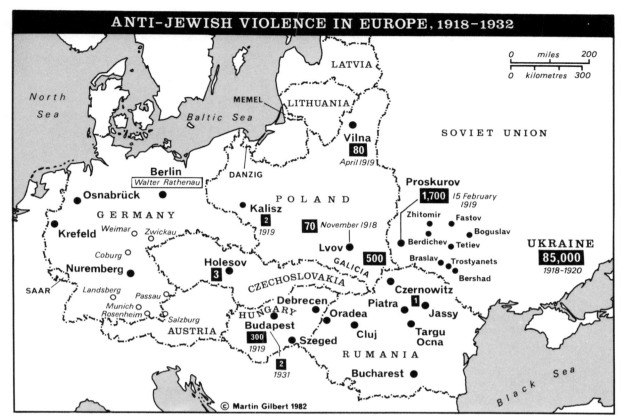

ANTI-JEWISH VIOLENCE IN EUROPE, 1918-1932

North Sea

Baltic Sea

LATVIA

MEMEL

LITHUANIA

SOVIET UNION

DANZIG

Vilna
80
April 1919

Proskurov
1,700 *15 February 1919*

Berlin
Walter Rathenau

Osnabrück •

P O L A N D

Zhitomir   Fastov

GERMANY

Kalisz
2
1919

70 *November 1918*

Berdichev   Tetiev   Boguslav

Krefeld •

Weimar ○   Zwickau ○

Lvov •

500

Braslav   Trostyanets

UKRAINE
85,000
1918-1920

Coburg ○

GALICIA

Bershad

Nuremberg •

Holesov
3

CZECHOSLOVAKIA

Czernowitz
1

SAAR   Landsberg ○   Passau ○

Debrecen   Piatra

Jassy

Munich ○
Rosenheim ○   Salzburg ○

Oradea

Cluj

Targu
Ocna

AUSTRIA

HUNGARY

Budapest
300
1919

Szeged

R U M A N I A

2
1931

Bucharest •

Black Sea

© Martin Gilbert 1982

the Jew as part of his National Socialist, or 'Nazi', philosophy. 'It is our duty', he declared in 1920, 'to arouse, to whip up, and to incite our people to instinctive repugnance of the Jews.'

In Berlin, in 1922, anti-semites murdered Walter Rathenau, the German Foreign Minister, and in 1923 Jewish houses in Berlin were attacked.

In the Moravian town of Holesov, in 1918, three Jews had been murdered. In eastern Poland, in 1918 and 1919, Jews were attacked and killed in Vilna, Lvov and throughout Galicia, where more than 500 Jews were killed.

In Rumania, in December 1922, restrictions were imposed on the percentage of Jewish students at Cluj University; then at universities in Jassy, Bucharest and Czernowitz, where Jewish students were attacked. Three years later at Piatra, synagogues and schools were looted and the Jewish cemetery desecrated. In 1926 a Jewish student was murdered at Czernowitz, and his murderer acquitted. In 1927, during anti-Jewish riots in Oradea, four synagogues were wrecked, while prayer houses were plundered in Jassy, Targu Ocna and Cluj.

But it was in Germany that anti-semitism gained its greatest hold. Between 1922 and 1933 there were 200 instances in Nuremberg alone of desecration of Jewish graves. Also in Nuremberg, the first issue of a vicious anti-semitic newspaper, *Der Stürmer,* was published in 1923. The newspaper proclaimed as its banner slogan 'The Jews are our misfortune'.

Following his unsuccessful attempt to seize power in Munich in 1924, Hitler was imprisoned at Landsberg. From there, on 18 July 1925, he published the first part of *Mein Kampf (My Struggle),* in which he wrote with venom of the Jews. The second part was published on 10 December 1926.

Out of prison, Hitler rebuilt his Nazi party, and at 'Party Day' in Weimar in 1926, and again at Nuremberg in 1927, many speakers advocated driving the Jews out of German life. In 1927 Jewish cemeteries were desecrated by Nazi gangs: at Osnabrück and Krefeld the synagogues were wrecked. In Berlin, on 12 September 1931, the eve of the Jewish New Year, Nazi gangs attacked Jews returning from synagogue.

On 30 January 1933, Adolf Hitler became Chancellor of Germany. He was to rule Germany for nearly twelve years, until his suicide in Berlin on 30 April 1945.

Map 5

TWO THOUSAND YEARS OF JEWISH LIFE IN EUROPE BY 1933

NORWAY
82 years

ESTONIA
600 years

DENMARK
311 years

LATVIA
400 years

HOLLAND
800 years

MEMEL
269 years

LITHUANIA
600 years

BELGIUM
700 years

WHITE RUSSIA
550 years

DANZIG
400 years

Wlodawa

GERMANY
1,612 years

UKRAINE
816 years

POLAND
800 years

LUXEMBOURG
647 years

CZECHOSLOVAKIA
1,000 years

CRIMEA
1,900 years

SAAR
312 years

AUSTRIA
1,030 years

HUNGARY
1,900 years

FRANCE
1,930 years

RUMANIA
1,800 years

ITALY
2,100 years

YUGOSLAVIA
1,000 years

BULGARIA
1,900 years

GREECE
2,233 years

RHODES
2,000 years

0 miles 300
0 kilometres 400

© Martin Gilbert 1982

From the moment that Hitler became Chancellor of Germany, he worked to transform one of Europe's most civilised states into a totalitarian dictatorship, and to deny Germany's half million Jews the basic rights of citizenship. Yet Jews had lived on German soil since the time of the Roman Empire. Despite often savage persecution in medieval times, and frequent expulsions from town to town, they had continued, over a period of sixteen centuries, to make their contribution to the development of

Map 6

THE JEWS OF GERMANY AND THE TRIUMPH OF NAZISM, 1933-1938

North Sea

Baltic Sea

MEMEL

DANZIG

EAST PRUSSIA

Hamburg 19,794

Esterwegen *concentration camp 1933*

Sachsenhausen *concentration camp 1933*

HOLLAND

Berlin 172,672

GERMANY

POLAND

BELGIUM

Cologne 16,093

Sachsenburg *concentration camp 1933*

Breslau 23,240

UPPER SILESIA

Buchenwald *concentration camp 1937*

Leipzig 12,594

Frankfurt 29,385

LUXEMBOURG

SAAR

CZECHOSLOVAKIA

FRANCE

Nuremberg 8,603

Dachau *concentration camp 1933*

Munich 10,068

45 *Jews murdered 1933-1935*

SWITZERLAND

AUSTRIA

HUNGARY

0 miles 100
0 kilometres 160

© Martin Gilbert 1982

modern Germany. Elsewhere in Europe the earliest Jewish communities dated back even further: the map opposite shows the age of those communities in countries which were to come under German rule or influence between 1933 and 1945.

The photograph, taken in 1980, is of a seventeenth-century synagogue in the present-day Polish town of Wlodawa.

From the very first days of Nazi rule in Germany, concentration camps were set up (*above*). Critics of the regime were sent to these camps, as were thousands of individuals against whom Nazi hatred was directed, including homosexuals, for whom the law was particularly severe, socialists, dissident clergymen, and Jews. Brutality by guards led to many deaths in these camps from the first days of Hitler's rule.

In July 1935 the *Manchester Guardian*

published the following description of the interrogation of a prisoner at the hands of the Gestapo: 'His head was wrapped in a wet cloth that was knotted so tightly across his mouth that his teeth cut into his lips and his mouth bled profusely. He was held by three assistants while the official and another assistant took turns in beating him with a flexible leather-covered steel rod (*Stahlrute*). When he fainted from pain and loss of blood he was brought to by means of various other tortures . . . He was told that he might write a letter to his wife, as he would never see her again. The assistants fingered their pistols and discussed which of them should shoot the prisoner. But he remained silent. He was released some time afterwards.' Similar press reports appeared regularly outside Germany: by 1935 at least 45 Jews had been murdered in Dachau alone.

Map 7

THE JEWS OF THE SAAR, 1 MARCH 1935

GERMANY

LUXEMBOURG

Sötern
95

Bosen
25

Bettingen
25

Neunkirchen
213

Tholey
41

Brotdorf
26

Hilbringen
28

Merzig
204

SAAR

Saint
Wendel
130

Ottweiler
55

Diefflen
29

Nalbach
29

Dillingen
135

Pachten
3

Saarwellingen
151

Illingen
107

Saarlouis
274

Fraulautern
37

Merchweiler
26

Waldmohr
21

FRANCE

Bous
5

Wadgassen
6

River Saar

Homburg
128

Differten
8

Saint Ingbert
76

Saarbrücken
2,650

Blieskastel
8

| 0 | miles | 10 |

| 0 | kilometres | 15 |

©Martin Gilbert 1982

The first territory outside Hitler's control to be incorporated inside Nazi Germany was the Saar (*above*). This small but prosperous province had been separated from Germany in 1919, under the Treaty of Versailles, but was then returned, as a result of a plebiscite, overwhelmingly in Germany's favour. The plebiscite, held under the auspices of the League of Nations, took place on 13 January 1935. Jews had lived in the city of Saarbrücken since the fourteenth century. Under the League of Nations administration between 1920 and 1935, their civil, political and personal rights had been protected by the minority statutes of the League. Outside Saarbrücken itself, there were some 25 rural communities with Jewish inhabitants, ranging in size from the 274 Jews of Saarlouis, to single Jewish families.

On 1 March 1935, six weeks after the plebiscite, the Saar became an integral part

of Germany (*opposite, below*) and was at once subjected to all the rigours of Nazism, including the anti-Jewish legislation, the rule of the Gestapo, and the concentration camps. Almost all the Jews of the Saar chose French or Belgian citizenship. By 1938, when the Saarbrücken synagogue was burned down during the 'night of broken glass' (*page 26*), only 177 Jews were still living in the city.

In Upper Silesia (*opposite*), the first record of a Jewish community dates back to the eleventh century when, in 1060 a synagogue near Ratibor was seized by the town authorities and transformed into a church. There is also a record of Jews being persecuted in Leobschütz a century later, in 1163. Many of the earliest Jewish settlers in this region were poor; fugitives from the crusades or from persecution further east.

Despite more than six centuries of persecution, the Jews of Upper Silesia

THE JEWS OF UPPER SILESIA, 15 JULY 1937

Pitschen
31

Landsberg
20

Kreuzburg
160

Rosenberg
102

Jellowa

Königshuld

Hitler Sea

Guttentag
145

LOWER SILESIA

GERMANY

POLAND

Malapane

Grottkau
40

Falkenburg
51

Oppeln
607

UPPER SILESIA
to Germany

Tworog
5

Patschkau Ottmachau

Niesse
220

Gogolin

Gross Strehlitz
145

Tost

Beuthen
3,500

Oberglogau
50

Peiskretscham
45

Neustadt
100

Cosel
80

Gleiwitz
1,899

Ziegenhals

Stanitz

Hindenburg
1,200

Leobschütz
111

Bauerwitz
4

EAST UPPER SILESIA
to Poland

Katscher
42

Ratibor
640

CZECHOSLOVAKIA

© Martin Gilbert 1982

emerged in the nineteenth century as a small but progressive community. When, after the First World War, the region was returned to Germany, the minority rights of the Jews shown here were protected. This was a result of the German-Polish Convention of 15 May 1922. Even after Hitler came to power in 1933, these minority rights were upheld by the League of Nations, and the imposition of Nazi racial laws was prevented, following a Jewish petition, the 'Bernheim Petition', to the League. But the Convention itself expired on 15 July 1937, bringing the Jews of Upper Silesia, like those of the Saar two years before, within the full rigour of Nazi rule.

THE GERMAN REICH, 1935-1937

North Sea

Baltic Sea

Sachsenhausen

Berlin
GERMANY

Warsaw

UPPER SILESIA

SAAR

Dachau

Prague

Cracow

Munich

© Martin Gilbert 1982

0 ____ miles ____ 200
0 ____ kilometres ____ 400

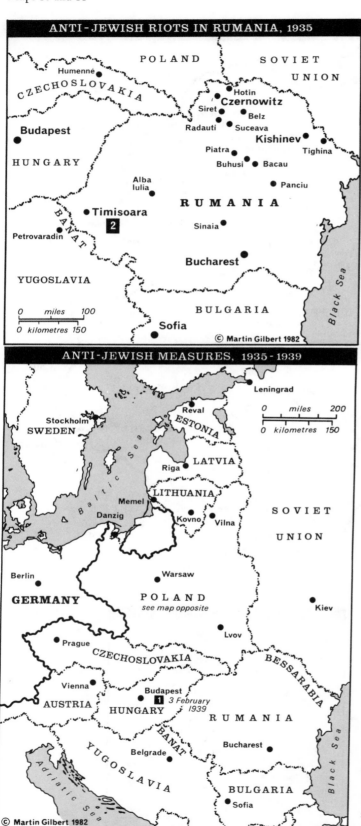

ANTI-JEWISH RIOTS IN RUMANIA, 1935

POLAND

SOVIET UNION

CZECHOSLOVAKIA

Humenné

Hotin

Czernowitz

Siret

Belz

Radauti

Suceava

Budapest

Kishinev

HUNGARY

Piatra

Tighina

Buhusi

Bacau

Alba Iulia

Panciu

R U M A N I A

Timisoara

2

Sinaia

Petrovaradin

BANAT

Bucharest

YUGOSLAVIA

BULGARIA

Black Sea

Sofia

| 0 | miles | 100 |
| 0 | kilometres | 150 |

© Martin Gilbert 1982

ANTI-JEWISH MEASURES, 1935-1939

Leningrad

Reval

| 0 | miles | 200 |
| 0 | kilometres | 150 |

Stockholm

SWEDEN

ESTONIA

Baltic Sea

LATVIA

Riga

LITHUANIA

Memel

SOVIET UNION

Danzig

Kovno

Vilna

Berlin

Warsaw

GERMANY

POLAND

see map opposite

Kiev

Lvov

Prague

CZECHOSLOVAKIA

BESSARABIA

Vienna

Budapest

1 3 February 1939

AUSTRIA

HUNGARY

RUMANIA

BANAT

Adriatic Sea

Belgrade

Bucharest

YUGOSLAVIA

Black Sea

BULGARIA

Sofia

© Martin Gilbert 1982

In the 1930s anti-Jewish violence spread through eastern Europe. It was particularly fierce in Rumania, where attacks on Jews took place in each of the towns shown on the map *(left)*. In universities throughout Rumania, student members of an influential anti-semitic organization, the Iron Guard, prevented Jewish students from attending lectures. From 1934, no new Jewish lawyers were allowed to enter the legal profession. In 1936 the Iron Guard exploded a bomb in a Jewish theatre in Timisoara, killing two Jews, and injuring many more.

In November 1936, at Petrovaradin in Yugoslavia, the editor of an anti-semitic paper modelled on the Nazi *Der Stürmer,* was tried and acquitted. In August 1937, at Humenne in Czechoslavakia, Jews were accused of sacrilege.

In Lithuania *(left, below),* severe restrictions were imposed on the number of Jews allowed to enter universities; in the 1936 university entrance, not a single Jewish student was granted admittance to study medicine.

Anti-Jewish laws now began to appear in the statute books of several countries. On 21 January 1938 Rumania formally abrogated the minority right of Jews, and revoked the citizenship of many Jews who had been resident there since the end of the war.

On 29 May 1938 the Hungarian Government passed its first law specifically restricting the number of Jews in the liberal professions, administration, commerce and industry to 20 per cent, while on 3 May 1939 a second 'Jewish Law' forbade any Hungarian Jew to become a judge, a lawyer, a schoolteacher, or a member of Parliament.

Such laws encouraged anti-semitism and led to violence. On 3 February 1939 a bomb thrown into a Budapest synagogue killed one worshipper and injured many more.

But it was in Poland that violence against the Jews was most widespread between 1935 and 1937. In every town and village shown on the map opposite, Jews were attacked in the streets, and Jewish houses and shops were broken up and looted. It was necessary, a Polish Jesuit periodical asserted in 1936, 'to provide separate schools for Jews, so that our children will not be infected with their lower moralty'. On 29 February 1936 Cardinal Hlond declared in a public letter: 'It is true that the Jews are committing frauds, practising usury, and dealing in white slavery. It is true that in schools, the influence of the Jewish youth upon the

Map 12

ANTI-JEWISH VIOLENCE AND JEWISH SELF-DEFENCE IN POLAND, 1935-1937

LITHUANIA

EAST PRUSSIA

DANZIG

Suwalki

Grodno

Jasionowka

Bydgoszcz

Lomza

Bialystok

Wysokie Mazowieckie

Suraz

Raciaz

Dybek

Bransk

Wloclawek

Plonsk

Stok

Serock

Sterdyn

River Vistula

Stoczek

Warsaw

Kaluszyn

Brest-Litovsk

Zyrardow

Otwock

Minsk Mazowiecki

Lukow

Warka

POLAND

River Bug

Nowe Miasto

Odrzywol

Piotrkow

Opoczno

Przytyk

3

Lublin

Kleszcow

Kamiensk

Dzialoszyn

Radomsko

Przedborz

79

Czestochowa

Jews killed throughout Poland between 1935 and 1937

Koniecpol

Jedrzejow

SILESIA

Zarki

Imielno

Stawiany

Mierzwin

Stawy

5

River Vistula

Katowice

Lvov

Myslenice

| 0 | miles | 40 |
| 0 | kilometres | 60 |

© Martin Gilbert 1982

Catholic youth is generally evil, from a religious and ethical point of view. But let us be just. Not all Jews are like that. One does well to prefer his own kind in commercial dealings and to avoid Jewish stores and Jewish stalls in the markets, but it is not permissable to demolish Jewish businesses, break windows, torpedo their houses . . .'

On 9 March 1936, in the village of Przytyk (*above*), the murder of three Jews sent further fears through Poland's three million Jews. A few days later, five Jews were murdered in the village of Stawy. Despite Jewish self-defence, as shown here in the Warsaw region and indicated by the star symbol, 79 Jews were killed, and 500 injured.

During 1937 there were further attacks on Jews throughout Poland: 350 attacks in August alone, and in Katowice bombs were thrown into Jewish-owned shops. Tens of thousands of Polish Jews emigrated: to France, Belgium, Holland and Palestine.

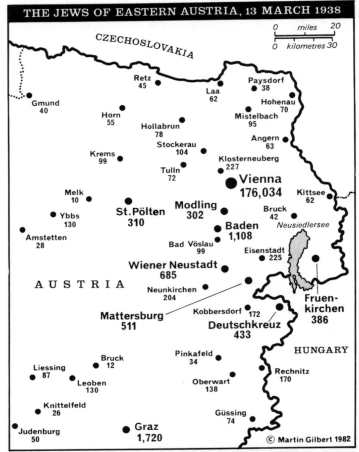

THE JEWS OF EASTERN AUSTRIA, 13 MARCH 1938

CZECHOSLOVAKIA

0   miles   20
0   kilometres   30

- Gmund 40
- Retz 45
- Paysdorf 38
- Laa 62
- Hohenau 70
- Horn 55
- Mistelbach 95
- Hollabrun 78
- Angern 63
- Stockerau 104
- Krems 99
- Klosterneuberg 227
- Tulln 72
- Melk 10
- **Vienna 176,034**
- Kittsee 62
- Ybbs 130
- **Modling 302**
- Bruck 42
- **St.Pölten 310**
- *Neusiedlersee*
- Amstetten 28
- **Baden 1,108**
- Bad Vöslau 99
- Eisenstadt 225
- **Wiener Neustadt 685**
- A U S T R I A
- Neunkirchen 204
- **Fruen-kirchen 386**
- **Mattersburg 511**
- Kobbersdorf 172
- **Deutschkreuz 433**
- HUNGARY
- Liessing 87
- Bruck 12
- Pinkafeld 34
- Leoben 130
- Rechnitz 170
- Knittelfeld 26
- Oberwart 138
- Güssing 74
- Judenburg 50
- **Graz 1,720**

© Martin Gilbert 1982

ANTI-JEWISH RIOTS IN POLAND. APRIL-JUNE 1938

- *Baltic Sea*
- LITHUANIA
- GREATER GERMANY
- EAST PRUSSIA
- Vilna 29 April
- SOVIET UNION
- Warsaw 8 to 15 June
- P O L A N D
- Dabrowa 15 April
- Przemysl 13 June
- CZECHOSLOVAKIA
- EASTERN GALICIA
- Tarnopol 11 and 12 June
- Vienna

0   miles   100
0   kilometres   150

© Martin Gilbert 1982

Jews had lived in Austria since Roman times. In 1867, following the abolition of all laws based on religious discrimination, Jews had risen to prominence in Austrian life and culture. They had come to Vienna from all over the Austro-Hungarian Empire, especially from the impoverished province of Eastern Galicia.

In 1919 the Treaty of St Germain guaranteed minority rights to the Jews of Austria. Most lived in Vienna *(left)*, but as the map shows, some were to be found in the towns and villages of every region: the Austrian census of 22 March 1934 listed 769 localities with Jewish inhabitants.

Following the violent suppression of the Social Democrat parties in 1934, anti-Jewish discrimination grew, and Austrian Nazism was encouraged by the German Nazis in power across the border.

On 13 March 1938 Germany annexed Austria, and a further 183,000 Jews came under German rule. The activities of all Jewish organizations and congregations were at once forbidden. Many Jewish leaders were imprisoned; several were taken to Dachau and murdered. The Great Synagogue of Vienna was first desecrated by organized hooligans, then 'occupied' by the German army. Many Jews were forced to turn their property over to the Gestapo. Individual Jews were seized in the streets, beaten, and even killed. More then 500 Jews, driven to despair, committed suicide.

In Poland a further spate of anti-Jewish activity broke out within three weeks of the imposition of Nazi rule in Austria *(left, below)*. Starting in Dabrowa on April 15, hundreds of Jews had been injured, and much Jewish property destroyed.

From Poland, and from Greater Germany, which now included Austria, tens of thousands of Jews sought safety elsewhere *(opposite, above)*. More than 85,000 Austrian Jews found havens in Britain, the United States, and in countries which were later to fall under Nazi rule. From Germany almost half of the country's 500,000 Jews emigrated or fled abroad *(opposite, above)*, including more than 33,000 to Palestine, where they joined tens of thousands of recent Jewish immigrants from Poland. But on 5 July 1938, with the opening of the Evian Conference, it became clear that more and more countries wanted to restrict the number of Jewish refugees. The Australian delegate at Evian declared: 'since we have no racial problem, we are not desirous of importing one'.

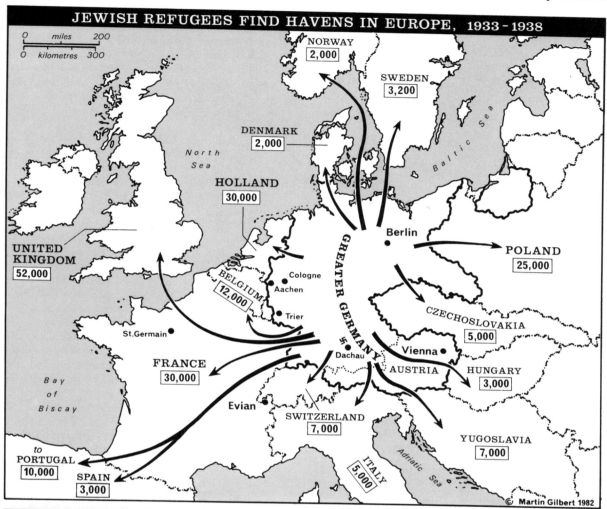

JEWISH REFUGEES FIND HAVENS IN EUROPE, 1933-1938

0 miles 200
0 kilometres 300

NORWAY
2,000

SWEDEN
3,200

DENMARK
2,000

North Sea

Baltic Sea

HOLLAND
30,000

Berlin

GREATER GERMANY

POLAND
25,000

UNITED KINGDOM
52,000

BELGIUM
12,000

Cologne
Aachen
Trier

CZECHOSLOVAKIA
5,000

St.Germain

Vienna

HUNGARY
3,000

FRANCE
30,000

Dachau

AUSTRIA

Bay of Biscay

Evian

SWITZERLAND
7,000

YUGOSLAVIA
7,000

ITALY
5,000

Adriatic Sea

to PORTUGAL
10,000

SPAIN
3,000

© Martin Gilbert 1982

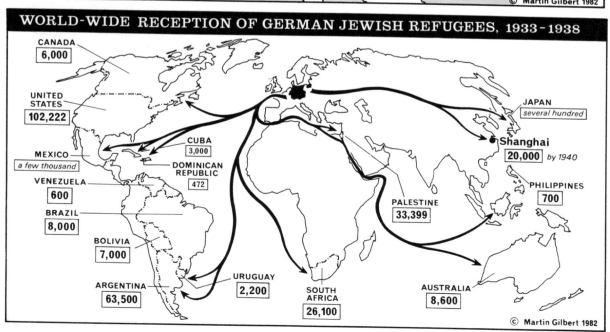

WORLD-WIDE RECEPTION OF GERMAN JEWISH REFUGEES, 1933-1938

CANADA
6,000

UNITED STATES
102,222

JAPAN
several hundred

CUBA
3,000

MEXICO
a few thousand

DOMINICAN REPUBLIC
472

Shanghai
20,000 by 1940

PHILIPPINES
700

VENEZUELA
600

BRAZIL
8,000

PALESTINE
33,399

BOLIVIA
7,000

URUGUAY
2,200

ARGENTINA
63,500

SOUTH AFRICA
26,100

AUSTRALIA
8,600

© Martin Gilbert 1982

Map 17

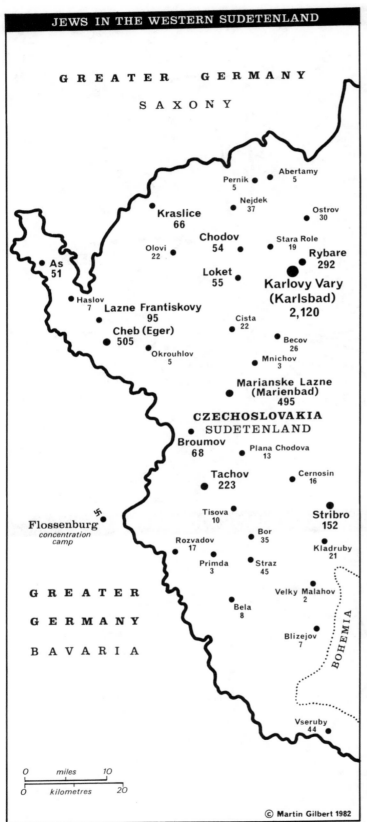

JEWS IN THE WESTERN SUDETENLAND

GREATER GERMANY

SAXONY

Pernik
5

Abertamy
5

Nejdek
37

Ostrov
30

Kraslice
66

Chodov
54

Stara Role
19

Rybare
292

Olovi
22

Karlovy Vary
(Karlsbad)
2,120

As
51

Loket
55

Haslov
7

Lazne Frantiskovy
95

Cista
22

Cheb (Eger)
505

Becov
26

Okrouhlov
5

Mnichov
3

Marianske Lazne
(Marienbad)
495

CZECHOSLOVAKIA
SUDETENLAND

Broumov
68

Plana Chodova
13

Tachov
223

Cernosin
16

Tisova
10

Stribro
152

Flossenburg
concentration camp

Bor
35

Rozvadov
17

Kladruby
21

Primda
3

Straz
45

Velky Malahov
2

GREATER

Bela
8

GERMANY

Blizejov
7

BAVARIA

BOHEMIA

Vseruby
44

0   miles   10

0   kilometres   20

© Martin Gilbert 1982

In October 1938, only six months after the German annexation of Austria, Germany annexed the Sudeten-German region of Czechoslovakia *(opposite)*. The area inside the broken line is shown in detail in the map on the left. Here, too, was a long-established Jewish community, whose origins went back, in Cheb for example, to the thirteenth century.

Between the wars the Jews of the Sudetenland were protected by the democratic and egalitarian laws of Czechoslovakia, and were living in towns and villages throughout the region. The map on the left, based on the national census of 1930, shows the Jewish communities in the western areas. The largest of these towns, Karlsbad, known in Czech as Karlovy Vary, had long been a popular resort town and meeting place for Jews. Two Zionist Congresses had been held there in 1921 and 1923. At Marienbad, known in Czech as Marianske Lazne, Jewish doctors had contributed to the development of the spa, whose cures had been popular with Russian Jews during the nineteenth century. In 1937 the Great Assembly of the union of orthodox Jews had been held there.

Beginning in 1933, the Jews of the Sudetenland were increasingly harassed by local, German-speaking, Nazis. During the Sudeten crisis in the autumn of 1938, many synagogues were burned down, including the synagogues at both Cheb and Marienbad on September 23. As the Germans prepared to occupy the region, almost all the 20,000 Sudetenland Jews fled into the still independent Czechoslovak provinces of Bohemia and Moravia. Those who remained were arrested by the Nazis, and sent to concentration camps.

Following the German occupation of the Sudetenland in October 1938, the borders of Greater Germany, as shown opposite, were extended yet again. So too was the concentration camp system, with the opening of a new camp at Flossenbürg, and the enlargement of Dachau. Another new camp, Buchenwald, had been opened on 19 July 1937, for professional criminals. In June 1938 many political prisoners, including Jews, were sent there, followed shortly afterwards by a further 2,200 Austrian Jews.

The photograph shows a rollcall at Dachau in 1938. Often during such rollcalls the prisoners, Jews and non-Jews alike, were forced to stand for many hours, hungry and cold, and were savagely beaten if they fell.

Map 18

THE JEWS OF THE SUDETENLAND, OCTOBER 1938

North Sea

Baltic Sea

MEMEL

DANZIG

EAST PRUSSIA

Sachsenhausen

Berlin

Warsaw

HOLLAND

GREATER GERMANY

P O L A N D

Buchenwald

SAAR

SUDETENLAND

Prague

Flossenburg

BOHEMIA

TESCHEN

20,000

MORAVIA

Zilina

CZECHOSLOVAKIA

F R A N C E

SLOVAKIA

RUTHENIA

Dachau

Munkacs

Munich

Bratislava

Vienna

A U S T R I A

H U N G A R Y

RUMANIA

0   miles   100

0   kilometres   150

© Martin Gilbert 1982

Map 19

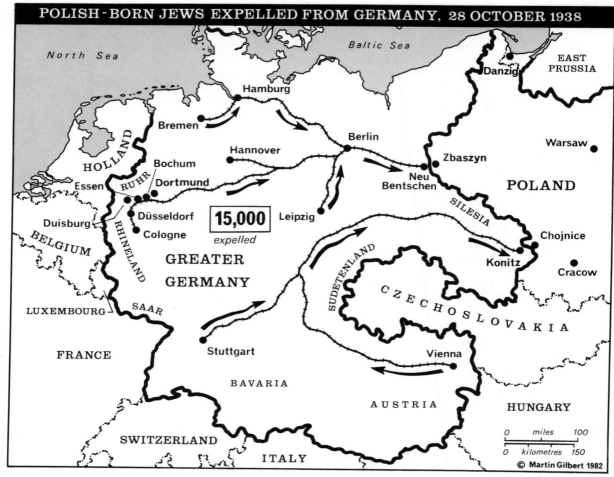

POLISH-BORN JEWS EXPELLED FROM GERMANY, 28 OCTOBER 1938

The next group of Jews to suffer under German policy were 15,000 Polish-born Jews who had been living and working in Germany for 10, 20 and even 30 years. Early in October 1938 the Polish Government announced that all Jews who had lived outside Poland for more than five years would have their passports revoked, and they would thereupon become 'stateless'. The Germans at once announced there would no longer be a place inside Germany for these 15,000 'stateless' Jews.

On October 18 these 15,000 Jews were forced to leave their homes throughout Germany, and to go, with only a single suitcase, to the nearest railway station. The rest of their belongings had to be left behind. Then they were taken through the night to the German-Polish border, and forced over the border at gun point.

At first the Polish Government was reluctant to take them in. Conditions, especially at the border town of Zbaszyn (above), were appalling. Learning of this, a member of one of the families which had been expelled, a young man named Herszel Grynszpan, who was living in France, shot and killed a German diplomat in Paris.

Using the diplomat's death as their excuse, the Nazis launched a campaign of terror against all the Jews of Greater Germany. On 9 November 1938, in one night, the so-called 'night of broken glass', hundreds of synagogues were set on fire, Jewish shops looted, and Jews beaten up in the streets. By morning, 91 Jews had been killed. All the towns shown in the map opposite (above) were the scene of anti-Jewish violence, as were hundreds of smaller towns, villages and hamlets throughout Greater Germany.

The lower map shows the towns in one small region of Germany, with their Jewish populations of 1932. Each of these little communities was likewise attacked during the 'night of broken glass'.

The photograph shows the fire raging in the principal synagogue in Berlin.

DESTRUCTION OF THE SYNAGOGUES, 9 NOVEMBER 1938

91 Jews killed

© Martin Gilbert 1982

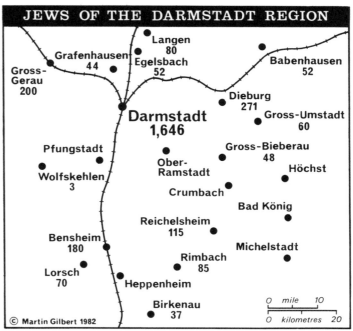

JEWS OF THE DARMSTADT REGION

Langen 80
Grafenhausen 44
Egelsbach 52
Babenhausen 52
Gross-Gerau 200
Dieburg 271
Gross-Umstadt 60
Darmstadt 1,646
Pfungstadt
Gross-Bieberau 48
Ober-Ramstadt
Höchst
Wolfskehlen 3
Crumbach
Bad König
Reichelsheim 115
Michelstadt
Bensheim 180
Rimbach 85
Lorsch 70
Heppenheim
Birkenau 37

© Martin Gilbert 1982

Map 22

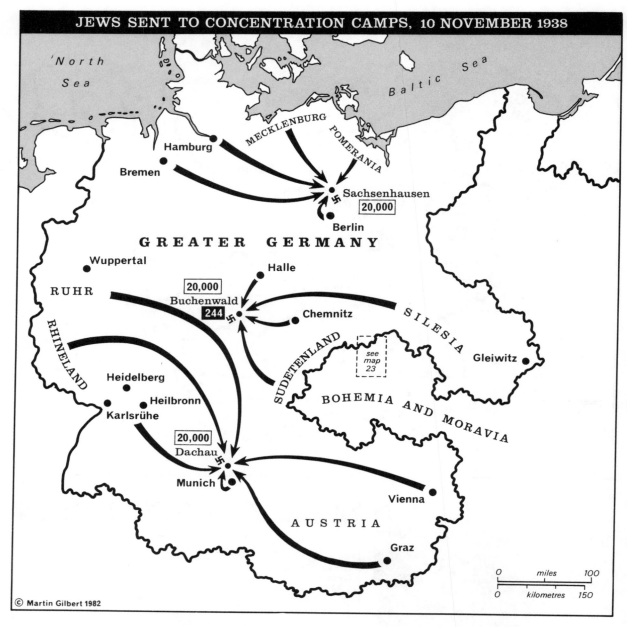

JEWS SENT TO CONCENTRATION CAMPS, 10 NOVEMBER 1938

'North Sea

Baltic Sea

Hamburg

Bremen

MECKLENBURG

POMERANIA

Sachsenhausen
20,000

Berlin

GREATER GERMANY

Wuppertal

Halle

RUHR

20,000
Buchenwald
244

Chemnitz

SILESIA

Gleiwitz

RHINELAND

SUDETENLAND

Heidelberg

see map 23

Heilbronn

Karlsrühe

BOHEMIA AND MORAVIA

20,000
Dachau

Munich

Vienna

AUSTRIA

Graz

0   miles   100

0   kilometres   150

© Martin Gilbert 1982

Immediately following the 'night of broken glass', more than 35,000 Jews were seized throughout Germany, and sent to concentration camps, bringing to more than 60,000 the total number of Jews in the camps (*above*). Hundreds died of ill-treatment, including 244 at Buchenwald alone in the first month of their imprisonment. Hundreds more committed suicide as a result of the harsh conditions and the brutality of the guards.

In March 1939 Hitler ordered his armies to enter the Bohemian and Moravian provinces of Czechoslovakia (*opposite, below*). Tens of thousands of Jews were trapped, many of them refugees from Germany and Austria who had fled to Bohemia and Moravia a year before. Other Jews fled from Slovakia to Poland, as the Slovak province, where anti-semitic activities had been growing, declared its independence.

Jews had first been mentioned in Prague in AD 970, the first settled community in 1091. They survived repeated expulsions in the seventeenth century, to enjoy religious liberty and their own civil jurisdiction by 1700. Forbidden to follow many of the trades of the time, they had come to excel as

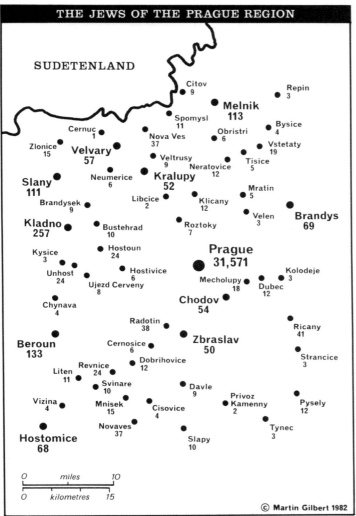

THE JEWS OF THE PRAGUE REGION

SUDETENLAND

Citov 9
Repin 3
Melnik 113
Spomysl 11
Bysice 4
Cernuc 1
Nova Ves 37
Obristri 6
Vstetaty 19
Zlonice 15
Velvary 57
Veltrusy 9
Neratovice 12
Tisice 5
Neumerice 6
Kralupy 52
Mratin 5
Slany 111
Brandysek 9
Libcice 2
Klicany 12
Kladno 257
Bustehrad 10
Roztoky 7
Velen 3
Brandys 69
Kysice 3
Hostoun 24
Prague 31,571
Unhost 24
Hostivice 6
Mecholupy 18
Kolodeje 3
Ujezd Cerveny 8
Dubec 12
Chynava 4
Chodov 54
Radotin 38
Ricany 41
Beroun 133
Cernosice 6
Zbraslav 50
Strancice 3
Liten 11
Revnice 24
Dobrihovice 12
Svinare 10
Davle 9
Privoz Kamenny 2
Pysely 12
Vizina 4
Mnisek 15
Cisovice 4
Novaves 37
Tynec 3
Hostomice 68
Slapy 10

Scale: 0 miles 10 / 0 kilometres 15

© Martin Gilbert 1982

BOHEMIA AND MORAVIA ANNEXED, 15 MARCH 1939

North Sea
Baltic Sea
MEMEL
DANZIG
EAST PRUSSIA
Berlin
RUHR
GREATER GERMANY
POLAND
SUDETENLAND
SAAR
Prague
BOHEMIA
RUTHENIA
MORAVIA
SUDETENLAND
SLOVAKIA
BAVARIA
Vienna
HUNGARY
AUSTRIA

Scale: 0 miles 100 / 0 kilometres 200

© Martin Gilbert 1982

THE JEWS OF MEMEL, 21 MARCH 1939

Scale: 0 miles 30 / 0 kilometres 40

Memel 2,470
LITHUANIA 7,000
Baltic Sea
MEMELLAND
River Nieman
River Nova
GREATER GERMANY
EAST PRUSSIA
● Königsberg

© Martin Gilbert 1982

shoemakers, tailors, hatters, furriers and goldsmiths. Jewish musicians often played at banquets in the palaces of the nobility. Known as excellent fire-fighters, a group of 400 Jewish firemen were present at all festivities, and at coronations. But no Jew was allowed to call himself a citizen of Prague, and outside the Jewish quarter all Jews were compelled to wear yellow badges and peaked yellow hats.

Slowly, the situation improved: in 1677 a royal edict had been issued against throwing stones at Jews. By 1800 Prague had become a centre of Hebrew printing, learning and scholarship, and in the century before 1938 the Jews of Prague knew emancipation, cultural vitality, prosperity, and hope.

When German troops entered Prague on 15 March 1939, the city's 31,571 Jews, ten per cent of the total population, had been joined by a further 25,000 refugees from the towns and villages of Bohemia shown here (*above, left*), whose Jewish populations are given according to the census of 1930.

Thousands of Czech Jews sought to escape, both by legal and illegal means. By the end of 1939 more than 19,000 had succeeded in leaving Europe altogether. But the rest were trapped.

Six days after the German occupation of Prague, Hitler sent his forces into Memel (*above, right*). Here, the local Jewish community could trace its origins back to the sixteenth century. In 1924 Memel had become an autonomous region under Lithuanian sovereignty. Its minorities were protected by the League of Nations. By 1939, the 2,470 Jews of Memel had been joined by 7,000 Lithuanian Jews.

With the German occupation of Memel, most Jews fled into Lithuania.

Map 26

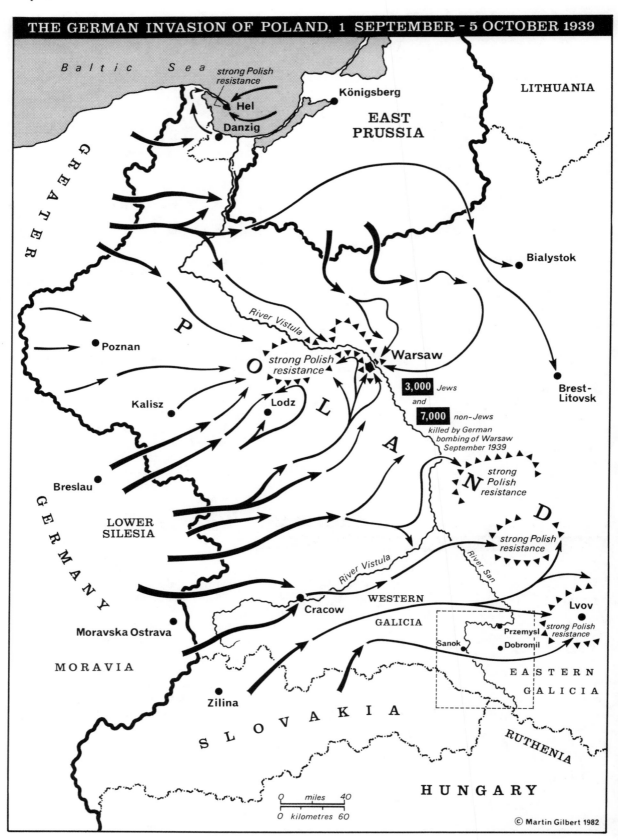

THE GERMAN INVASION OF POLAND, 1 SEPTEMBER - 5 OCTOBER 1939

Baltic Sea

LITHUANIA

strong Polish resistance

Königsberg

Hel

Danzig

EAST PRUSSIA

GREATER

Bialystok

River Vistula

Poznan

strong Polish resistance

Warsaw

Brest-Litovsk

P

O

L

A

N

D

3,000 *Jews*

and

7,000 *non-Jews*

killed by German bombing of Warsaw September 1939

Kalisz

Lodz

strong Polish resistance

strong Polish resistance

Breslau

LOWER SILESIA

GERMANY

River Vistula

River San

strong Polish resistance

Lvov

WESTERN GALICIA

Cracow

Przemysl

strong Polish resistance

Moravska Ostrava

Sanok

Dobromil

MORAVIA

Zilina

EASTERN GALICIA

S L O V A K I A

RUTHENIA

O   *miles*   40

O   *kilometres*   60

© **Martin Gilbert** 1982

HUNGARY

Map 27

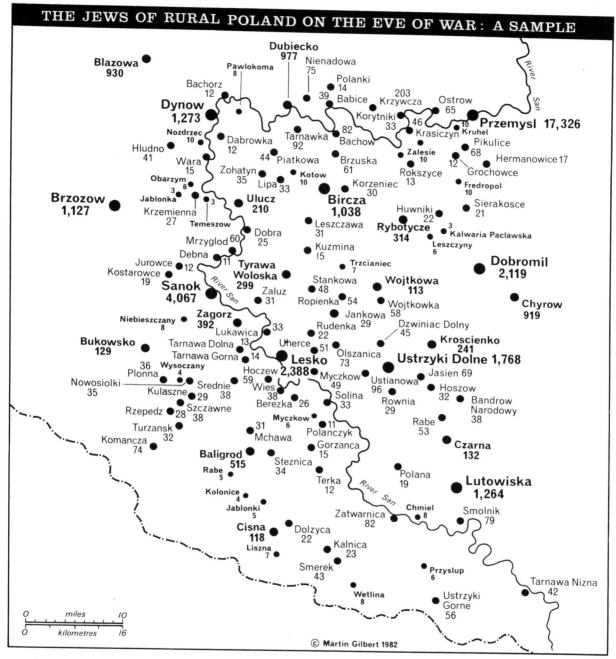

THE JEWS OF RURAL POLAND ON THE EVE OF WAR: A SAMPLE

© Martin Gilbert 1982

On 1 September 1939 the German army invaded Poland, advancing across a land where Jews had lived for over 800 years. The map above shows the number of Jews living in a small area of Poland, which in September 1939, was on one of the lines of advance of the German army as it drove through Poland.

The map on the left shows the main line of advance of the German army: the thicker arrows show the advance in the first five days of September, the thinner arrows, the advance in the next two weeks.

Rapid though the German advance was, the Polish forces fought with skill and bravery at many points, checking the German forces in a series of fierce battles. During the fighting, more than sixty thousand Polish soldiers were killed, of whom some 6,000 were Jews. In addition 3,000 Jewish civilians were among those killed during the bombing of Warsaw.

Map 28

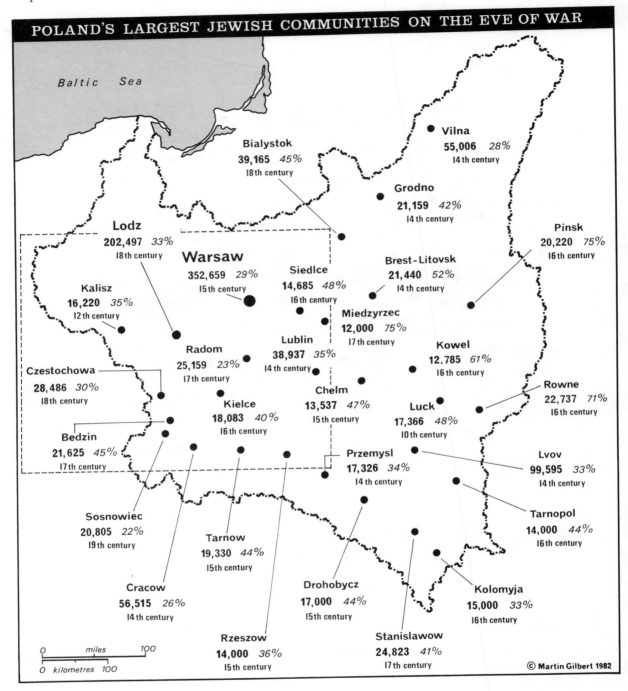

POLAND'S LARGEST JEWISH COMMUNITIES ON THE EVE OF WAR

Baltic Sea

Vilna
55,006 *28%*
14th century

Bialystok
39,165 *45%*
18th century

Grodno
21,159 *42%*
14th century

Pinsk
20,220 *75%*
16th century

Lodz
202,497 *33%*
18th century

Warsaw
352,659 *29%*
15th century

Siedlce
14,685 *48%*
16th century

Brest-Litovsk
21,440 *52%*
14th century

Kalisz
16,220 *35%*
12th century

Miedzyrzec
12,000 *75%*
17th century

Radom
25,159 *23%*
17th century

Lublin
38,937 *35%*
14th century

Kowel
12,785 *61%*
16th century

Czestochowa
28,486 *30%*
18th century

Chelm
13,537 *47%*
15th century

Rowne
22,737 *71%*
16th century

Kielce
18,083 *40%*
16th century

Luck
17,366 *48%*
10th century

Bedzin
21,625 *45%*
17th century

Przemysl
17,326 *34%*
14th century

Lvov
99,595 *33%*
14th century

Sosnowiec
20,805 *22%*
19th century

Tarnopol
14,000 *44%*
16th century

Tarnow
19,330 *44%*
15th century

Drohobycz
17,000 *44%*
15th century

Kolomyja
15,000 *33%*
16th century

Cracow
56,515 *26%*
14th century

Rzeszow
14,000 *36%*
15th century

Stanislawow
24,823 *41%*
17th century

0   *miles*   100

0   *kilometres*   100

© **Martin Gilbert 1982**

The map above shows those Polish cities with 12,000 or more Jewish inhabitants at the time of the census of 1931. Also given is the percentage of Jews among the total population of the town.

On the map opposite are some of the towns in which, from the first days of the German occupation, Jews were singled out for abuse, violence, and death. The figures show only some of those killed, mostly in savage attacks on Jews at prayer, or in random shootings. Thousands of Jews, and thousands of non-Jews, were killed during these early days of German rule. Jews, who formed a tenth of the Polish population, accounted for nearly a third of those killed. The photograph, taken by a German soldier, shows a typical incident, 'mocking a Jew'.

Map 29

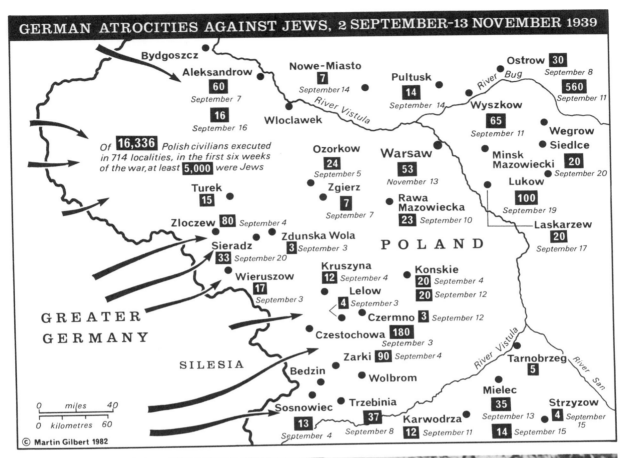

GERMAN ATROCITIES AGAINST JEWS, 2 SEPTEMBER–13 NOVEMBER 1939

Bydgoszcz

Aleksandrow
60
September 7
16
September 16

Nowe-Miasto
7
September 14

Pultusk
14
September 14

Ostrow **30**
September 8
560
September 11

River Bug

River Vistula

Wloclawek

Wyszkow
65
September 11

Wegrow
Siedlce

Of **16,336** *Polish civilians executed in 714 localities, in the first six weeks of the war, at least* **5,000** *were Jews*

Ozorkow
24
September 5

Warsaw
53
November 13

Minsk
Mazowiecki

20
September 20

Lukow
100
September 19

Turek
15

Zgierz
7
September 7

Rawa
Mazowiecka
23 *September 10*

P O L A N D

Laskarzew
20
September 17

Zloczew **80** *September 4*

Sieradz
33 *September 20*

Zdunska Wola
3 *September 3*

Wieruszow
17
September 3

Kruszyna
12 *September 4*

Lelow
4 *September 3*

Czermno **3** *September 12*

Konskie
20 *September 4*
20 *September 12*

G R E A T E R
G E R M A N Y

Czestochowa **180**
September 3

River Vistula

River San

S I L E S I A

Bedzin

Zarki **90** *September 4*

Wolbrom

Tarnobrzeg
5

Mielec
35
September 13

Strzyzow
4 *September 15*

0 miles 40
0 kilometres 60

Sosnowiec
13
September 4

Trzebinia
37
September 8

Karwodrza
12 *September 11*

14 *September 15*

© **Martin Gilbert 1982**

Map 30

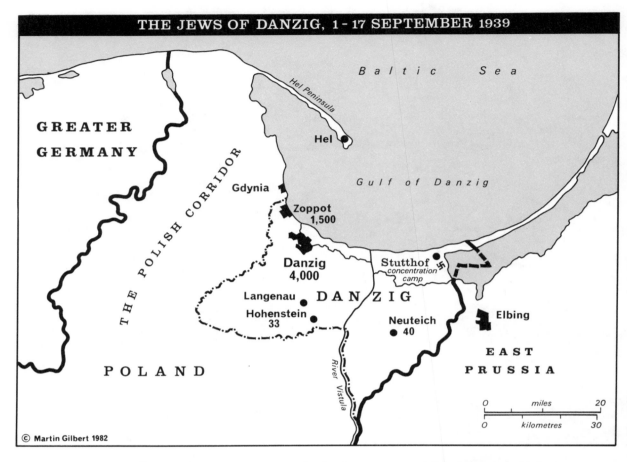

THE JEWS OF DANZIG, 1-17 SEPTEMBER 1939

Following the German invasion of Poland, and even while that invasion was in progress, German troops entered the Free City of Danzig, which was immediately annexed to the German Reich. With the dominance of the local Nazi Party in Danzig in 1937, many of Danzig's 9,000 Jews had managed to emigrate to western Europe, Britain, the United States and Palestine. But more than 5,000 Jews, many of them old people, were trapped in the city as the German army entered on 1 September 1939 (above).

On September 2, as German control was imposed throughout the Danzig territory, a concentration camp was opened at Stutthof, and two weeks later several hundred leading Danzig Jews, including the writer and journalist, Jacob Lange, and the cantor of the Danzig synagogue, Leopold Shufflan, were deported there. Within a week most of them had died as a result of deliberate brutality.

On September 9, while German troops still battled with Polish forces, all Jewish men in the small Ruhr town of Gelsenkirchen (opposite, above) were deported to the concentration camp of Sachsenhausen, near Berlin. Of the original Jewish community of 1,400 in 1933, nearly 700 had managed to emigrate by 1939. Now, scarcely a week after the outbreak of war, the men were sent eastwards, and the women and children left to fend for themselves.

By the end of the German-Polish campaign, 6,000 Jewish soldiers had been killed and as many as 400,000 Polish soldiers had been captured, of whom some 61,000 were Jews. The Jews were at once separated from the Poles: thousands were sent to prisoner-of-war camps inside Germany, where they were denied the basic rights of prisoners-of-war and treated instead as if they were concentration camp inmates, with less rations than other prisoners, forced to do especially heavy work. At Lamsdorf 5,000 Jewish prisoners were housed in barns, 700 or 800 to each barn, without any floor covering, and one loaf of bread had to be shared by six or eight men. At Rathorn the two days' ration for five men was one loaf of bread and half a jar of soup. At Stablack, as a result of savage beatings by the German overseers at the various construction works

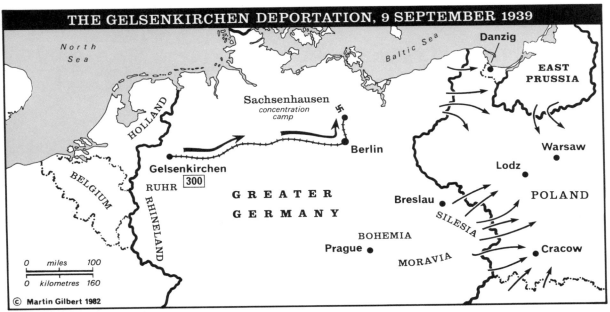

THE GELSENKIRCHEN DEPORTATION, 9 SEPTEMBER 1939

© Martin Gilbert 1982

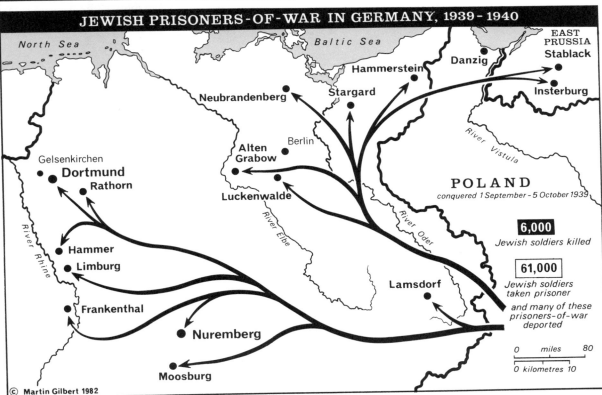

JEWISH PRISONERS-OF-WAR IN GERMANY, 1939-1940

POLAND
conquered 1 September – 5 October 1939

6,000
Jewish soldiers killed

61,000
Jewish soldiers taken prisoner

and many of these prisoners-of-war deported

© Martin Gilbert 1982

to which they were sent, 10 to 15 Jews died each day. At Neubrandenburg the German commander issued instructions in October 1939 to the effect that all 'Aryan' prisoners-of-war were entitled to the uniforms and personal effects of their fellow Jewish prisoners. As a result, the Jews were sent to work half-naked and barefoot, and many of them froze to death.

These Jewish prisoners-of-war were among the first victims of a Nazi policy that, while severe at all times against conquered peoples, singled out Jews for particularly savage treatment. For the fate of some surviving Jewish prisoners-of-war in 1944 and 1945, see pages 204, 211 and 217.

Map 33

THE GERMAN-SOVIET PARTITION OF POLAND, 28 SEPTEMBER 1939

On 28 September 1939 Poland was partitioned between Nazi Germany and the Soviet Union, while Lithuania annexed the Vilna region. In the following two months, before the border was sealed, more than a quarter of a million Jews escaped from the German to the Soviet side. These Jews were to constitute the majority of the survivors of Polish Jewry by the end of the war (page 242).

The map above shows the number of Jews living in the three principal divisions of Poland at the time of the German invasion. With the eastward extension of the frontiers of Greater Germany, nearly two million more Jews were brought under German rule: four times the number of Jews who had been living in Germany when Hitler came to power in January 1933.

The first German acts of terror in Poland had been the September murders (page 33). Now a new policy was put briefly and brutally into operation: expulsion. The figures shown on the map opposite give some of the main expulsions eastward, where figures are available. By the end of 1939, tens of thousands of Jews had been driven to the border rivers and forced to swim them. Hundreds had been drowned as they tried to cross. Others had been shot and killed as they swam.

Of the 1,800 Jews driven from Chelm, only 400 survived the perils of expulsion. Hundreds of others were denied refuge at the last moment when Soviet soldiers refused to allow them to cross into Soviet territory.

Map 34

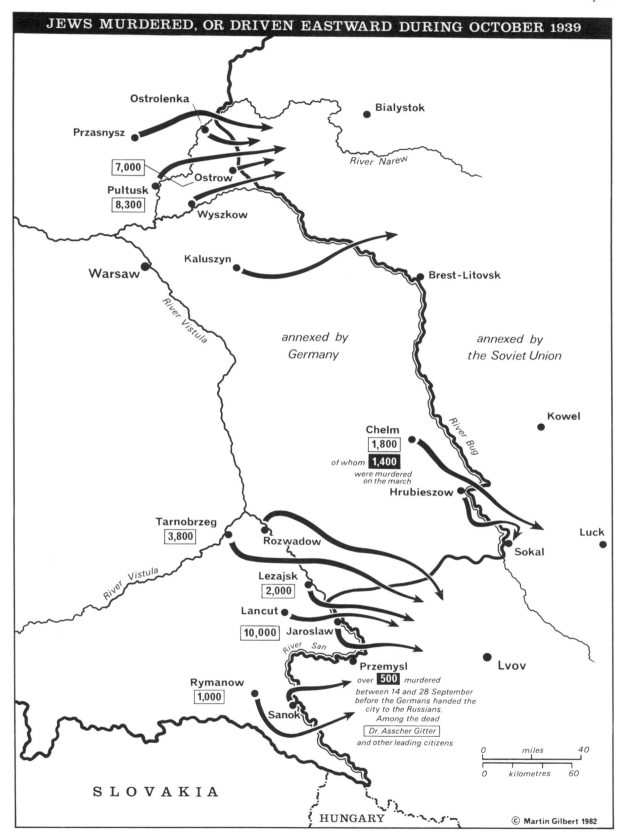

JEWS MURDERED, OR DRIVEN EASTWARD DURING OCTOBER 1939

Ostrolenka

Bialystok

Przasnysz

River Narew

7,000 — Ostrow

Pultusk

8,300

Wyszkow

Warsaw

Kaluszyn

Brest-Litovsk

River Vistula

annexed by
Germany

annexed by
the Soviet Union

Kowel

River Bug

Chelm

1,800

of whom 1,400

*were murdered
on the march*

Hrubieszow

Luck

Tarnobrzeg

3,800

Rozwadow

Sokal

River Vistula

Lezajsk

2,000

Lancut

10,000 Jaroslaw

River San

Przemysl

Lvov

over 500 *murdered*

Rymanow

1,000

*between 14 and 28 September
before the Germans handed the
city to the Russians.
Among the dead*

Sanok

Dr. Asscher Gitter

and other leading citizens

0 ___ *miles* ___ 40

0 ___ *kilometres* ___ 60

S L O V A K I A

HUNGARY

© Martin Gilbert 1982

Map 35

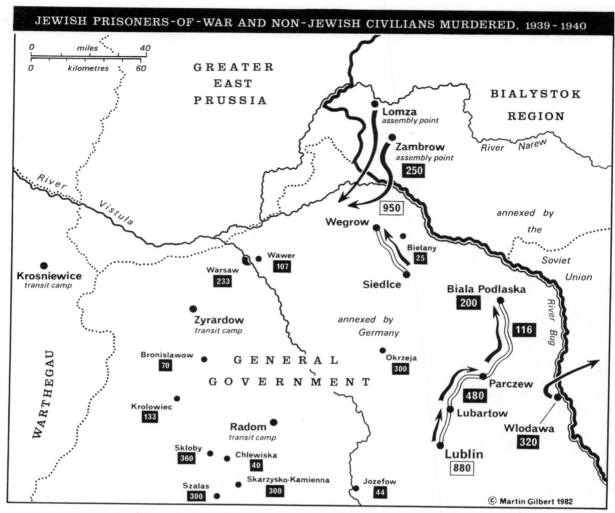

JEWISH PRISONERS-OF-WAR AND NON-JEWISH CIVILIANS MURDERED, 1939-1940

In the opening months of the Second World War the Germans particularly ill-treated Jewish soldiers who had been taken prisoner while fighting with the Polish army. Some were sent to Germany *(page 35)*. Others, kept in Poland, were also treated savagely from the first days of their capture. Those at the assembly points of Lomza and Zambrow *(above)* were to be transferred under German escort to the German side of the partition line. But of the 1,200 assembled at Zambrow, 250 were murdered on the spot.

At the transit camp at Zyrardow, the Jewish prisoners-of-war were kept in the local stadium for 10 days without food, surviving only because local Poles managed to throw food in to them. On the Day of Atonement, 24 September 1939, these Jewish prisoners-of-war were forced to clean the latrines with their bare hands, and treated with particular brutality.

Another group that suffered terribly were

the Jewish soldiers whom the Germans took prisoner during the Polish campaign, whose birthplaces were in those parts of eastern Poland which had just been annexed by the Soviet Union. One train load was brought to Wlodawa, to be sent eastward across the border; 200 had died of hunger or had frozen to death during the journey from central Poland. Near Wlodawa, the survivors were made to take the corpses out of the train. The SS guards then opened fire, killing 120 more of the prisoners.

A further group of Polish Jewish prisoners-of-war was brought to Lublin. They were told that they were to be sent to Soviet Russia. On the march northwards, ostensibly towards the border, almost all of them were killed. The survivors were held in the prisoner-of-war camp at Biala Podlaska, where another 200, denied medical attention, died of typhus. Extreme brutality against Jewish prisoners-

Map 36

of-war was also recorded at transit camps set up at Krosniewice, Zyrardow and Radom.

Thousands of non-Jews, as well as Jews, suffered cruelty during these early days of the German occupation of western Poland. Between September 1939 and June 1940, in each of the towns and villages shown in small type (*left*), Polish civilians were shot, some at random, some because they were the political, religious, or intellectual leaders of their community: as many as 360 at Skloby. As with the killing of Jews, the method was barbaric. At Szalas, for example, all 300 males over the age of 15 were seized, many machine-gunned, and the rest locked in a school which was then set on fire. The list, even for the region shown here, is incomplete. Elsewhere in the occupied regions, the scale of killing of non-Jews was similar; more than 16,000 in the first month and a half of the occupation (*page 33*), and continually increasing during 1940. At Torun (*right*), twelve young boys aged 11 to 16 were shot as a reprisal for the breaking of a window in the local police station.

On 12 December 1939 two years' forced labour was made compulsory for all Jewish males between the ages of 14 and 60. Labour camps were set up throughout the General Government and in the Warthegau (*right*). At first Jews were seized in the streets in order to fill the camps. Later, organized conscription took place. Many died in the camps of brutality, and exhaustion. The photograph shows part of the barracks of one such labour camp, near Dabrowa.

EASTERN LABOUR CAMPS BY JANUARY 1940

Baltic Sea

LITHUANIA

0 miles 60
0 kilometres 100

Danzig
1 camp

GREATER EAST PRUSSIA

GREATER DANZIG AND WEST PRUSSIA

THE SOVIET UNION

Bydgoszcz
4 camps
Torun

Poznan
25 camps

WARTHEGAU

Warsaw
14 camps

VOLHYNIA

Lodz
6 camps

THE GENERAL GOVERNMENT

GREATER GERMANY

SILESIA

Lublin
28 camps

Kielce
21 camps

Dabrowa Gornicza
6 camps

Rzeszow
10 camps

EAST UPPER SILESIA

Cracow
12 camps

EASTERN GALICIA

BOHEMIA & MORAVIA

SLOVAKIA

RUTHENIA

HUNGARY

© Martin Gilbert 1982

Map 37

'LUBLINLAND' DEPORTATIONS, OCTOBER 1939 - APRIL 1940

© Martin Gilbert 1982

Even before the new German-Soviet border had been fixed, the Germans were planning to drive the Jews from hundreds of towns and villages in the nearly annexed territories. As Hitler himself declared: 'Out with them from all the professions and into the ghetto with them: fence them in somewhere, where they can perish as they deserve.'

On 21 September 1939 it was decreed that all communities with less than 500 Jews were to be dissolved, and that the Jews were hereafter to live in certain restricted areas in the larger cities, or in a special area set aside for them in the poor village region between Lublin and Nisko, the so-called 'Lublinland reservation' (above).

Even Jews waiting at Hamburg for the next ship to the United States, then neutral, were deported eastwards, as shown here. Also deported were Jews from Vienna, from three former Czechoslovak towns, Prague, Brno and Moravska Ostrava, as well as from the Baltic ports of Stralsund and Stettin.

By the end of the winter, lacking proper housing, food or medical help, hundreds, if not thousands of these deportees to Lublinland had died. Others worked in harsh conditions, savagely beaten by guards, in a forced labour camp set up near Zarzecze, and many died. Some, who managed to escape eastwards into the Soviet Union, were immediately deported to labour camps in Siberia, where many of them also died.

Meanwhile, on 30 October 1939, the head

JEWS WEST OF OZORKOW

0 — miles — 7
0 — kilometres — 12

Drzewce 3
Besiekiery 12
Zalesie 3
Grabow 31
Chelmno 33
Siedlec 4
Chorki 6
Dabie 1,163
Blonie 13
Leczyca 4,051
Stawiszyn 672
Wilczkowice 5
Topola 14
Uniejow 1,100
Jankow 5
Ozorkow 4,949
Niewiesz 10
Parzeczew 174
Druzbin 4
Poddebice 1,333
Bratkow 16

River Warta
River Ner

© Martin Gilbert 1982

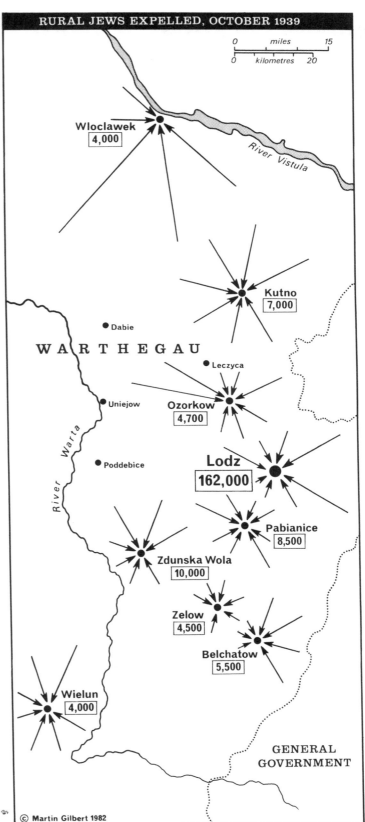

RURAL JEWS EXPELLED, OCTOBER 1939

0 — miles — 15
0 — kilometres — 20

Wloclawek 4,000
River Vistula
Kutno 7,000
W A R T H E G A U
Dabie
Leczyca
Uniejow
Ozorkow 4,700
Lodz 162,000
River Warta
Poddebice
Pabianice 8,500
Zdunska Wola 10,000
Zelow 4,500
Belchatow 5,500
Wielun 4,000
GENERAL GOVERNMENT

© Martin Gilbert 1982

of the SS, Heinrich Himmler, had fixed the following three months as the period during which all Jews had to be cleared out of the rural areas of western Poland. In the Poznan region, 50 communities were at once uprooted: seven of them are named opposite.

From Lodz, hundreds of women, children and old people were deported eastward by train in sealed freight-cars, mostly to the Lublin region. At the same time, Jews living in the rural areas of western Poland were forced to leave their homes, taking with them only what they could carry in sacks or bundles, and to go to the towns and cities shown on the right-hand map. An idea of the numbers of those uprooted can be seen in the boxes: 4,700 Jews, for example, were forced into the city of Ozorkow, bringing the total population to more than 9,000. Hundreds of communities were involved: those from the region west of Ozorkow are shown above. In some of the smaller villages, such as Drzewce, there was only a single Jewish family. They too were driven out. In one of these villages, Chelmno, lived a total of 33 Jews, all of whom were forced to leave. Just over a year later, their village became the site of the first death camp (*page 82*).

In the cities to which Jews were driven, overcrowding was severe. Poverty followed swiftly for tens of thousands of families, already stripped of their possessions, and now without a livelihood. The photograph (*left*) is of one such deportee, a Jewish boy in Lublin.

41

POLISH JEWS EXPELLED FROM WESTERN POLAND, SEPTEMBER - NOVEMBER 1939

Baltic   *Sea*

Strzelno
1

Puck
31

*Gulf
of
Danzig*

Wejherowo
62

Chylonia
5

Danzig

┉┉ Borders of 1919
to 1939

POMERANIA

THE POLISH CORRIDOR

Kartuzy
35

Skarszewy
40

Tczew
93

EAST
PRUSSIA

Koscierzyna

Zblewo
12

Starogard
125

Gniew
20

Brusy
24

Karsin
3

Skorcz
19

Chojnice
110

Czersk
5

POLAND

Nowe
31

Lubawa
26

Kamien
12

Osie
26

Tuchola
118

Grudziadz
297

Lasin
23

Nowe
Miasto
61

Sepolno
183

Bukowiec
12

Swiecie
171

Radzyn
12

Sypniewo
3

Wiebork
64

Chelmno
74

Lisewo
9

Wabrzezno
92

Brodnica
56

Lidzbark
60

Dziadlowo
35

Chelmza
72

Golub
104

Gorzno
1

| 0 | miles | 5 |
| 0 | kilometres | 40 |

Torun
354

Mlyniec
3

© Martin Gilbert 1982

JEWS EXPELLED INTO WARSAW, NOVEMBER - DECEMBER 1939

DANZIG WEST PRUSSIA

GREATER
EAST
PRUSSIA

SOVIET
UNION

Bydgoszcz

River Vistula

Zuromin

Sierpc

Biezun

Lipno

Raciaz

40,000
expelled

Poznan

Kaluszyn

WARTHEGAU

Konin

Warsaw

Konstancin

GENERAL

Aleksandrow

GOVERNMENT

Kalisz

Brzeziny

Lodz

Sieradz

Kozienice

| 0 | miles | 40 |
| 0 | kilometres | 60 |

© Martin Gilbert 1982

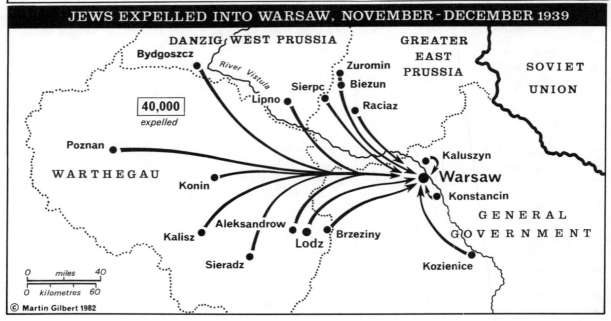

As the eastward expulsion of Jews continued, incredible distress was caused, both in the uprooting of settled communities, and in the disruption of life in the towns to which they were sent. The German plan was carefully prepared and ruthlessly pursued. As Hitler had made clear to the Reichstag on 6 October 1939, strict measures were needed for what he descibed as 'adapting and regulating the Jewish problem'. By the end of January 1940 some 78,000 Polish Jews had been driven out of their homes.

The map on the right shows the new German administrative division, and the first three provinces — Greater Danzig and West Prussia, Greater East Prussia, and the Warthegau — from which Jews were expelled during the first few months of the German conquest of Poland. The map below, with figures for the number of inhabitants at the time of the 1931 census, shows how Jews from the city of Poznan, and from several of the villages around it, were first driven westwards to a central collecting point, then eastwards into the General Government, and then dispersed. Also dispersed were the Polish Jews of the new Greater Danzig region (*opposite, above*). This region had been part of the German Empire before 1914.

But the largest single destination for those who had been uprooted was Warsaw (*opposite, below*), a city that was already the home of more than 350,000 Jews.

DEPORTATION REGIONS

© Martin Gilbert 1982

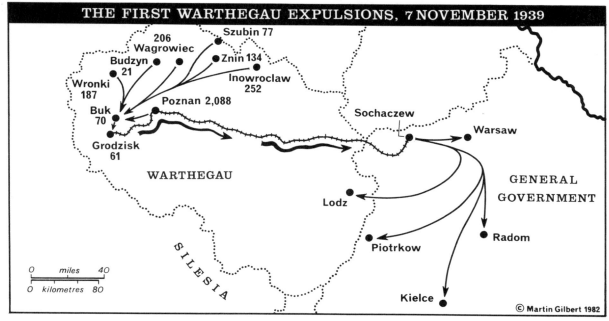

THE FIRST WARTHEGAU EXPULSIONS, 7 NOVEMBER 1939

© Martin Gilbert 1982

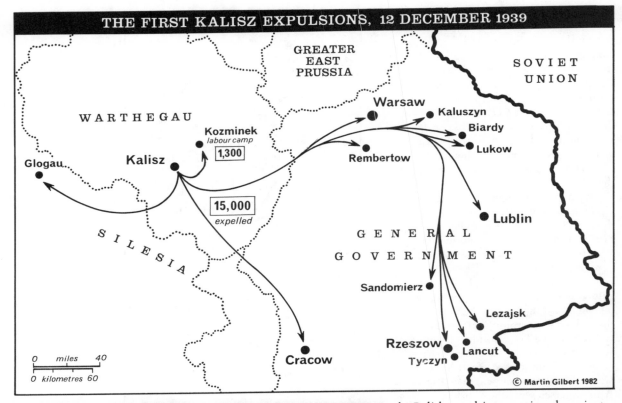

THE FIRST KALISZ EXPULSIONS, 12 DECEMBER 1939

GREATER
EAST
PRUSSIA

SOVIET
UNION

WARTHEGAU

Kozminek
labour camp
1,300

Warsaw

Kaluszyn

Biardy

Lukow

Glogau

Kalisz

Rembertow

15,000
expelled

Lublin

SILESIA

GENERAL

GOVERNMENT

Sandomierz

Lezajsk

0   miles   40
0   kilometres   60

Cracow

Rzeszow

Lancut

Tyczyn

© Martin Gilbert 1982

GERMANY MOVES NORTH, APRIL 1940

0   miles   200
0   kilometres   400

North
Atlantic
Ocean

FINLAND

NORWAY

S W E D E N

Oslo

EST.

North
Sea

LAT.

LIT.

Baltic Sea

EIRE

BRITAIN

DENMARK

SOVIET UNION

HOLLAND

Berlin

GREATER GERMANY

BELGIUM

SLOV.

FRANCE

HUNGARY

SWITZ.

© Martin Gilbert 1982

As the Polish expulsions continued, ancient communities were dispersed. The map above shows the first expulsions from Kalisz, where Jews had first come from the Rhineland more than seven centuries before. In 1919, at the beginning of Polish rule, two Kalisz Jews had been killed by local anti-semites (*page 15*). At the outbreak of the Second World War, 20,000 Jews in the town made up almost half the population. Of those expelled, some 7,000 Kalisz Jews reached Warsaw by the end of the year. But more than 1,000 able-bodied men were sent to a nearby labour camp at Kozminek.

In April 1940 the German army moved again, northwards into Denmark and Norway (*left*). In Denmark, 6,000 Jews were left unmolested at the insistence of the Danish authorities, as were the 1,400 Jewish refugees who had reached Denmark from Germany, Austria and Czechoslovakia, in 1938 and 1939. In Norway (*right*), some 1,400 Norwegian Jews, and about 300 refugees, were likewise unmolested, but only for six months. In October 1940 they were forbidden to continue in all academic or other professions. There were, however, none of the killings, beatings, forced labour and expulsion which had become daily events in German-occupied Poland.

Map 46

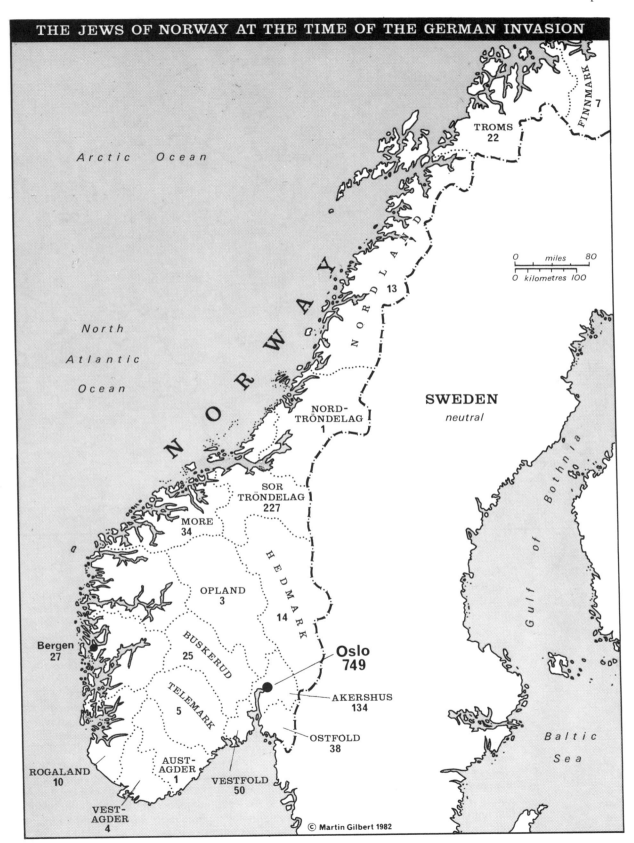

THE JEWS OF NORWAY AT THE TIME OF THE GERMAN INVASION

Arctic Ocean

FINNMARK 7

TROMS 22

North Atlantic Ocean

N O R W A Y

NORDLAND 13

0   miles   80
0   kilometres   100

SWEDEN
neutral

NORD-TRÖNDELAG 1

SOR TRÖNDELAG 227

MORE 34

HEDMARK

OPLAND 3

14

Gulf of Bothnia

BUSKERUD 25

Oslo 749

Bergen 27

TELEMARK 5

AKERSHUS 134

OSTFOLD 38

Baltic Sea

ROGALAND 10

AUST-AGDER 1

VESTFOLD 50

VEST-AGDER 4

© Martin Gilbert 1982

Map 47

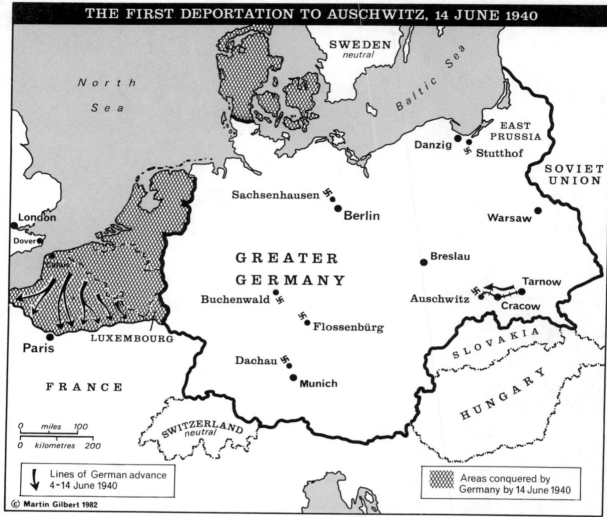

THE FIRST DEPORTATION TO AUSCHWITZ, 14 JUNE 1940

Lines of German advance
4-14 June 1940

Areas conquered by
Germany by 14 June 1940

© Martin Gilbert 1982

On 10 May 1940 the German army invaded Holland, Belgium, Luxembourg and France (*above*). Within five weeks, on June 14, as German forces approached Paris, yet another concentration camp was being set up in German-occupied Poland. Situated just outside the town of Auschwitz, it was intended as a punishment camp for Polish political prisoners, not as a concentration camp for Jews. But in order to prepare the old barracks, 300 Jewish forced labourers had been brought from Auschwitz town.

The first inmates were mostly non-Jewish Poles, 728 in all, from a prison in Tarnow. Many of them had been caught at the eastern border trying to get to France through Hungary. Other Poles taken in that first train to Auschwitz were schoolteachers and priests. Three Jews were also among these first inmates: Emil Wieder and Isaac Holzer, both lawyers, and Maximilian Rosenbusch,

the Director of the Hebrew school in Tarnow. As the deportees' train was passing through Cracow, they heard the station announcer report the fall of Paris.

Like all concentration camp inmates, these first Auschwitz prisoners were put to forced labour, often doing heavy work that was not needed, such as digging ditches. At times they were tormented by having to queue on their knees for their daily bowl of soup. After the first successful escape, on July 6, there was a punitive 20-hour rollcall. After a second escape on October 28, a rollcall was held in bitter weather from 12 noon to 9 p.m., during which 200 prisoners died.

Elsewhere in Poland, thousands of Jews were being sent to forced labour camps, mostly to build fortifications along the new Soviet frontier (*opposite*). Thousands of other Jews were brought from Slovakia to these labour camp regions.

Map 48

SLAVE LABOUR ON THE GERMAN BORDER, MAY–DECEMBER 1940

Baltic Sea

Danzig

EAST PRUSSIA

SOVIET-OCCUPIED POLAND

Mlawa

Rypin

River Vistula

Pultusk

Nasielsk

Serock

Warsaw
May 1940

Miedzyrzec

border fortifications

POLESIA

GERMAN-OCCUPIED POLAND

Radom
May 1940

2,000

almost none survived

Lublin
May 1940

River Bug

VOLHYNIA

Czestochowa
August 1940

1,000

almost none survived

Zamosc

S I L E S I A

River Vistula

Belzec

Cieszanow

Cracow

Mielec

the 'Otto line'

Tarnow

Auschwitz

EASTERN GALICIA

PROTECTORATE OF BOHEMIA & MORAVIA

Zilina

Ruzomberok

Presov

Humenne

S L O V A K I A

Banska Bystrica

Kosice

HUNGARIAN-OCCUPIED RUTHENIA

HUNGARY

© Martin Gilbert 1982

O   miles   40
O   kilometres   60

JEWS DEPORTED FROM GERMANY TO THE PYRENEES, 22 OCTOBER 1940

© Martin Gilbert 1982

On 22 October 1940 the German Government deported more than 15,000 German Jews from the Rhineland to internment camps in France, at the foothills of the Pyrenees. As a result of the conditions in the camps, nearly 2,000 of the deportees died. The towns shown on the map above are the birthplaces of some of the deportees, including Danzig, Warsaw, and even Auschwitz.

The small map (right) shows the numbers deported to Gurs from part of the upper Rhine. These Jews had been German patriots. From Mannheim alone, 126 Jews had died fighting for Germany in the First World War: among them five soldiers with the common Jewish surname Mayer.

The map on the far right gives the birthplaces, names and ages of deportees with the surname Mayer who died while in Gurs internment camp.

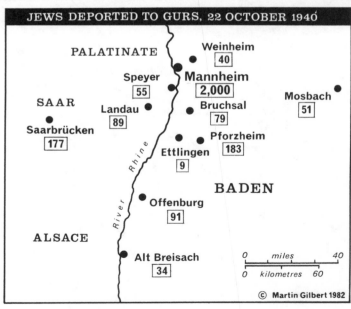

JEWS DEPORTED TO GURS, 22 OCTOBER 1940

© Martin Gilbert 1982

Map 51

TWENTY JEWS WITH THE SURNAME MAYER WHO DIED IN GURS

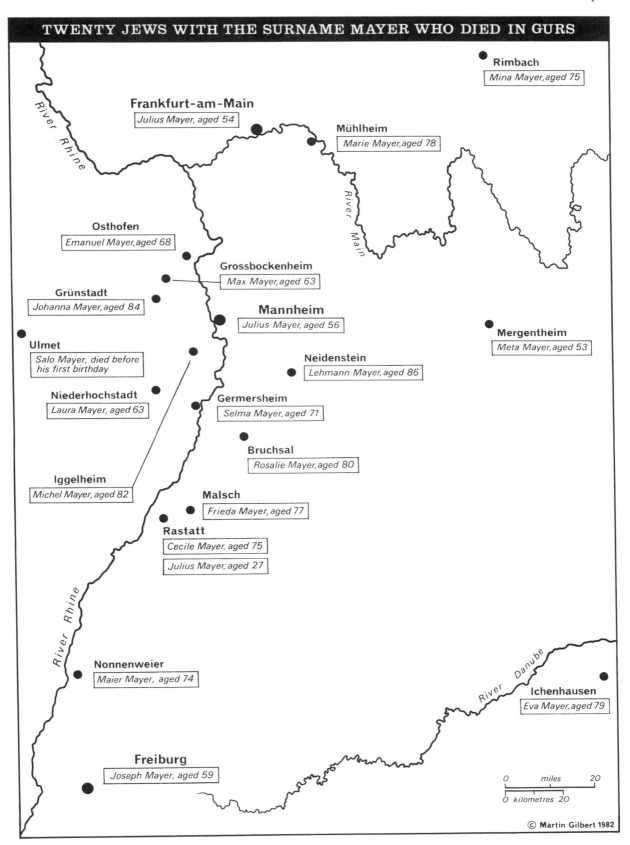

Rimbach
Mina Mayer, aged 75

Frankfurt-am-Main
Julius Mayer, aged 54

Mühlheim
Marie Mayer, aged 78

River Rhine

River Main

Osthofen
Emanuel Mayer, aged 68

Grossbockenheim
Max Mayer, aged 63

Grünstadt
Johanna Mayer, aged 84

Mannheim
Julius Mayer, aged 56

Mergentheim
Meta Mayer, aged 53

Ulmet
Salo Mayer, died before his first birthday

Neidenstein
Lehmann Mayer, aged 86

Niederhochstadt
Laura Mayer, aged 63

Germersheim
Selma Mayer, aged 71

Bruchsal
Rosalie Mayer, aged 80

Iggelheim
Michel Mayer, aged 82

Malsch
Frieda Mayer, aged 77

Rastatt
Cecile Mayer, aged 75

Julius Mayer, aged 27

River Rhine

River Danube

Nonnenweier
Maier Mayer, aged 74

Ichenhausen
Eva Mayer, aged 79

Freiburg
Joseph Mayer, aged 59

0   miles   20

0 kilometres 20

© Martin Gilbert 1982

Map 52

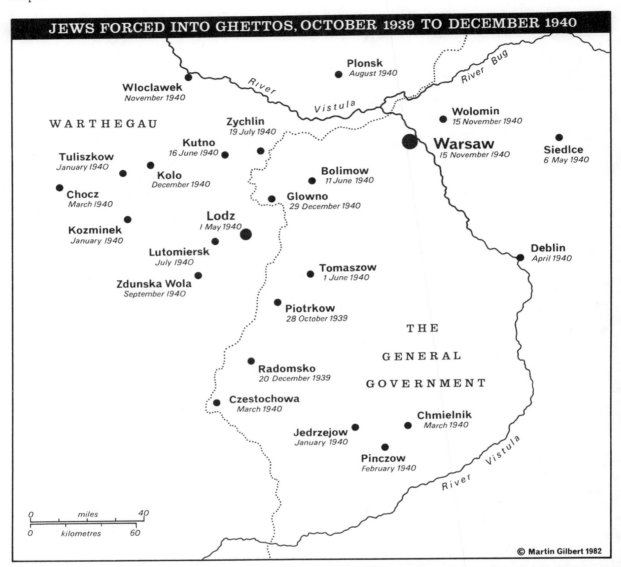

JEWS FORCED INTO GHETTOS, OCTOBER 1939 TO DECEMBER 1940

Plonsk
August 1940

River Bug

Wloclawek
November 1940

River

Vistula

Wolomin
15 November 1940

WARTHEGAU

Zychlin
19 July 1940

Warsaw
15 November 1940

Siedlce
6 May 1940

Kutno
16 June 1940

Tuliszkow
January 1940

Kolo
December 1940

Bolimow
11 June 1940

Chocz
March 1940

Glowno
29 December 1940

Kozminek
January 1940

Lodz
I May 1940

Deblin
April 1940

Lutomiersk
July 1940

Tomaszow
1 June 1940

Zdunska Wola
September 1940

Piotrkow
28 October 1939

T H E

G E N E R A L

G O V E R N M E N T

Radomsko
20 December 1939

Czestochowa
March 1940

Chmielnik
March 1940

Jedrzejow
January 1940

Pinczow
February 1940

River Vistula

miles	
0	40
0	60
kilometres	

© **Martin Gilbert 1982**

Starting with the town of Piotrkow on 28 October 1939, the Germans began to confine the Jews in Poland to a particular area of each town in which they lived. Sometimes this area was the already predominantly Jewish quarter. But often it was a poor or neglected part of the town, away from the centre. Jews from the rest of the town were then forced to leave their homes, and to move into this other, often much smaller area, in which even the basic amenities were not available.

Not only the Jews of each of the towns shown in the map on the left, but also deportees from the Warthegau, and from the surrounding rural communities, were forced to move into these new ghetto confines; at Piotrkow 8,000 local Jews were joined by a further 8,000 deportees.

In each ghetto food supplies and medical provisions were restricted. Intense overcrowding, hunger and disease led to widespread suffering, and death. The photograph was taken in the Lodz ghetto, where 5,000 were to die from starvation in the first six months of 1941 (page 54).

Meanwhile, in Germany itself, experiments had been tried on non-Jewish, and also on some Jewish patients from mental homes and old people's homes. The aim of the experiments was to kill all whom the Nazis judged unfit to live. The victims, including the children, were killed by gas in the euthanasia centres shown here.

After the German conquest of Poland more than 1,000 Poles were taken from nearby psychiatric clinics to a wood outside the Polish village of Piasnica Wielki, where they were shot. In October 1940, 290 Jews, old people, cripples, and the mentally ill from the Old Age Home in Kalisz, were put in a lorry to be taken to the town of 'Padernice' (below). No such town existed. Just outside Kalisz, in the woods at Winiary, all 290 were gassed inside the lorry by exhaust fumes, and buried in the woods.

GERMAN EUTHANASIA CENTRES, 1940

Baltic Sea

North Sea

Piasnica Wielki
1,200
October-December 1939

Kalisz

Brandenberg
Bernberg

Sonnenstein

Hadamar
over **10,000**

total killed **70,273**
by November 1941

Grafeneck

Schloss Hartheim
13,000

0 miles 200
0 kilometres 300

© Martin Gilbert 1982

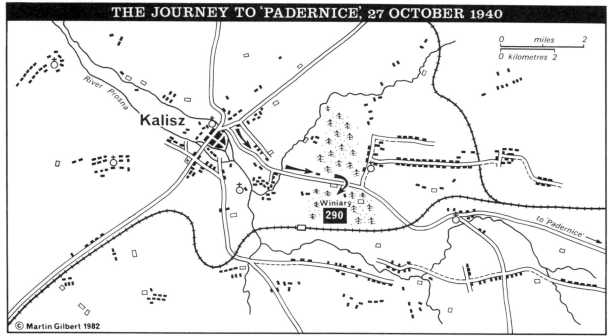

THE JOURNEY TO 'PADERNICE', 27 OCTOBER 1940

0 miles 2
0 kilometres 2

River Prosna

Kalisz

Winiary
290

to 'Padernice'

© Martin Gilbert 1982

Map 55

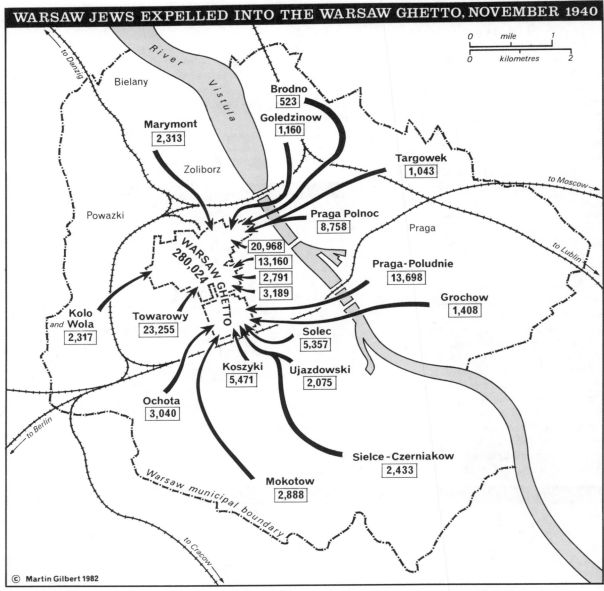

WARSAW JEWS EXPELLED INTO THE WARSAW GHETTO, NOVEMBER 1940

Bielany

River Vistula

to Danzig

Marymont
2,313

Zoliborz

Powazki

Brodno
523

Goledzinow
1,160

Targowek
1,043

to Moscow

Praga Polnoc
8,758

Praga

WARSAW GHETTO
280,024

20,968
13,160
2,791
3,189

Praga-Poludnie
13,698

to Lublin

Kolo *and* Wola
2,317

Towarowy
23,255

Grochow
1,408

Solec
5,357

Koszyki
5,471

Ujazdowski
2,075

to Berlin

Ochota
3,040

Sielce - Czerniakow
2,433

Warsaw municipal boundary

Mokotow
2,888

to Cracow

© **Martin Gilbert 1982**

0   mile   1
0   kilometres   2

Just over a year after the establishment of the first ghetto, at Piotrkow *(page 50)*, orders were given to confine all the Jews of Warsaw, as well as all the Jews who had already been deported to Warsaw, inside one section of the city. The Warsaw ghetto was to become the largest of all the ghettos established by the Germans in Poland. The section of the city chosen for it was one in which more than 280,000 Jews were already living.

In October 1940 a wall was built around the area designated for the ghetto. Jews were made both to build the wall and to pay for it. As soon as it was built, the thousands of Jews who lived elsewhere in Warsaw were forced to leave their homes, to abandon most of their possessions, and to move into the new ghetto area *(above)*. One Warsaw Jew, Chaim Kaplan, wrote in his diary of the expulsion from the Praga suburbs: 'By the thirty-first of October, Praga must be empty of its Jewish inhabitants, who were rooted to its soil for hundreds of years. Most of them are poor. They have no money to move their belongings. And where would they move them to?' Many Poles, Kaplan added, 'drove the Praga Jews from their apartments in advance, before the fixed date'.

Early in 1941, 72,000 Jews were expelled from towns throughout the Warsaw region

Map 56

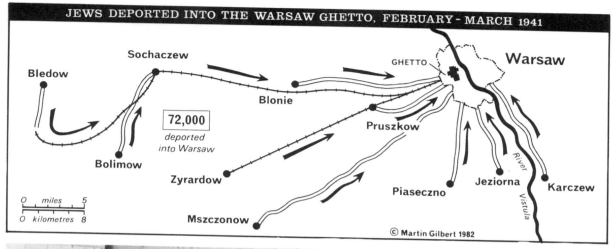

JEWS DEPORTED INTO THE WARSAW GHETTO, FEBRUARY – MARCH 1941

Bledow

Sochaczew

Blonie

72,000
*deported
into Warsaw*

Bolimow

Zyrardow

Pruszkow

Mszczonow

Piaseczno

Jeziorna

Karczew

GHETTO

Warsaw

River Vistula

© Martin Gilbert 1982

0 miles 5
0 kilometres 8

(*above*), and driven into the ghetto, bringing the total number of refugees to 150,000. Conditions inside the ghetto were appalling: terrible overcrowding, minimum rations, and almost no contact with the outside world for 400,000 people.

Under the ration scales imposed by the Germans, all Germans in Warsaw were entitled to 2,310 calories a day, foreigners to 1,790 calories, Poles to 934 calories, and Jews to a mere 183 calories. Yet Jews had to pay twice as much as Poles, and nearly 20 times as much as Germans, for each calory. Inside the ghetto, food distribution was organized by the Jews themselves. The photograph, one of more than 300 photographs taken by a member of the Warsaw photographic studio, Studio Forbert, was entitled simply 'meal time'. More than 13,000 Jews died of starvation in Warsaw between January and June 1941 (*page 54*).

Attempts to make conditions as bearable as possible were made by a special Jewish Council, set up by the Germans. The Council provided what relief it could, and arranged cultural activities, concerts, and education. There were many orphanages in the ghetto, their difficult work inspired by the leadership of their directors, including Janusz Korczak. On 12 August 1942 he was to insist on accompanying his children in one of the Warsaw deportations (*page 112*).

53

Map 57

THE SPREAD OF TERROR AND DEATH, JANUARY TO JUNE 1941

Amsterdam
400
22 February 1941

Bremen
hundreds
early 1941

Kalisz
439
gassed 1 January 1941

Warsaw
13,000
died of starvation and disease January - June 1941

Biala Podlaska
12
prisoners of war 15 May 1941

Lodz
5,000
died of starvation and disease January - June 1941

Lublin

Kielce **Opole**
Lagow **Modliborzyce**
Cracow

GREATER
GERMANY

Mauthausen

Paris
3,600
interned 14 May 1941

Suresnes
GERMAN-
OCCUPIED
FRANCE

VICHY
FRANCE

Vienna
5,004
15 February - 12 March 1941

Zagreb
6
April 1941

RUMANIA
Bucharest
120
murdered in the streets 22-23 January 1941

Noé
Le Vernet
Les Milles
Gurs
Rivesaltes
Argelés
internment camps

SPAIN
neutral

Adriatic Sea

Mediterranean Sea

Black Sea

TURKEY
neutral

791
on board the "Darien" reached Palestine by sea 9 March 1941

0 miles 200
0 kilometres 300

several thousand deported to the Sahara, for slave labour see page 56

© Martin Gilbert 1982

North Sea
Baltic Sea
BELGIUM

Map 58

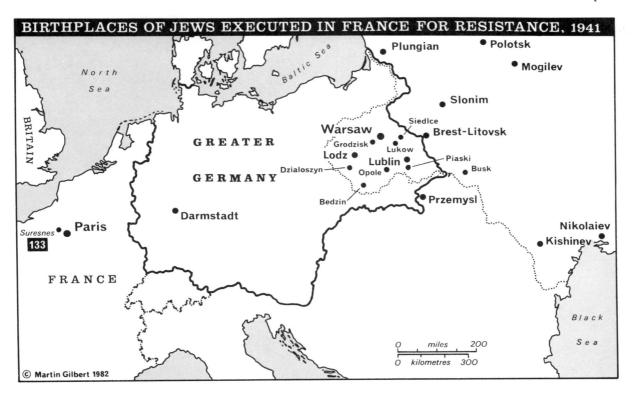

BIRTHPLACES OF JEWS EXECUTED IN FRANCE FOR RESISTANCE, 1941

During the first six months of 1941, the rigour of Germany's policy towards the Jews was constant and severe. On 1 January 1941 a further 439 old and sick Jews were taken from the Old People's Home at Kalisz, and gassed by exhaust fumes in a nearby wood (*see also page 51*). At Biala Podlaska, 12 more defenceless Jewish prisoners-of-war were savagely murdered. In each of the ghettos shown on page 50, death from starvation and disease was a daily occurrence, with more than 18,000 dead in Warsaw and Lodz. From 22 February 1941 any Pole selling food to a Jew outside the Warsaw ghetto was automatically sentenced to three months' hard labour, and the ghetto ration was reduced to three ounces of bread a day. 'Although the ghetto of Lodz was intended as a mere trial,' the Cologne *Zeitung* reported on 5 April 1941, 'a mere prelude to the solution of the Jewish question, it has turned out to be the best and most perfect temporary solution of the Jewish problem.' Nine days later, any Jew leaving the Lodz ghetto was ordered to be shot on sight.

More than 40,000 German and Belgian Jews were deported into the Warsaw ghetto. New ghettos were also set up in Cracow, Lublin and Kielce. From Vienna, more than 5,000 Jews were deported to these eastern ghettos and labour camps, while from Amsterdam, more than 400 Jews were seized as hostages and deported to the stone quarries of Mauthausen concentration camp; the events leading to this deportation are described on pages 78-9.

In Paris, several thousand foreign-born Jews were seized and interned in May 1941. At the same time, thousands of Polish- and German-born Jews, who had fought in the French Foreign Legion against Germany in 1940, were deported to slave labour camps in the Sahara. Outside Paris, at Suresnes, 133 Jews were shot for resistance during 1941, the first executions taking place on 16 April 1941. The map above shows the birthplaces of some of those shot, as recorded by the Gestapo: 10 had been born in Warsaw, and almost all had been born within the borders (shown here dotted) of the former Russian Empire. Many, like Charles Weinberg from Kishinev, were in their fifties. One of those shot, Antoine Hajje, had been born in Cyprus; another, Elias Salomon, in Beirut.

Outside Greater Germany, anti-semitic violence in Bucharest left 120 Jews dead in the streets (*left*): men, women and children who had been hunted down by armed gangs. A few survivors managed to reach Palestine by sea.

The photograph shows work on the Sahara railroad (*see also page 56*).

Map 59

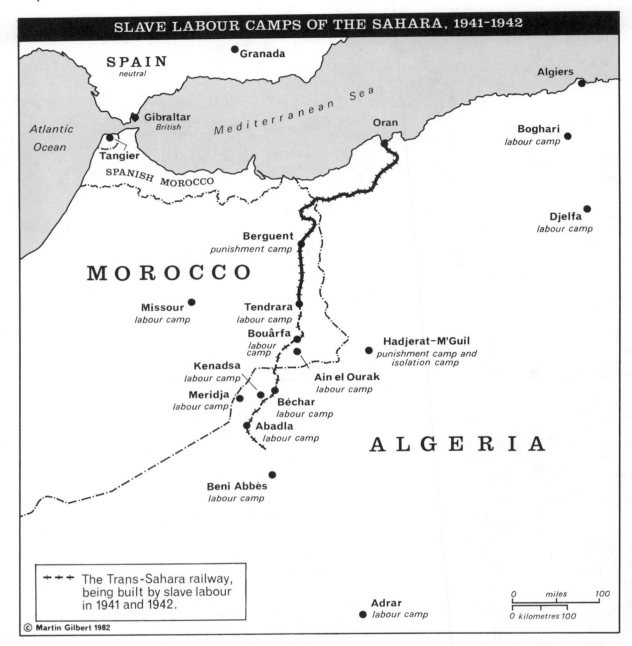

SLAVE LABOUR CAMPS OF THE SAHARA, 1941-1942

SPAIN
neutral

Granada

Algiers

Mediterranean Sea

Gibraltar
British

Oran

Boghari
labour camp

Atlantic
Ocean

Tangier

SPANISH MOROCCO

Djelfa
labour camp

MOROCCO

Berguent
punishment camp

Missour
labour camp

Tendrara
labour camp

Bouârfa
labour camp

Hadjerat-M'Guil
punishment camp and isolation camp

Kenadsa
labour camp

Ain el Ourak
labour camp

Meridja
labour camp

Béchar
labour camp

Abadla
labour camp

ALGERIA

Beni Abbès
labour camp

+ + + The Trans-Sahara railway,
being built by slave labour
in 1941 and 1942.

Adrar
labour camp

0 _____ miles _____ 100

0 kilometres 100

© Martin Gilbert 1982

In April 1940 more than 1,500 Jews were serving in the French Foreign Legion, hoping to fight against Nazi Germany. But with the German conquest of France in June 1940 they were first 'demobilized', then interned, and finally sent to labour camps in French North Africa (*above*). Many of these Jews were refugees from Germany and Austria who had been in France at the outbreak of war.

A law of 4 October 1940 gave Vichy France the power to intern Jews even inside the Unoccupied Zone, and on 22 March 1941 a law signed by Marshal Pétain authorized the construction of a Trans-Sahara railway. The work was done, in harsh conditions, by all who had been interned: former Spanish Republican soldiers, Poles, Czechs, Greeks and Jews.

The camp at Hadjerat-M'Guil was opened on 1 November 1941, as a punishment and isolation camp. It contained 170 prisoners, nine of whom were tortured and murdered in conditions of the worst brutality. Two of those murdered were Jews, one of whom had earlier been in a concentration camp in Germany but had been released in 1939 and

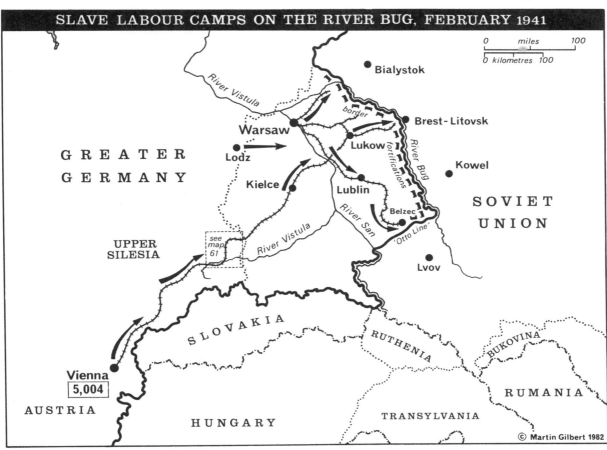

SLAVE LABOUR CAMPS ON THE RIVER BUG, FEBRUARY 1941

GREATER
GERMANY

UPPER
SILESIA

see map 61

AUSTRIA

Vienna
5,004

SLOVAKIA

HUNGARY

Bialystok

River Vistula

Warsaw

Lodz

Kielce

Lukow

Lublin

River San

Belzec

'Otto Line'

Brest-Litovsk

River Bug fortifications

border

Kowel

SOVIET
UNION

Lvov

RUTHENIA

BUKOVINA

RUMANIA

TRANSYLVANIA

© Martin Gilbert 1982

had fled to France. This young man's parents had become refugees in London. On learning of their son's murder in the Sahara, they committed suicide.

Shown above is the deportation of more than 5,000 Jews from Vienna to the Kielce and Lublin ghettos, and to the labour camps along the River Bug (*above*). There, together with Jews deported from Warsaw and Lodz, they were forced to drain marshes and build fortifications on the Soviet border, the 'Otto Line', intended to act as a barrier against Soviet tanks. One of the main labour camps, at Belzec, was later to become one of the four eastern death camps (*page 90*).

Another group of Jews who were sent to forced labour were skilled workers living in the region of the Upper Silesian coalfields. There were 93,628 Jews living in this region, in 32 communities, the six largest of which, among them the town of Auschwitz, are shown here (*right*). Thousands of able-bodied Jews were rounded up in these towns and sent to work in German mining, metallurgy and textile plants and factories in the region, as many as 5,000 men from Bedzin.

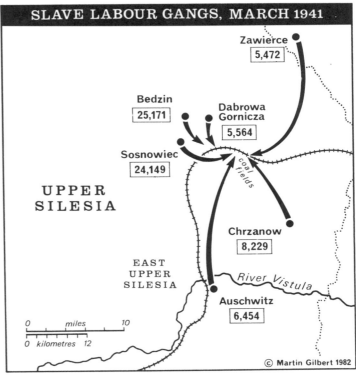

SLAVE LABOUR GANGS, MARCH 1941

Zawierce
5,472

Bedzin
25,171

Dabrowa
Gornicza
5,564

Sosnowiec
24,149

UPPER
SILESIA

coal fields

Chrzanow
8,229

EAST
UPPER
SILESIA

River Vistula

Auschwitz
6,454

© Martin Gilbert 1982

Map 62

THE GERMAN CONQUEST OF YUGOSLAVIA AND GREECE, APRIL 1941

On 6 April 1941 the German armies invaded Yugoslavia and Greece, and by the end of the month a further 145,000 Jews had been brought under Nazi tyranny (*above*). Those of the Banat, shown opposite according to the Yugoslav census of 31 March 1931, lived in small and scattered communities north of Belgrade, between the River Tisa and the Rumanian border. Numbering over 3,000 people, they were all driven from their homes by the Germans in August 1941, within four months of the German conquest of Yugosalvia. Taken to Tasmajdan camp, near Belgrade, they were shot in the camp itself, and on the banks of the Danube, in daily executions: on 20 August 1941 the whole Banat region was declared *Judenrein*, 'purged of Jews'.

Map 63

THE JEWS OF THE BANAT

HUNGARY

Krstr 11

Arandelovo 39

Nova Kanjiza 46

Coka 49

Mokrin 38

Sajan 9

Kikinda 100

Padej 28

RUMANIA

Novi Becej 167

Torda 10

Kumani 14

Melenci 32

Jasa Tomic 56

Veliki Beckerek 1,352

Boka 3

Aradac 4

Ecka 33

Jarkovac 5

BACSKA

BANAT

Vrsac 404

Perlez 18

Seleus 5

Kovacica 37

Padina 33

Alibunar 31

Novo Selo 1

Bela Crkva 67

YUGOSLAVIA

Delibiato 10

Pancevo 507

Gaj 6

SREM

Kovin 75

Tasmajdan
concentration camp
3,000

Belgrade
Sajmiste
concentration camp

SERBIA

River Tisa

River Danube

River Danube

© Martin Gilbert 1982

0 miles 10

0 kilometres 20

By the end of October 1941 almost no Banat Jews were left alive in Tasmajdan: the life, the culture and the achievements of more than 30 communities had been destroyed for all time.

East of the Banat, the towns of Subotica and Novi Sad were occupied by Hungarian forces on 11 April 1941. In Subotica the Germans executed 250 members of a Jewish youth movement who had carried out the first acts of sabotage against the occupation forces. In Novi Sad, Hungarian troops and local Germans murdered at random 250 Jews and 250 Serbs.

From the outset of the war, Jews were active in the Yugoslav resistance. The first secret radio in Zagreb was operated by two Jewish brothers. More than 2,000 Yugoslav Jews later fought with Tito's partisans, and a specifically Jewish unit of 250 men, formed in 1943, lost more than 200 fighting against the Germans. One leading resistance fighter, Moša Pijade, a Jew, later became a Vice-President of Yugoslavia.

Map 64 and 65

THE JEWS OF WESTERN CROATIA ON THE EVE OF WAR

Cakovac 533
HUNGARY
Varazdin 486
Ludbrijeg 74
Koprivnica 339
Krapina
Zlata 13
Virje 15
Djurdjevac 29
River
Drava
Donji Miholjac 119
Klanjec
Zabok 6
Krizevci 126
Loka 1
Sevnica 4
Zagreb 8,702
Dugo Selo 23
Bjelovar 360
Virovitica 233
Slatina 174
Osijek
see map 66
Samobor 8
Klostar Ivanic 5
Daruvar 136
Nasice 161
Jastrebarsko
Ivanic 16
Lekenik 11
CROATIA
Pakrac 209
Pozega 248
Pisarovina 15
Petrinja 14
Sisak 230
Jasenovac 2
Vinica 23
Karlovac 347
Sunja 9
River Sava
Slavonski Brod 462
Leskovac 93
Kostajnica
Nova Gradiska 207
Ogulin 21
Dvor 1
BOSNIA see page 75
Cazin 1
Bihac 149

© Martin Gilbert 1982

0 miles 30
0 kilometres 40

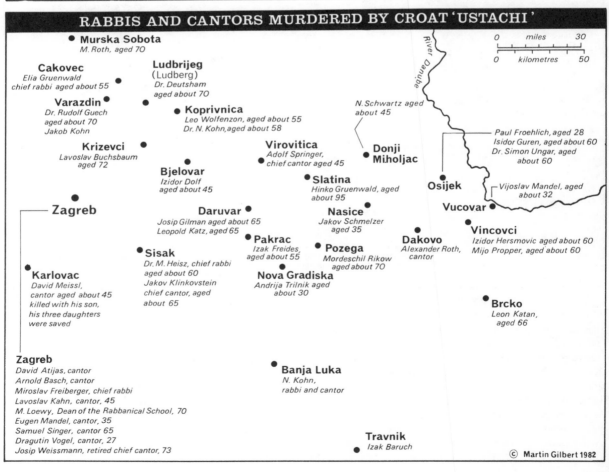

RABBIS AND CANTORS MURDERED BY CROAT 'USTACHI'

Murska Sobota
M. Roth, aged 70

Cakovec
Elia Gruenwald chief rabbi aged about 55

Ludbrijeg (Ludberg)
Dr. Deutsham aged about 70

River Danube

0 miles 30
0 kilometres 50

Varazdin
Dr. Rudolf Guech aged about 70 Jakob Kohn

Koprivnica
Leo Wolfenzon, aged about 55 Dr. N. Kohn, aged about 58

N. Schwartz aged about 45

Krizevci
Lavoslav Buchsbaum aged 72

Virovitica
Adolf Springer, chief cantor aged 45

Donji Miholjac

Paul Froehlich, aged 28
Isidor Guren, aged about 60
Dr. Simon Ungar, aged about 60

Bjelovar
Izidor Dolf aged about 45

Slatina
Hinko Gruenwald, aged about 95

Osijek

Zagreb

Daruvar
Josip Gilman aged about 65 Leopold Katz, aged 65

Nasice
Jakov Schmelzer aged 35

Vucovar

Vijoslav Mandel, aged about 32

Pakrac
Izak Freides, aged about 55

Pozega
Mordeschil Rikow aged about 70

Dakovo
Alexander Roth, cantor

Vincovci
Izidor Hersmovic aged about 60 Mijo Propper, aged about 60

Karlovac
David Meissl, cantor aged about 45 killed with his son, his three daughters were saved

Sisak
Dr. M. Heisz, chief rabbi aged about 60 Jakov Klinkovstein chief cantor, aged about 65

Nova Gradiska
Andrija Trilnik aged about 30

Brcko
Leon Katan, aged 66

Zagreb
*David Atijas, cantor
Arnold Basch, cantor
Miroslav Freiberger, chief rabbi
Lavoslav Kahn, cantor, 45
M. Loewy, Dean of the Rabbinical School, 70
Eugen Mandel, cantor, 35
Samuel Singer, cantor 65
Dragutin Vogel, cantor, 27
Josip Weissmann, retired chief cantor, 73*

Banja Luka
N. Kohn, rabbi and cantor

Travnik
Izak Baruch

© Martin Gilbert 1982

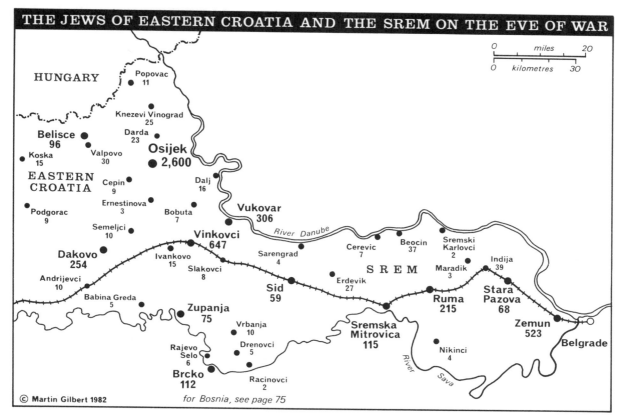

THE JEWS OF EASTERN CROATIA AND THE SREM ON THE EVE OF WAR

HUNGARY

Popovac 11

Knezevi Vinograd 25

Belisce 96

Darda 23

Koska 15

Valpovo 30

Osijek 2,600

EASTERN CROATIA

Cepin 9

Dalj 16

Podgorac 9

Ernestinova 3

Bobuta 7

Vukovar 306

Semeljci 10

Vinkovci 647

River Danube

Cerevic 7

Beocin 37

Sremski Karlovci 2

Dakovo 254

Ivankovo 15

Sarengrad 4

SREM

Maradik 3

Indija 39

Andrijevci 10

Slakovci 8

Erdevik 27

Ruma 215

Stara Pazova 68

Babina Greda 5

Sid 59

Zemun 523

Zupanja 75

Vrbanja 10

Sremska Mitrovica 115

Belgrade

Rajevo Selo 6

Drenovci 5

Nikinci 4

River Sava

Brcko 112

Racinovci 2

© Martin Gilbert 1982   *for Bosnia, see page 75*

Following the German conquest of Yugosalvia on 17 April 1941, Croatia became an independent State, ruled by the pro-Nazi 'Ustachi'. The top maps show the Jewish communities of Croatia and the Srem according to the Yugoslavia census of 1931. The areas plotted are shown on the small map (*right*).

Persecution of the Jews began at once. In Ruma, the synagogue was demolished. In Vukovar, the community leaders were arrested, and then 'ransomed' back to the community. In Osijek, German soldiers, local Germans and Croat 'Ustachi' burned the main synagogue, destroyed the Jewish cemetery, looted Jewish property, and imposed a crippling 'fine' on the Jewish community.

The map opposite (*below*) gives the names of some rabbis and cantors who were murdered during the late spring and early summer: some were venerable rabbis, scholars and teachers; others were young men embarking upon their careers. Doctors, nurses, midwives, chemists, dentists and vets, whose work had been for the whole Croatian community, were also killed. Many young Croat Jews were to fight with Tito's partisans.

GERMANY AND CROATIA

Baltic Sea

Berlin

GREATER GERMANY

Warsaw

Prague

Lvov

Vienna

SLOVAKIA

Budapest

HUNGARY

RUMANIA

CROATIA

YUGOSLAVIA

Banja Luka

Travnik

Belgrade

DALMATIA

BOSNIA

SERBIA

Adriatic Sea

ITALY

© Martin Gilbert 1982

Map 68

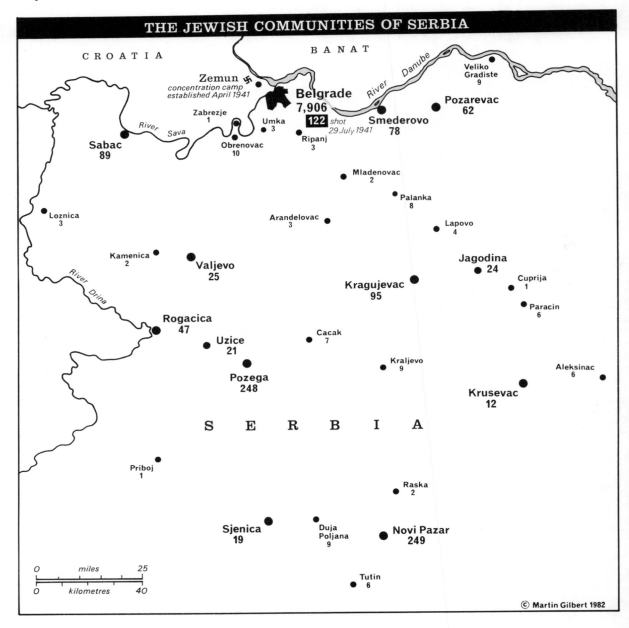

THE JEWISH COMMUNITIES OF SERBIA

CROATIA

BANAT

River Danube

Zemun
concentration camp
established April 1941

Belgrade
7,906

122 *shot*
29 July 1941

Veliko
Gradiste
9

Pozarevac
62

Zabrezje
1

Umka
3

Smederovo
78

River Sava

Obrenovac
10

Ripanj
3

Sabac
89

Mladenovac
2

Palanka
8

Loznica
3

Arandelovac
3

Lapovo
4

Kamenica
2

Valjevo
25

Jagodina
24

Cuprija
1

River Drina

Kragujevac
95

Paracin
6

Rogacica
47

Cacak
7

Uzice
21

Kraljevo
9

Aleksinac
6

Pozega
248

Krusevac
12

S E R B I A

Priboj
1

Raska
2

Sjenica
19

Duja
Poljana
9

Novi Pazar
249

Tutin
6

miles 25
0

0 kilometres 40

© Martin Gilbert 1982

After 500 years of struggle, persecution and expulsion, the Jews of Belgrade achieved full civil rights in 1878 in the newly independent Serbia. Between the wars they were active in Serbian professional and business life. Smaller Jewish communities settled throughout Serbia, as in the region south of Belgrade (*above*).

On 14 April 1941, within a few hours of the German occupation of Belgrade, Jewish shops were looted, and within a few weeks all Jewish communal activity was forbidden.

On 29 July 1941 the Germans executed 122 'Communists and Jews' for resistance.

Undeterred, Jews from the youth movement joined the resistance, sabotaging German military installations.

By November 1941 more than 15,000 Jews had been deported from throughout Serbia to the concentration camp at Zemun, where by June 1942 they had been killed in mobile gas units, disguised as Red Cross vans.

On 29 August 1942 Berlin was informed officially that the Jewish problem was 'totally solved' in Serbia, 'the only community', the report boasted, 'in which this has been achieved'. Of Serbia's 23,000 Jews, 20,000 had been murdered.

Map 69

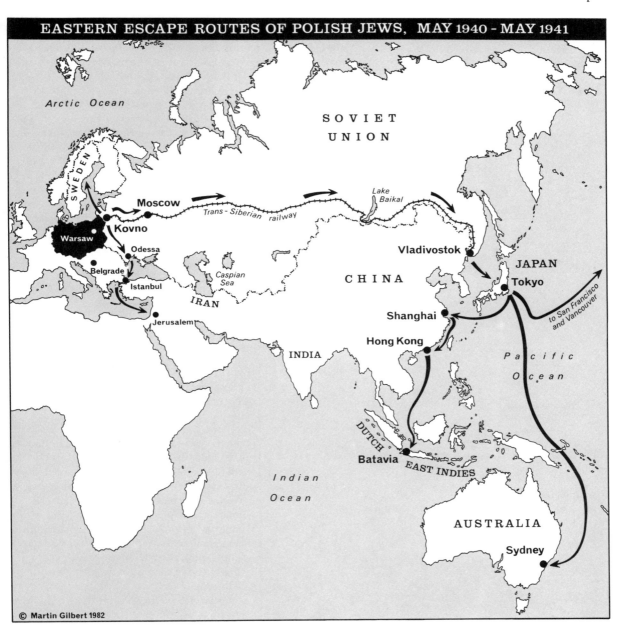

EASTERN ESCAPE ROUTES OF POLISH JEWS, MAY 1940 - MAY 1941

In the year before the German invasion of
the Soviet Union, hundreds of Jews living in
the Soviet-annexed regions of Poland and
the Baltic States, as well as refugees from
German-occupied Poland, tried to escape to
potentially safer regions. In the Lithuanian
city of Kovno, the British Consul, Thomas
Preston, helped provide 400 'illegal' Palestine certificates for Jews who were
then able to make their way through Istanbul
to Jerusalem, while a further 800 received
legal certificates. A few hundred Jews were
able to cross the Baltic Sea to Sweden. The
leaders of several Jewish youth movements,

however, decided to return to Warsaw, to
help organize resistance there.

Several hundred Polish and Lithuanian
Jews managed to get permission to enter
Japan. A few others received transit visas,
issued between 20 and 31 August 1940 by
Sugehara, the Japanese Consul in Kovno,
enabling them to cross the Trans-Siberian
railway to Japan, ostensibly for the Dutch
East Indies. They were then able to move on
to Australia, the United States and Canada.

But those who managed to escape were
only a fragment of those trapped in eastern
Poland, the Baltic States and western Russia.

Map 70

RUSSIAN JEWRY, A SAMPLE

On 22 June 1941 German forces invaded the Soviet Union. As they advanced they moved through areas of dense Jewish settlement, in which lived more than 2,700,000 Jews as well as several hundred thousand Jewish refugees from western Poland.

The figures shown here (*left*) of the number of Jews in some of the cities, towns and villages of western Russia are taken from the Soviet census of 1926. In cities such as Kharkov Jews constituted more than 20 per cent of the total population, and between 1926 and the outbreak of war, the Jewish population of most of the towns shown here had increased. Some had almost doubled: there were as many as 150,000 Jews in Kharkov on the eve of the German invasion. In the Crimea, ancient Jewish communities dating back to Greek and Roman times, and Jewish collective farms set up in the 1920s, existed side by side.

The Jews of several towns shown on the left-hand map had lived through the pogroms in Tsarist times (*page 14*). Many more had been the victims of the massacres of 1918 and 1919, which had claimed 85,000 lives (*page 15*). Some of the towns, such as Starodub, had taken a lead in organizing Jewish self-defence during that period. Others, a few years later, had been at the centre of the famine region, when millions of Soviet citizens had perished.

During the early 1920s tens of thousands of Russian Jews had emigrated, some to avoid Communist persecution, others to escape the all-pervading poverty. But the majority had no choice but to remain in their homes and with their families, working in shops and offices, tilling the fields, and simply trying to exist in the harsh world of Stalinism.

Hitler had other plans for these millions of Jews. He wanted them neither as subjects, nor as slaves. He had made his plans before the German invasion: in May 1941, at Pretzsch, in Saxony, special mobile killing squads, the 'Einsatzgruppen', were set up. Each squad had been allocated a particular area of the Soviet Union for its future activities. Thus Einsatzgruppe A was to be responsible for the murder of Jews in the Baltic States, while Einsatzgruppe D was to work in the Ukraine and the Crimea.

Just as the German army was confident that it could defeat the Soviet Union, and conquer all of western Russia, so the SS was convinced that it could, by mass executions on the spot, 'solve' the Jewish question in

Map 71

THE GERMAN INVASION OF RUSSIA, AND MASS MURDER PLANS, 22 JUNE 1941

© Martin Gilbert 1982

Russia, by murdering all the Jews it could catch. No family was to be spared. Nor were any resources to be wasted in setting up ghettos, nor in the deportation of Jews to distant camps or murder sites. The killing was to be done in the towns and villages, at the moment of military victory.

When the German army invaded Russia in June 1941, its advance was so rapid that less than 300,000 Jews were able to escape eastward, to safety beyond the Volga.

The photograph, taken from the personal album of one of the officers in the picture, shows the arrival of a detachment of Einsatzgruppe D in the town of Drohobycz, in the Polish province of Eastern Galicia, which Russia had annexed in October 1939. Part of the task of these killing squads was to recruit local anti-semites, whether Ukrainians, Lithuanians, or Latvians, who could help them to round up, terrorize and destroy each Jewish community, however small. For the work of this particular detachment in Drohobycz itself, see page 67.

The map above shows the regions allocated to the different killing squads, and the initial points of attack of the German army and its Rumanian ally on 22 June 1941.

Map 72

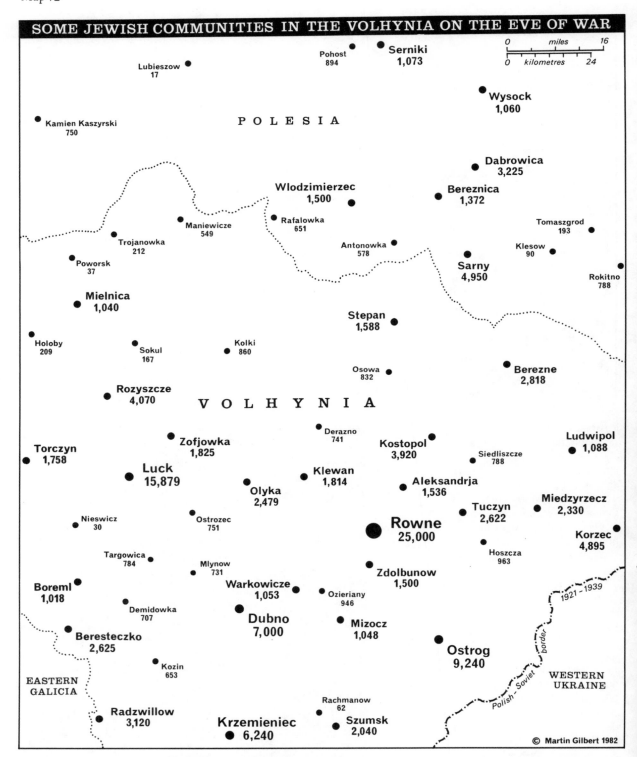

SOME JEWISH COMMUNITIES IN THE VOLHYNIA ON THE EVE OF WAR

0 — miles — 16
0 — kilometres — 24

Pohost 894

Serniki 1,073

Lubieszow 17

Wysock 1,060

P O L E S I A

Kamien Kaszyrski 750

Dabrowica 3,225

Bereznica 1,372

Wlodzimierzec 1,500

Rafalowka 651

Tomaszgrod 193

Maniewicze 549

Antonowka 578

Klesow 90

Trojanowka 212

Sarny 4,950

Rokitno 788

Poworsk 37

Mielnica 1,040

Stepan 1,588

Holoby 209

Sokul 167

Kolki 860

Osowa 832

Berezne 2,818

Rozyszcze 4,070

V O L H Y N I A

Derazno 741

Ludwipol 1,088

Torczyn 1,758

Zofjowka 1,825

Kostopol 3,920

Siedliszcze 788

Luck 15,879

Klewan 1,814

Aleksandrja 1,536

Miedzyrzecz 2,330

Olyka 2,479

Tuczyn 2,622

Nieswicz 30

Ostrozec 751

Rowne 25,000

Korzec 4,895

Hoszcza 963

Targowica 784

Mlynow 731

Zdolbunow 1,500

Boreml 1,018

Warkowicze 1,053

Ozieriany 946

1921-1939

Demidowka 707

Dubno 7,000

Mizocz 1,048

Beresteczko 2,625

Kozin 653

Ostrog 9,240

EASTERN GALICIA

WESTERN UKRAINE

Radzwillow 3,120

Rachmanow 62

Szumsk 2,040

Polish-Soviet border

Krzemieniec 6,240

© Martin Gilbert 1982

In the first three weeks of their invasion of the Soviet Union, the German forces made rapid advances. In their wake, the specially trained mobile killing squads began the systematic murder of Jews, in every city, town and village of western Russia. The map above shows the number of Jews living in the larger towns and villages of part of the Volhynia, an area inside the Russian Empire until 1914, and within the independent Polish

Map 73

JEWS MASSACRED BETWEEN 22 JUNE AND 16 JULY 1941

Gulf of Riga

Baltic Sea

Riga **400**

Jelgava 2,000

Jekabpils **700**

Siauliai 3,000

Rietavas **500**

Vandziogala **34**

Widze **200**

Virbalis **500**

Kovno 3,000

Swieciany **100**

Vilna 5,000
4-20 July

Wilejka **150**

THE

Marijampole **70**

Moscow

R.=Radzilow **1,500**

J=Jedwabne **1,000**

S=Szczuczyn **1,900**

Grodno **80**

Lida **200**

Minsk 2,000

W=Wasosz **1,185**

Augustow 1,000
S
W
R
J

Krynki **30**

Nowogrodek **50**

Baranowicze **400**

German forces advancing

Warsaw

Bialystok 5,200

Kobryn **70**

Brest-Litovsk 5,000

Janow **400**

SOVIET

GREATER GERMANY

David Grodek 1,000

see map 72

Sokal **200**

Tuczyn **70**

Toporow **180**

German forces advancing

Lvov 3,000

Kamionka Strumilowa **200**

Zloczow 3,500

Kiev

Sambor **100**

Drohobycz **400**

Tarnopol 5,000

UNION

SLOVAKIA

Boryslaw **200**

Jezierna **180**

Skalat **560**

Stryj **300**

Czortkow **200**

HUNGARY

Czernowitz 2,400

Hotin 2,000

Novoselitsa **800**

Marculesti 1,000

Jassy **2,421** in two death trains organized by Rumanian fascists

Odessa

RUMANIA

0 — miles — 100
0 — kilometres — 150

© Martin Gilbert 1982

state between the wars. The Volhynia was annexed by Russia at the time of the Nazi-Soviet partition of Poland in October 1939. In the area shown here, there were also more than 100 smaller Jewish communities.

In all, more than a quarter of a million Jews were living in the Volhynia in 1939. The figures above show some of the German killing squad massacres during the first three weeks following the invasion.

Map 74

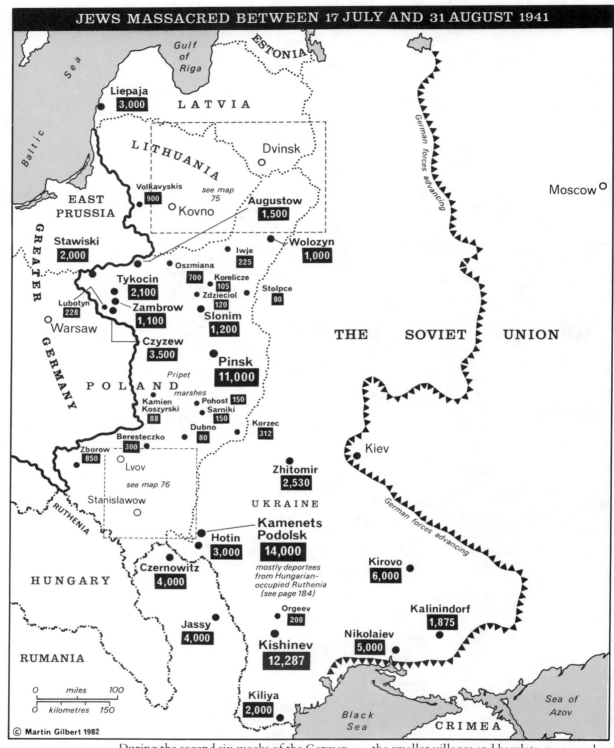

JEWS MASSACRED BETWEEN 17 JULY AND 31 AUGUST 1941

Gulf of Riga

Baltic Sea

ESTONIA

Liepaja 3,000

LATVIA

LITHUANIA

Dvinsk

Moscow

EAST PRUSSIA

Volkavyskis 900

see map 75

Kovno

Augustow 1,500

German forces advancing

Stawiski 2,000

Iwje 225

Wolozyn 1,000

Oszmiana 700

Korelicze 105

Stolpce 80

Tykocin 2,100

Zdzieciol 120

Lubotyn 228

Zambrow 1,100

Slonim 1,200

THE   SOVIET   UNION

Warsaw

GERMANY

Czyzew 3,500

Pripet marshes

Pinsk 11,000

POLAND

Kamien Koszyrski 88

Pohost 150

Sarniki 150

Dubno 80

Korzec 312

Beresteczko

Zborow 300

Lvov

Kiev

Zhitomir 2,530

see map 76

Stanislawow

UKRAINE

German forces advancing

RUTHENIA

Hotin 3,000

Kamenets Podolsk 14,000

mostly deportees from Hungarian-occupied Ruthenia (see page 184)

Kirovo 6,000

Czernowitz 4,000

HUNGARY

Orgeev 200

Kalinindorf 1,875

Jassy 4,000

Kishinev 12,287

Nikolaiev 5,000

RUMANIA

0 miles 100

0 kilometres 150

Kiliya 2,000

Black Sea

CRIMEA

Sea of Azov

© Martin Gilbert 1982

During the second six weeks of the German advance into Russia, the work of the killing squads continued without respite. This map, like the previous map and the maps on the right, shows only a small percentage of the total killings. For many places, particularly the smaller villages and hamlets, no record survives. Nor was the killing confined to SS units. In Lithuania local non-Jews were among the most savage killers, while in the south, Rumanian troops and militia murdered thousands of Jews in the area of

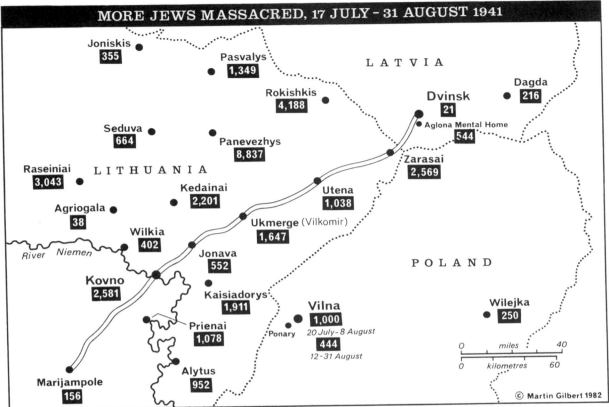

MORE JEWS MASSACRED, 17 JULY - 31 AUGUST 1941

Joniskis **355**

Pasvalys **1,349**

Rokishkis **4,188**

L A T V I A

Dagda **216**

Dvinsk **21**

Aglona Mental Home **544**

Seduva **664**

Panevezhys **8,837**

Zarasai **2,569**

Raseiniai **3,043**

L I T H U A N I A

Kedainai **2,201**

Utena **1,038**

Agriogala **38**

Ukmerge (Vilkomir) **1,647**

Wilkia **402**

P O L A N D

River Niemen

Jonava **552**

Kovno **2,581**

Kaisiadorys **1,911**

Vilna **1,000**
Ponary
20 July - 8 August **444**
12 - 31 August

Wilejka **250**

Prienai **1,078**

0 miles 40
0 kilometres 60

Marijampole **156**

Alytus **952**

© Martin Gilbert 1982

Rumanian military advance. Throughout Eastern Galicia *(right)* Ukrainian peasants frequently set upon the Jews, murdering hundreds before the German killing squads arrived. But it was the German squads whose work was on the larger scale, including the first 'five figure' massacre of Jews by Einsatzgruppe D in Kishinev between 17 and 31 July 1941 *(page 71)*. A second 'five figure' massacre took place on August 27 and 28, of Jews who had earlier been deported to Kamenets Podolsk from Hungary. These were not Hungarian citizens but Jewish refugees who had fled to Hungary and Ruthenia in 1938 and 1939 from Germany, Austria, Slovakia and Poland. Some had lived in Hungary as 'Aryans', on false identity papers. Others had obtained the right to live in Hungary as 'transients' on their way to Palestine. Rounded up and deported eastward during July, over 18,000 had been sent to camps in and around Kamenets Podolsk. On 27 August 1941 heavily armed SS units, with Ukrainian militia support, marched 14,000 of these refugees some 10 miles to a series of bomb craters, ordered them to undress, and opened fire with machine-guns. Many of those who died had been buried alive.

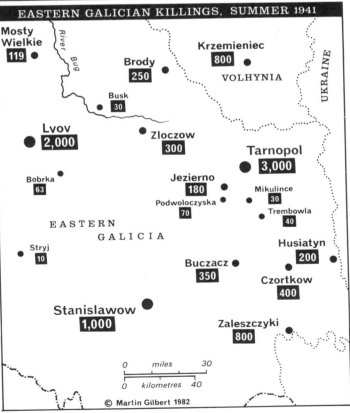

EASTERN GALICIAN KILLINGS, SUMMER 1941

Mosty Wielkie **119**

River Bug

Brody **250**

Krzemieniec **800**

VOLHYNIA

Busk **30**

U K R A I N E

Lvov **2,000**

Zloczow **300**

Tarnopol **3,000**

Bobrka **63**

Jezierno **180**

Mikulince **30**

Podwoloczyska **70**

Trembowla **40**

E A S T E R N

G A L I C I A

Husiatyn **200**

Stryj **10**

Buczacz **350**

Czortkow **400**

Stanislawow **1,000**

Zaleszczyki **800**

0 miles 30
0 kilometres 40

© Martin Gilbert 1982

Map 77

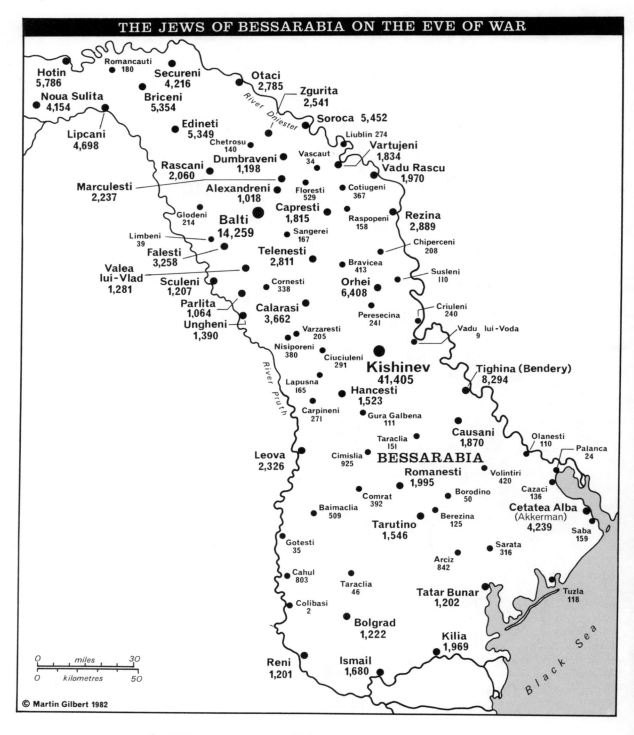

THE JEWS OF BESSARABIA ON THE EVE OF WAR

Hotin 5,786
Romancauti 180
Secureni 4,216
Otaci 2,785
Zgurita 2,541
Noua Sulita 4,154
Briceni 5,354
Soroca 5,452
Liublin 274
Lipcani 4,698
Edineti 5,349
Chetrosu 140
Vascaut 34
Vartujeni 1,834
Vadu Rascu 1,970
Rascani 2,060
Dumbraveni 1,198
Alexandreni 1,018
Floresti 529
Cotiugeni 367
Marculesti 2,237
Glodeni 214
Balti 14,259
Capresti 1,815
Raspopeni 158
Rezina 2,889
Limbeni 39
Sangerei 167
Chiperceni 208
Falesti 3,258
Telenesti 2,811
Bravicea 413
Susleni 110
Valea lui-Vlad 1,281
Sculeni 1,207
Cornesti 338
Orhei 6,408
Parlita 1,064
Calarasi 3,662
Peresecina 241
Criuleni 240
Ungheni 1,390
Varzaresti 205
Vadu lui-Voda 9
Nisiporeni 380
Ciuciuleni 291
Kishinev 41,405
Tighina (Bendery) 8,294
Lapusna 165
Hancesti 1,523
Carpineni 271
Gura Galbena 111
Causani 1,870
Olanesti 110
Palanca 24
Taraclia 151
Leova 2,326
Cimislia 925
BESSARABIA
Volintiri 420
Cazaci 136
Romanesti 1,995
Borodino 50
Comrat 392
Cetatea Alba (Akkerman) 4,239
Baimaclia 509
Berezina 125
Saba 159
Tarutino 1,546
Gotesti 35
Arciz 842
Sarata 316
Cahul 803
Taraclia 46
Tatar Bunar 1,202
Tuzla 118
Colibasi 2
Bolgrad 1,222
Kilia 1,969
Reni 1,201
Ismail 1,680
Black Sea

River Dniester

River Pruth

0 miles 30
0 kilometres 50

© Martin Gilbert 1982

Until 1941 Bessarabia was part of the Tsarist Empire. The murder of 49 Jews during the Kishinev pogrom in 1903 *(page 14)* had led to protest demonstrations in London, Paris and New York, and a letter of rebuke from Theodore Roosevelt to the Tsar. In 1918 the region became part of Rumania but remained strongly anti-semitic. The city of Kishinev was a focal point of Jewish culture and political life, while Jewish agricultural communities thrived throughout the province.

With the return of Soviet rule to Bessarabia in June 1940, all Jewish

Map 78

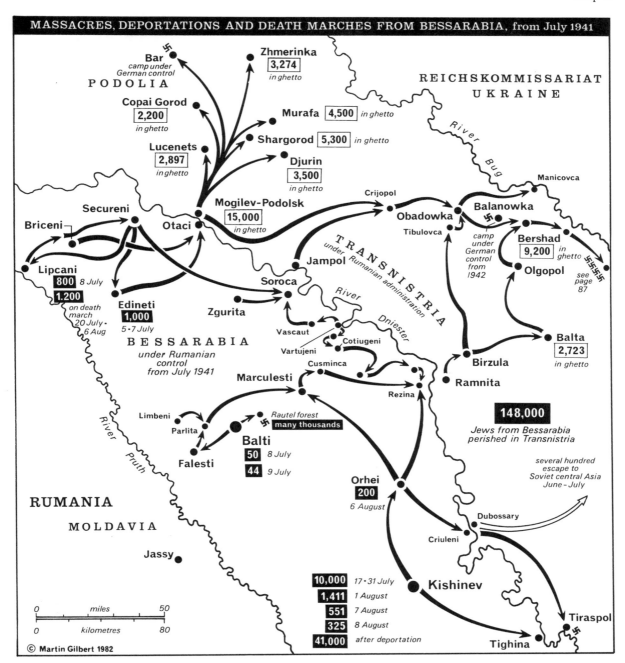

MASSACRES, DEPORTATIONS AND DEATH MARCHES FROM BESSARABIA, from July 1941

REICHSKOMMISSARIAT UKRAINE

PODOLIA

Bar
camp under German control

Zhmerinka
3,274 *in ghetto*

Copai Gorod
2,200 *in ghetto*

Murafa **4,500** *in ghetto*

Shargorod **5,300** *in ghetto*

Lucenets
2,897 *in ghetto*

Djurin
3,500 *in ghetto*

Mogilev-Podolsk
15,000 *in ghetto*

Crijopol

Manicovca

Obadowka

Balanowka

camp under German control from 1942

Bershad
9,200 *in ghetto*

Olgopol

see page 87

Secureni

Otaci

Briceni

Jampol

TRANSNISTRIA
under Rumanian administration

Tibulovca

Lipcani
800 *8 July*
1,200 *on death march 20 July - 6 Aug*

Edineti
1,000 *5-7 July*

Zgurita

Soroca

Vascaut

Vartujeni

Cotiugeni

River Dniester

Birzula

Balta
2,723 *in ghetto*

BESSARABIA
under Rumanian control from July 1941

Marculesti

Cusminca

Rezina

Ramnita

148,000
Jews from Bessarabia perished in Transnistria

Limbeni

Parlita

Rautel forest
many thousands

Balti
50 *8 July*
44 *9 July*

Falesti

Orhei
200 *6 August*

several hundred escape to Soviet central Asia June - July

Dubossary

RUMANIA

MOLDAVIA

Jassy

Criuleni

Kishinev

River Pruth

10,000 *17-31 July*
1,411 *1 August*
551 *7 August*
325 *8 August*
41,000 *after deportation*

Tiraspol

Tighina

0 ——— miles ——— 50
0 ——— kilometres ——— 80

© Martin Gilbert 1982

institutions were closed and on 13 June 1941 many of the Jewish leaders, as well as wealthy Jews, were exiled to Siberia, where many died. But with the arrival of the Nazi killing squads in July 1941, the scale of murder, as indicated above, exceeded anything previously known.

Following the initial killings, internment camps were set up throughout the province. At the camp in Edineti, after the initial slaughter, 70 to 100 people died every day in July and August 1941, mostly of starvation.

Then in September the Jews of Bessarabia were forced out of the province in hundreds of death marches, some of which are shown above. In all, more than 148,000 Bessarabian Jews perished in the ghettos and camps of Transnistria. During these marches more than half of the victims died: of exposure, disease, hunger, thirst and the savage brutality of the Rumanian and German guards, who would often pick a group of marchers at random, order them aside, and shoot them.

Map 79

THE JEWS OF THE BUKOVINA ON THE EVE OF WAR

miles 0 — 10

kilometres 0 — 20

Kolomyja

GREATER GERMANY (EASTERN GALICIA)

Sniatyn

RUMANIA (BESSARABIA)

Cincau **57**

Dorosauti **58**

Ocna **115**

Zastavna **635**

Davidesti **48**

Cozmeni **640**

Lujeni **381**

Sadagura **1,488**

River

Banila pe Ceremus **517**

Stanestii **622**

Broscauti **115**

Milie **197**

Ispas **143**

Kuty

Vijnita **2,666**

Costesti **274**

Cabesti **120**

Jadova **50**

Panca **25**

Czernowitz (Cernauti) **42,932**

Pruth

Berhomet **979**

Nova Jadova **325**

Mihova **243**

Storojinet **2,482**

River

Iordanesti **99**

Rastoace **71**

Mareniceni **25**

Gura Putilei **115**

Dintinet **56**

Banila **688**

Cires **100**

Budinet **8**

Siret

RUMANIA (MOLDAVIA)

Ciudeiu **570**

Petrauti **138**

Toraceni **58**

Putila **382**

Crasna Putnei **169**

Crasna Iliesti **97**

Igesti **100**

Fradautii Noui **104**

Siret **2,121**

Sarghieni **204**

Vicovul de Sus **334**

Bainet **23**

Zamostea **129**

Plosca **99**

Seletin **737**

Brodina **234**

Straja **134**

Putna **214**

Dornesti **84**

Zvorastea **28**

BUKOVINA

Argel **11**

Sucevita **10**

Marginea **23**

Radauti **5,647**

Serbauti **14**

Clit **4**

Granicesti **9**

Moldovita **452**

Poiana **11**

Darmanesti **92**

River Ceremos

River Ceremos

Moldova Sulita **55**

Vatra **136**

Frumosul **88**

Ilisesti **131**

Suceava **3,533**

Breaza **94**

Vama **392**

Liteni **11**

Carlibaba **154**

Campulung-Moldovenesc **1,488**

Frasin **156**

Gura Humoruliu **1,951**

Paltinoasa **14**

HUNGARY (TRANSYLVANIA)

Ciocanesti **7**

Stulpicani **151**

River Moldova

Iacobeni **228**

Vatra Dornei **1,750**

Ostra **10**

RUMANIA

© Martin Gilbert 1982

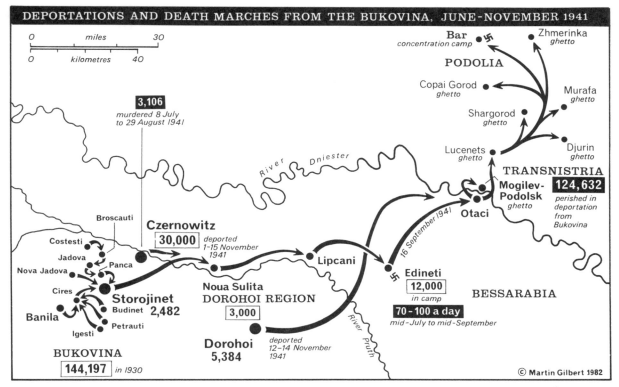

DEPORTATIONS AND DEATH MARCHES FROM THE BUKOVINA, JUNE–NOVEMBER 1941

miles 0 30
kilometres 0 40

Bar
concentration camp

Zhmerinka
ghetto

PODOLIA

Copai Gorod
ghetto

Murafa
ghetto

3,106
murdered 8 July
to 29 August 1941

Shargorod
ghetto

River Dniester

Lucenets
ghetto

Djurin
ghetto

TRANSNISTRIA **124,632**
perished in
deportation
from
Bukovina

Mogilev-
Podolsk
ghetto

Broscauti

Czernowitz **30,000** deported
1–15 November
1941

Otaci

16 September 1941

Costesti

Jadova

Panca

Lipcani

Edineti **12,000**
in camp

70 – 100 a day
mid-July to mid-September

BESSARABIA

Nova Jadova

Cires

Storojinet
Budinet 2,482

Noua Sulita
DOROHOI REGION
3,000

River Pruth

Banila

Igesti

Petrauti

Dorohoi
5,384
deported
12–14 November
1941

BUKOVINA
144,197 in 1930

© Martin Gilbert 1982

THE BUKOVINA

North Sea

Oslo
Stockholm

Leningrad

Moscow

miles 0 300
kilometres 0 500

Berlin

Warsaw

Kiev

Paris

GREATER
GERMANY

Vienna

Lvov

BUKOVINA

HUNGARY

Black
Sea

Rome

RUMANIA

Belgrade

Istanbul

Athens

CRETE

© Martin Gilbert 1982

The Jews of the Bukovina, like those of
Bessarabia, were driven eastwards to ghettos
in Transnistria. Uprooted from more than
100 communities, they too were marched
away, interned, and then marched off again.
Within a year more than 120,000 had died
(page 87). The photograph was taken at the
start of a Bukovina death march.

THE JEWS OF ESTONIA ON THE EVE OF WAR

FINLAND

Helsinki

Gulf of Finland

Leningrad

German front line
1 September 1941

Baltic
Sea

Tallinn
4,213

Paldiski
1

Nõmme
109

Keila
1

Rakvere
100

Johvi
8

Narva
370

Tapa
16

Mustvee
6

ESTONIA

Haapsalu
11

Türi
2

Paide
31

DAGO
10

Jõgeva
5

Lake
Peipus

SOVIET

UNION

Karuse
37

Põltsamaa
2

Pärnu
500

Viljandi
226

OSEL

Kuressaare
37

Kilingi-
Nõmme
1

Mõisaküla
1

Tõrva
1

Tartu
1,766

Lake
Pskov

Valga
521

Anstla
3

Võru
199

Petseri
5

Pskov

Gulf of
Riga

LATVIA

0   miles   40
0   kilometres   60

© Martin Gilbert 1982

ESTONIA CONQUERED, 3 SEPTEMBER 1941

Oslo

Helsinki

Leningrad

Stockholm

Pskov

ESTONIA

Moscow

North
Sea

Baltic
Sea

Vilna

Berlin

GREATER
GERMANY

Warsaw

German front line

1 September 1941

Vienna

Czernowitz

0   miles   200
0   kilometres   400

Budapest

Loborgrad

BOSNIA

Bucharest

Black Sea

Sarajevo

Belgrade

Rome

Sofia

Ankara

© Martin Gilbert 1982

The Jewish community of Estonia owed its origins to the Cantonists: Jewish boy soldiers conscripted for the army of Tsar Nicholas I at the age of 12, and sometimes even at eight or nine. These boys served a compulsory 25 years, a system which had started in 1827 and which continued for more than 20 years. On demobilization, many Cantonists settled in Tallin, known in Russian as Reval. A further 2,000 Russian Jews came in Tsarist times to live in the university town of Tartu, known to the Jews by its German name, Dorpat.

In the inter-war years Estonia was the only country in eastern Europe to adhere to the minority treaties of the League of Nations. Jewish autonomous institutions, set up in 1926, were controlled by a Jewish Cultural Council. For ten years Jewish life flourished. But from 1934, a local fascist movement encouraged anti-semitism.

In 1940 Estonia was annexed by the Soviet Union. Five hundred Jewish communal leaders, as well as many 'capitalist' Jews, were then deported to Siberia, where many died. But following the German invasion of Russia in June 1941, some 3,000 Estonian

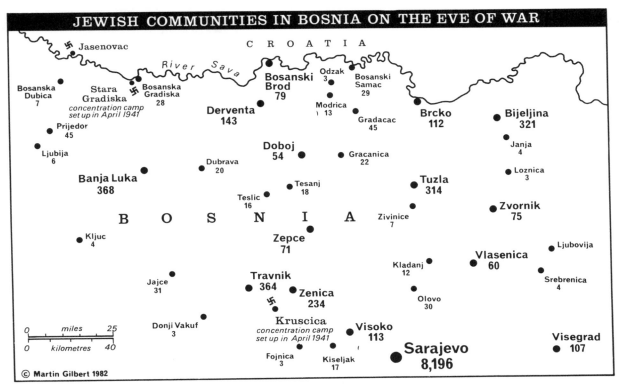

JEWISH COMMUNITIES IN BOSNIA ON THE EVE OF WAR

C R O A T I A

River Sava

Jasenovac

Bosanska Dubica 7

Stara Gradiska
concentration camp set up in April 1941

Bosanska Gradiska 28

Bosanski Brod 79

Odzak 3

Bosanski Samac 29

Derventa 143

Modrica 13

Gradacac 45

Brcko 112

Bijeljina 321

Prijedor 45

Ljubija 6

Doboj 54

Gracanica 22

Janja 4

Loznica 3

Banja Luka 368

Dubrava 20

Tesanj 18

Teslic 16

Tuzla 314

Zvornik 75

B O S N I A

Zivinice 7

Ljubovija

Kljuc 4

Zepce 71

Kladanj 12

Vlasenica 60

Srebrenica 4

Jajce 31

Travnik 364

Zenica 234

Olovo 30

Donji Vakuf 3

Kruscica
concentration camp set up in April 1941

Visoko 113

Visegrad 107

Fojnica 3

Kiseljak 17

Sarajevo 8,196

miles 0–25
kilometres 0–40

© Martin Gilbert 1982

Jews found refuge in the Soviet Union. After the German occupation of Tallin in September, the remaining 1,000 Jews were murdered by the SS killing squads.

After the German invasion of Bosnia, a few Jews managed to flee over the mountains into Italian-occupied territory, but the majority were deported to concentration camps controlled by the Croat fascist 'Ustachi'. The majority died in the camps.

The Jewish community of Sarajevo had been built up during the sixteenth century by Jewish refugees from Spain. These 'Sephardi' Jews spoke their own language, Ladino, and helped, as merchants and traders, to link Bosnia with the outside world. After the Austrian annexation of Bosnia in 1878, hundreds of Ashkenazi Jews, from Vienna, Prague and Budapest, joined the local communities. Between the wars, during the 'Yugoslav era', the Jews of Bosnia enjoyed full civil liberties. But disaster struck from the first days of the German occupation, with the burning down of the synagogue by German troops and local Muslims.

By November 1941 a total of 14,000 Bosnian Jews had been deported to the camps shown here *(right)*. Less than 1,000 survived the war.

THE JEWS OF BOSNIA MURDERED

miles 0–40
kilometres 0–60

Loborgrad
4,000
women

C R O A T I A

Jasenovac
4,000
men

Stara Gradiska
6,000
children

children

men

women

Tuzla

B O S N I A

Travnik

Kruscica

Sarajevo

Italian zone

D A L M A T I A

Mostar
1,600

Adriatic Sea

© Martin Gilbert 1982

Map 86

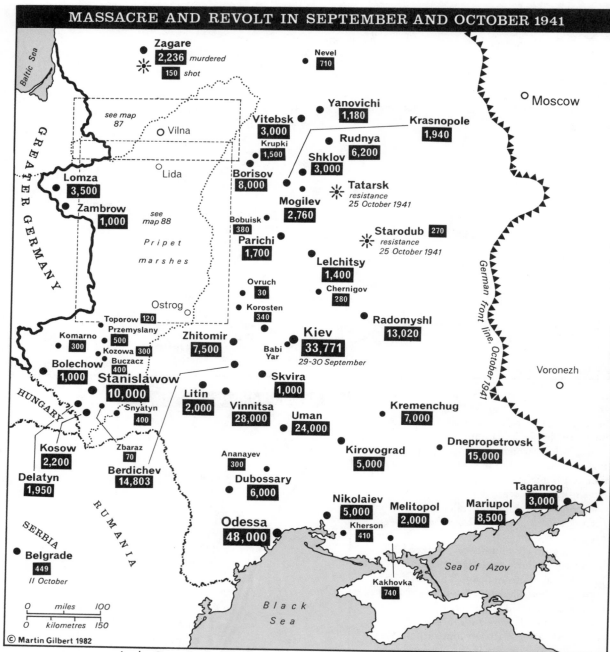

MASSACRE AND REVOLT IN SEPTEMBER AND OCTOBER 1941

Baltic Sea

Zagare 2,236 *murdered* 150 *shot*

Nevel 710

O Moscow

GREATER GERMANY

see map 87

O Vilna

Yanovichi 1,180

Vitebsk 3,000

Krupki 1,500

Krasnopole 1,940

O Lida

Rudnya 6,200

Lomza 3,500

Borisov 8,000

Shklov 3,000

Zambrow 1,000

see map 88

Tatarsk *resistance 25 October 1941*

Mogilev 2,760

P r i p e t   m a r s h e s

Bobuisk 380

Starodub 270 *resistance 25 October 1941*

Parichi 1,700

O Ostrog

Lelchitsy 1,400

German front line, October 1941

Ovruch 30

Chernigov 280

Toporow 120

Korosten 340

Radomyshl 13,020

Komarno 300

Przemyslany 500

Zhitomir 7,500

Kiev 33,771 *29-30 September*

Kozowa 300

Babi Yar

Voronezh O

Bolechow 1,000

Buczacz 400

Stanislawow 10,000

Litin 2,000

Skvira 1,000

HUNGARY

Snyatyn 400

Vinnitsa 28,000

Uman 24,000

Kremenchug 7,000

Dnepropetrovsk 15,000

Zbaraz 70

Kosow 2,200

Berdichev 14,803

Ananayev 300

Kirovograd 5,000

Delatyn 1,950

Dubossary 6,000

R U M A N I A

Nikolaiev 5,000

Melitopol 2,000

Mariupol 8,500

Taganrog 3,000

SERBIA

Odessa 48,000

Kherson 410

Sea of Azov

Belgrade 449 *II October*

0 miles 100
0 kilometres 150

Kakhovka 740

Black Sea

© Martin Gilbert 1982

As the German armies approached Moscow, the killing squads continued their work behind the lines. The map above shows some of the main killings. The map opposite (*above*) shows the details in the Vilna region of Lithuania, where a German lieutenant carefully recorded for his superiors the precise number of those killed on each day of his squad's activities, dividing his statistics into men, women and children.

The killing squads were heavily armed and had strong local support. The Jews were unarmed, and surrounded by an extremely hostile peasantry, who sometimes attacked them even before the killing squads had arrived. In some cases this random butchery of so many Jews led the SS to order the locals to stop the killing, in order to put it on a 'systematic' basis, according to the killing squad schedules. Despite the overwhelming odds against them the Jews rose in revolt wherever they could. The first revolts, as shown above, were at Tatarsk and Starodub. To crush this resistance, German regular

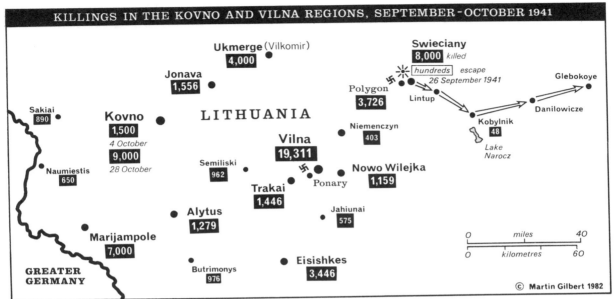

KILLINGS IN THE KOVNO AND VILNA REGIONS, SEPTEMBER – OCTOBER 1941

Sakiai 890

Kovno 1,500
4 October
9,000
28 October

Naumiestis 650

GREATER GERMANY

Marijampole 7,000

Butrimonys 976

Alytus 1,279

Trakai 1,446

Semiliski 962

Ponary

LITHUANIA

Jonava 1,556

Ukmerge (Vilkomir) 4,000

Vilna 19,311

Niemenczyn 403

Nowo Wilejka 1,159

Jahiunai 575

Eisishkes 3,446

Swieciany 8,000 killed
hundreds escape 26 September 1941
Lintup

Polygon 3,726

Kobylnik 48
Lake Narocz

Danilowicze

Glebokoye

miles 40
kilometres 60

© Martin Gilbert 1982

army units were brought in. Where necessary, as resistance spread, the Germans used artillery fire, and even air support.

At Kiev the Jews were driven into Babi Yar, a ravine in the suburbs, and then machine-gunned by an SS killing squad, helped by Ukrainian militiamen.

At Vilna the Jews were confined to a ghetto inside the city, where hundreds were murdered. Others were taken away in batches of a thousand and more to pits eight miles away, at the village of Ponary. Here too, they were shot.

Any Jews who managed to escape from their executioners at the pits were killed by a special unit of Germans and Lithuanians. Hundreds of other Jews were murdered inside Vilna itself, and in the notorious Lukiszki prison. In two months, throughout the former eastern provinces of Poland (*right, below*), more than 20,000 Jews were murdered.

On 26 September 1941 the Jews of Swieciany were rounded up and taken to a former army camp in the nearby Polygon woods, where they were massacred. On the evening before, several hundred young men and women had managed to break through the Lithuanian police cordon and escape eastwards, to towns not yet reached by the killing squads. These Jewish communities were liable at any moment to be subjected to the activities of the killing squads, for, as the map opposite shows, the front line, with its chaos and confusion had long since moved much further east.

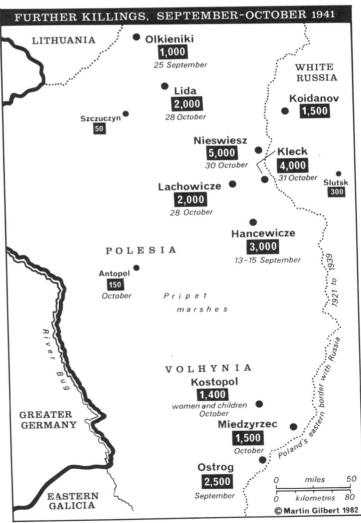

FURTHER KILLINGS, SEPTEMBER – OCTOBER 1941

LITHUANIA

Olkieniki 1,000
25 September

Szczuczyn 50

Lida 2,000
28 October

WHITE RUSSIA

Koidanov 1,500

Nieswiesz 5,000
30 October

Kleck 4,000
31 October

Slutsk 300

Lachowicze 2,000
28 October

POLESIA

Antopol 150
October

Pripet marshes

Hancewicze 3,000
13–15 September

River Bug

GREATER GERMANY

EASTERN GALICIA

VOLHYNIA

Kostopol 1,400
women and children
October

Miedzyrzec 1,500
October

Ostrog 2,500
September

Poland's eastern border with Russia
1921 to 1939

miles 50
kilometres 80

© Martin Gilbert 1982

Map 89

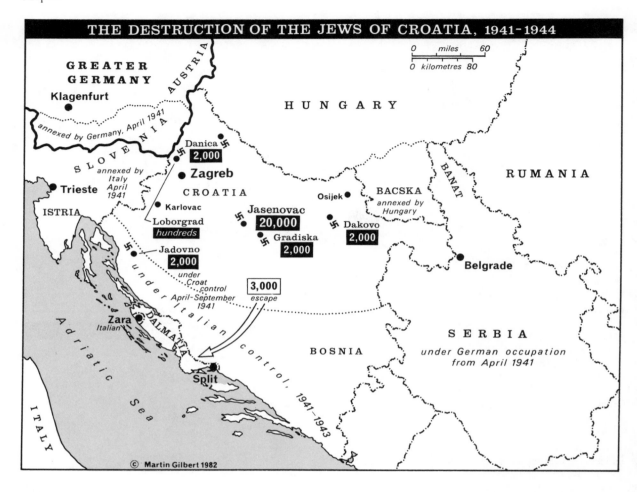

THE DESTRUCTION OF THE JEWS OF CROATIA, 1941-1944

Following the German army's conquest of Yugoslavia, a pro-German regime was established in Croatia, with its capital at Zagreb (*above*). On 30 April 1941 this new Croat State introduced its first racial laws, removing Jews from public office and ordering all Jews to wear a yellow badge. Within a few weeks, several wealthy Jews had been seized in Zagreb and held as hostages until local Jews could provide 100 kilogrammes of gold for their release, thus impoverishing the community. By the end of May all Jewish cultural institutions had been closed, synagogues ransacked, and cemeteries destroyed.

In May 1941 the first Croat concentration camp was set up, at Danica. It was quickly followed by four more camps, at Jadovno, Gradiska, Loborgrad, and Dakovo. More than 6,000 Croat Jews were deported to these camps, and during July and August almost all of them were murdered. On 1 October 1941 a further camp was established at Jasenovac.

By the end of 1942 the remaining 20,000 Croat Jews had been rounded up and sent to Jasenovac, where most of them were starved to death, beaten to death or shot. By the spring of 1945, as the Soviet army and Yugoslav partisan forces approached the camp, only a few hundred were still alive (*page 220*).

Between April 1941 and April 1942 more than 3,000 Croatian Jews escaped over the mountains to Italy and the Italian-controlled coastal zone. But by a law of 30 April 1941, people with only one Jewish parent were 'protected' from deportation.

Because of the successful intervention by the Catholic Church and the Papal Nuncio to save the Jewish partners in mixed marriages, 1,000 Croat Jews survived the war.

In Holland the Jews had been confined to special parts of the towns, denied the right to teach or to remain in the civil service, and ordered to wear a yellow star. Nazi agitators repeatedly raided the Jewish quarter of

Amsterdam, beating up Jews in the streets. At the beginning of February 1941 a Dutch Nazi had been killed when the Jews resisted one such attack. At the same time the Germans accused a Jewish tavern owner, Ernst Cahn, of daring to resist a German patrol. Cahn was shot, the first Dutch citizen to die in front of a German firing-squad. A few days later, on 22 February 1941, the SS raided the Jewish quarter of Amsterdam as a reprisal for the earlier resistance: 425 Jews were arrested, beaten, and deported to Buchenwald (*above, right*). Some died there. The rest, among them the distinguished Czech pharmacologist, Emil Starckenstein, were transferred shortly afterwards to Mauthausen. Within three days of their arrival, they were killed in the stone quarry, the centre of Mauthausen's forced labour network (*right*).

The photograph is of the gallows at Mauthausen, photographed at liberation (*pages 234-5*).

Map 92

TWELVE EASTWARD DEPORTATIONS, 16 OCTOBER–29 NOVEMBER 1941

North Sea

Baltic Sea

Riga
LATVIA

REICHSKOMMISSARIAT
OSTLAND

Minsk
WHITE
RUSSIA

Hamburg
`1,034`

Emden

Berlin
`4,187`
GREATER GERMANY

Lodz

Warsaw

RUHR
Düsseldorf
`984`
Cologne
`2,007`

Würzburg
`202`

BOHEMIA

Prague
`5,000`

Lublin
GENERAL
GOVERNMENT

EASTERN
GALICIA

Frankfurt
`1,113`

Brno
`3,000`

Luxembourg
`512`

Nuremberg
`618`

Vienna
`5,000`

Munich
`1,000`

AUSTRIA

© Martin Gilbert 1982

0   *miles*   150
0 *kilometres* 200

In the autumn of 1941 the SS decided to deport more than 22,000 Jews to the ghettos of Lodz, Warsaw and Lublin, and to the former Soviet cities of Riga and Minsk *(above)*. The first of these deportation trains left on 16 October 1941. On reaching the ghettos, the Jews were faced with starvation. On reaching Riga and Minsk, many were taken to nearby woods and shot.

Meanwhile, beginning on 10 October 1941, thousands of Slovak Jews were sent to labour camps at Sered, Vyhne and Novaky, while the remaining Jews living in what had once been Czechoslovakia were ordered out of their homes and sent to specially designated 'ghetto areas' in 14 selected towns *(opposite, above)*. Already, on 1 September 1941, these Jews had been

ordered to wear the yellow star, and to cease all business activity. In Slovakia alone more than 10,000 Jewish shops and businesses had been closed down.

The largest of the new ghettos was established on 24 November 1941 in the small fortress town of Theresienstadt, known in Czech as Terezin. By the end of the war, 73,614 Jews had been deported to Theresienstadt from Bohemia and Moravia, and thousands more from elsewhere in Greater Germany.

In November the eastward deportations continued, as did the work of the mobile killing squads *(right)*. At the same time, as an experiment, 1,200 prisoners at Buchenwald were taken to the euthanasia institute at Bernberg, and gassed.

BOHEMIAN, MORAVIAN AND SLOVAK JEWS FORCED INTO GHETTOS, 10 OCTOBER 1941

SUDETENLAND

GERMANY

Cheb

Teplice
Usti
Theresienstadt

Karlovy
Vary

Mlada Boleslav

Marianske
Lazne

Brandys

Hradec Kralove

Plana

Prague

Plzen

Pardubice

Kolin

BOHEMIA

Klatovy

MORAVIA

Unicov

Moravska Ostrava

Olomouc

Boskovice

Lipnik

Trebic

Kromeriz

Holesov

Brno

Zilina

Bardejov

Uhersky
Brod

Ruzomberok

Poprad

Presov

GREATER

Ivancice

Trencin

SLOVAKIA

Kosice

Mikulov

Novaky

Vyhne

Breclav

Trnava

Sered

Nitra

Bratislava

Levice

Galanta

FELVIDEK
annexed by Hungary

Dunajska
Streda

Komarno

| 0 | miles | 60 |
| 0 | kilometres | 80 |

© Martin Gilbert 1982

MASSACRE AND DEPORTATION, NOVEMBER 1941

North
Sea

Baltic Sea

Borisov
7,000

Monastyrshchina
1,010

GERMAN-OCCUPIED-RUSSIA

Riga
10.000
Rumbuli forest

Vitebsk
4,090

Kovno
5,000

Berezino
1,000

Lyubavichi
700

Ponary

Vilna
1,341

Minsk
12,000

Mogilev
3,730

Berlin

Nowogrodek
400

Wolozyn
300

Rogachev
3,500

RUHR
Essen
252

Bernberg

Swierzen
500

Mir
1,500

Bobruisk
20,000

Gomel
4,000

Lodz

Slonim
9,000

Düsseldorf
489

Buchenwald
1,200

Bayreuth
50

Theresienstadt

Rowne
15,000

Kremenchug
8,000

RHINELAND

Kamionka Strumilowa
500

Berdichev
2,000

TRANSNISTRIA

UKRAINE

BAVARIA

Boryslaw
1,500

Czernowitz
30,000

Lvov
3,000

Stryj
1,200

Odessa
25,000

Nadworna
2,500

Przemyslany
400

Kolomyja
1,000

Belgrade

Black
Sea

| 0 | miles | 100 |
| 0 | kilometres | 200 |

© Martin Gilbert 1982

Map 95

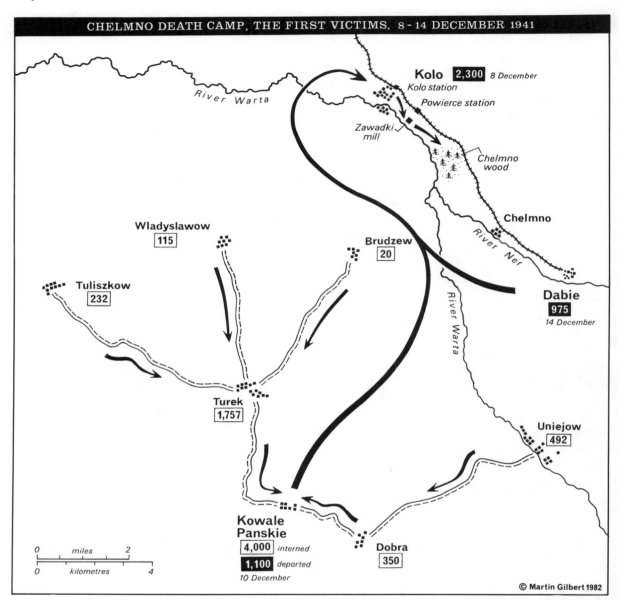

CHELMNO DEATH CAMP, THE FIRST VICTIMS, 8-14 DECEMBER 1941

Kolo `2,300` *8 December*
Kolo station
Powierce station
Zawadki mill
Chelmno wood
Chelmno
River Ner

River Warta

Wladyslawow
`115`

Brudzew
`20`

Dabie
`975`
14 December

Tuliszkow
`232`

River Warta

Turek
`1,757`

Uniejow
`492`

Kowale Panskie
`4,000` *interned*
`1,100` *deported*
10 December

Dobra
`350`

| 0 | miles | 2 |
| 0 | kilometres | 4 |

© Martin Gilbert 1982

Map 96

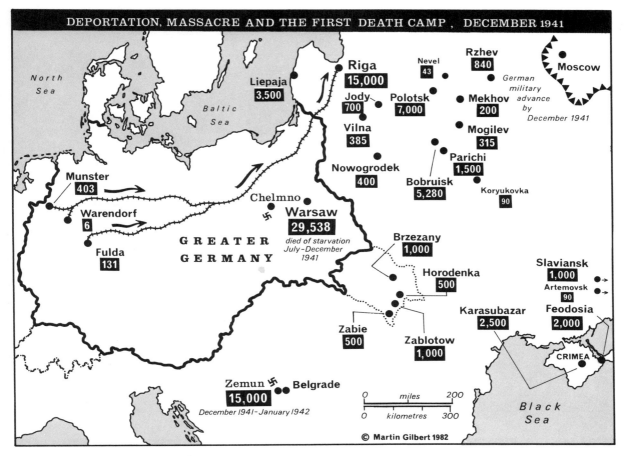

DEPORTATION, MASSACRE AND THE FIRST DEATH CAMP, DECEMBER 1941

The successful gassing of 1,200 Jews from Buchenwald in November 1941 was followed two weeks later by a second gassing experiment. The place chosen was a wood near the Polish village of Chelmno; the victims were Jewish villagers from several nearby communities (opposite). The method chosen was to bring the Jews by narrow guage railway from Kolo to Powierce, drive them with whips to the river, lock them overnight, without food or water, in the mill at the hamlet of Zawadki (seen here in a photograph taken in 1980), and then, in the morning, drive them in lorries to the woods near Chelmno, gassing them by exhaust fumes during the journey. The bodies were then thrown into deep pits, while the lorries returned to the mill for more victims. In all, five lorries were used, three of which held up to 150 people, and two up to 100. By noon, the whole trainload had usually been destroyed.

The first gassing at Chelmno took place on 8 December 1941. It was judged a success, and was continued on an ever widening scale. The next 1,000 victims had already been taken by truck from six villages to Kowale Panskie, and were held there until the journey to Chelmno on 10 December 1941.

Even as the gassings at Chelmno began, the deportations from Germany to Riga continued, as did the mass murder of deportees almost immediately after their arrival (above). Thus on 13 December 1941 the last six Jews living in Warendorf were deported to Riga and killed: their small community dated back to 1387, and had been 41 strong in 1933. Most had managed to emigrate by 1939. In the south-east, German forces had conquered the Crimea. Here too, community after community was being wiped out by the killing squads.

It was not only at Chelmno that mobile gas vans were being used. At the concentration camp at Zemun, just outside Belgrade, some 15,000 Jews from all over Serbia were gradually but systematically being gassed in vans disguised as Red Cross vehicles. By June 1942 all had been killed: an average of 120 every day. No sooner had the vans completed their task at Zemun than they were transferred to Riga (page 104).

83

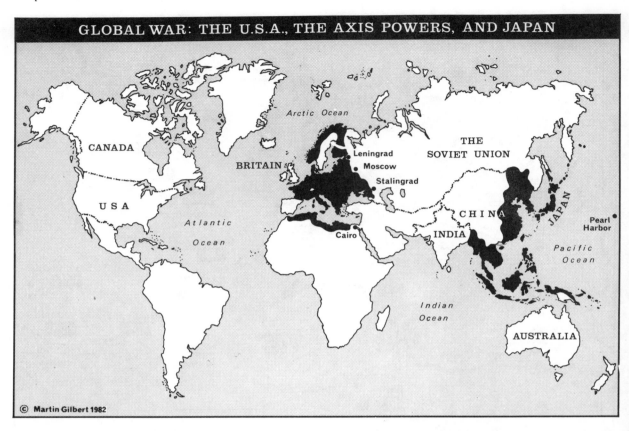

GLOBAL WAR: THE U.S.A., THE AXIS POWERS, AND JAPAN

CANADA

BRITAIN

USA

Atlantic Ocean

Arctic Ocean

Leningrad
Moscow
Stalingrad

THE SOVIET UNION

CHINA

INDIA

JAPAN

Pearl Harbor

Cairo

Pacific Ocean

Indian Ocean

AUSTRALIA

© Martin Gilbert 1982

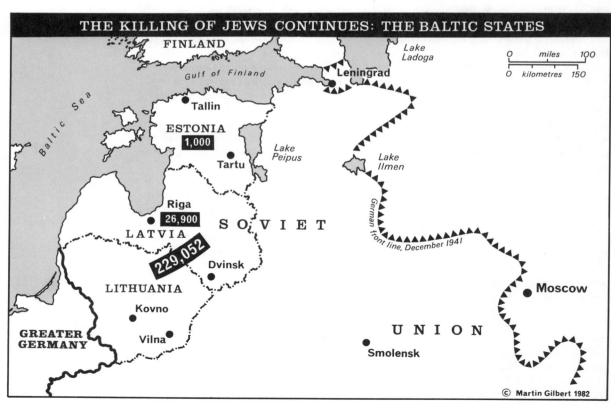

THE KILLING OF JEWS CONTINUES: THE BALTIC STATES

FINLAND

Lake Ladoga

Gulf of Finland

Leningrad

0   miles   100
0   kilometres   150

Baltic Sea

Tallin

ESTONIA
1,000

Tartu

Lake Peipus

Lake Ilmen

Riga
26,900

S O V I E T

LATVIA

229,052

Dvinsk

German front line, December 1941

Moscow

LITHUANIA

Kovno

U N I O N

GREATER GERMANY

Vilna

Smolensk

© Martin Gilbert 1982

Map 99

JEWS MARKED OUT FOR DEATH, 20 JANUARY 1942

NORWAY
1,300

ESTONIA
"Free of Jews"

USSR
5 million

DENMARK
5,600

LATVIA
3,500

HOLLAND
160,800

BIALYSTOK
DISTRICT
400,000

BALTIC STATES

LITHUANIA
34,000

BELGIUM
43,000

WHITE
RUSSIA
446,484

Berlin
Wannsee

GERMANY
131,800

GENERAL
GOVERNM.ᴺᵀ
2,284,000

EASTERN TERRITORIES

420,000

FRANCE
OCCUPIED ZONE
165,000

BOHEMIA
& MORAVIA
74,200

UKRAINE
2,994,684

88,000

AUSTRIA

SLOVAKIA

FRANCE
UNOCCUPIED ZONE
700,000
including
French North Africa

HUNGARY
742,800

43,700

SERBIA

10,000

RUMANIA
342,000

CROATIA
40,000

ITALY
58,000

BULGARIA
48,000

ALBANIA
200

MOROCCO

ALGERIA
French North Africa

TUNISIA

GREECE
69,600

KOS

RHODES

0   miles   200
0 kilometres 300

CRETE

© Martin Gilbert 1982

By December 1941 the German armies were masters of Europe, and on 7 December 1941 the Japanese entered the war against the United States and Britain (*opposite, above*).

From Estonia the killing squads reported to Berlin with their usual precision the murder over the previous six months of 229,052 Jews in Latvia and Lithuania (*opposite, below*). All 1,000 Jews caught in Estonia had also been killed.

At the Wannsee suburb of Berlin, German officials gathered on 20 January 1942 to discuss the final destruction of European Jewry. They also noted, as seen on the map above, what they believed to be the precise number of Jews still to be killed. The 'low' figures for the Baltic States indicate their knowledge that so many thousands had been killed already. At the Wannsee Conference plans were made for what was called the 'Final Solution', to be carried out by means of slave labour for all able-bodied Jews, the separation of men from women, and mass deportation.

Map 100

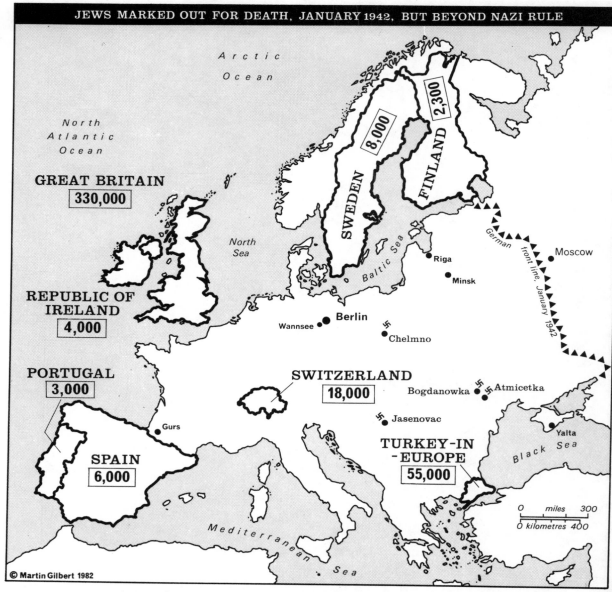

JEWS MARKED OUT FOR DEATH, JANUARY 1942, BUT BEYOND NAZI RULE

© Martin Gilbert 1982

Among the statistics presented by the SS to the Wannsee Conference were the number of Jews in Britain and Finland, as well as in all the neutral countries of Europe, whom the Gestapo hoped eventually to bring within the scope of the 'Final Solution'.

In 1942 the Finns agreed to deport 11 Jewish refugees. But when these 11 were murdered by the Gestapo, the Finnish Government refused to allow any further deportations *(page 244)*.

Meanwhile, the gassings at Chelmno, and the killing squad slaughter in Russia, continued, as did the deaths from starvation in the Warsaw ghetto, and the death marches from the Bukovina *(opposite, above)*.

Those Jews in Odessa who had not been murdered earlier were deported to concentration camps, where thousands died of brutality, starvation and disease. At Novi Sad, on 23 January 1942, Hungarian fascists drove 550 Jews and 292 Serbs to the river and on to the ice, and, after firing on the ice to break it up, shot all those who managed to stay afloat. In Titel 35 of the 36 Jews of the town were shot.

In the Crimea *(opposite, below)* ancient communities and modern collective farms were being wiped out so thoroughly that on 16 April 1942 Berlin was officially informed by the local SS: 'the Crimea is purged of Jews' *(page 97)*.

DEPORTATION AND MASSACRE, JANUARY 1942

WHITE RUSSIA

German front line, January 1942

0 miles 150
0 kilometres 200

Izbica Kujawska **1,000** 14 January

Brdow **600** 12 January

Bugaj **600** 12 January

Chelmno

Klodawa **1,140** 9 January

Lodz **3,000** 16 January

Warsaw

River Vistula

Pripet

Mozyr **1,500**

Pripet marshes

Kiev **8,000**

Kharkov **14,000**

Drobitzky Yar

Artemovsk **3,000**

Northern Bug

Brzezany **400**

Khmelnik **6,800**

Vinnitsa **5,000**

Novomoskovsk **140**

River Dnieper

Pavlovgrad **3,670**

5,123 deaths from starvation

Mielec **500**

Dolina **2,000**

Southern Bug

TRANSNISTRIA

Dniester River

Dumanovka **18,000**
Bogdanovka **48,000**
Atmicetka **5,000**
Vertugen **23,000**

1942 to 1943

Sea of Azov

HUNGARY

in all **2,550** Serbs and **700** Jews

killed by Hungarian fascists in occupied Yugoslavia

Titel

Novi Sad

BUKOVINA deportations continue

BESSARABIA deportations continue

Odessa **19,852** 12 January to 23 February

CRIMEA

Black Sea

© Martin Gilbert 1982

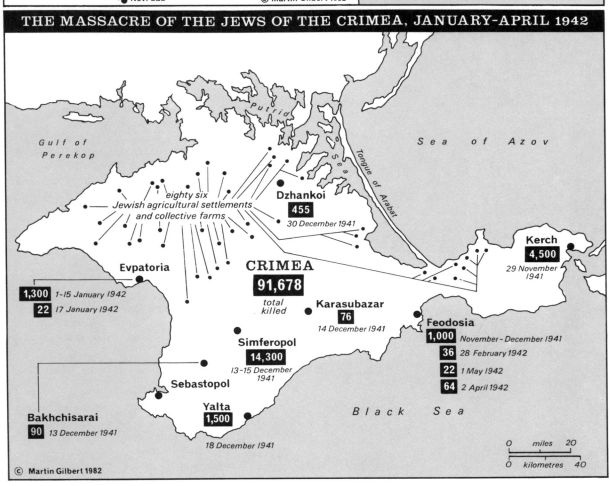

THE MASSACRE OF THE JEWS OF THE CRIMEA, JANUARY–APRIL 1942

Gulf of Perekop

Putrid

Sea of Azov

Sivash

Tongue of Arabat

eighty six Jewish agricultural settlements and collective farms

Dzhankoi **455** 30 December 1941

Kerch **4,500** 29 November 1941

Evpatoria

1,300 1–15 January 1942
22 17 January 1942

CRIMEA **91,678** total killed

Karasubazar **76** 14 December 1941

Feodosia **1,000** November–December 1941
36 28 February 1942
22 1 May 1942
64 2 April 1942

Simferopol **14,300** 13–15 December 1941

Sebastopol

Bakhchisarai **90** 13 December 1941

Yalta **1,500** 18 December 1941

Black Sea

0 miles 20
0 kilometres 40

© Martin Gilbert 1982

Map 103

EASTERN KILLINGS, AND THE 'STRUMA'

WHITE RUSSIA

Lepel
`1,000` 28 February

SOVIET UNION

Pyshno
`26`

Cherven
`1,800`
1 February

Kursk
`100`
1 February

VOLHYNIA

under German occupation

Shamovo
`500` 2 February

UKRAINE

Brailov
`3,000` 12 February

Hulievca
`650`
13 March

Czernowitz

Cihrin
`722`
9 March

Taganrog

Jassy

Sea of Azov

RUMANIA

CRIMEA

Caucasus

Bucharest

Simferopol
`300`

Constanta
12 December 1941

Black Sea

BULGARIA

sunk 24 February 1942

Istanbul
arrived 15 December 1941

`709` drowned

`1` saved

Sile

Sea of Marmara

T U R K E Y
neutral

KOS under German occupation

RHODES
under German occupation

SYRIA

CYPRUS

CRETE
under German occupation

intended route

Mediterranean Sea

Haifa

Tel Aviv

PALESTINE
British Mandate

Alexandria

EGYPT

TRANS-JORDAN

SAUDI ARABIA

```
0        miles      150
0      kilometres    300
```

© Martin Gilbert 1982

German front line: January 1942

The eastern killings continued during February 1942, with shootings such as those at Radom, and the deportation by lorry from Sierpc to Mlawa, when hundreds were murdered on the journey itself.

Hundreds of Jews were also deported to slave labour camps, such as the one at Cieszanow (right), where conditions were so harsh that almost no one survived.

Jewish resistance also grew. A group of Jews from Tomaszow Lubelski (right) organized a partisan unit which fought the Germans for some months, until it was betrayed by local Poles. Elsewhere, small groups of Jews still managed to escape, and to maintain themselves in the woods. Thus the four Jewish families living in the village of Hola (opposite, below), who were about to be deported to the ghetto in Wlodawa, escaped to the woods east of Zamolodycze, where they found several families already in hiding. Within a short time, armed Ukrainian peasants forced the families out of the forest, locked them into a barn, and then betrayed them to the Germans. Only four Jews managed to escape, to the Skorodnica forest. There they found 100 other Jews in hiding, but when German troops attacked them 75 were shot. The survivors fled to the woods near Maryanka, and managed to acquire a rifle from Lubien village. Later they helped smuggle 75 Jews from the Wlodawa ghetto, and a further 46 men, women and girls from the village of Adampol. The group then set up its base deep in the Skorodnica forest, built up an armoury of 15 rifles and, in an ambush on a German truck, killed 10 Germans. Later the group joined other Jewish partisans in the Parczew forest (pages 122 to 123).

The SS killing squads were also still at work (left), in White Russia and the Ukraine in February, and in the Transnistrian deportee camps in March. Meanwhile, the Jews of neighbouring Rumania, as well as thousands of Jewish refugees who had managed to reach Rumania from Poland and Czechoslovakia, sought boats in which to escape across the Black Sea, and on to Palestine. Boats were scarce, German submarines patrolled the Black Sea, and British officials pressed the Turkish Government not to allow the boats through the Sea of Marmara, hoping thereby not to offend Arab opinion in Palestine.

One such ship was the 'Struma', which had left Rumania on 12 December 1941. The ship was flying the neutral Panamanian flag,

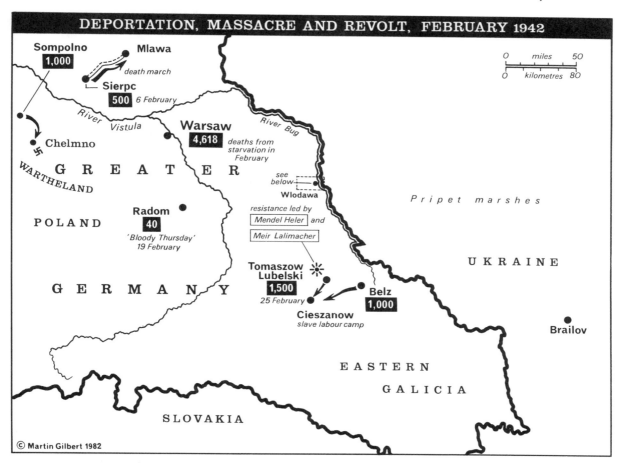

DEPORTATION, MASSACRE AND REVOLT, FEBRUARY 1942

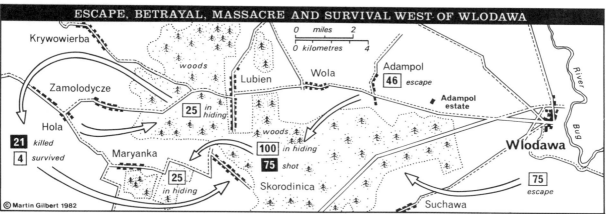

ESCAPE, BETRAYAL, MASSACRE AND SURVIVAL WEST OF WLODAWA

but while it was still in the Black Sea, Germany and Italy declared war on Panama, following the United States' entry into the war a week earlier. As a result, the ship was flying, in German eyes, an 'enemy' flag. After four days in the Black Sea, it reached Istanbul. But under British pressure, the Turks ordered the ship back into the Black Sea, where it was sunk, probably by the Germans, on 24 February 1942. All but one refugee was drowned. 'Palestine', commented the British High Commissioner in Jerusalem, 'was under no obligation to them', and he went on to explain, that he was acting in accordance with the 'basic principle that enemy nationals from enemy or enemy-controlled territory should not be admitted to this country during the war', a principle, he insisted, that applied even to refugees from enemy territory.

Map 106

FOUR DEATH CAMPS AND THE ACCELERATION OF MURDER

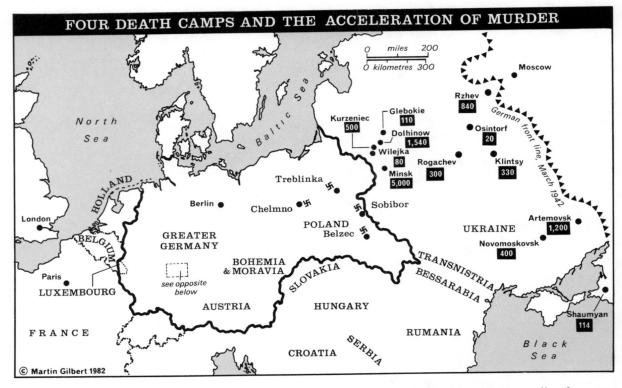

The death camp at Chelmno had been in operation for more than six weeks by the time of the Wannsee Conference of 20 January 1942 (page 85). In March 1942 the town-by-town killings in the east continued (above), while at the same time (also above), three new death camps were being prepared, at Belzec, Treblinka and Sobibor, where, as at Chelmno, no-one was kept alive for slave labour. These four camps had a single purpose: to kill every Jew within a few hours of arrival.

As soon as these four 'death' camps were in operation, thousands of Jewish communities were marked out for deportation, first from German-occupied Poland, then from elsewhere in Greater Germany, and finally, from western and southern Europe. The deportees were told they were going to Poland to be 'resettled' in farms and labour camps. In fact, their only destination was a death camp and immediate death.

Between 8 December 1941 and 28 February 1942, more than 13,000 Jews had been deported to Chelmno and gassed. Adolf Eichmann himself had witnessed this process. Then, on 17 March 1942 the first deportations took place to the second of the death camps, just south of the village of Belzec. The deportees came from as far west

as Mielec (opposite above), as well as from Lublin, and from the village of Belzec itself. In all, 6,786 Jews were murdered in this first set of deportations. A group of a dozen or so Jews from the nearby village of Lubycza Krolewska, who had been at work for more than a month finishing construction in the camp, were also killed.

The gas chambers at Belzec operated for more than nine months, the killing process being supervised by SS men, assisted by Ukrainian and Estonian guards. A special rail spur from the main line to the unloading ramp could take 20 goods wagons at a time: these wagons were shunted on, leaving the rest of each train to wait its turn.

Hardly had the first Jews been gassed at Belzec, than the German authorities began a search throughout the western provinces of Germany for those Jews, often only a single family, living in isolated communities in remote country regions. From one such region, in the hills above Bad Kissingen (opposite, below), 83 Jews were seized, as well as 23 in Bad Kissingen itself. Deported eastward across Germany, Bohemia and Poland to Belzec, they were first held in two nearby internment camps, Izbica Lubelska and Piaski, and then sent on to Belzec, where they were gassed (pages 92 and 93). Not a single one of these deportees survived.

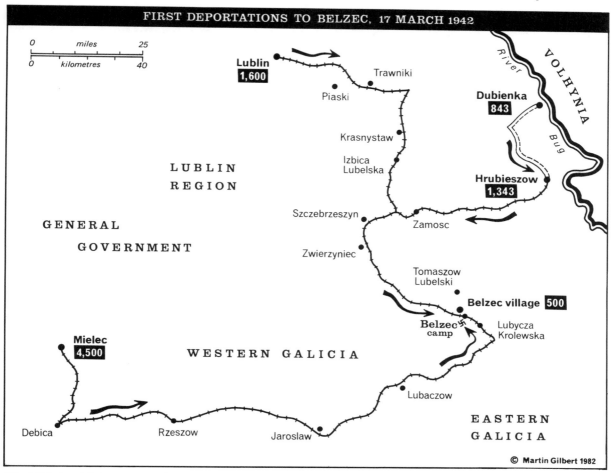

FIRST DEPORTATIONS TO BELZEC, 17 MARCH 1942

0 miles 25
0 kilometres 40

Lublin 1,600
Trawniki
Piaski

Dubienka 843

VOLHYNIA

River

Bug

LUBLIN
REGION

Krasnystaw

Izbica
Lubelska

Hrubieszow 1,343

GENERAL
GOVERNMENT

Szczebrzeszyn

Zamosc

Zwierzyniec

Tomaszow
Lubelski

Belzec village 500

Belzec camp

Lubycza
Krolewska

Mielec 4,500

WESTERN GALICIA

Lubaczow

EASTERN
GALICIA

Debica

Rzeszow

Jaroslaw

© Martin Gilbert 1982

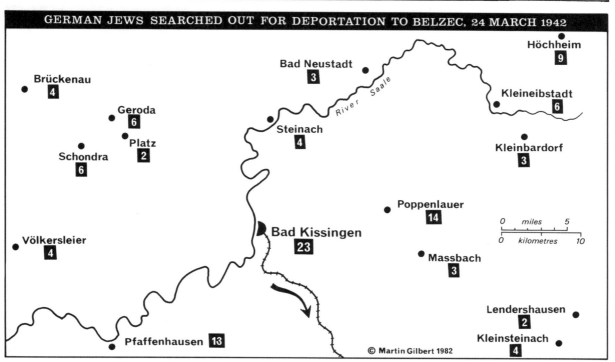

GERMAN JEWS SEARCHED OUT FOR DEPORTATION TO BELZEC, 24 MARCH 1942

Höchheim 9

Bad Neustadt 3

River Saale

Kleineibstadt 6

Brückenau 4

Geroda 6

Platz 2

Steinach 4

Kleinbardorf 3

Schondra 6

Poppenlauer 14

0 miles 5
0 kilometres 10

Völkersleier 4

Bad Kissingen 23

Massbach 3

Lendershausen 2

Pfaffenhausen 13

Kleinsteinach 4

© Martin Gilbert 1982

91

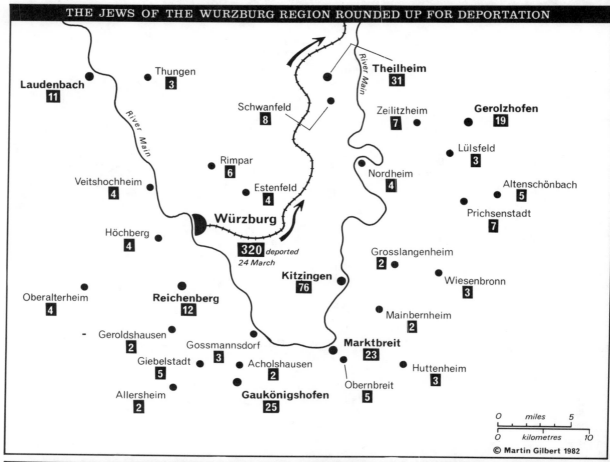

THE JEWS OF THE WURZBURG REGION ROUNDED UP FOR DEPORTATION

Laudenbach
11

Thungen
3

Schwanfeld
8

River Main

Theilheim
31

Zeilitzheim
7

Gerolzhofen
19

Lülsfeld
3

Nordheim
4

Altenschönbach
5

Prichsenstadt
7

Rimpar
6

Veitshochheim
4

Estenfeld
4

Würzburg

320 deported
24 March

Grosslangenheim
2

Wiesenbronn
3

Höchberg
4

Kitzingen
76

Mainbernheim
2

Oberalterheim
4

Reichenberg
12

Geroldshausen
2

Gossmannsdorf
3

Acholshausen
2

Marktbreit
23

Huttenheim
3

Giebelstadt
5

Obernbreit
5

Allersheim
2

Gaukönigshofen
25

0 miles 5
0 kilometres 10

© Martin Gilbert 1982

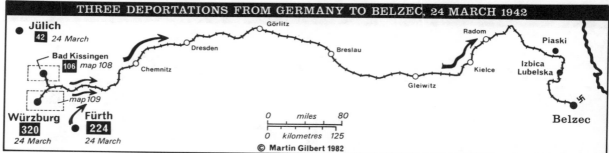

THREE DEPORTATIONS FROM GERMANY TO BELZEC, 24 MARCH 1942

Jülich
42 24 March

Görlitz

Radom

Piaski

Bad Kissingen
106 map 108

Dresden

Breslau

Chemnitz

Izbica
Lubelska

Würzburg
320
24 March

map 109

Fürth
224
24 March

Kielce

Gleiwitz

Belzec

0 miles 80
0 kilometres 125

© Martin Gilbert 1982

The search for the remaining Jews of Germany continued during the last week of March 1942 and the first three weeks of April. Throughout the Würzburg region *(top)* single families and small communities were seized and taken to Würzburg, from where, on 24 March 1942 the first of three deportations took place, with 320 deportees. Together with the Jews collected at Bad Kissingen, Jülich and Fürth, all were deported eastwards *(above),* held for a few days in the village of Piaski, and then taken to Belzec *(opposite);* not one survived.

Throughout March Jews were also deported to Belzec from Eastern Galicia and the Lublin region. From Lublin itself almost all the city's large Jewish community was deported within two weeks.

The deportation of Jews to Chelmno also continued *(opposite).* In the deportations from Opole were many Austrian-born Jews who had been deported from Vienna to Poland two years before *(page 40).*

In Warsaw thousands of Jews continued to die of starvation. In other towns, such as Rohatyn and Tarnopol, the Jews were driven to nearby woods, and murdered. Near Ilja, on March 14, Jews who had been sent to

Map 111

MASS MURDER, DEPORTATION AND REVOLT, MARCH 1942

Baltic Sea

REICHSKOMMISSARIAT OSTLAND

resistance led by | Josef Rodblat | *and* | David Rubin | **Ilja** ☀
900
17 March

resistance led by | R.M.Bromberg | M.P.Malkevich | *and* | Hersh Smolar | **Minsk** ☀
5,000
2 March

GREATER GERMANY

Baranowicze
3,000
4 March

WARTHEGAU

Krosniewice
900
2 March

Kutno
7,000

Chelmno

Zychlin
3,200
3 March

Warsaw
at least **4,000** *deaths from starvation in March*

Ozorkow
500

Kazimierz Dolny
2,000

Lublin
10,000
18–25 March

REICHSKOMMISSARIAT UKRAINE

Radoszkowicze
850
11 March

Poddebice
2,000

Kozminek
1,000

Wawolnica
1,500

Piaski
3,400

Opole Lubelskie
3,000
31 March

Izbica Lubelska
2,200
24 March

Siennica Rozana
272

Zamosc
hundreds

GENERAL GOVERNMENT

Bilgoraj
2,500

Tomaszow Lubelski
hundreds

Belzec

Rawa Ruska
1,500
20 March

Zolkiew
700
15 March

Lvov
15,000

Drohobycz
1,500

Rohatyn
2,000
20 March

EASTERN GALICIA

Tarnopol
1,000
25 March

Stanislawow
6,000
31 March

0 — miles — 40
0 — kilometres — 80

© Martin Gilbert 1982

work on a farm joined a group of Soviet partisans, and went into hiding in the forest. Three days later two Jewish leaders at Ilja, who had refused to hand over partisan sympathizers to the SS, themselves escaped to the forest to join the partisans. As a reprisal, the Germans shot all old and sick Jews in the street, then forced 900 more into a building, locked it, and set it on fire. All 900 perished.

In Minsk 5,000 Jews were taken from the ghetto to a newly dug pit on the outskirts of the town and machine-gunned. No ammunition was wasted on the hundreds of Jewish children seized that day: they were thrown into the pit alive to die of suffocation. The Jews of Minsk tried to organize a resistance group. But on 31 March 1942 the Gestapo raided the ghetto, capturing several of the resistance leaders.

FIRST DEPORTATIONS TO AUSCHWITZ, 26-27 MARCH 1942

BIRTHPLACES OF SOME OF THE FIRST PARIS DEPORTEES

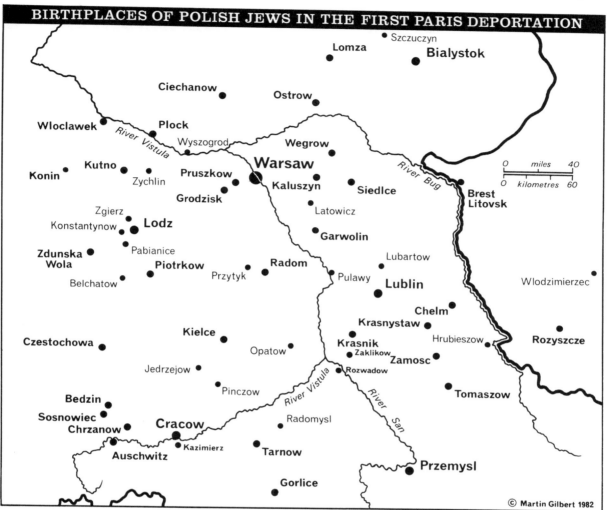

Map 114

BIRTHPLACES OF POLISH JEWS IN THE FIRST PARIS DEPORTATION

Szczuczyn
Lomza
Bialystok
Ciechanow
Ostrow
Wloclawek
Plock
River Vistula
Wyszogrod
Wegrow
Konin
Kutno
Pruszkow
Warsaw
River Bug
Zychlin
Kaluszyn
Siedlce
Brest Litovsk
Grodzisk
Zgierz
Latowicz
Konstantynow
Lodz
Garwolin
Zdunska Wola
Pabianice
Lubartow
Piotrkow
Radom
Wlodzimierzec
Belchatow
Przytyk
Pulawy
Lublin
Chelm
Kielce
Krasnystaw
Czestochowa
Opatow
Krasnik
Hrubieszow
Rozyszcze
Zaklikow
Zamosc
Jedrzejow
Rozwadow
River Vistula
Pinczow
River San
Tomaszow
Bedzin
Radomysl
Sosnowiec
Chrzanow
Cracow
Kazimierz
Tarnow
Przemysl
Auschwitz
Gorlice

© Martin Gilbert 1982

The first deportations from western Europe to Belzec had taken place on 24 March 1942 (*page 91*). Two days later, the first deportations of Jews to Auschwitz began, first from Slovakia, and on the following day from France (*opposite*). At Auschwitz, all were sent to the barracks. No gassings took place there until 4 May 1942 (*page 100*).

The first Jews deported to Auschwitz from France on 27 March 1942 were all foreign-born Jews who had been rounded up in Paris seven months earlier, and interned. Their birthplaces ranged from Marrakech to Haifa, and from London to Simferopol (*opposite, below*). Many had left their birthplaces between the wars, to seek a new livelihood in France. Others had reached France as refugees. The majority had been born in Poland (*above*), within the area that had now become a part of Greater Germany. One of these first Paris deportees, Israel Chlebowski, had been born in the village of

Przytyk, scene of the pogrom of 1936 in which three Jews had died (*page 21*). Another, Henry Eckstein, had been born in London 26 years before. Lazare Mnouchine had been born in Tatarsk, one of the first towns in which the Jews had challenged SS killing squads in the autumn of 1941 (*page 76*). The 41-year-old Moses Schneider had been born in Auschwitz itself, then a market town in the Austro-Hungarian Empire.

The Paris deportation of 27 March 1942 was timed by the SS with precision. The train left Paris at 17.00 hours, reaching the border of Greater Germany at 13.59 on the following day, and arriving at Auschwitz at 5.33 in the morning of March 31.

Even French-born Jews were now subjected to the full rigours of anti-Jewish legislation. On 29 May 1942 all Jews were forbidden access to all public places, squares, restaurants, cafés, libraries, public baths, gardens and sports grounds.

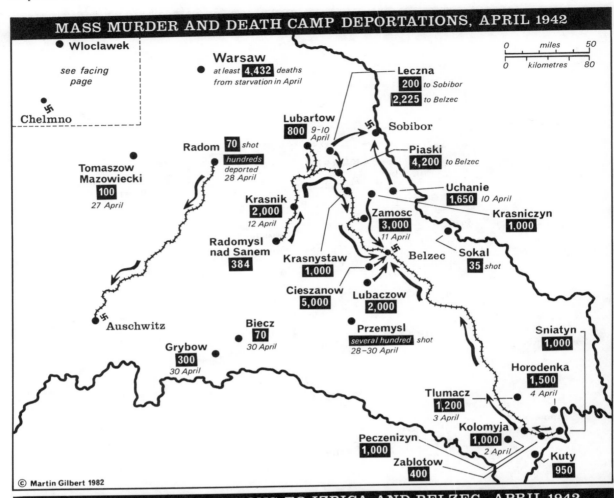

MASS MURDER AND DEATH CAMP DEPORTATIONS, APRIL 1942

Wloclawek

see facing page

Chelmno

Warsaw
at least **4,432** deaths from starvation in April

Leczna
200 to Sobibor
2,225 to Belzec

Lubartow
800 9-10 April

Sobibor

Piaski
4,200 to Belzec

Radom **70** shot
hundreds deported 28 April

Uchanie
1,650 10 April

Tomaszow Mazowiecki
100
27 April

Krasnik
2,000
12 April

Zamosc
3,000
11 April

Krasniczyn
1,000

Radomysl nad Sanem
384

Krasnystaw
1,000

Belzec

Sokal
35 shot

Auschwitz

Cieszanow
5,000

Lubaczow
2,000

Biecz
70
30 April

Przemysl
several hundred shot
28-30 April

Sniatyn
1,000

Grybow
300
30 April

Horodenka
1,500
4 April

Tlumacz
1,200
3 April

Peczenizyn
1,000

Kolomyja
1,000
2 April

Kuty
950

Zablotow
400

© Martin Gilbert 1982

0 — miles — 50
0 — kilometres — 80

FURTHER DEPORTATIONS TO IZBICA AND BELZEC, APRIL 1942

GREATER GERMANY

Poppenlauer
14

Schweinfurt
30

Bamberg
105 25 April

Piaski

Bad Kissingen
23

Coburg
27

Nuremberg
650 24 April

Izbica Lubelska

Hammelberg
13

Belzec

Karlbach
27

Hassfurt
16

BOHEMIA

EASTERN GALICIA

Nordlingen
25

Ceske Budejovice
909
18 April

Krumbach
16

BAVARIA

Landshut
11 2 April

SLOVAKIA

Lindau
3

Fischach
56

Augsburg
129
3 April

Memmingen
22

SWITZERLAND
neutral

© Martin Gilbert 1982

0 — miles — 150
0 — kilometres — 200

TEN DEPORTATIONS TO CHELMNO, APRIL 1942

Radzejow **600**

Brzesc Kujawski **200** *30 April*

Wloclawek **3,000** *22 April*

Piotrkow Kujawski **550**

Lubraniec **100**

River Vistula

Gostynin **2,000** *16 April*

Gabin **2,000**

Sanniki **250** *17 April*

WARTHEGAU

narrow gauge railways

River Warta

Kolo

standard gauge railway

River Bzura

Powierce station
Zawadki mill

Chelmno *death camp*

Grabow **1,240**

Chelmno village

River Ner

Leczyca **1,700** *10 April*

0 miles 20 / 0 kilometres 30

© Martin Gilbert 1982

NAZI-DOMINATED EUROPE, APRIL - MAY 1942

Throughout April 1942 the eastern killings continued (*right*), as did the deportations to the death camps of Belzec (*opposite, above*), Chelmno (*above*), and Auschwitz.

From Bavaria and Bohemia, the remnants of once flourishing communities were sent to be 'resettled' in the east (*opposite, below*). Their destination was not, however, an eastern labour camp or ghetto, but two transit camps, Izbica and Piaski, from where they were sent the few further miles to Belzec, and its gas chamber. With the deportation of 3 April 1942, the once 1,000-strong Jewish community of Augsburg ceased to exist. Jews had lived in the town since AD 1212, and in the fifteenth century it had been a centre of Jewish culture.

In Warsaw, thousands more Jews died of starvation during April (*opposite, above*).

Two thousand miles to the south (*right*), the 38,000 Jews of Libya, having been briefly under British control at the end of 1941, had come once more under Italian rule in February 1942. Jewish shops were at once plundered, and 2,600 Jews deported to a camp at Giado, for forced labour, building military roads. The death toll was high: in 14 months 562 died of starvation and typhus.

In April 1942 a further 1,750 Jews were taken from Tripoli to forced labour sites at Homs, Benghazi and Derna. Hundreds perished from hunger and the heat. Others, forbidden to use the air-raid shelters, were killed during Allied bombing raids.

97

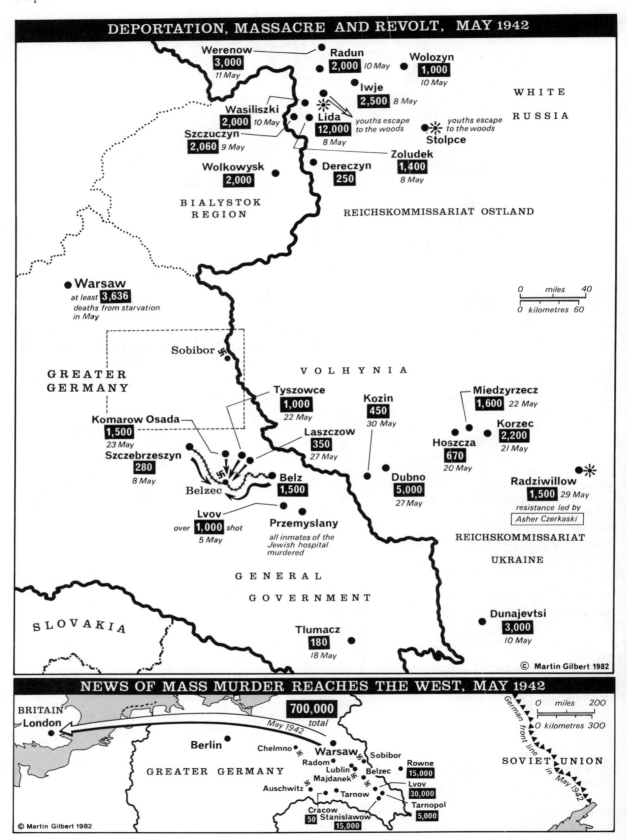

DEPORTATION, MASSACRE AND REVOLT, MAY 1942

Werenow 3,000 *11 May*

Radun 2,000 *10 May*

Wolozyn 1,000 *10 May*

Iwje 2,500 *8 May*

WHITE

RUSSIA

Wasiliszki 2,000 *10 May*

Lida 12,000 *8 May*

youths escape to the woods

youths escape to the woods

Stolpce

Szczuczyn 2,060 *9 May*

Zoludek 1,400 *8 May*

Wolkowysk 2,000

Dereczyn 250

BIALYSTOK
REGION

REICHSKOMMISSARIAT OSTLAND

Warsaw at least 3,636 *deaths from starvation in May*

0 miles 40

0 kilometres 60

Sobibor

VOLHYNIA

GREATER
GERMANY

Tyszowce 1,000 *22 May*

Kozin 450 *30 May*

Miedzyrzecz 1,600 *22 May*

Korzec 2,200 *21 May*

Komarow Osada 1,500 *23 May*

Laszczow 350 *27 May*

Hoszcza 670 *20 May*

Szczebrzeszyn 280 *8 May*

Belzec

Belz 1,500

Dubno 5,000 *27 May*

Radziwillow 1,500 *29 May*

resistance led by Asher Czerkaski

Lvov over 1,000 shot *5 May*

Przemyslany *all inmates of the Jewish hospital murdered*

REICHSKOMMISSARIAT

UKRAINE

GENERAL

GOVERNMENT

Dunajevtsi 3,000 *10 May*

SLOVAKIA

Tlumacz 180 *18 May*

© Martin Gilbert 1982

NEWS OF MASS MURDER REACHES THE WEST, MAY 1942

BRITAIN
London

700,000 *total*

May 1942

0 miles 200

0 kilometres 300

German front line in May 1942

Berlin

Chelmno

Warsaw

Sobibor

GREATER GERMANY

Radom

Lublin

Belzec

Rowne 15,000

SOVIET UNION

Auschwitz

Majdanek

Lvov 30,000

Tarnow

Cracow 50

Stanislawow 15,000

Tarnopol 5,000

© Martin Gilbert 1982

Map 121

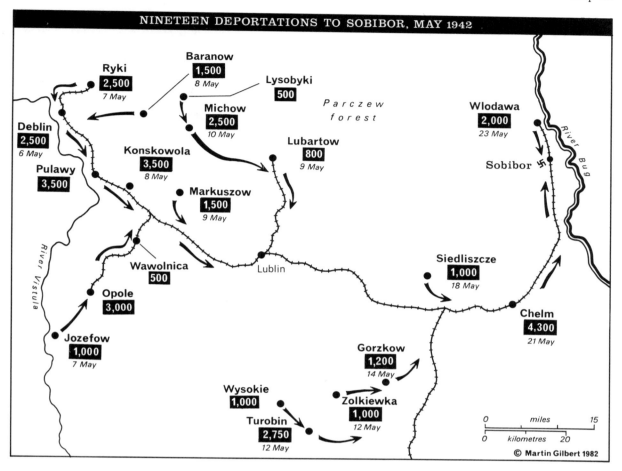

NINETEEN DEPORTATIONS TO SOBIBOR, MAY 1942

Ryki 2,500 7 May

Baranow 1,500 8 May

Lysobyki 500

Parczew forest

Wlodawa 2,000 23 May

Deblin 2,500 6 May

Michow 2,500 10 May

Konskowola 3,500 8 May

Lubartow 800 9 May

Sobibor

Pulawy 3,500

Markuszow 1,500 9 May

River Bug

Wawolnica 500

Lublin

Siedliszcze 1,000 18 May

Opole 3,000

Chelm 4,300 21 May

River Vistula

Jozefow 1,000 7 May

Gorzkow 1,200 14 May

Wysokie 1,000

Zolkiewka 1,000 12 May

Turobin 2,750 12 May

0 miles 15
0 kilometres 20

© Martin Gilbert 1982

Throughout May 1942 the killings east of the General Government continued (*opposite, above*). So also did the deportations to Sobibor (*above*), Belzec, Chelmno and Auschwitz (*pages 100-1*). In Przemyslany all the inmates of the Jewish hospital were dragged from their beds and shot. At Dubno 5,000 Jews, judged 'non-productive' for the German war effort, were taken outside the town and killed. At Chelm local Jews, and Slovakian Jews who had been deported there two years before, were deported to Sobibor and gassed.

At that very moment, the first news had reached London (*opposite, below*), smuggled out of Poland by the underground Jewish Socialist Party in Warsaw, telling of the mass murder of 700,000 Jews in Eastern Galicia and the east. Specific figures were given of mass killings in four towns, as well as of other killings in Radom, Lublin, Cracow and Tarnow. Throughout Eastern Galicia, the report stated, 'men, fourteen to sixty years old, were driven to a single place, a square or a cemetery, where they were

slaughtered or shot by machine-guns or killed by hand grenades. They had to dig their own graves. Children in orphanages, inmates in old-age homes, the sick in hospitals were shot, women were killed in the streets. In many towns the Jews were carried off to "an unknown destination" or killed in adjacent woods.'

Only one death camp, Belzec, was named in the report. But it warned that mass killings were still in progress.

Although the victims were weak from hunger and privation, always unarmed against machine-guns and grenades, alone among hostile local populations, and facing vicious torture if they challenged Nazi power, many Jews attempted nevertheless to break out of the SS and local police cordons. In the three examples shown opposite (*above*), some young men and women did succeed in reaching the woods, and in forming, or joining, partisan groups. Some record survives of these particular acts of resistance. Many other such acts went unrecorded.

Map 122

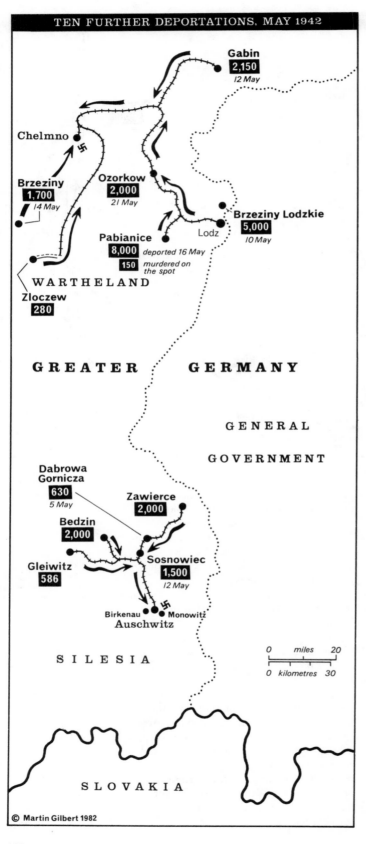

TEN FURTHER DEPORTATIONS, MAY 1942

Gabin
2,150
12 May

Chelmno

Brzeziny
1,700
14 May

Ozorkow
2,000
21 May

Brzeziny Lodzkie
5,000
10 May

Lodz

Pabianice
8,000 *deported 16 May*
150 *murdered on the spot*

WARTHELAND

Zloczew
280

GREATER   GERMANY

GENERAL

GOVERNMENT

Dabrowa Gornicza
630
5 May

Zawierce
2,000

Bedzin
2,000

Sosnowiec
1,500
12 May

Gleiwitz
586

Birkenau   Monowitz
Auschwitz

SILESIA

0   miles   20

0   kilometres   30

SLOVAKIA

© Martin Gilbert 1982

The gassing of more than two million Jews at Auschwitz began on 4 May 1942, first at Auschwitz itself, then at the nearby camp of Birkenau, where four gas chambers and crematoria were built during 1942 and early 1943 for the purpose of mass murder. A few Jews from each deportation were selected to 'live' as slave labourers, some in barracks at Birkenau itself, others at nearby factories, including a synthetic oil and rubber plant later built at Monowitz. While at Birkenau, many Jews, and in particular Jewish women, were selected by SS doctors for medical experiments.

Because Birkenau became known during the war as Auschwitz II, and the slave labour camp in Monowitz as Auschwitz III, most accounts of the deportation of Jews to Birkenau name 'Auschwitz' as the destination, rather than Birkenau, to which they were in fact deported. For nearly two years, all deportees to Birkenau were brought to the railway sidings just outside Auschwitz station, and marched or taken by truck to Birkenau. In April 1944 a direct rail spur was built to Birkenau, almost to the gates of two of the four gas chambers there.

Throughout May 1942 the deportations to Chelmno continued unabated. The map on the left shows six communities destroyed there in one month. Of the Jews of Ozorkow, 2,000 were gassed, while 800 able-bodied men and women were sent to factories in the Lodz ghetto. At Pabianice all 150 patients in the Jewish hospital were murdered on the spot, before the rest of the community was sent to death at Chelmno.

Jewish resistance continued. But the chances of success were remote, as heavily armed SS units moved from town to town. Each Jewish community was unarmed and isolated; forbidden contact with all neighbouring communities, cut off from every normal means of communication, terrified by rumours of slaughter, but having no real knowledge of the fate of the Jews elsewhere.

Sometimes whole villages were able to escape *(opposite, above)*. But once they had reached the immediate safety of nearby woods, the families and their leaders had to begin the desperate search for food. Often they were refused food by villagers who were themselves hungry, or even hostile. Then, in their own time, the Germans were able to launch full-scale military attacks: those shown here by heavy black arrows, the

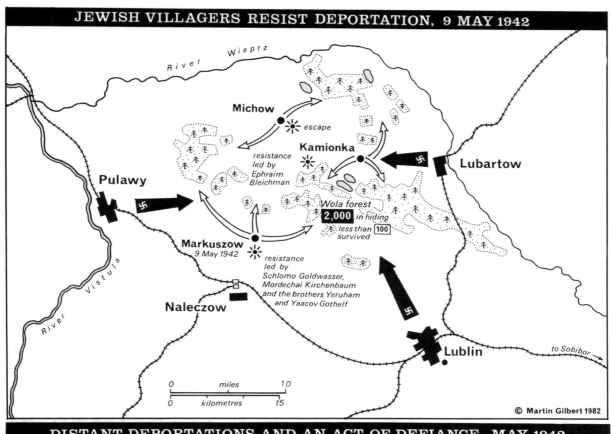

JEWISH VILLAGERS RESIST DEPORTATION, 9 MAY 1942

River Wieprz

Michow

escape

Kamionka

resistance
led by
Ephraim
Bleichman

Lubartow

Pulawy

Wola forest
2,000 *in hiding*
less than 100 *survived*

Markuszow
9 May 1942

resistance
led by
Schlomo Goldwasser,
Mordechai Kirchenbaum
and the brothers Yeruham
and Yaacov Gothelf

Naleczow

River Vistula

Lublin

to Sobibor

0   miles   10
0   kilometres   15

© Martin Gilbert 1982

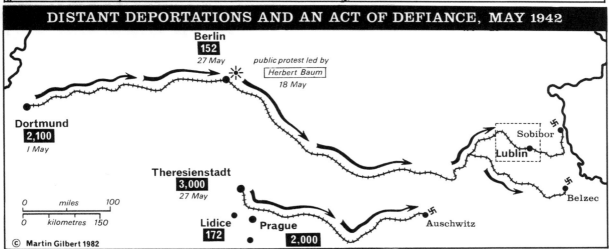

DISTANT DEPORTATIONS AND AN ACT OF DEFIANCE, MAY 1942

Berlin
152
27 May

public protest led by
Herbert Baum
18 May

Dortmund
2,100
I May

Sobibor

Lublin

Belzec

Theresienstadt
3,000
27 May

0   miles   100
0   kilometres   150

© Martin Gilbert 1982

Lidice
172

Prague
2,000

Auschwitz

first in October 1942, the second in December 1942, were on three separate fronts, supported by artillery, armoured vehicles, grenades, machine-guns, and carried out by armed men who had been trained for military combat and were now being sent to destroy small groups of isolated Jewish families on the verge of starvation.

There was also Jewish defiance in Berlin (*above*). A public display of anti-Nazi posters by a student group led to the capture of one group; all 152 were shot.

As a reprisal for the shooting of the SS chief, Reinhardt Heydrich, in Prague, on May 27, the SS launched 'Operation Reinhardt' against both Czechs and Jews. Some 2,000 Czechs were killed in Prague as well as in the village of Lidice. From the Theresienstadt ghetto, 3,000 Jews were deported to Auschwitz and gassed.

Map 125

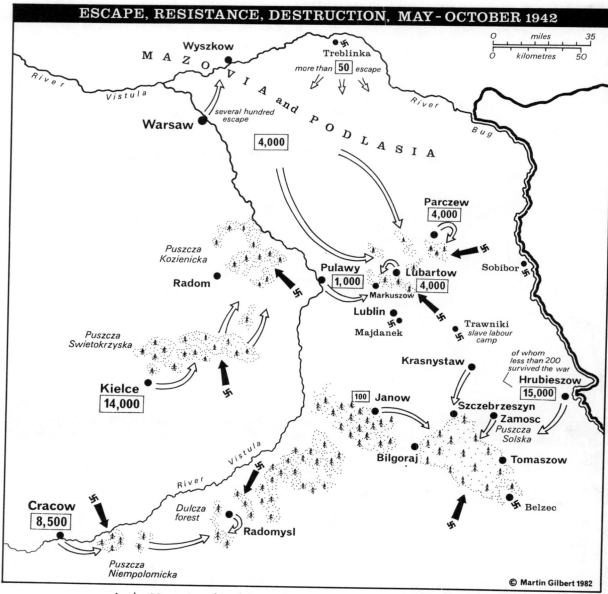

ESCAPE, RESISTANCE, DESTRUCTION, MAY - OCTOBER 1942

M A Z O V I A and P O D L A S I A

Wyszkow

River Vistula

Treblinka
more than 50 *escape*

Warsaw
several hundred escape

4,000

River Bug

Parczew
4,000

Sobibor

Puszcza Kozienicka

Radom

Pulawy
1,000

Lubartow
4,000

Markuszow

Lublin

Majdanek

Trawniki
slave labour camp

Puszcza Swietokrzyska

Kielce
14,000

Krasnystaw

of whom less than 200 survived the war

Hrubieszow
15,000

Janow
100

Szczebrzeszyn

Zamosc
Puszcza Solska

Vistula

River

Bilgoraj

Tomaszow

Cracow
8,500

Dulcza forest

Radomysl

Belzec

Puszcza Niempolomicka

© Martin Gilbert 1982

As the SS continued its drive to deport Jews to death camps and labour camps, the Jews themselves continued to try to escape to the woods and forests *(above)*. These were not escapes of the young and strong, leaving behind the women, children, the old and the sick. Rather, many of the escape leaders sought to save whole families. Once in the woods, survival for more than a few months was virtually impossible. Those who did manage to escape faced full-scale German military campaigns, local peasant hostility and betrayal. The terrible privations of forest life took their toll: no medical help, hardly any food, brackish water, and the ravages of extremes of climate – summer heat and insects, followed by autumn storms and sub-zero winter temperatures. Of more than 100 Jews who escaped from Janow to the Puszcza Solska, for example, no more than ten survived the war.

Nevertheless, the spirit of resistance was strong. These were not 'sheep to the slaughter', but brave men and women, willing, unarmed, to challenge the armed strength of a victorious army. No outside State supported them, while only a few local villagers were prepared to give them haven.

The photographs *(right),* taken by the author in 1980, show one such forest area: the Parczew forest, the story of which is told on pages 122-3.

DISTANT DEPORTATIONS AND MASSACRES, JUNE 1942

Riga

Smolensk `2,000`

Lysa Gora *slave labour camp* `400` *15 June*

Priluki `1,210` *15 May–15 June*

Duisburg `146` *25 June*

TRANSNISTRIA

Theresienstadt — Auschwitz

Drancy

Paris

`933` *5 June*
`934` *22 June*
`999` *25 June*
`965` *28 June*

SLOVAKIA
`52,000`
March–June

Czernowitz
`4,000` *deported*
17–27 June
`3,500` *perished*
after deportation

Black Sea

© Martin Gilbert 1982

A GAS VAN ORDERED NORTH, 9 JUNE 1942

Riga
Kaiserwald
Tilsit

Berlin
GREATER GERMANY
Dresden
Prague
Vienna

Zemun **Belgrade**

Adriatic Sea

Black Sea

© Martin Gilbert 1982

June 1942 saw no relaxation in the SS deportation plan, or in the executions in the east. Hardly had the German army reached the Russian cities of Smolensk and Priluki, than more than 3,000 Jews were murdered. From Czernowitz, in the Bukovina (*pages 72-3*), a further 4,000 were deported eastwards to Transnistria (*above, top*), of

whom less than half survived the war. The deportations to Auschwitz continued without pause, with four from Paris, 50 from Slovakia in four months, and five from the Auschwitz region (*opposite*). In Warsaw a further 4,000 Jews died of starvation during June. At Belzec and Sobibor more than 23,000 Jews were gassed.

Among those deported to Belzec, from Cracow, was the 65-year-old Mordechai Gebirtig, a carpenter whose Yiddish songs and melodies were sung throughout Poland. His best known, 'Our town is burning', was written after the Przytyk pogrom (*page 21*). Gebirtig was deported and killed with his wife and two daughters. Another distinguished Cracow Jew, the writer Abraham Naumann, aged 70, was shot in the street during the round-up.

On 9 June 1942 a special gas van, used earlier at Zemun for the murder of Serbian Jews (*page 83*), was sent to Riga (*left*), for the continuing killing not only of Riga's Jews, but of tens of thousands of Jews deported to Riga from Greater Germany six months before. So heavy was its task, that on 15 June 1942 the SS in Riga ordered a second van.

As the killings continued, so did the attempts at resistance: at Dzisna (*opposite*) 2,000 Jews managed to break out of the ghetto. Many were caught, but some reached Russian partisan units, and fought with the Red Army against the Germans.

Map 128

DEPORTATION, MASS MURDER AND REVOLT, JUNE 1942

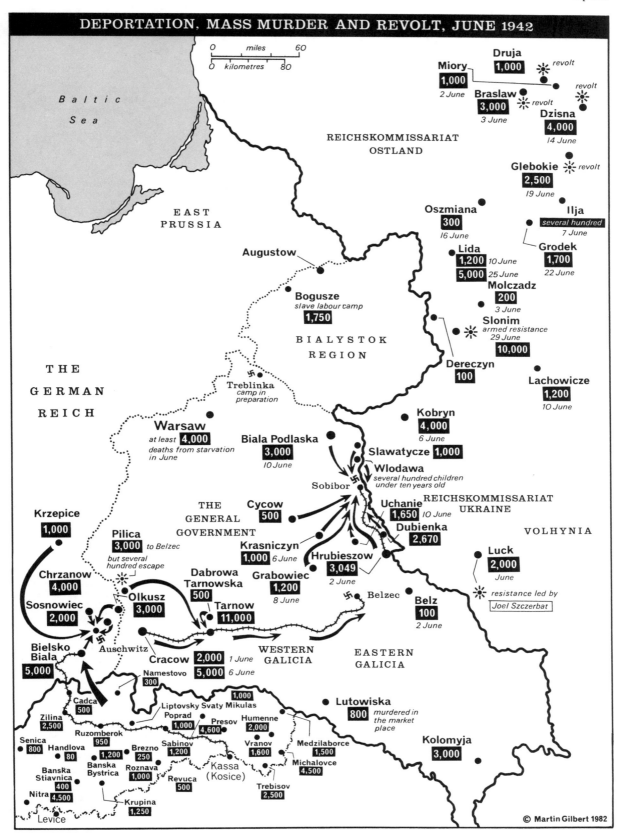

miles 60
kilometres 80

Baltic Sea

EAST PRUSSIA

REICHSKOMMISSARIAT OSTLAND

Miory 1,000 *2 June*

Druja 1,000 ☀ *revolt*

☀ *revolt*

Braslaw 3,000 *3 June* ☀ *revolt*

Dzisna 4,000 *14 June*

Glebokie 2,500 ☀ *revolt* *19 June*

Oszmiana 300 *16 June*

Ilja *several hundred* *7 June*

Grodek 1,700 *22 June*

Lida 1,200 *10 June* / 5,000 *25 June*

Molczadz 200 *3 June*

Slonim ☀ *armed resistance 29 June* 10,000

Dereczyn 100

Lachowicze 1,200 *10 June*

Augustow

Bogusze *slave labour camp* 1,750

BIALYSTOK REGION

THE GERMAN REICH

Treblinka *camp in preparation* ✠

Warsaw *at least* 4,000 *deaths from starvation in June*

Biala Podlaska 3,000 *10 June*

Kobryn 4,000 *6 June*

Slawatycze 1,000

Wlodawa *several hundred children under ten years old* ✠

Sobibor

Krzepice 1,000

Pilica 3,000 *to Belzec but several hundred escape* ☀

THE GENERAL GOVERNMENT

Cycow 500

Uchanie 1,650 *10 June*

REICHSKOMMISSARIAT UKRAINE

VOLHYNIA

Dubienka 2,670

Krasniczyn 1,000 *6 June*

Grabowiec 1,200 *8 June*

Hrubieszow 3,049 *2 June*

Luck 2,000 *June*

☀ *resistance led by* Joel Szczerbat

Chrzanow 4,000

Dabrowa Tarnowska 500

Sosnowiec 2,000

Olkusz 3,000

Tarnow 11,000

✠ Belzec

Belz 100 *2 June*

Bielsko Biala 5,000

Auschwitz ☀

Cracow 2,000 *1 June* / 5,000 *6 June*

WESTERN GALICIA

EASTERN GALICIA

Namestovo 300

Lutowiska 800 *murdered in the market place*

Cadca 500

Liptovsky Svaty Mikulas 1,000

Poprad 1,000

Presov 4,600

Humenne 2,000

Kolomyja 3,000

Zilina 2,500

Ruzomberok 950

Sabinov 1,200

Vranov 1,600

Medzilaborce 1,500

Senica 800

Handlova 80

Brezno 250

Kassa (Kosice)

Michalovce 4,500

Banska Stiavnica 400

Banska Bystrica 1,200

Roznava 1,000

Revuca 500

Trebisov 2,500

Nitra 4,500

Krupina 1,250

Levice

© Martin Gilbert 1982

Map 129

THE JEWS OF HOLLAND ON THE EVE OF DEPORTATION

N o r t h

S e a

GRONINGEN
4,708
Leeuwarden • **Groningen**
• Winschoten

FRIESLAND
852
• Assen

Westerbork

DRENTE
2,498
• Meppel
• Hoogeveen

NORTH
HOLLAND
87,566

• Alkmaar

• Zaandam

• Zwolle

OVERIJSSEL
4,385
• Almelo

Bloemendaal
Zandvoort
Haarlem
• Heemstede
• Naarden
Bussum
• Laren
Hilversum

Apeldoorn
• Deventer
Hengelo
Enschede

Voorburg
• Leiden
de Bilt
• Amersfoort
• Zutphen
Lochem

The Hague
SOUTH
HOLLAND
25,648
• Rijswijk
Utrecht
• Zeist
GELDERLAND
6,642
Arnhem
• Winterswijk

• Gouda

• Schiedam
Rotterdam
UTRECHT
3,802
• Nijmegen

• Dordrecht
• Oss
• Hertogenbosch

NORTH BRABANT
2,281
• Tilburg

ZEELAND
174

• Eindhoven

LIMBURG
1,441

B E L G I U M

G R E A T E R   G E R M A N Y

• Towns with **300** to **700** Jewish inhabitants
• Towns with **1,000** to **3,000** Jewish inhabitants
● Towns with **8,000** to **14,000** Jewish inhabitants
● Amsterdam: **80,000** Jewish inhabitants

© **Martin Gilbert 1982**

| 0 | miles | 30 |
| 0 | kilometres | 50 |

The figures show the
number of Jews in the
Dutch Provinces in 1941

• Maastricht

Since May 1940 the 140,000 Jews of Holland (*above*) had been deliberately cut off from the community around them. On 9 May 1942 the yellow star was made compulsory.

On 14 July 1942 thousands of Dutch Jews were arrested in Amsterdam, and on the following day the first train, with 1,135 Dutch Jews on board, left Holland for an 'unknown destination' (*opposite*). By the end of the month, nearly 6,000 had, in fact, reached Auschwitz, where the majority were gassed.

The photograph shows the special railway spur being built from the internment camp at Westerbork to the main railway line.

From Germany, hundreds of Jews were deported to the Theresienstadt ghetto, and kept there, isolated and starving.

Map 130

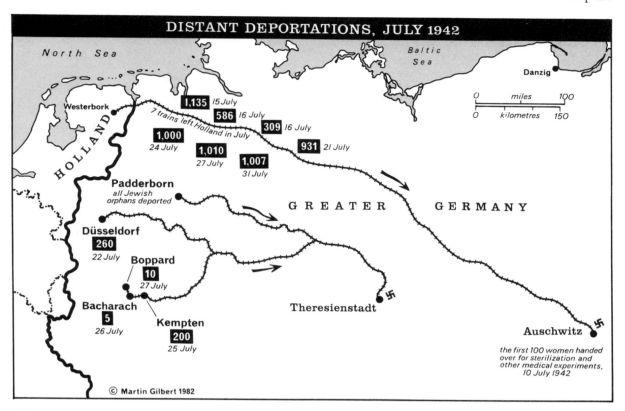

DISTANT DEPORTATIONS, JULY 1942

7 trains left Holland in July

1,135 *15 July*
586 *16 July*
309 *16 July*
931 *21 July*
1,000 *24 July*
1,010 *27 July*
1,007 *31 July*

North Sea

Baltic Sea

Danzig

Westerbork

HOLLAND

GREATER   GERMANY

Padderborn
all Jewish orphans deported

Düsseldorf
260
22 July

Boppard
10
27 July

Bacharach
5
26 July

Kempten
200
25 July

Theresienstadt

Auschwitz
the first 100 women handed over for sterilization and other medical experiments, 10 July 1942

© Martin Gilbert 1982

O miles 100
O kilometres 150

Map 131

DEPORTATION, MASSACRE AND REVOLT, JULY 1942

Danzig

GREATER GERMANY

Szarkowszczyzna
revolt **600** *killed 18 July*
900 *escape*

Minsk
25,000
28-30 July

Molczadz
1,000
15 July

Nieswiez
600
ghetto revolt 15 July *22 July*

revolt led by Shalom Cholawsky

Dereczyn
3,000 *24 July*

Bialystok

Treblinka

Kosow
1,200 *25 July*

Kleck
1,000
21 July

revolt

Antopol
1,100

Bereza Kartuska
1,000
15 July

Byten
840
25 July

Pinsk

Kobryn
2,000
25 July

Drohiczyn
1,700
26 June

all patients in the Jewish hospital murdered

REICHSKOMMISSARIAT UKRAINE

Chelmno

Warsaw
66,701 *deported*
and at least
4,000
died of starvation in July

Sobibor

Kowel
24,000
mid July

Luck
4,000
4 July

Lutomiersk
700

GENERAL GOVERNMENT

Chelm **300**

Kowale Panskie
3,000
20 July

Jozefow
1,500 *shot 13 July*

Czestochowa

12,000
21-25 July

Rozwadow

Brody

Olyka
5,673
27-28 July

Rowne
5,000
14-15 July

Pilica

Tarnobrzeg

Baranow

Belzec

Uhnow
1,000

Bedzin

Radomysl

Sokolow

Ropczyce

Rawa Ruska
2,000 *27 July*

Cracow

Debica

Niemirow
500

Pilzno

Rzeszow
22,000
7-13 July

Sasow
1,000
15 July

Bochnia

Wielopole

Strzyzow

Zimgrod
1,000 *murdered in nearby woods*

Sambor
50 *shot*

Tluste
200
mid July

murdered at an 'unknown destination' possibly Belzec, or a nearby wood

Stanislawow
1,000 *shot*

SLOVAKIA

© Martin Gilbert 1982

On 22 July 1942 the Germans embarked upon their most ambitious project: the deportation of more than half a million Jews from the Warsaw ghetto. The death camp prepared for them was at Treblinka, scarcely more than 40 miles from the ghetto. In one month alone, 66,701 Jews were deported from Warsaw to Treblinka, and gassed on arrival.

In an attempt to warn of what was happening, to organize armed resistance, and to link the scattered and isolated ghettos, a Jewish Fighters' Organization, known by its Polish initials ZOB, was set up in Warsaw, Bialystok, Brody, and in five of the ghettos south-west of Warsaw (*above*).

The deportations to Chelmno and Belzec continued (*above*). Further east, as the killing squads continued their executions, the last Jews alive in Nieswiez, 600 artisans, fought

with sticks and clubs to resist their killers. Most were murdered. At Kleck a few dozen, fortunate to possess a pistol or two, broke away from the ghetto and were able to join the partisans in the forests.

During August 1942 the Dutch and French deportations continued (*opposite, below*). Now, for the first time, Jews from Luxembourg and Belgium were deported to Auschwitz.

To prevent the Swedish Government from giving its protection to Dutch Jews, the Germans had decided, on 17 July 1942, to deprive all Jews in Holland of their Dutch citizenship. Two weeks later, to forestall a further Swedish effort to help the Jews of Holland, the Germans decided not to disclose the whereabouts of the deportees. Thus Auschwitz remained an 'unknown destination', 'somewhere in the east'.

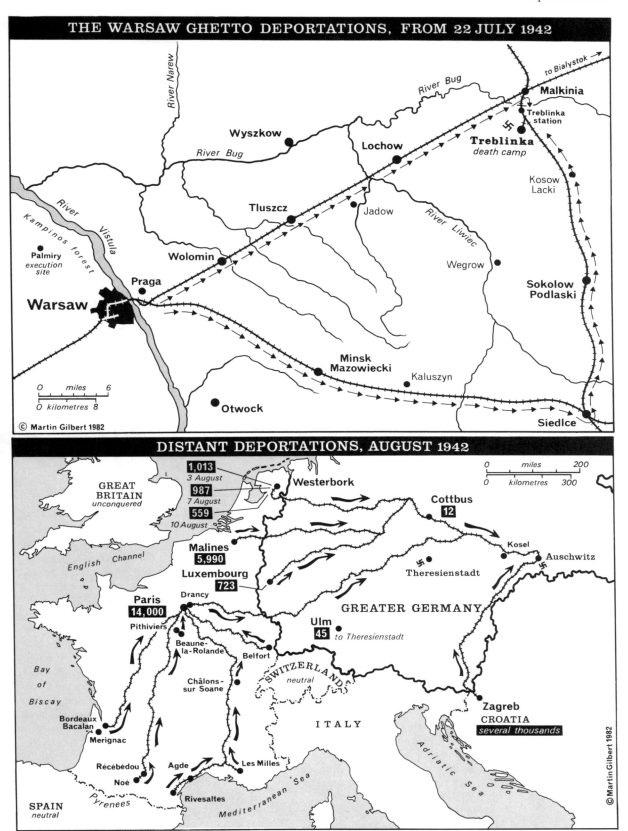

THE WARSAW GHETTO DEPORTATIONS, FROM 22 JULY 1942

River Narew

to Bialystok →

River Bug

Malkinia

Wyszkow

Treblinka station

Lochow

Treblinka
death camp

River Bug

Kosow
Lacki

Tluszcz

Jadow

River Liwiec

Kampinos forest

River Vistula

Palmiry
execution
site

Wolomin

Wegrow

Sokolow
Podlaski

Praga

Warsaw

Minsk
Mazowiecki

Kaluszyn

O   miles   6

O kilometres 8

Otwock

Siedlce

© Martin Gilbert 1982

DISTANT DEPORTATIONS, AUGUST 1942

O   miles   200

O kilometres 300

1,013
3 August

987
7 August

559
10 August

Westerbork

Cottbus
12

GREAT
BRITAIN
unconquered

Kosel

Auschwitz

English Channel

Malines
5,990

Luxembourg
723

Theresienstadt

Paris
14,000

Drancy

GREATER GERMANY

Pithiviers

Ulm
45
to Theresienstadt

*Bay
of
Biscay*

Beaune-
la-Rolande

Belfort

SWITZERLAND
neutral

Châlons-
sur Soane

I T A L Y

Zagreb
CROATIA
several thousands

Bordeaux
Bacalan

Merignac

Récébédou

Agde

Les Milles

Adriatic Sea

Noé

Rivesaltes

SPAIN
neutral

Pyrenees

Mediterranean Sea

© Martin Gilbert 1982

Map 134

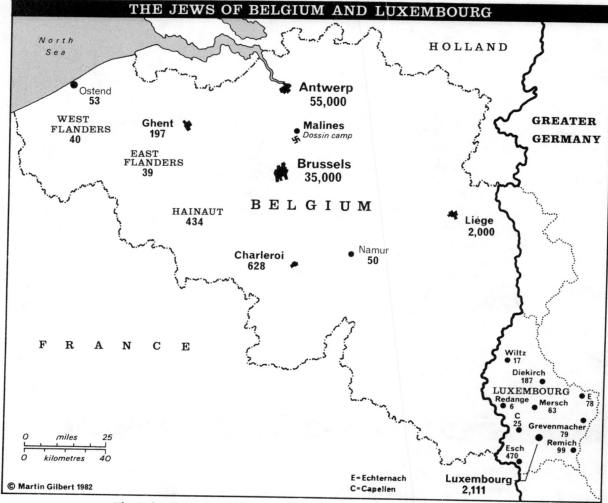

THE JEWS OF BELGIUM AND LUXEMBOURG

North Sea

HOLLAND

Ostend
53

WEST
FLANDERS
40

Ghent
197

Antwerp
55,000

Malines
Dossin camp

GREATER
GERMANY

EAST
FLANDERS
39

Brussels
35,000

B E L G I U M

HAINAUT
434

Liége
2,000

Charleroi
628

Namur
50

F R A N C E

Wiltz
17

Diekirch
187

LUXEMBOURG
Redange
6

Mersch
63

E
78

C
25

Grevenmacher
79

Esch
470

Remich
99

Luxembourg
2,111

0   miles   25
0   kilometres   40

E=Echternach
C=Capellen

© Martin Gilbert 1982

The Belgian and Luxembourg Jews, now seized and deported, came from many cities, towns and villages *(above)*. The first deportations from Belgium took place on 4 August 1942 *(page 109)*. Henceforth, over a period of two years, a total of 26 trains set off to the 'unknown destination' from the internment camp at Dossin, near Malines. The destination was in fact, Auschwitz.

The Germans ignored protests from the Catholic Church, including one by Jean Hérinckx, a leading right-wing Catholic, and one by Cardinal van Roey, Archbishop of Malines.

The local Belgian population was active in helping Jews, of whom more than 25,000 were hidden in private homes and orphanages, and thereby saved. But of the 25,631 Belgian Jews who were deported, only 1,244 survived the war.

More than 1,000 Belgian Jews fought with the Belgian partisans; 140 of them were killed in action. Other Jews were smuggled across France, to Spain and Switzerland. But on 13 August 1942 the Swiss police began to turn back Jewish refugees who had managed to cross into Switzerland. 'Under current practice', a Police Instruction of 25 September 1942 read, 'refugees on the grounds of race alone are not political refugees'.

From France, the deportations continued without pause. On 17 August 1942, among 997 mainly Polish-born Jews deported from Paris to Auschwitz, 27 were children under the age of four, almost all of whom had been born in France, and most of whom were deported without their parents. Marguerite Jakubovitch was deported with her six brothers and sisters, the oldest of whom was only ten years old: all had been born in Paris, and were deported without their parents. All 27 young children named here *(right)* were gassed within hours of reaching Auschwitz.

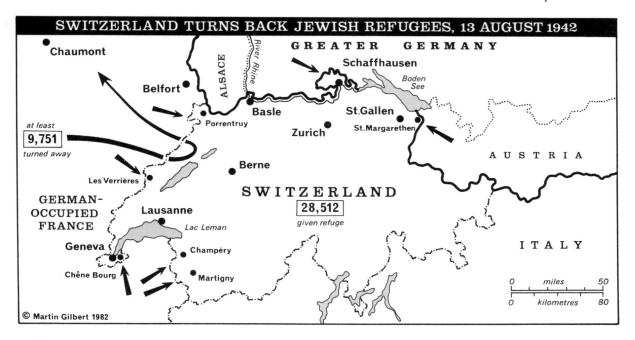

SWITZERLAND TURNS BACK JEWISH REFUGEES, 13 AUGUST 1942

Chaumont

GREATER GERMANY

ALSACE

River Rhine

Schaffhausen

Boden See

Belfort

Basle

Porrentruy

St.Gallen

St.Margarethen

Zurich

AUSTRIA

at least **9,751** turned away

Les Verrières

Berne

SWITZERLAND

28,512 given refuge

GERMAN-OCCUPIED FRANCE

Lausanne

Lac Leman

ITALY

Geneva

Champéry

Chêne Bourg

Martigny

miles 50

kilometres 80

© Martin Gilbert 1982

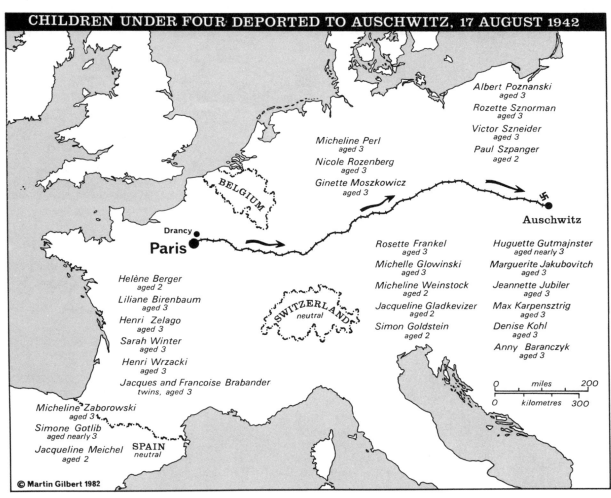

CHILDREN UNDER FOUR DEPORTED TO AUSCHWITZ, 17 AUGUST 1942

Albert Poznanski
aged 3

Rozette Sznorman
aged 3

Victor Szneider
aged 3

Paul Szpanger
aged 2

Micheline Perl
aged 3

Nicole Rozenberg
aged 3

Ginette Moszkowicz
aged 3

Auschwitz

BELGIUM

Drancy
Paris

SWITZERLAND
neutral

Rosette Frankel
aged 3

Huguette Gutmajnster
aged nearly 3

Michelle Glowinski
aged 3

Marguerite Jakubovitch
aged 3

Helène Berger
aged 2

Micheline Weinstock
aged 2

Jeannette Jubiler
aged 3

Liliane Birenbaum
aged 3

Jacqueline Gladkevizer
aged 2

Max Karpensztrig
aged 3

Henri Zelago
aged 3

Simon Goldstein
aged 2

Denise Kohl
aged 3

Sarah Winter
aged 3

Anny Baranczyk
aged 3

Henri Wrzacki
aged 3

Jacques and Francoise Brabander
twins, aged 3

Micheline Zaborowski
aged 3

Simone Gotlib
aged nearly 3

Jacqueline Meichel
aged 2

SPAIN
neutral

miles 200

kilometres 300

© Martin Gilbert 1982

111

Map 137

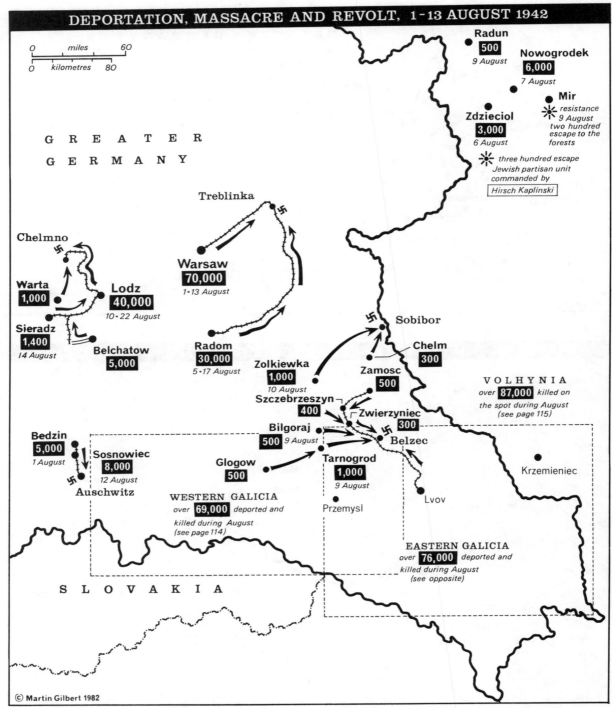

DEPORTATION, MASSACRE AND REVOLT, 1-13 AUGUST 1942

miles 0 — 60
kilometres 0 — 80

Radun 500 *9 August*

Nowogrodek 6,000 *7 August*

Mir ☀ resistance 9 August two hundred escape to the forests

Zdzieciol 3,000 *6 August*

☀ three hundred escape Jewish partisan unit commanded by Hirsch Kaplinski

GREATER GERMANY

Treblinka

Chelmno

Warta 1,000

Lodz 40,000 *10·22 August*

Warsaw 70,000 *1·13 August*

Sieradz 1,400 *14 August*

Belchatow 5,000

Radom 30,000 *5·17 August*

Sobibor

Chelm 300

Zolkiewka 1,000 *10 August*

Zamosc 500

VOLHYNIA over 87,000 killed on the spot during August (see page 115)

Szczebrzeszyn 400

Zwierzyniec 300

Bilgoraj 500 *9 August*

Belzec

Bedzin 5,000 *1 August*

Sosnowiec 8,000 *12 August*

Glogow 500

Tarnogrod 1,000 *9 August*

Krzemieniec

Auschwitz

WESTERN GALICIA over 69,000 deported and killed during August (see page 114)

Przemysl

Lvov

EASTERN GALICIA over 76,000 deported and killed during August (see opposite)

SLOVAKIA

© Martin Gilbert 1982

In the first two weeks of August nearly a quarter of a million Jews were killed at Chelmno, Auschwitz, Treblinka and Belzec *(above),* and by the killing squads in the east. In preparation for a single deportation to Chelmno, Jews were brought to Wielun *(opposite)* from nine nearby communities.

More than 76,000 Jews were deported from Eastern Galicia to Belzec *(opposite, below).* All were killed within a few hours, as were a further 74,000 Jews from Western Galicia *(page 114).* East of Greater Germany, killing on the spot continued, 87,000 Jews being murdered in the Volhynia *(page 115).* Resistance had also led, at both Mir and Zdzieciol, to mass escapes.

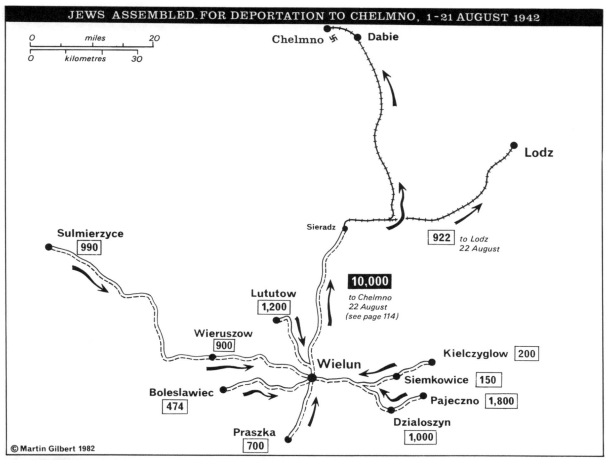

JEWS ASSEMBLED FOR DEPORTATION TO CHELMNO, 1-21 AUGUST 1942

miles 20
kilometres 30

Chelmno
Dabie
Lodz
Sulmierzyce 990
Sieradz
922 to Lodz 22 August
10,000 to Chelmno 22 August (see page 114)
Lututow 1,200
Wieruszow 900
Wielun
Kielczyglow 200
Siemkowice 150
Boleslawiec 474
Pajeczno 1,800
Dzialoszyn 1,000
Praszka 700

© Martin Gilbert 1982

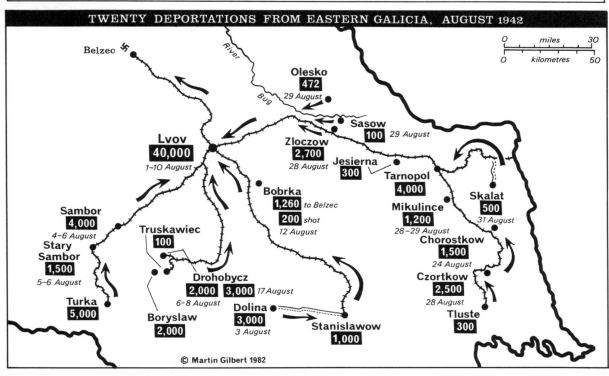

TWENTY DEPORTATIONS FROM EASTERN GALICIA, AUGUST 1942

miles 30
kilometres 50

Belzec
River Bug
Olesko 472 29 August
Sasow 100 29 August
Lvov 40,000 1-10 August
Zloczow 2,700 28 August
Jesierna 300
Tarnopol 4,000
Skalat 500 31 August
Sambor 4,000 4-6 August
Truskawiec 100
Bobrka 1,260 to Belzec 200 shot 12 August
Mikulince 1,200 28-29 August
Stary Sambor 1,500 5-6 August
Drohobycz 2,000 3,000 17 August 6-8 August
Chorostkow 1,500 24 August
Czortkow 2,500 28 August
Turka 5,000
Boryslaw 2,000
Dolina 3,000 3 August
Stanislawow 1,000
Tluste 300

© Martin Gilbert 1982

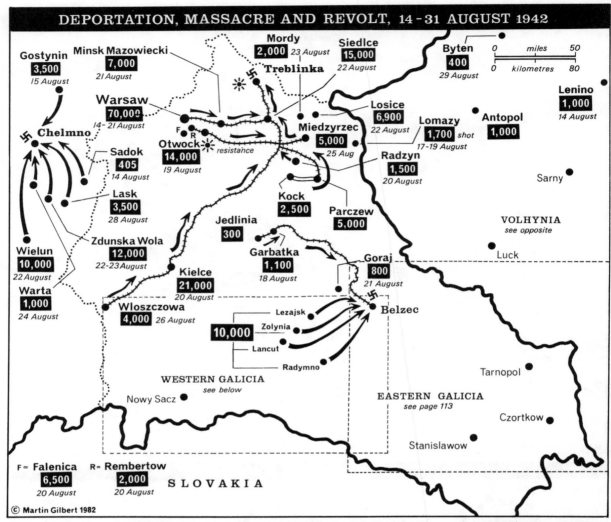

DEPORTATION, MASSACRE AND REVOLT, 14-31 AUGUST 1942

Gostynin 3,500 15 August

Minsk Mazowiecki 7,000 21 August

Mordy 2,000 23 August

Siedlce 15,000 22 August

Byten 400 29 August

0 miles 50 / 0 kilometres 80

Treblinka

Lenino 1,000 14 August

Warsaw 70,000 14-21 August

Chelmno

Losice 6,900 22 August

Lomazy 1,700 shot 17-19 August

Antopol 1,000

Sadok 405 14 August

Otwock 14,000 19 August

F R resistance

Miedzyrzec 5,000 25 Aug

Radzyn 1,500 20 August

Sarny

Lask 3,500 28 August

Kock 2,500

Parczew 5,000

VOLHYNIA see opposite

Zdunska Wola 12,000 22-23 August

Jedlinia 300

Garbatka 1,100 18 August

Goraj 800 21 August

Luck

Wielun 10,000 22 August

Warta 1,000 24 August

Kielce 21,000 20 August

Belzec

Wloszczowa 4,000 26 August

10,000

Lezajsk
Zolynia
Lancut
Radymno

Tarnopol

WESTERN GALICIA see below

Nowy Sacz

EASTERN GALICIA see page 113

Czortkow

Stanislawow

F = **Falenica** 6,500 20 August

R = **Rembertow** 2,000 20 August

S L O V A K I A

© Martin Gilbert 1982

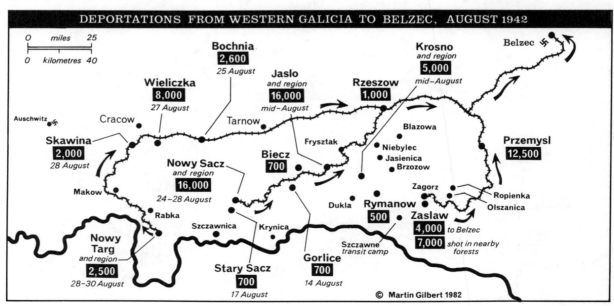

DEPORTATIONS FROM WESTERN GALICIA TO BELZEC, AUGUST 1942

0 miles 25 / 0 kilometres 40

Bochnia 2,600 25 August

Jaslo and region 16,000 mid-August

Krosno and region 5,000 mid-August

Belzec

Rzeszow 1,000

Wieliczka 8,000 27 August

Tarnow

Blazowa

Przemysl 12,500

Auschwitz

Cracow

Frysztak

Niebylec
Jasienica
Brzozow

Skawina 2,000 28 August

Nowy Sacz and region 16,000 24-28 August

Biecz 700

Zagorz

Ropienka

Olszanica

Makow

Dukla

Rymanow 500

Zaslaw 4,000 to Belzec 7,000 shot in nearby forests

Rabka

Szczawnica

Krynica

Szczawne transit camp

Nowy Targ and region 2,500 28-30 August

Stary Sacz 700 17 August

Gorlice 700 14 August

© Martin Gilbert 1982

114

Map 142

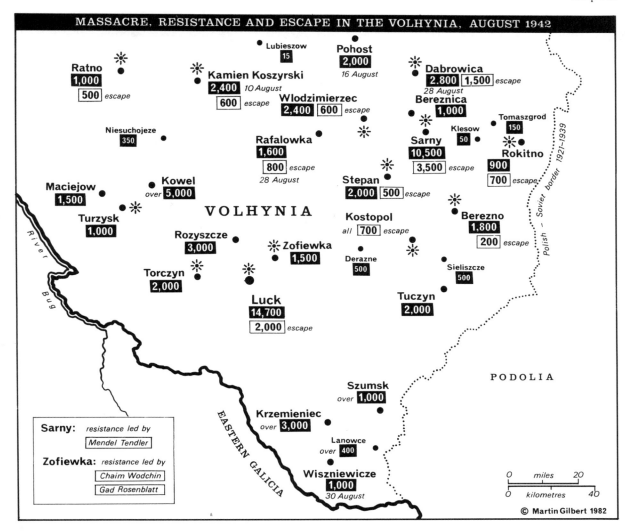

MASSACRE, RESISTANCE AND ESCAPE IN THE VOLHYNIA, AUGUST 1942

Lubieszow **15**

Pohost **2,000** *16 August*

Ratno **1,000** **500** *escape*

Kamien Koszyrski **2,400** *10 August* **600** *escape*

Dabrowica **2,800** **1,500** *escape* *28 August*

Wlodzimierzec **2,400** **600** *escape*

Bereznica **1,000**

Tomaszgrod **150**

Niesuchojeze **350**

Klesow **50**

Rafalowka **1,600** **800** *escape* *28 August*

Sarny **10,500** **3,500** *escape*

Rokitno **900** **700** *escape*

Maciejow **1,500**

Kowel *over* **5,000**

VOLHYNIA

Stepan **2,000** **500** *escape*

Berezno **1,800** **200** *escape*

Turzysk **1,000**

Kostopol *all* **700** *escape*

Rozyszcze **3,000**

Zofiewka **1,500**

Derazne **500**

Sieliszcze **500**

Torczyn **2,000**

Luck **14,700** **2,000** *escape*

Tuczyn **2,000**

PODOLIA

Szumsk *over* **1,000**

Sarny: *resistance led by* Mendel Tendler

Zofiewka: *resistance led by* Chaim Wodchin / Gad Rosenblatt

Krzemieniec *over* **3,000**

Lanowce *over* **400**

Wiszniewicze **1,000** *30 August*

River Bug

EASTERN GALICIA

Polish – Soviet border 1921-1939

0 miles 20
0 kilometres 40

© Martin Gilbert 1982

During the last two weeks of August, more than 200,000 Jews were murdered in German-occupied Poland, most of them deported to the three death camps of Chelmno, Treblinka and Belzec. These deportations were dominated by the relentless rounding up and deportation of Jews from Warsaw to Treblinka.

For every deportation, a precise time-table was devised, and copies sent to every station en route. After the deportees had been taken off, the trains were cleaned, and returned empty along the same routes, and with the same careful planning.

Resistance also continued: at Treblinka itself, on 26 August 1942, a young deportee fom the town of Kielce, having been forbidden by one of the Ukrainian guards to say farewell to his mother, attacked the guard with a knife. Hardly had he done so, than the whole trainload of deportees was machine-gunned.

In the Volhynia (*above*) over 87,000 Jews were murdered in August 1942. As German units came to kill them, as many as 15,000 managed to escape. But less than 1,000 of the escapees, who included men, women and children, were able to survive nearly two years of intense hunger, severe winter cold, sickness, and repeated German and Ukrainian attacks. Some of the men later joined the small Soviet partisan units which were later parachuted into the Volhynia.

Between May and December 1942 more than 140,000 Volhynia Jews were murdered. Some, who had been given refuge in Polish homes, were murdered together with their Polish protectors in the spring of 1943, when, of 300,000 Poles living in the Volhynia, 40,000 were murdered by Ukrainian 'bandits'. In many villages, Poles and Jews fought together against the common foe.

Map 143

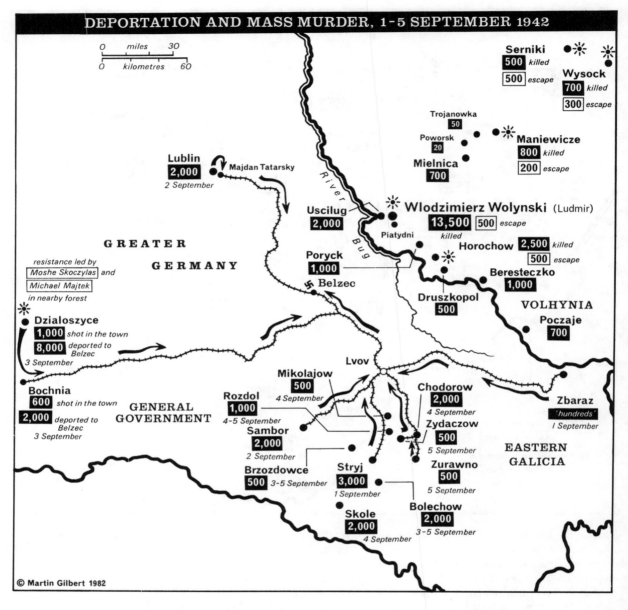

DEPORTATION AND MASS MURDER, 1-5 SEPTEMBER 1942

0 miles 30
0 kilometres 60

Serniki
500 killed
500 escape

Wysock
700 killed
300 escape

Trojanowka
50

Poworsk
20

Maniewicze
800 killed
200 escape

Mielnica
700

Lublin
2,000
2 September
Majdan Tatarsky

Uscilug
2,000

Wlodzimierz Wolynski (Ludmir)
13,500 500 escape
killed
Piatydni

Horochow 2,500 killed
500 escape

GREATER

GERMANY

Poryck
1,000

Belzec

Beresteczko
1,000

Druszkopol
500

VOLHYNIA

Poczaje
700

resistance led by
Moshe Skoczylas and
Michael Majtek
in nearby forest

Dzialoszyce
1,000 shot in the town
8,000 deported to Belzec
3 September

Mikolajow
500
4 September

Lvov

Chodorow
2,000
4 September

Zbaraz
'hundreds'
1 September

Bochnia
600 shot in the town
2,000 deported to Belzec
3 September

GENERAL

GOVERNMENT

Rozdol
1,000
4-5 September

Sambor
2,000
2 September

Zydaczow
500
5 September

Zurawno
500
5 September

EASTERN
GALICIA

Brzozdowce
500 3-5 September

Stryj
3,000
1 September

Skole
2,000
4 September

Bolechow
2,000
3-5 September

© Martin Gilbert 1982

Throughout September 1942, deportation to the death camps continued. For the Wloszczowa deportation (*opposite*) an intricate timetable, typical of hundreds more, was devised:

Wloszczowa		depart 16.38
Kielce	arrive 19.06	depart 19.55
Skarzysko	arrive 21.41	depart 22.43
Radom	arrive 0.03	depart 0.13
Deblin	arrive 2.00	depart 3.10
Lukow	arrive 5.17	depart 6.08
Siedlce	arrive 6.58	depart 8.34
Treblinka	arrive 11.24	(depart empty) 15.59

Following the empty train's despatch from Treblinka, an equally intricate timetable was devised, to return it to the next deportation point.

East of the border of Greater Germany, the killings continued to take place, as shown above, in or near the towns themselves: at Wlodzimierz Wolynski 4,000 Jews were shot in the prison courtyard, and 14,000 driven to the gravel pits at Piatydni, and machine-gunned. Even inside the General Government, as at Warsaw (*opposite*) and Dzialoszyce (*above*), thousands were shot in the streets while the deportations were in progress.

Map 144

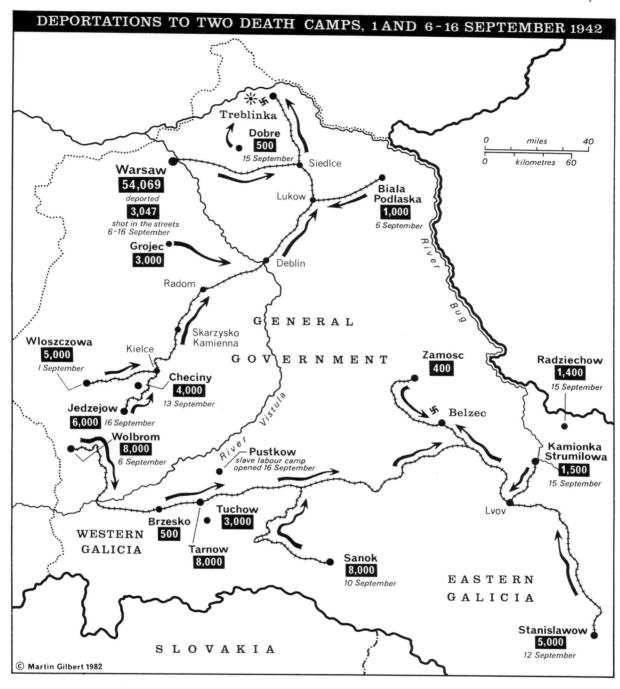

DEPORTATIONS TO TWO DEATH CAMPS, 1 AND 6–16 SEPTEMBER 1942

Treblinka

Dobre
500
15 September

Siedlce

Warsaw
54,069
deported
3,047
shot in the streets
6–16 September

Lukow

Biala Podlaska
1,000
6 September

River Bug

Grojec
3,000

Deblin

Radom

G E N E R A L

Skarzysko Kamienna

G O V E R N M E N T

Wloszczowa
5,000
1 September

Kielce

Zamosc
400

Radziechow
1,400
15 September

Checiny
4,000
13 September

Belzec

Jedzejow
6,000 *16 September*

River Vistula

Wolbrom
8,000
6 September

Pustkow
slave labour camp
opened 16 September

River

Kamionka Strumilowa
1,500
15 September

Lvov

Brzesko
500

Tuchow
3,000

WESTERN GALICIA

Tarnow
8,000

Sanok
8,000
10 September

E A S T E R N G A L I C I A

Stanislawow
5,000
12 September

S L O V A K I A

© Martin Gilbert 1982

0 miles 40
0 kilometres 60

At Treblinka, there was a further act of resistance on 11 September 1942, by a young Jew from the Argentine, who had been trapped in Warsaw at the outbreak of war. The young man, Meir Berliner, having been deported in one of the daily September transports to Treblinka, stabbed an SS officer to death with his penknife.

Meir Berliner's action saved no lives. But it was an act of considerable courage. So too was the decision of a number of Jews from Dzialoszyce (*opposite*) to try to break out on the eve of deportation to Belzec, and make for the forests. Some of them succeeded. Led by Moshe Skoczylas and Michael Majtek, they formed two small but effective partisan units. Majtek helped to organize resistance in Pinczow (*page 131*). Within three months, however, both had been hunted down and destroyed by German troops.

Map 145

NINE DEPORTATIONS TO BELZEC, 7 SEPTEMBER 1942

REICHSKOMMISSARIAT
UKRAINE

Belzec

GENERAL
GOVERNMENT

Lvov

Janowska
*slave labour
camp*

GREATER GERMANY

EASTERN
GALICIA

Zablotow
250

Kolomyja
8,700

Jablonow
800

Sniatyn
2,000

Pistyn
500

Kosow
600

Roznow
100

Kuty
800

RUTHENIA

HUNGARY

Zabie
200

BUKOVINA

miles
0   30

kilometres
0   40

© Martin Gilbert 1982

TRANSYLVANIA

The map above shows nine deportations to Belzec in a single day. The only Jews not sent to their deaths were a group of young people from Kuty. While the rest of their community was sent to Belzec, they were sent to the Janowska slave labour camp in Lvov: a camp where brutality was so savage that almost no-one survived.

In the east (*opposite, above*), German troops had reached the Caucasus. Killing squads at once rounded up the local Jews, murdering them on the spot, or deporting them to nearby execution sites.

In the west (*opposite, below*), the deportations to Auschwitz continued with eight trains from Holland, five from

Belgium, and 13 from Paris. The French deportees included many German Jews who had been deported to the Pyrenees two years before (*page 48*). Deportations also continued to Theresienstadt; there, as in the Polish ghettos, tens of thousands died of starvation and disease. Of 533 Jews deported from Nuremberg in September 1942, only 27 survived the war.

Resistance also continued: at Lachwa, where all 820 Jews fought against the 'liquidation', most were killed, but a few managed to escape and join a Soviet partisan unit. At Stolin local Ukrainians handed over to the SS the two leaders of the revolt, who were then shot.

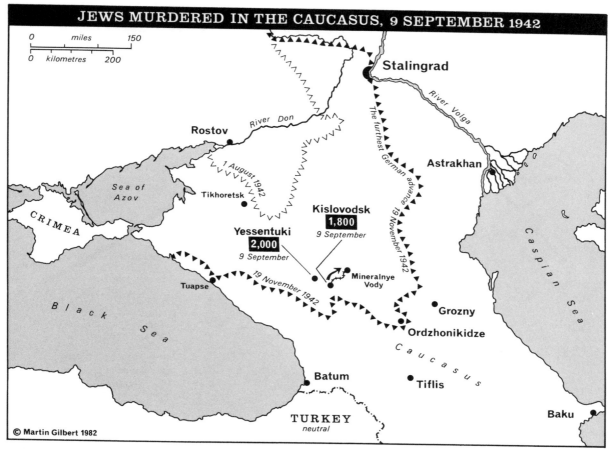

JEWS MURDERED IN THE CAUCASUS, 9 SEPTEMBER 1942

0 miles 150
0 kilometres 200

River Don

Rostov

Sea of Azov

CRIMEA

Tikhoretsk

1 August 1942

Kislovodsk
1,800
9 September

Yessentuki
2,000
9 September

Mineralnye Vody

Tuapse

19 November 1942

The furthest German advance

19 November 1942

Stalingrad

River Volga

Astrakhan

Caspian Sea

Grozny

Ordzhonikidze

Black Sea

Caucasus

Batum

Tiflis

Baku

TURKEY
neutral

© Martin Gilbert 1982

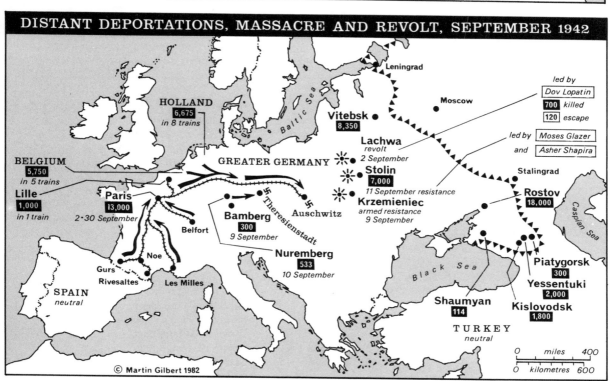

DISTANT DEPORTATIONS, MASSACRE AND REVOLT, SEPTEMBER 1942

HOLLAND
6,675
in 8 trains

BELGIUM
5,750
in 5 trains

Lille
1,000
in 1 train

Paris
13,000
2·30 September

Belfort

Gurs
Rivesaltes

Noe

Les Milles

SPAIN
neutral

GREATER GERMANY

Theresienstadt

Auschwitz

Bamberg
300
9 September

Nuremberg
533
10 September

Baltic Sea

Leningrad

Moscow

Vitebsk
8,350

Lachwa
revolt
2 September

Stolin
7,000
11 September resistance

Krzemieniec
armed resistance
9 September

led by
Dov Lopatin
700 killed
120 escape

led by   Moses Glazer
and   Asher Shapira

Stalingrad

Rostov
18,000

Caspian Sea

Black Sea

Piatygorsk
300

Yessentuki
2,000

Shaumyan
114

Kislovodsk
1,800

TURKEY
neutral

0 miles 400
0 kilometres 600

© Martin Gilbert 1982

Map 148

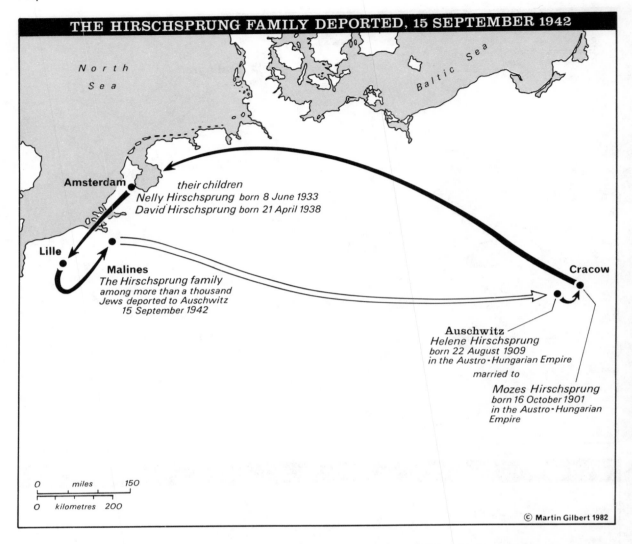

The map above tells of a single family deported from Belgium in September 1942. Hélène Hirschsprung, born in Auschwitz itself, had married a man from Cracow, and then had emigrated to Holland, where both their children were born. With the coming of war they had fled for refuge to Lille, in north-eastern France. But on 15 September 1942 they were among 1,000 Jews who were seized by the SS, transferred to Malines, and then deported to Auschwitz.

The deportees of September 15 (opposite, above) included many Jews born in the Polish provinces of Tsarist Russia, and others from the former Austro-Hungarian Empire.

The SS deportation lists from Paris record a total of 25 Auschwitz-born Jews, deported back to Auschwitz between 1942 and 1944. Among them was Frajdla Leiber, who had left Auschwitz with her parents shortly after

her birth in September 1932, but was deported back to Auschwitz and gassed, when she was only 11 years old.

The Lille deportation of September 15 included the 21-year-old Bernice Winer, born in neutral Switzerland (page 144), and the 28-year-old Fanny Yerkowski, born in London. On the following day, from Paris, a further deportation to Auschwitz contained 40 Bulgarian-born Jews who had been seized in the French capital. The fact that no Jew had yet been deported to Auschwitz from Bulgaria itself could not save them. The names and ages of 14 of them are given opposite. Also deported was the 42-year-old Flora Landsman, born in Britain, and the 28-year-old Londoner, Lea Cohen, as well as Jews with Dutch, Estonian, Lithuanian, Latvian, Yugoslav, and even neutral Turkish citizenship.

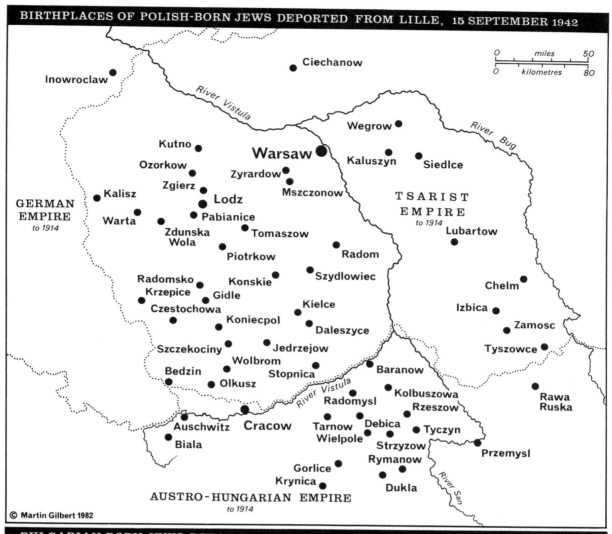

BIRTHPLACES OF POLISH-BORN JEWS DEPORTED FROM LILLE, 15 SEPTEMBER 1942

Ciechanow

Inowroclaw

River Vistula

miles 50
kilometres 80

Wegrow

Kutno

Ozorkow

Zgierz

Zyrardow

Warsaw

Kaluszyn

Siedlce

River Bug

GERMAN EMPIRE
to 1914

Kalisz

Warta

Lodz

Mszczonow

Pabianice

Zdunska Wola

Tomaszow

TSARIST EMPIRE
to 1914

Lubartow

Piotrkow

Radom

Radomsko

Konskie

Szydlowiec

Chelm

Krzepice

Gidle

Izbica

Czestochowa

Kielce

Zamosc

Koniecpol

Daleszyce

Tyszowce

Szczekociny

Jedrzejow

Wolbrom

Bedzin

Stopnica

Baranow

Olkusz

River Vistula

Kolbuszowa

Rawa Ruska

Radomysl

Rzeszow

Auschwitz

Cracow

Tarnow

Debica

Tyczyn

Biala

Wielpole

Strzyzow

Przemysl

Rymanow

Gorlice

River San

Krynica

Dukla

AUSTRO-HUNGARIAN EMPIRE
to 1914

© Martin Gilbert 1982

BULGARIAN-BORN JEWS DEPORTED FROM PARIS TO AUSCHWITZ, 16 SEPTEMBER 1942

miles 75
kilometres 90

River Danube

Ruschuk (Ruse)
Anna Mayer aged 45
Djamba Mayer aged 21
Djoia Mayer aged 14

Jacques Sabetai aged 41
Jeanne Tadger aged 42
Marcel Mayer aged 15
Avram Ninio aged 40
Daniel Ninio aged 37
Esther Ninio aged 37
Moshe Ninio aged 16

Varna
Bellina Mitrani aged 47
Rebecca Ninio aged 34
Elizer Papo aged 45

Sofia

B l a c k

B U L G A R I A

S e a

Kustendil
David Alkali aged 33

Plovdiv
Leon Seliktar aged 37
Joseph Illel aged 53
Israel Cohen aged 40

TURKEY
neutral

borders of 1940

G R E E C E

Sea of Marmara

© Martin Gilbert 1982

Map 151

DEPORTATIONS AND REVOLT, 17-20 SEPTEMBER 1942

Treblinka

Byten
50
19 September

miles 0 — 50
kilometres 0 — 80

River Bug

Parczew
5,000
19 September

'Altana' and 'Tabor'
family camps
hideout and
resistance group led by
Yehiel Grynszpan

Sokal
2,500
17 September

Belzec

mass break out from
deportation train;
almost all the would-
be escapees machine
gunned

Brody
3,000
19 September

EASTERN
GALICIA

Zaleszczyki
2,000
20 September

© Martin Gilbert 1982

In only three days, over 10,000 Jews were deported to Belzec and Treblinka *(left)*. All were murdered. The photograph shows a group of Jews being deported from Eastern Galicia; their bundles contained everything they were allowed to take with them. At Belzec all these belongings were taken from them, sorted, and sent to Germany.

As the Parczew round-ups were in progress, several thousand Jews managed to break through the cordon, escape southwards to the hamlet of Makoszka *(opposite),* and reach the dense woods, thickets and swamps of the Parczew forest *(photographs on page 103)*. Most of them were hunted down by German armed units, and shot. Three particular German hunts, one in November and two in December 1942, led to hundreds of Jewish families being massacred in the forest itself. Others died of starvation, cold and disease. Those few hundred who survived the repeated searches, and the ravages of winter, remained hidden in the forest, in two family camps.

One particularly unpleasant and unexpected hazard for the Jewish families hiding in the Parczew forest was the activity of a group of former Red Army soldiers, prisoners-of-war who had formed their own partisan unit. These Russians promised to give the Jews guns in return for money and jewelry, but simply took the money and disappeared. Others raped the Jewish women, one of whom, Sarah, from Parczew, was murdered by a Russian partisan when she resisted his attempt to rape her. Her murderer was killed by a Jewish partisan.

Only 200 Jews of the family camps survived the war in the Parczew forest, emerging in July 1944 as the Red Army liberated the region.

Map 152

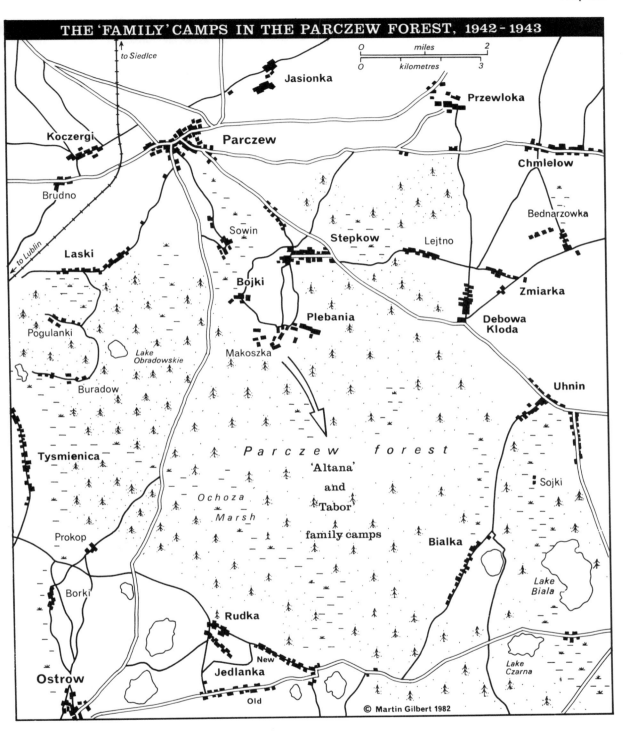

THE 'FAMILY' CAMPS IN THE PARCZEW FOREST, 1942-1943

During the final year of the war, a Polish partisan battalion, commanded by a Jewish officer, Alexander Skotnicki, was also to make the Parczew forest its base of operations, attacking German military trains on the Lublin-Siedlce railway line. Under his command, Skotnicki had one entirely Jewish company, led by Yehiel Grynszpan. At first, Grynszpan's company had only two rifles and one pistol: but by a series of raids on German military posts, he managed to acquire seven rifles, ammunition, and even a number of grenades. About 150 of these Jewish partisans survived the war.

Map 153

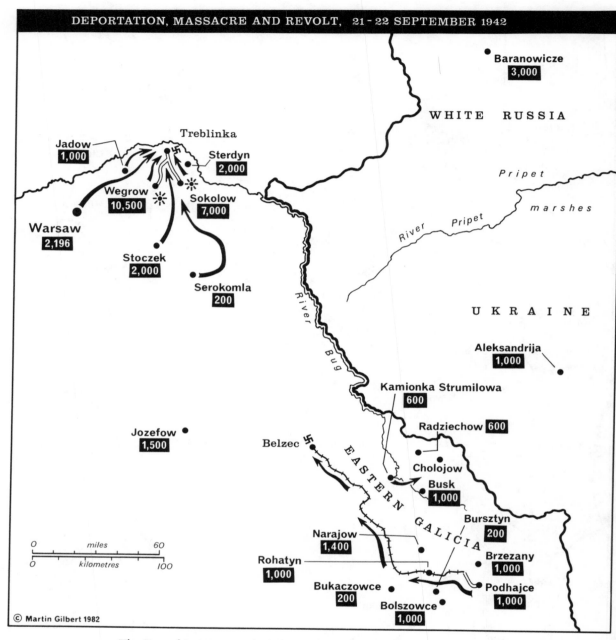

DEPORTATION, MASSACRE AND REVOLT, 21-22 SEPTEMBER 1942

Baranowicze
3,000

WHITE RUSSIA

Treblinka

Jadow
1,000

Sterdyn
2,000

Wegrow
10,500

Sokolow
7,000

Warsaw
2,196

Stoczek
2,000

Serokomla
200

Pripet

River Pripet

marshes

River Bug

UKRAINE

Aleksandrija
1,000

Kamionka Strumilowa
600

Radziechow 600

Jozefow
1,500

Belzec

EASTERN GALICIA

Cholojow

Busk
1,000

Bursztyn
200

Narajow
1,400

Rohatyn
1,000

Brzezany
1,000

Podhajce
1,000

Bukaczowce
200

Bolszowce
1,000

miles 60

kilometres 100

0   0

© Martin Gilbert 1982

The Day of Atonement, the holiest day in the Jewish calendar, fell in 1942 on September 21. During that day and the following day, more than 30,000 Jews were murdered in eastern Europe. From Wegrow and Sokolow hundreds managed to escape to nearby woods but most were quickly hunted down and shot. In the following week (*opposite, above*) thousands more were killed or deported. At Tuczyn 2,000 Jews managed to escape. At Korzec 50 Jews who escaped built up a small partisan unit.

On September 25 the SS seized more than 700 Rumanian-born Jews in Paris, and deported them to Auschwitz. The deportees had been born throughout Rumania (*opposite, below*), among them the 46-year-old Estera Bercovici and her six children. Many children were deported without parents or relatives, among them two 8-year-olds, Suzanne Sloim and Raymond Toutman. Sarah Sepolghi, aged 33, was deported with her ten-month-old baby, Paul. Of the 1,594 deportees on this single train, only 15 able-bodied men, who had been among those 'selected' for slave labour, survived the war.

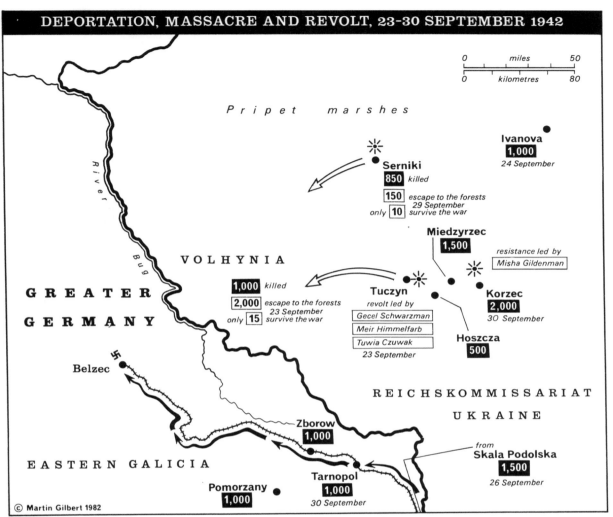

DEPORTATION, MASSACRE AND REVOLT, 23-30 SEPTEMBER 1942

0 — miles — 50
0 — kilometres — 80

Pripet marshes

Ivanova
1,000
24 September

☀ Serniki
850 *killed*
150 *escape to the forests*
29 September
only **10** *survive the war*

Miedzyrzec
1,500

resistance led by
Misha Gildenman

☀

VOLHYNIA

1,000 *killed*
2,000 *escape to the forests*
23 September
only **15** *survive the war*

Tuczyn
revolt led by
Gecel Schwarzman
Meir Himmelfarb
Tuwia Czuwak
23 September

Korzec
2,000
30 September

Hoszcza
500

G R E A T E R

G E R M A N Y

River Bug

Belzec ⚑

R E I C H S K O M M I S S A R I A T

U K R A I N E

Zborow
1,000

from
Skala Podolska
1,500
26 September

E A S T E R N   G A L I C I A

Tarnopol
1,000
30 September

Pomorzany
1,000

© Martin Gilbert 1982

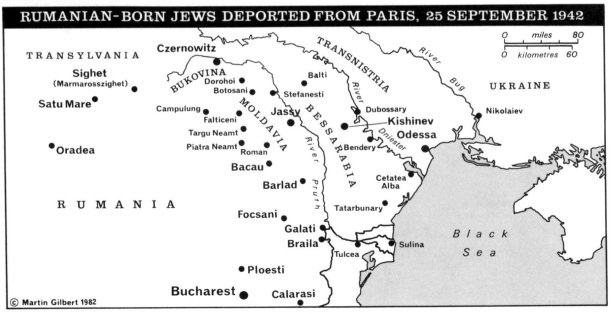

RUMANIAN-BORN JEWS DEPORTED FROM PARIS, 25 SEPTEMBER 1942

0 — miles — 80
0 — kilometres — 60

T R A N S Y L V A N I A

Czernowitz

BUKOVINA

TRANSNISTRIA

River Bug

UKRAINE

Sighet
(Marmarosszighet)

Dorohoi
Botosani

Balti

Stefanesti

Satu Mare

Campulung
Falticeni
Targu Neamt
Piatra Neamt
Roman

MOLDAVIA

Jassy

River

Dubossary

Kishinev

Nikolaiev

BESSARABIA

Odessa

Bendery

Dniester

Oradea

Bacau

Barlad

River Pruth

Cetatea
Alba

R U M A N I A

Focsani

Tatarbunary

Galati
Braila

Tulcea

Sulina

*Black
Sea*

Ploesti

Bucharest

Calarasi

© Martin Gilbert 1982

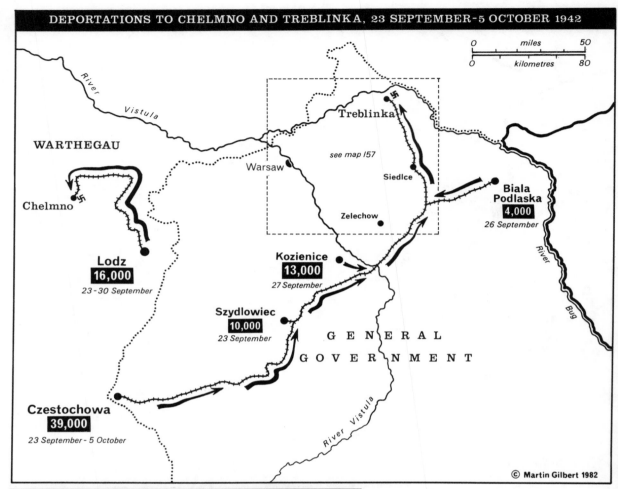

DEPORTATIONS TO CHELMNO AND TREBLINKA, 23 SEPTEMBER–5 OCTOBER 1942

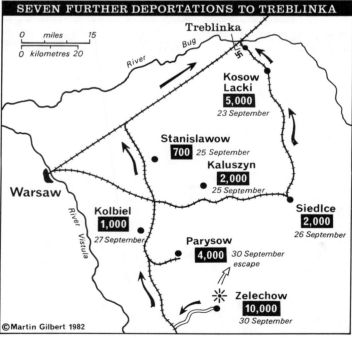

SEVEN FURTHER DEPORTATIONS TO TREBLINKA

In the middle of September the SS, having decided to make the Lodz ghetto an entirely 'working' ghetto, launched the 'Gehsperre' action, aimed at deporting to Chelmno all children up to the age of 10, all men and women over 60, and all who were sick or emaciated. In all, 16,000 Jews were deported and gassed within two weeks (*above*). East of Warsaw (*left*) more than 24,000 Jews were deported to Treblinka and killed.

The deportations from the General Government also continued on a massive scale (*above*). From one town, Zelechow, a few hundred young Jews managed to escape into the woods and form a partisan group. But most Jews were trapped by the overwhelming German military might.

From Paris the deportations to Auschwitz continued, bringing to the gas chambers Jews born throughout Asia (*opposite, above*), the Dutch East Indies and North Africa (*opposite, below*); men and women who had sought a new life in Paris before 1939.

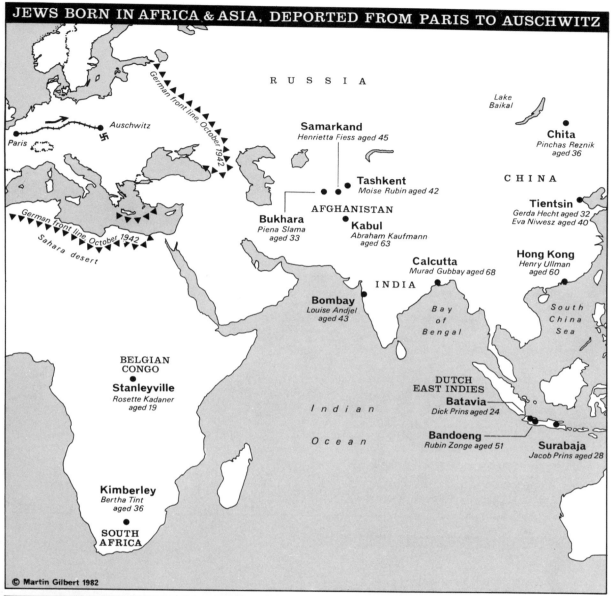

JEWS BORN IN AFRICA & ASIA, DEPORTED FROM PARIS TO AUSCHWITZ

RUSSIA

German front line, October 1942

Auschwitz

Paris

German front line, October 1942

Sahara desert

Lake Baikal

Chita
Pinchas Reznik aged 36

Samarkand
Henrietta Fiess aged 45

Tashkent
Moise Rubin aged 42

CHINA

AFGHANISTAN

Bukhara
Piena Slama aged 33

Kabul
Abraham Kaufmann aged 63

Tientsin
*Gerda Hecht aged 32
Eva Niwesz aged 40*

Calcutta
Murad Gubbay aged 68

Hong Kong
Henry Ullman aged 60

INDIA

Bombay
Louise Andjel aged 43

Bay of Bengal

South China Sea

BELGIAN CONGO

Stanleyville
Rosette Kadaner aged 19

Indian Ocean

DUTCH EAST INDIES

Batavia
Dick Prins aged 24

Bandoeng
Rubin Zonge aged 51

Surabaja
Jacob Prins aged 28

Kimberley
Bertha Tint aged 36

SOUTH AFRICA

© Martin Gilbert 1982

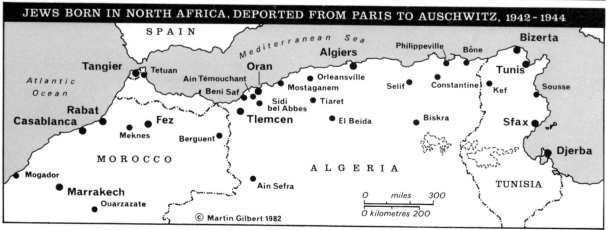

JEWS BORN IN NORTH AFRICA, DEPORTED FROM PARIS TO AUSCHWITZ, 1942-1944

SPAIN

Mediterranean Sea

Bizerta

Tangier
Tetuan

Ain Témouchant

Oran

Algiers

Philippeville

Bône

Tunis

Atlantic Ocean

Orléansville
Mostaganem

Beni Saf

Sidi bel Abbès

Selif

Constantine

Kef

Sousse

Rabat
Casablanca

Fez

Meknes

Berguent

Tlemcen

Tiaret

El Beida

Biskra

Sfax

Djerba

Mogador

MOROCCO

Marrakech
Ouarzazate

Ain Sefra

ALGERIA

TUNISIA

0 miles 300
0 kilometres 200

© Martin Gilbert 1982

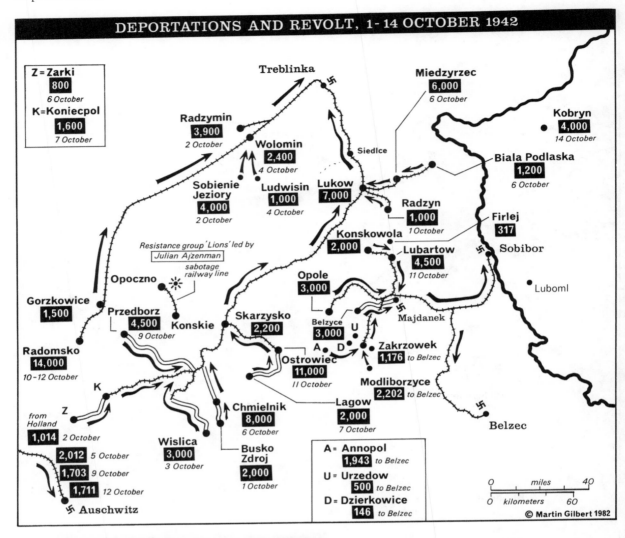

DEPORTATIONS AND REVOLT, 1–14 OCTOBER 1942

Z = Zarki
800
6 October

K = Koniecpol
1,600
7 October

Treblinka

Miedzyrzec
6,000
6 October

Kobryn
4,000
14 October

Radzymin
3,900
2 October

Wolomin
2,400
4 October

Siedlce

Biala Podlaska
1,200
6 October

Sobienie Jeziory
4,000
2 October

Ludwisin
1,000
4 October

Lukow
7,000

Radzyn
1,000
1 October

Firlej
317

Sobibor

Resistance group 'Lions' led by
Julian Ajzenman
sabotage
railway line

Konskowola
2,000

Lubartow
4,500
11 October

Luboml

Opoczno

Opole
3,000

Gorzkowice
1,500

Przedborz
4,500
9 October

Konskie

Skarzysko
2,200

Belzyce
3,000

U

Majdanek

Zakrzowek
1,176 *to Belzec*

Radomsko
14,000
10–12 October

K

Ostrowiec
11,000
11 October

A   D

Modliborzyce
2,202 *to Belzec*

Z

Chmielnik
8,000
6 October

Lagow
2,000
7 October

Belzec

from Holland
1,014 *2 October*

2,012 *5 October*

1,703 *9 October*

1,711 *12 October*

Wislica
3,000
3 October

Busko Zdroj
2,000
1 October

A = Annopol
1,943 *to Belzec*

U = Urzedow
500 *to Belzec*

D = Dzierkowice
146 *to Belzec*

Auschwitz

0   miles   40
0   kilometers   60

© Martin Gilbert 1982

MORE KILLINGS, SEPTEMBER – OCTOBER 1942

0   miles   100
0   kilometres   150

Baltic Sea

Koziany
400 *30 September*

Korzeniec
2,000
9 Sept

Kobylnik
150 *29 September*

Grodek
1,600 *11 September*

Wolozyn
1,000 *29 September*

Rakow
112 *21 September*

Danzig

GREATER GERMANY

Warsaw

Janow
2,000
24 August

Kiev

CZORTKOW REGION
Jezierzany **900**
Kopyczynce **1,500**
Korolowka **700**
Mielnica **1,000**
Probuzna **1,500**

Belzec

to Belzec

Buczacz
1,500

Horodenka
1,500 *8–10 September*

© Martin Gilbert 1982

Among the Jews murdered in September 1942 *(left)* were 1,000 from the town of Wolozyn, formerly a centre of Jewish spiritual learning. In Eastern Galicia Jews had been deported to Belzec from seven communities, some of them small villages in the Czortkow region.

Throughout October 1942 the deportations continued. From Holland *(above)* and Belgium *(opposite, above)*, Jews were brought to Auschwitz *(see also page 130)*. From central Poland and Theresienstadt they were deported to Treblinka, with as many as 30 deportations during the last two weeks of October *(opposite, below)*; and from eastern Galicia to Belzec *(opposite, above)*. East of Greater Germany, the Jews were killed in the streets, or in nearby woods and quarries, including 10,000 in the Volhynian town of Luboml.

DEPORTATION, MASSACRE AND REVOLT, 1–31 OCTOBER 1942

Baltic Sea

German front line

Bystrzycza
hundreds

Kiemieliszki
hundreds

Oszmiana
406
23 October

Nowogrodek
50 Jews escape to join resistance led by
Tobias Bielski

from Belgium

Bielsk Podlaski
11,000
2 October

Kosow **300** *14 October*

Antopol **1,000**

Treblinka

Drohiczyn **2,500**
15 October

GREATER

Siedlce

Ryki

Szack
150

Kamien Koszyrski
300 *14 October*

999 *10 October* **675** *16 October*

995 *20 October* **476** *24 October*

822 *31 October* **875** *31 October*

GERMANY

Parczew
108

Luboml
Warkowicze

Zdolbunow
1,000

Mizocz
Ostrog

Luboml
10,000 *1 October*
hundreds escape but later hunted down

Belzec

EASTERN GALICIA

Theresienstadt
1,000 **1,998**
5 October *15 October*

2,018 **1,000** **1,984**
22 October *8 October* *19 October*

Auschwitz

Czortkow
500

Tluste

Warkowicze
400 *killed*
1,600 *escape*

Mizocz
850
850

Ostrog
2,200
800 *escape*

Kolomyja
4,500
3 October

Bar
12,000

1,000
5 October

0 — miles — 150
0 — kilometres — 200

© Martin Gilbert 1982

THIRTY DEPORTATIONS TO TREBLINKA, 15–31 OCTOBER 1942

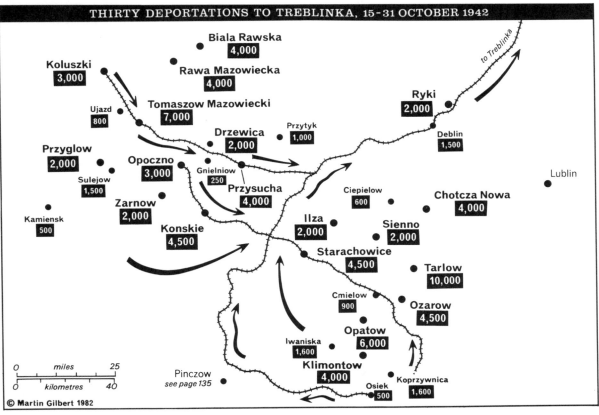

to Treblinka

Biala Rawska
4,000

Koluszki
3,000

Rawa Mazowiecka
4,000

Ryki
2,000

Ujazd
800

Tomaszow Mazowiecki
7,000

Drzewica
2,000

Przytyk
1,000

Deblin
1,500

Przyglow
2,000

Opoczno
3,000

Gnielniow
250

Lublin

Sulejow
1,500

Przysucha
4,000

Ciepielow
600

Chotcza Nowa
4,000

Zarnow
2,000

Ilza
2,000

Sienno
2,000

Kamiensk
500

Konskie
4,500

Starachowice
4,500

Tarlow
10,000

Cmielow
900

Ozarow
4,500

Iwaniska
1,600

Opatow
6,000

Klimontow
4,000

Koprzywnica
1,600

Pinczow
see page 135

Osiek
500

0 — miles — 25
0 — kilometres — 40

© Martin Gilbert 1982

Map 164

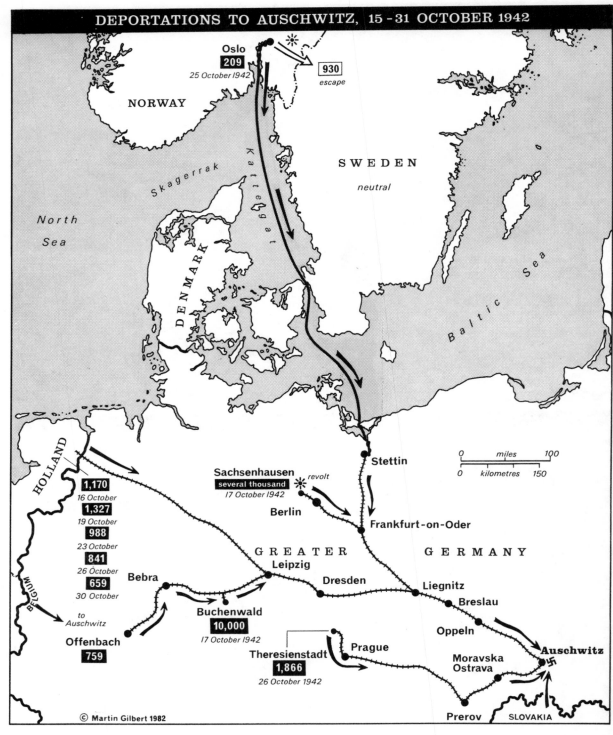

DEPORTATIONS TO AUSCHWITZ, 15-31 OCTOBER 1942

Oslo
209
25 October 1942

930
escape

NORWAY

SWEDEN
neutral

Skagerrak

Kattegat

North Sea

DENMARK

Baltic Sea

HOLLAND

1,170
16 October
1,327
19 October
988
23 October
841
26 October
659
30 October

BELGIUM

to Auschwitz

Offenbach
759

Bebra

Sachsenhausen
several thousand *revolt*
17 October 1942

Berlin

Stettin

Frankfurt-on-Oder

GREATER
Leipzig

GERMANY

Dresden

Liegnitz

Breslau

Buchenwald
10,000
17 October 1942

Oppeln

Theresienstadt
1,866
26 October 1942

Prague

Moravska Ostrava

Auschwitz

Prerov   SLOVAKIA

0 ___ miles ___ 100
0 ___ kilometres ___ 150

© Martin Gilbert 1982

The map above shows ten of the deportations from western Europe and Norway to Auschwitz in the second half of October 1942. In addition to these deportations, and four from Belgium (*page 129*), the Auschwitz calendar records a further train reaching the camp from Slovakia on October 23.

Within six months of the German occupation of Norway in April 1940 (*page 45*), Jews had been forbidden to participate in professional life. Forcible registration of

Map 165

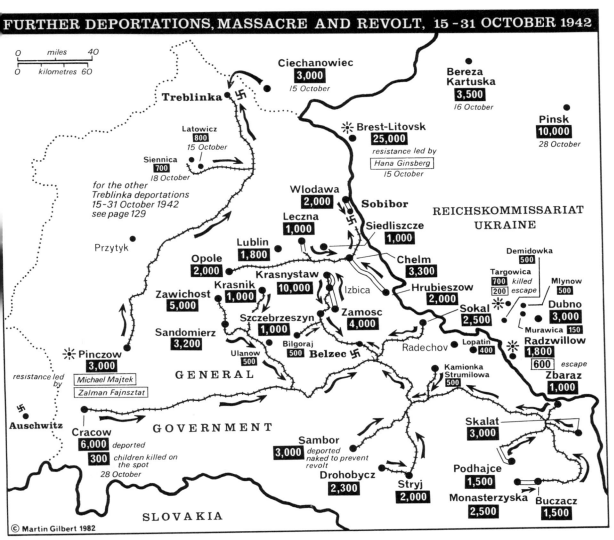

FURTHER DEPORTATIONS, MASSACRE AND REVOLT, 15–31 OCTOBER 1942

all Jews took place in June 1942, and the confiscation of all Jewish property in October 1942. Then, on October 25, all Jewish men and boys over the age of sixteen, some 209 in all, were seized throughout the country, sent by sea from Norway to Stettin, and then on by rail to Auschwitz. A further 531 women and children were seized on November 25 (*page 133*), and likewise sent to their deaths. Only 12 of the 740 deportees survived the war.

Helped by the Norwegian people, often at the risk of their own lives, as many as 930 Norwegian Jews succeeded in escaping into neutral Sweden. About 60 were imprisoned or interned inside Norway itself.

The map above shows some of the deportations to the eastern death camps during the same two-week period. Before the deportation from Drohobycz, nearly 200

old and sick Jews were shot in the streets of the town. Among the executions on the spot was the killing of 25,000 Jews in Brest-Litovsk. Almost all the other Jews of Brest, some 5,000, had been murdered in June 1941 (*page 67*). Most of the few hundred Jews still alive managed to join partisan units.

Among the deportations during these two weeks was one from Przytyk to Treblinka (*page 129*). It was the murder of three Jews in Przytyk before the Second World War (*page 21*) that had created such alarm among Polish Jewry, reviving memories of the Tsarist pogroms. But in the autumn of 1942 the deportation and immediate murder of 1,000 Jews from the same village, deaths horrific in themselves, were dwarfed by the total number of deaths in only two weeks, in eastern Poland alone, of more than 100,000 men, women and children.

Map 166

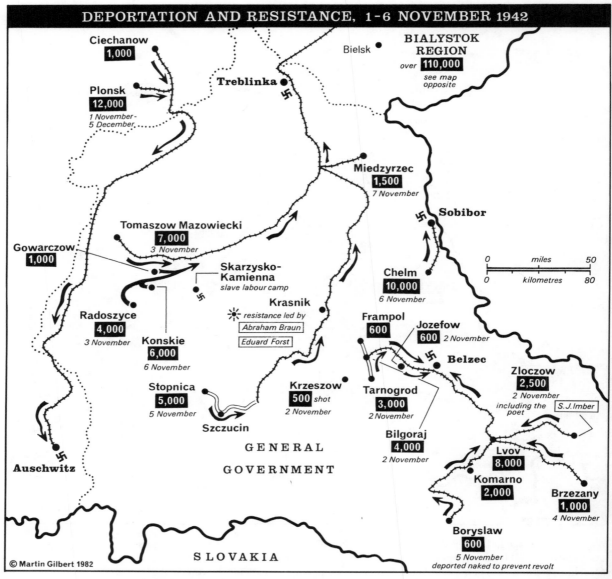

DEPORTATION AND RESISTANCE, 1-6 NOVEMBER 1942

Ciechanow
1,000

Bielsk

BIALYSTOK REGION
over **110,000**
see map opposite

Plonsk
12,000
1 November - 5 December

Treblinka

Miedzyrzec
1,500
7 November

Sobibor

Tomaszow Mazowiecki
7,000
3 November

Gowarczow
1,000

Skarzysko-Kamienna
slave labour camp

Chelm
10,000
6 November

0 — miles — 50
0 — kilometres — 80

Krasnik
☀ *resistance led by*
Abraham Braun
Eduard Forst

Frampol
600

Jozefow
600
2 November

Belzec

Zloczow
2,500
2 November including the poet
S. J. Imber

Radoszyce
4,000
3 November

Konskie
6,000
6 November

Stopnica
5,000
5 November

Krzeszow
500 *shot*
2 November

Tarnogrod
3,000
2 November

Szczucin

Bilgoraj
4,000
2 November

Lvov
8,000

Komarno
2,000

Brzezany
1,000
4 November

Auschwitz

GENERAL

GOVERNMENT

Boryslaw
600
5 November
deported naked to prevent revolt

© Martin Gilbert 1982

S L O V A K I A

In November 1942 the Dutch, French and Norwegian deportations continued (*opposite, above*). Further east, Jews were slaughtered at Slutsk; and at Proskurov, where 1,700 Jews had been killed in 1919 (*page 15*), the last 7,000 Jews were murdered.

On November 2 one of the most carefully organized and intensive round-ups of the war took place throughout the Bialystok region (*opposite, below*), where more than 20,000 Jews had already been murdered during the first two months of the German invasion (*pages 67 and 68*). The remaining 110,000 Jews, who had been strictly confined to their towns and villages, were now seized and sent to camps at Zambrow, Wolkowysk, Bogusze and Kielbasin, before being taken by train to Treblinka and Auschwitz. When the Jews of Marcinkance resisted deportation, all were shot in the village.

At Siemiatycze a few dozen Jews managed to escape to nearby forests and to form a small resistance group. Most were then killed by Polish partisan bands.

Further south, at Stopnica (*above*), 1,500 men were sent to the slave labour camps at Skarzysko Kamienna, while 400 children and old people were shot in the town cemetery. The remaining 3,000 Jews were marched to Szczucin, many being shot on the way, and the survivors sent on by train to Treblinka, at which, with Belzec and Auschwitz, more than 170,000 Jews were killed within one week (*above*).

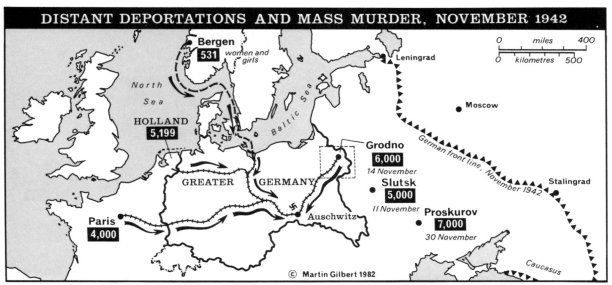

DISTANT DEPORTATIONS AND MASS MURDER, NOVEMBER 1942

Bergen
531
women and girls

North Sea

Baltic Sea

Leningrad

Moscow

HOLLAND
5,199

GREATER   GERMANY

Auschwitz

Grodno
6,000
14 November

Slutsk
5,000
11 November

Proskurov
7,000
30 November

German front line, November 1942

Stalingrad

Paris
4,000

Caucasus

© Martin Gilbert 1982

miles 0 — 400
kilometres 0 — 500

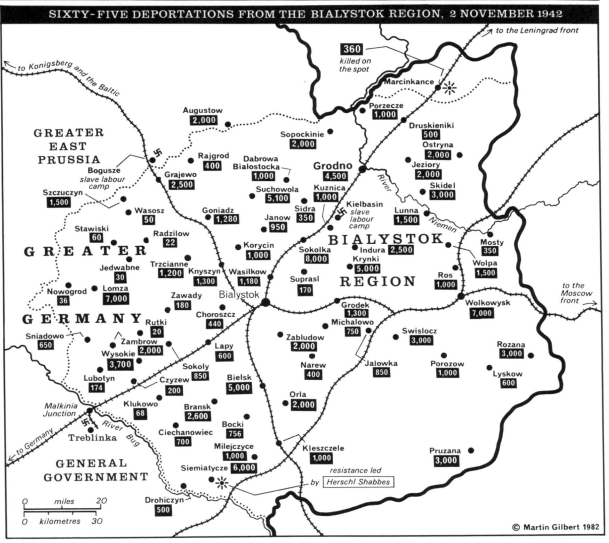

SIXTY-FIVE DEPORTATIONS FROM THE BIALYSTOK REGION, 2 NOVEMBER 1942

to the Leningrad front

360
killed on the spot

Marcinkance

to Konigsberg and the Baltic

Porzecze
1,000

Druskieniki
500

Augustow
2,000

Sopockinie
2,000

Ostryna
2,000

GREATER
EAST
PRUSSIA

Rajgrod
400

Dabrowa
Bialostocka
1,000

Grodno
4,500

Jeziory
2,000

Bogusze
slave labour camp

Grajewo
2,500

Kuznica
1,000

Skidel
3,000

Szczuczyn
1,500

Suchowola
5,100

Kielbasin
slave labour camp

Lunna
1,500

River Niemen

Wasosz
50

Goniadz
1,280

Sidra
350

Mosty
350

Stawiski
60

Radzilow
22

Janow
950

BIALYSTOK

Indura
2,500

Wolpa
1,500

G R E A T E R

Korycin
1,000

Sokolka
8,000

Krynki
5,000

to the Moscow front

Jedwabne
30

Trzcianne
1,200

Knyszyn
1,300

Wasilkow
1,180

Ros
1,000

Nowogrod
36

Lomza
7,000

Zawady
180

Suprasl
170

REGION

G E R M A N Y

Rutki
20

Choroszcz
440

Bialystok

Grodek
1,300

Wolkowysk
7,000

Sniadowo
650

Zambrow
2,000

Michalowo
750

Swislocz
3,000

Rozana
3,000

Wysokie
3,700

Lapy
600

Zabludow
2,000

Lubotyn
174

Sokoly
850

Narew
400

Jalowka
850

Porozow
1,000

Lyskow
600

Czyzew
200

Bielsk
5,000

Malkinia Junction

River Bug

Klukowo
68

Orla
2,000

Treblinka

Bransk
2,600

Bocki
756

to Germany

Ciechanowiec
700

Kleszczele
1,000

Pruzana
3,000

**GENERAL
GOVERNMENT**

Milejczyce
1,000

Siemiatycze
6,000

resistance led by | Herschl Shabbes |

Drohiczyn
500

miles 0 — 20
kilometres 0 — 30

© Martin Gilbert 1982

Map 169

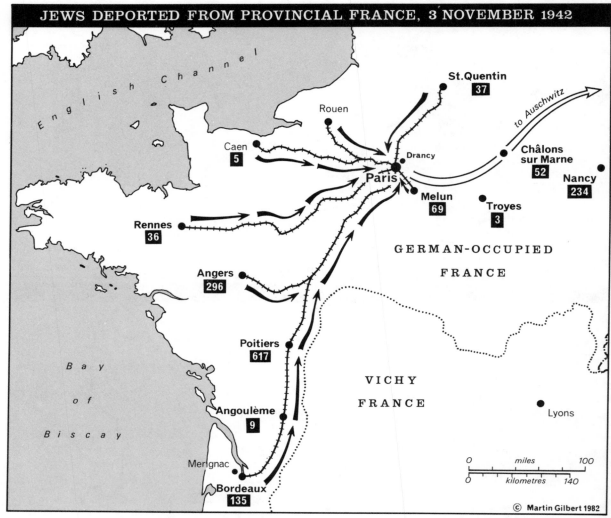

JEWS DEPORTED FROM PROVINCIAL FRANCE, 3 NOVEMBER 1942

English Channel

St.Quentin
37

Rouen

to Auschwitz

Caen
5

Drancy

Châlons
sur Marne
52

Paris

Nancy
234

Melun
69

Troyes
3

Rennes
36

GERMAN-OCCUPIED

FRANCE

Angers
296

Poitiers
617

Bay

of

VICHY

FRANCE

Lyons

Biscay

Angoulème
9

0   miles   100

Merignac

0   kilometres   140

Bordeaux
135

© Martin Gilbert 1982

Among the deportations to Auschwitz in November 1942 was one, from Paris on November 3, which included several hundred Jews who had been seized in provincial France (*above*).

Of the 1,000 Jews deported on that day, 200 were children, deported with their parents or grandparents; including the 4-year-old twins, Annie and Lydia Kirzner, the 2-year-old Jacques Wlademirski, the 4-year-old Daniel Szulc, and the Zajdenwerger children, David aged 4 and his sister, Solange, aged 3. All were gassed.

The map opposite (*top*) shows some of the other birthplaces of those deported from Paris to Auschwitz on November 3. Some were old people, such as Gabriel Erlich, from Warsaw, aged 70, deported with his wife, and his two daughters, aged 36 and 38.

Many of the deportees, like the Erlich daughters, were in the prime of life: Magalta

Poulios, from the Greek island of Chios, was 35; Jean Blumenthal, from Berlin, was 27; so also was Joseph Rozio from the Turkish port of Smyrna; Robert Geyer from Metz was just 20; Gabrielle Bruski from Budapest was only 18. Deported all alone was a boy, the 4-year-old Jankiel Ciesielski, who had been born in Lodz.

The two smaller maps (*opposite, below*) give the birthplaces and names of some of the hundreds of Jews deported from Paris to Auschwitz between 1942 and 1944 who had been born in the Americas. At least 10 were still United States citizens at the time of their deportation. Between the wars all had chosen to come to Europe; to teach, to work, to marry and to bring up children.

The photograph was taken during one of the Paris deportations; more than 80,000 Jews were deported from Paris to Auschwitz in little over two years.

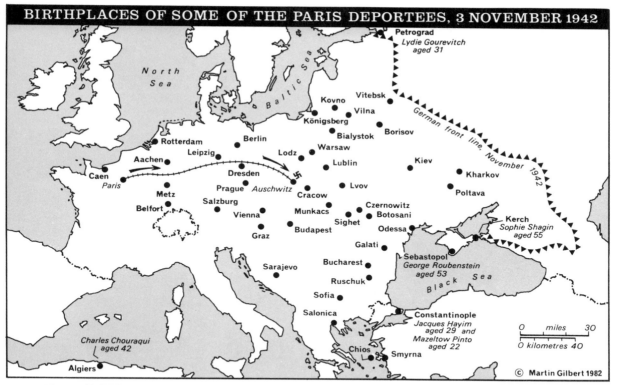

BIRTHPLACES OF SOME OF THE PARIS DEPORTEES, 3 NOVEMBER 1942

North Sea

Baltic Sea

Petrograd
Lydie Gourevitch aged 31

German front line, November 1942

Kovno

Vitebsk

Vilna

Königsberg

Borisov

Berlin

Bialystok

Rotterdam

Leipzig

Lodz

Warsaw

Aachen

Lublin

Kiev

Caen

Paris

Dresden

Auschwitz

Lvov

Kharkov

Metz

Prague

Cracow

Poltava

Belfort

Salzburg

Munkacs

Czernowitz

Botosani

Kerch
Sophie Shagin aged 55

Vienna

Sighet

Odessa

Graz

Budapest

Galati

Sarajevo

Bucharest

Sebastopol
George Roubenstein aged 53

Ruschuk

Black Sea

Sofia

Salonica

Constantinople
Jacques Hayim aged 29 and Mazeltow Pinto aged 22

Charles Chouraqui aged 42

Chios

Smyrna

Algiers

| 0 | miles | 30 |
| 0 | kilometres | 40 |

© Martin Gilbert 1982

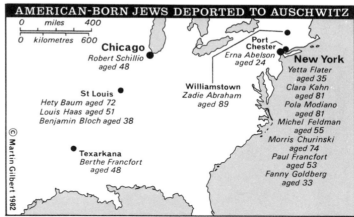

AMERICAN-BORN JEWS DEPORTED TO AUSCHWITZ

| 0 | miles | 400 |
| 0 | kilometres | 600 |

Chicago
Robert Schillio aged 48

Port Chester
Erna Abelson aged 24

New York
Yetta Flater aged 35
Clara Kahn aged 81
Pola Modiano aged 81
Michel Feldman aged 55
Morris Churinski aged 74
Paul Francfort aged 53
Fanny Goldberg aged 33

St Louis
Hety Baum aged 72
Louis Haas aged 51
Benjamin Bloch aged 38

Williamstown
Zadie Abraham aged 89

Texarkana
Berthe Francfort aged 48

© Martin Gilbert 1982

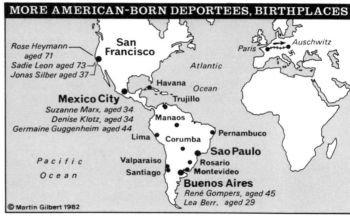

MORE AMERICAN-BORN DEPORTEES, BIRTHPLACES

Rose Heymann aged 71

San Francisco

Sadie Leon aged 73
Jonas Silber aged 37

Paris → *Auschwitz*

Atlantic Ocean

Havana

Mexico City
Suzanne Marx, aged 34
Denise Klotz, aged 34
Germaine Guggenheim aged 44

Trujillo

Manaos

Lima

Corumba

Pernambuco

Sao Paulo

Pacific Ocean

Valparaiso

Santiago

Rosario
Montevideo

Buenos Aires
René Gompers, aged 45
Lea Berr, aged 29

© Martin Gilbert 1982

135

Map 173

DEPORTATION, MASSACRE AND REVOLT, 7-30 NOVEMBER 1942

Mlawa
6,300
10 November

Makow
500
14 November

Treblinka

Wyszogrod
2,700
19 November

Warsaw

Danilowicze
900
21 November

Miedzyrzec
Podlaski
1,500 *7 November*

Serokomla
200 *shot*
22 November

Wisznice
120 *shot*
20 November

Lukow
3,000
7 November

Szydlowiec
10,000
23 November

Gniewoszow
1,000
15 November

Leczna
1,000
11 November

Komarow Osada
1,000
10 November

Konskie
4,500
7 November

Zwolen
10,000
29 November

Majdanek

Wlodzimierz Wolynski
2,500
*13 November
resistance*

Suchedniow
4,000
21 November

Piaski
4,000
9 November

Szczekociny
1,500
21 November

Goraj
30 *shot*
30 November

Zamosc
4,000
15 November

Belzec

Brody
250 *to Belzec*
20 *shot*
26 November

Sedziszow
1,000
21 November

Staszow
6,000
7 November

Zolkiew
2,500
22 November

Busk
1,000 *shot*

Zbaraz
1,000
8 November

Ksiaz
Wielki
500 *shot*

Cracow

Kolbuszowa
2,500

Lubaczow

Sasow
400
25 November

Bochnia
570
10 November

Tarnow
3,000
15 November

Rzeszow
2,000

Lvov
5,000
18 November

Skalat
1,100
9 November

Zakliczyn
500

Przemysl
4,000
18 November

Rudki
800

Buczacz
2,750
27 November

'Amsterdam' Jewish
resistance group active,
November 1942 –
November 1944

Stryj
1,500
to Belzec

Jaworow
1,500
7 November

Szczerzec
600

Tlumacz
2,000
27 November

SLOVAKIA

Mosciska
2,500
28 November

© Martin Gilbert 1982

During the last three weeks of November more than 50,000 Jews were deported to the death camps of Treblinka and Belzec, sent to the concentration camp at Majdanek, now a death camp; or, as in Wlodzimierz Wolynski, massacred in the streets (*above*).

In the course of a few hours ancient communities were totally destroyed: the Jews of Wyszogrod could trace their first settlement in the town to the early fifteenth century, those of Buczacz to the late sixteenth century.

It was in Buczacz that the author S. Y. Agnon, a Nobel prizewinner, had been born in 1907; at the age of 20, he had emigrated to Palestine. After a visit to Buczacz in 1930, he published a nightmarish picture of his home town, its synagogues empty, its society collapsed, its people shattered: a 'city of the dead'.

In Buczacz, following the first killings in August 1941 (*page 69*), and the deportations of October 1942 (*page 131*), young men and women had searched for arms, and tried to

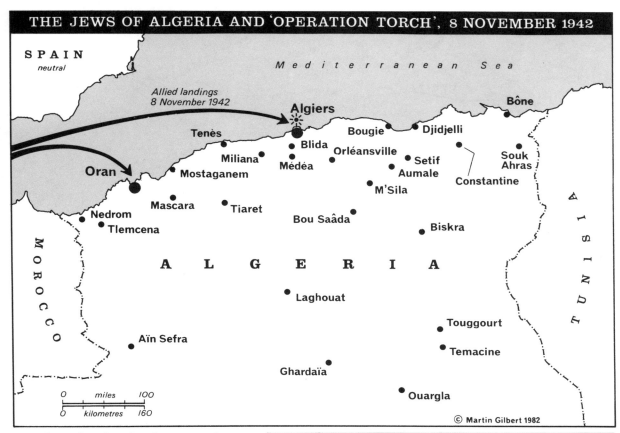

THE JEWS OF ALGERIA AND 'OPERATION TORCH', 8 NOVEMBER 1942

SPAIN
neutral

Mediterranean Sea

Allied landings 8 November 1942

Bône

Algiers

Tenès

Bougie · Djidjelli

Blida

Oran

Miliana · Médéa · Orléansville · Setif · Souk Ahras

Mostaganem · Aumale

Mascara · Tiaret · M'Sila · Constantine

Nedrom · Bou Saâda

Tlemcena

MOROCCO

Biskra

ALGERIA

Laghouat

TUNISIA

Aïn Sefra

Touggourt

Temacine

Ghardaïa

Ouargla

0 miles 100
0 kilometres 160

© Martin Gilbert 1982

train themselves for a breakout. In mid-1943 (*page 161*), when the SS liquidated the ghetto, some Jews managed to escape to the forest. But most were murdered near the Jewish cemetery on the outskirts of the town.

It was not only in Europe, but also in North Africa (*above*), that Jews were at risk. Jews were active throughout the Algerian resistance, and it was a Jew, Jose Abulker, who led the uprising in Algiers, tying down the German forces and 'neutralizing' the capital, as the Allies carried out 'Operation Torch', the landings of 8 November 1942 which ended German control of Algeria. For the 117,000 Jews of Algeria, the Allied landings brought security from deportation.

With the almost simultaneous German defeats at Stalingrad and El Alamein (*right*), the Allied landings in North Africa marked a major turning point of the war. But a full year and a half were to pass before the Red Army reached the first of the death camps on Polish soil, Majdanek (*page 200*), or the western Allies landed on the Normandy beaches (*page 201*). During those eighteen months the deportation of Jews continued without respite throughout Nazi-dominated Europe.

STALINGRAD, EL ALAMEIN, 'TORCH'

0 miles 400
0 kilometres 800

North Sea

Baltic Sea

Leningrad *besieged*

SOVIET RUSSIA

Atlantic Ocean

Warsaw

GREATER Cracow
GERMANY

Stalingrad *relieved*

Black Sea

Oran Algiers
Allied landings

Mediterranean Sea

EGYPT

El Alamein
Germans defeated

© Martin Gilbert 1982

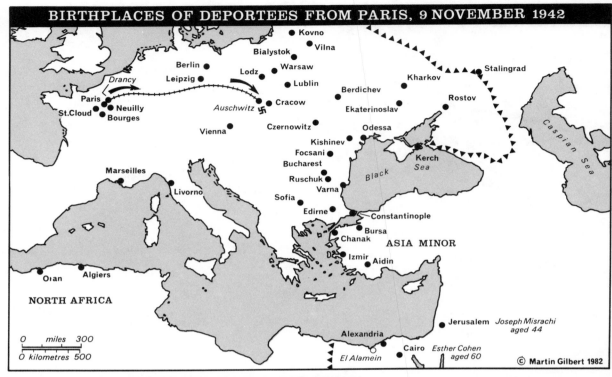

BIRTHPLACES OF DEPORTEES FROM PARIS, 9 NOVEMBER 1942

© Martin Gilbert 1982

GREEK-BORN DEPORTEES FROM PARIS

© Martin Gilbert 1982

On 9 November 1942 it was the turn of Jews who had been born in Greece to be seized in Paris and deported to Auschwitz. More than 800 of these deportees had been born in Salonica *(above)*: nearly 100 or them were children under 12. Among those from the ancient town of Drama were Jacques and Nicoula Benveniste, and their daughter Liza, aged 19. From Canea, in Crete, had come the 67-year-old Moise Cohen.

As with each of the previous Paris deportations, there were Jews who had been born throughout Europe *(above)*, North Africa and Asia Minor. Esther Cohen had been born in Cairo 60 years before, Joseph Misrahi in Jerusalem 44 years before, Solomon Moscowitz in the port of Kerch in 1877.

In the General Government several thousand Jews, from four communities, had been in hiding in the forests since the spring *(opposite, above)*. On November 10 a German promise of the security of a new ghetto led more than 6,000 of them to agree to come out in return for safe conduct. Starving and freezing, they were taken to Sandomierz: but two months later, on 10 January 1943, almost all of them were deported to Treblinka and gassed, only a few hundred being sent to labour camps at Skarzysko Kamienna and Sandomierz itself.

In the province of Zamosc *(opposite, below)* it was Poles who faced Nazi brutality. To enable SS men, ethnic Germans and Ukrainians to settle in the province's rich pastureland, tens of thousands of Poles were driven from their homes, and hundreds killed. At the same time, thousands of Polish children were deported to concentration camps. In all more than 100 villages were emptied of their inhabitants, and more than 40,000 Poles expelled.

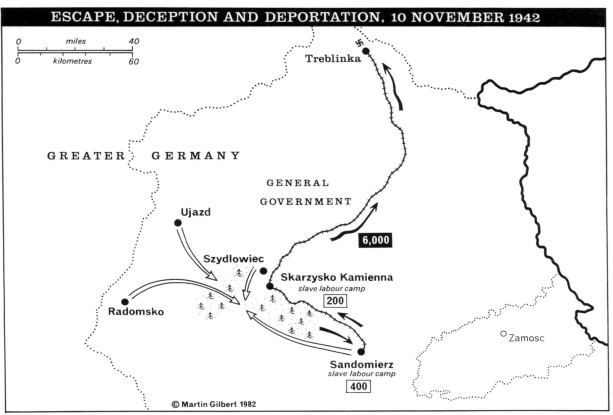

ESCAPE, DECEPTION AND DEPORTATION, 10 NOVEMBER 1942

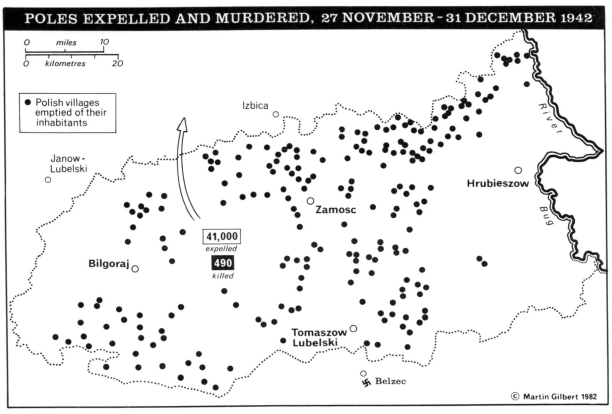

POLES EXPELLED AND MURDERED, 27 NOVEMBER – 31 DECEMBER 1942

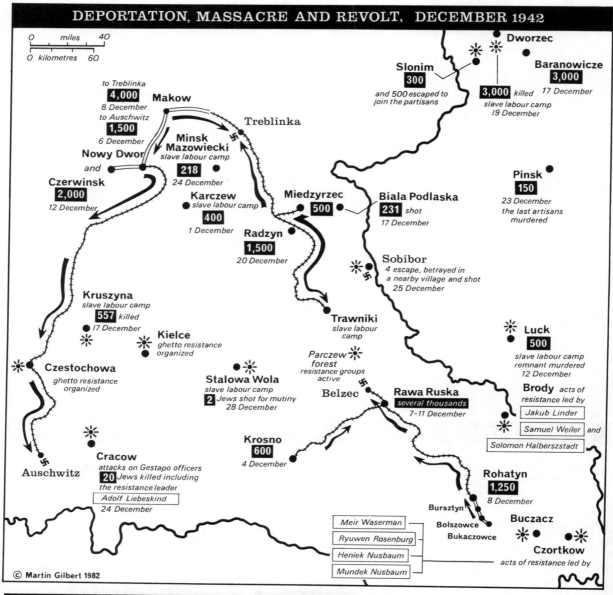

DEPORTATION, MASSACRE AND REVOLT, DECEMBER 1942

0 miles 40
0 kilometres 60

Dworzec

Slonim `300`
and 500 escaped to
join the partisans

`3,000` killed
slave labour camp
19 December

Baranowicze `3,000`
17 December

to Treblinka `4,000`
8 December
to Auschwitz `1,500`
6 December

Makow

Treblinka

Minsk Mazowiecki
slave labour camp `218`
24 December

Nowy Dwor and

Czerwinsk `2,000`
12 December

Karczew slave labour camp `400`
1 December

Miedzyrzec `500`

Biala Podlaska `231` shot
17 December

Pinsk `150`
23 December
the last artisans
murdered

Radzyn `1,500`
20 December

Sobibor
4 escape, betrayed in
a nearby village and shot
25 December

Kruszyna
slave labour camp `557` killed
17 December

Kielce
ghetto resistance
organized

Trawniki
slave labour camp

Parczew forest
resistance groups
active

Luck `500`
slave labour camp
remnant murdered
12 December

Czestochowa
ghetto resistance
organized

Stalowa Wola
slave labour camp
`2` Jews shot for mutiny
28 December

Belzec

Rawa Ruska
several thousands
7-11 December

Brody acts of
resistance led by
Jakub Linder
Samuel Weiler and
Solomon Halberszstadt

Auschwitz

Cracow
attacks on Gestapo officers
`20` Jews killed including
the resistance leader
Adolf Liebeskind
24 December

Krosno `600`
4 December

Rohatyn `1,250`
8 December

Bursztyn
Bolszowce
Bukaczowce

Meir Waserman
Ryuwen Rosenburg
Heniek Nusbaum
Mundek Nusbaum

Buczacz

Czortkow
acts of resistance led by

© Martin Gilbert 1982

THREE DEPORTATIONS, THREE MASSACRES

North Sea

Baltic Sea

Westerbork

Berlin

Postawy `2,500`
25 December 1942

Iwje `150`
31 December 1942

Korelicze `1,000`

Auschwitz

HOLLAND
`817` 4 December
`927` 8 December
`757` 12 December 1942

GREATER GERMANY

0 miles 300
0 kms 400

Black Sea

© Martin Gilbert 1982

From western Europe the deportations from Holland to Auschwitz continued (*left*). But by the end of 1942 the deportation of Polish Jews to Belzec and Treblinka had almost ended, and in many regions (*above*) only the remnants of communities now remained. In slave labour camps Jews were also murdered.

Throughout German-occupied Poland, as in the Parczew forest, Jewish resistance had become more organized. In Buczacz the Jews were preparing to break out of the ghetto. In Cracow the Jewish Fighters' Organization, set up in July 1942, carried out acts of sabotage. Elsewhere, acts of resistance, escape to the forests, preparation for uprisings, and even escape from the death camps, continued,

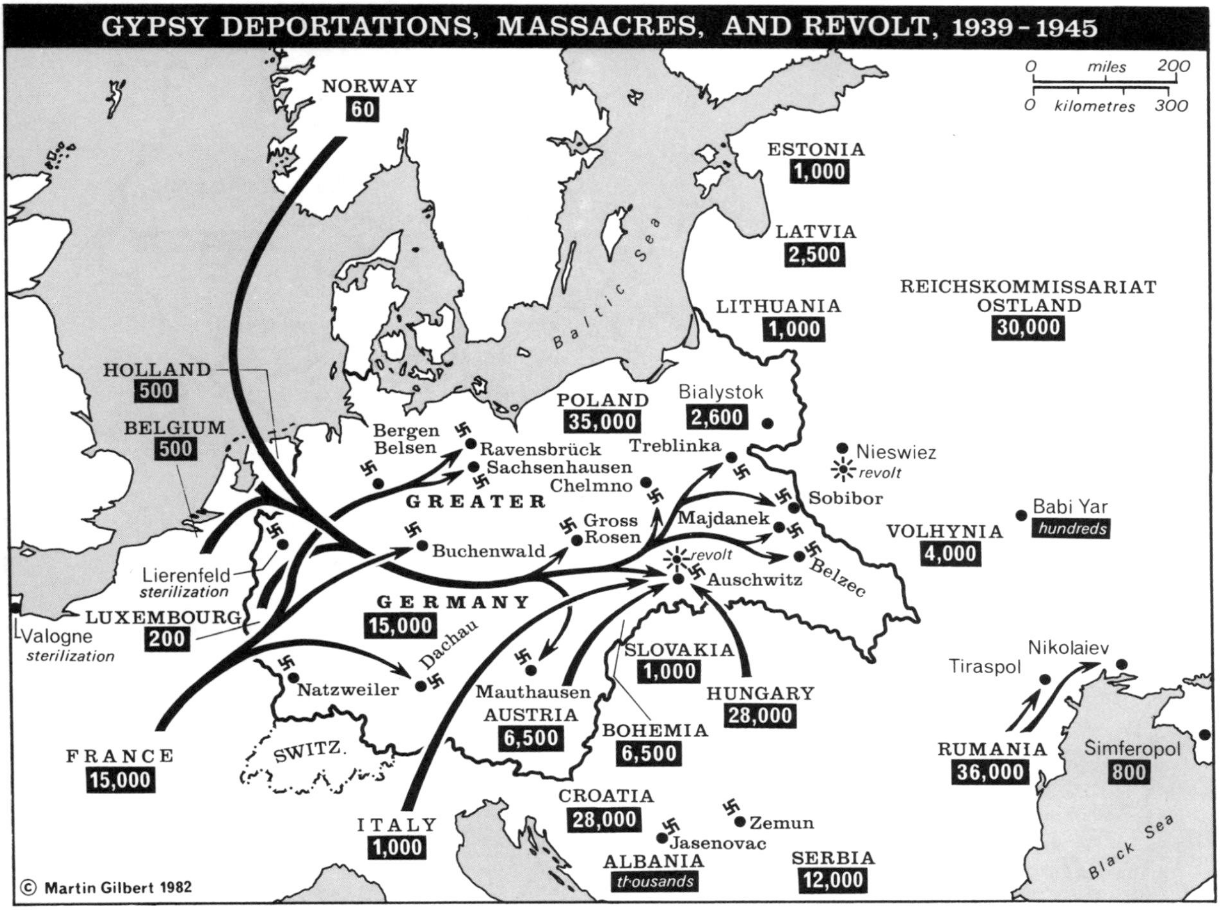
GYPSY DEPORTATIONS, MASSACRES, AND REVOLT, 1939-1945
0 miles 200
0 kilometres 300
NORWAY
60
ESTONIA
1,000
LATVIA
2,500
LITHUANIA
1,000
REICHSKOMMISSARIAT
OSTLAND
30,000
Baltic Sea
HOLLAND
500
BELGIUM
500
POLAND
35,000
Bialystok
2,600
Bergen Belsen
Ravensbrück
Sachsenhausen
Treblinka
Nieswiez
revolt
Chelmno
GREATER
Sobibor
Babi Yar
hundreds
Gross Rosen
Majdanek
VOLHYNIA
4,000
Buchenwald
revolt
Belzec
Lierenfeld
sterilization
Auschwitz
GERMANY
15,000
LUXEMBOURG
200
Valogne
sterilization
Dachau
SLOVAKIA
1,000
Nikolaiev
Tiraspol
Natzweiler
Mauthausen
HUNGARY
28,000
AUSTRIA
6,500
BOHEMIA
6,500
FRANCE
15,000
SWITZ.
RUMANIA
36,000
Simferopol
800
CROATIA
28,000
Zemun
ITALY
1,000
Jasenovac
ALBANIA
thousands
SERBIA
12,000
Black Sea
© Martin Gilbert 1982

against formidable odds.

Like the Jews, Europe's Gypsies were marked for destruction by the Nazis *(above)*. Following a decree of 16 December 1942, all German Gypsies were deported to Auschwitz. On 29 March 1943 the order was given to deport all Dutch Gypsies to Auschwitz. All over Europe, as shown above, Gypsy communities were destroyed. Several Gypsy revolts are recorded. But like the Jews, the Gypsies had to face a combination of artificially intensified 'race' hatred, meticulous planning, continual deception, and overwhelming military power.

Many Gypsies were deported to Jewish ghettos. In Lithuania the Gestapo locked 1,000 Gypsies in a synagogue until they died of starvation. Hundreds were killed alongside Jews, as at Babi Yar. At Valogne, Lierenfeld and Ravensbrück, hundreds of Gypsy women were sterilized. By 1945 more than 220,000 of Europe's 700,000 Gypsies had been murdered by the Nazis. The photograph is of a Gypsy family in Volhynia.

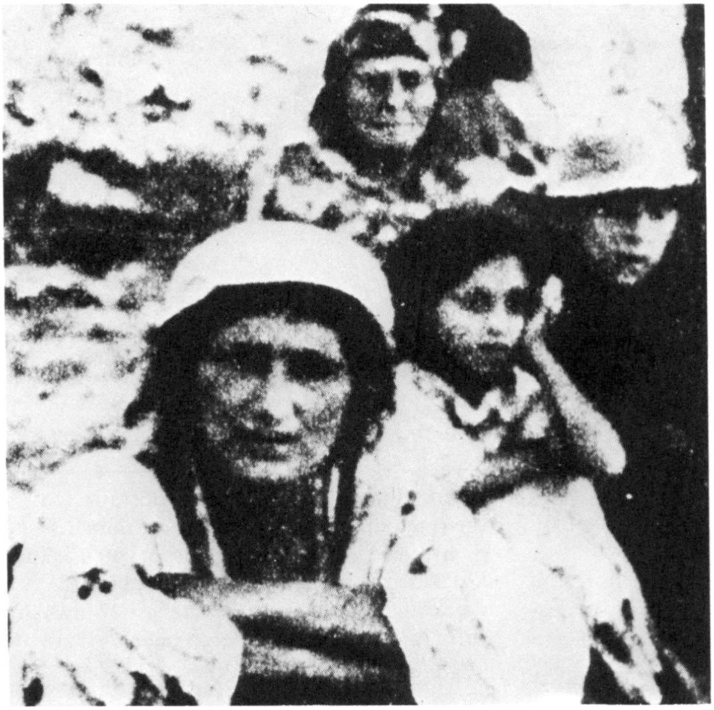

Map 183

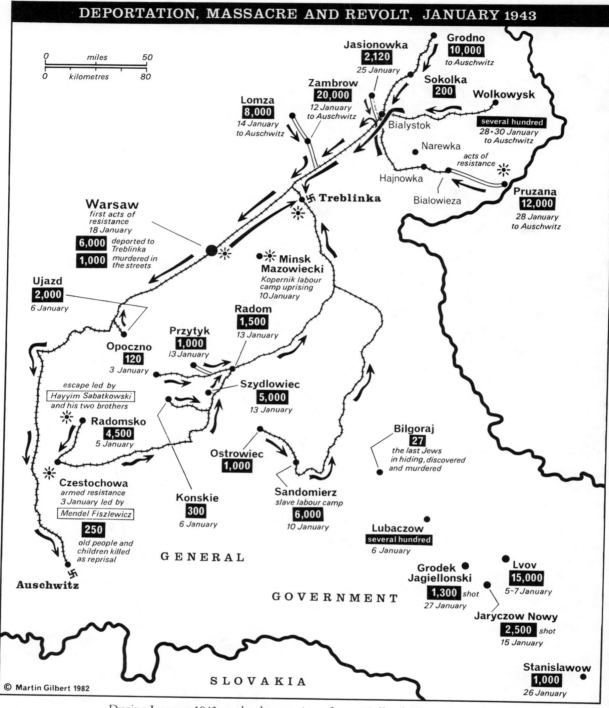

DEPORTATION, MASSACRE AND REVOLT, JANUARY 1943

Jasionowka 2,120 *25 January*

Grodno 10,000 *to Auschwitz*

Zambrow 20,000 *12 January to Auschwitz*

Sokolka 200

Wolkowysk

Lomza 8,000 *14 January to Auschwitz*

Bialystok

several hundred *28-30 January to Auschwitz*

Narewka

Hajnowka

Bialowieza

acts of resistance

Pruzana 12,000 *28 January to Auschwitz*

✠ **Treblinka**

Warsaw *first acts of resistance 18 January* 6,000 *deported to Treblinka* 1,000 *murdered in the streets*

Minsk Mazowiecki *Kopernik labour camp uprising 10 January*

Ujazd 2,000 *6 January*

Radom 1,500 *13 January*

Przytyk 1,000 *13 January*

Opoczno 120 *3 January*

escape led by Hayyim Sabatkowski *and his two brothers*

Szydlowiec 5,000 *13 January*

Bilgoraj 27 *the last Jews in hiding, discovered and murdered*

Radomsko 4,500 *5 January*

Ostrowiec 1,000

Czestochowa *armed resistance 3 January led by* Mendel Fiszlewicz 250 *old people and children killed as reprisal*

Konskie 300 *6 January*

Sandomierz *slave labour camp* 6,000 *10 January*

Lubaczow *several hundred* *6 January*

Grodek Jagiellonski 1,300 *shot 27 January*

Lvov 15,000 *5-7 January*

Jaryczow Nowy 2,500 *shot 15 January*

Auschwitz

G E N E R A L

G O V E R N M E N T

Stanislawow 1,000 *26 January*

S L O V A K I A

© Martin Gilbert 1982

0 — miles — 50
0 — kilometres — 80

During January 1943, as the deportation of the remaining Jews of Poland continued, many were murdered on the spot, such as the last 200 in Sokolka (*above*) who had been working in a boot factory, the last 27 Jews in Bilgoraj, and the last 17 craftsmen of Dzisna (*opposite*). Deported to Auschwitz (*opposite, above*) were more than 10,000 Jews from Holland, Theresienstadt and Belgium, as well as 2,000 from Berlin. The last Dutch transport contained 869 invalids and children; all were gassed on arrival.

Jewish resistance was also growing in scale and confidence. In Czestochowa a Jewish resistance group killed 25 German soldiers. But as a reprisal, the SS shot 250 old

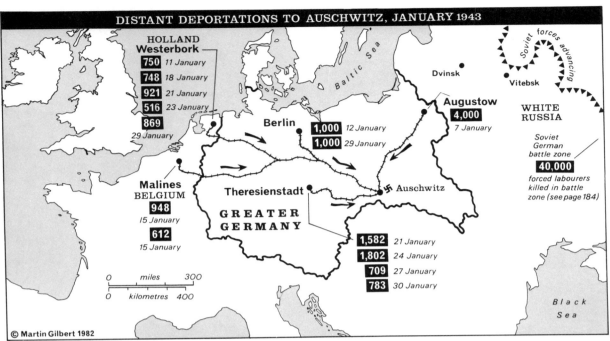

DISTANT DEPORTATIONS TO AUSCHWITZ, JANUARY 1943

HOLLAND
Westerbork

750	11 January
748	18 January
921	21 January
516	23 January
869	29 January

Baltic Sea

Dvinsk

Vitebsk

Soviet forces advancing

Berlin

1,000	12 January
1,000	29 January

Augustow

4,000 7 January

WHITE
RUSSIA

Soviet German battle zone

40,000

forced labourers killed in battle zone (see page 184)

Malines
BELGIUM

948 15 January

612 15 January

Theresienstadt

Auschwitz

GREATER
GERMANY

1,582	21 January
1,802	24 January
709	27 January
783	30 January

miles 0—300

kilometres 0—400

Black Sea

© Martin Gilbert 1982

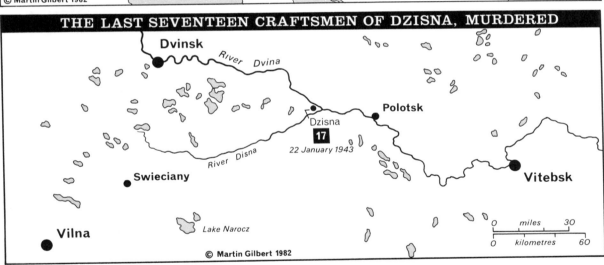

THE LAST SEVENTEEN CRAFTSMEN OF DZISNA, MURDERED

Dvinsk

River Dvina

Polotsk

Dzisna

17

22 January 1943

River Disna

Swieciany

Vitebsk

Vilna

Lake Narocz

miles 0—30

kilometres 0—60

© Martin Gilbert 1982

people and children. Reprisals on this scale made acts of resistance all the more perilous. At Pruzana a small group of Jews made contact with nearby Polish partisans, but even this course of action was not free from danger. When the three Sabatkowski brothers, Hayyim, Mordekhai and Herzke, finally reached the forests near Konskie, they were murdered by Polish partisans. While fleeing many Jews were killed by anti-semitic Poles, many other Jews were saved when Poles risked their lives to shelter them.

As the sealed trains reached Treblinka, the Ukrainian guards drove the starving, frightened passengers with whips and rifle butts along the short road to the gas chamber. The road itself was flanked by bogus shops, and the station disguised as a transit point. But by January 1943 it was no longer fear of the unknown but fear of death which filled the deportees, and when one of the trains from Grodno reached Treblinka late in the evening, 1,000 Jews turned on the guards and attacked them with wooden clubs torn from a nearby fence, with knives and with razors. The fight lasted several hours. In the morning all the Jews and the guards were found dead in the snow, killed by SS machine-gun fire and grenades aimed indiscriminately at both.

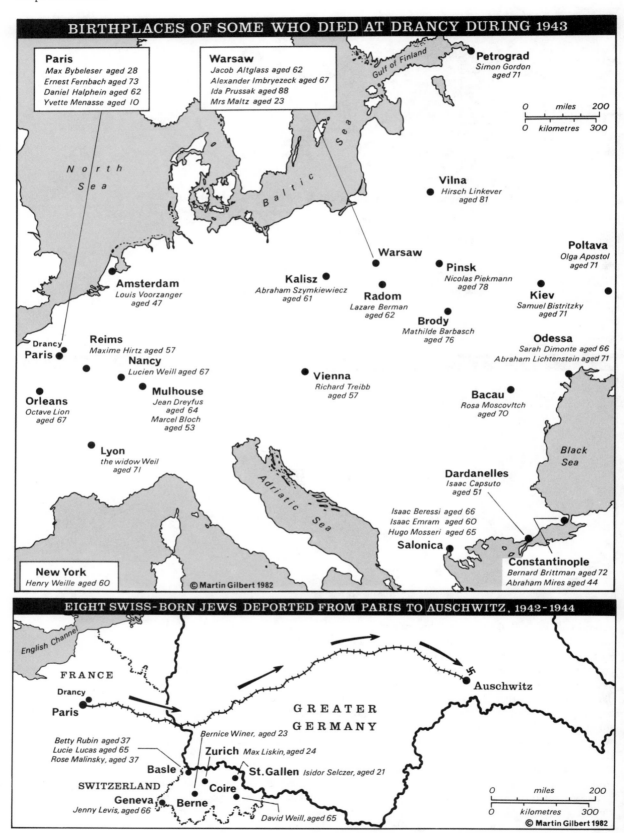

BIRTHPLACES OF SOME WHO DIED AT DRANCY DURING 1943

Paris
Max Bybeleser aged 28
Ernest Fernbach aged 73
Daniel Halphein aged 62
Yvette Menasse aged 10

Warsaw
Jacob Altglass aged 62
Alexander Imbryezeck aged 67
Ida Prussak aged 88
Mrs Maltz aged 23

Petrograd
Simon Gordon aged 71

Gulf of Finland

0   miles   200

0   kilometres   300

North Sea

Baltic Sea

Vilna
Hirsch Linkever aged 81

Warsaw

Poltava
Olga Apostol aged 71

Kalisz
Abraham Szymkiewiecz aged 61

Pinsk
Nicolas Piekmann aged 78

Radom
Lazare Berman aged 62

Kiev
Samuel Bistritzky aged 71

Amsterdam
Louis Voorzanger aged 47

Brody
Mathilde Barbasch aged 76

Odessa
Sarah Dimonte aged 66
Abraham Lichtenstein aged 71

Drancy
Paris

Reims
Maxime Hirtz aged 57

Nancy
Lucien Weill aged 67

Vienna
Richard Treibb aged 57

Bacau
Rosa Moscovitch aged 70

Orleans
Octave Lion aged 67

Mulhouse
Jean Dreyfus aged 64
Marcel Bloch aged 53

Adriatic Sea

Black Sea

Lyon
the widow Weil aged 71

Dardanelles
Isaac Capsuto aged 51

Isaac Beressi aged 66
Isaac Emram aged 60
Hugo Mosseri aged 65

Salonica

Constantinople
Bernard Brittman aged 72
Abraham Mires aged 44

New York
Henry Weille aged 60

© Martin Gilbert 1982

EIGHT SWISS-BORN JEWS DEPORTED FROM PARIS TO AUSCHWITZ, 1942-1944

English Channel

FRANCE

Drancy
Paris

**G R E A T E R
G E R M A N Y**

Auschwitz

Betty Rubin aged 37
Lucie Lucas aged 65
Rose Malinsky, aged 37

Bernice Winer, aged 23

Zurich *Max Liskin, aged 24*

St. Gallen *Isidor Selczer, aged 21*

Basle

SWITZERLAND

Coire

Geneva
Jenny Levis, aged 66

Berne

David Weill, aged 65

0   miles   200

0   kilometres   300

© Martin Gilbert 1982

THE JEWS OF TUNIS AT RISK

Bizerta

Mateur · Utica

Souk el Arba · Béja **Tunis** · Menzel Bou Zelfa

Chemtou · Testour · Soliman · Nabeul

Lekef

Ebba-Ksour

Thala · Kairouan **Sousse** · Monastir · Moknine · Mahdia

Hadjeb-el-Aioun

Sbeitla

under Axis military control **Sfax**

Gafsa

El Guettar

Nefta · Tozeur

El Hamma · Hara Kebira *Djerba Island* · Hara Sghira

Gabès

Kebili · Zarzis

Médenine

Foum Tatahouine · Ben Gardane

TUNISIA

ALGERIA

LIBYA

0 miles 100
0 kilometres 160

© Martin Gilbert 1982

In preparing to deport Jews from Paris, the Gestapo confined them at Drancy, where conditions were primitive. More than 100 Jews died there during 1943, including many old people (*opposite, above*) who could not stand the continuous privation. Henry Weille had been born in New York in 1883, and Ida Prussak had been born in Warsaw at the time of the Crimean War. Some young people also died in the camp, including the 10-year-old Yvette Menasse.

The photograph was taken by the Germans at Drancy detention camp in 1942.

Even Jews who had been born in neutral Switzerland were not immune from deportation. The Gestapo's own lists of those deported fom Paris record 39 Swiss-born Jews deported to Auschwitz between March 1942 and May 1944: their birthplaces are shown on the map opposite (*below*): both Max Liskin from Zurich and Bernice Winer from Berne were in their early twenties at the time of their deportation.

The Jews of Tunis (*right*) suffered five months of confiscation of property, plunder, forced labour, ill-treatment and execution under German rule. More than 4,000 of them had been sent to labour camps near the front lines, and many had died from ill-treatment, disease, and even during Allied aerial bombardments. Shown here are the principal towns in which more than 50,000 Tunisian Jews lived. Their suffering came to an end in May 1943, as the Allied armies drove the Germans from North Africa.

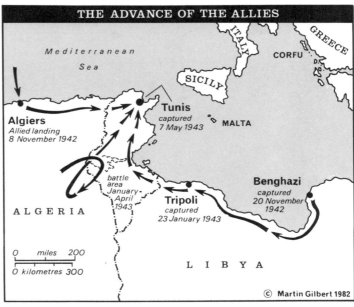

THE ADVANCE OF THE ALLIES

Mediterranean Sea

ITALY · GREECE

CORFU

SICILY

Tunis *captured 7 May 1943* · MALTA

Algiers *Allied landing 8 November 1942*

battle area January–April 1943

ALGERIA

Tripoli *captured 23 January 1943*

Benghazi *captured 20 November 1942*

LIBYA

0 miles 200
0 kilometres 300

© Martin Gilbert 1982

Map 190

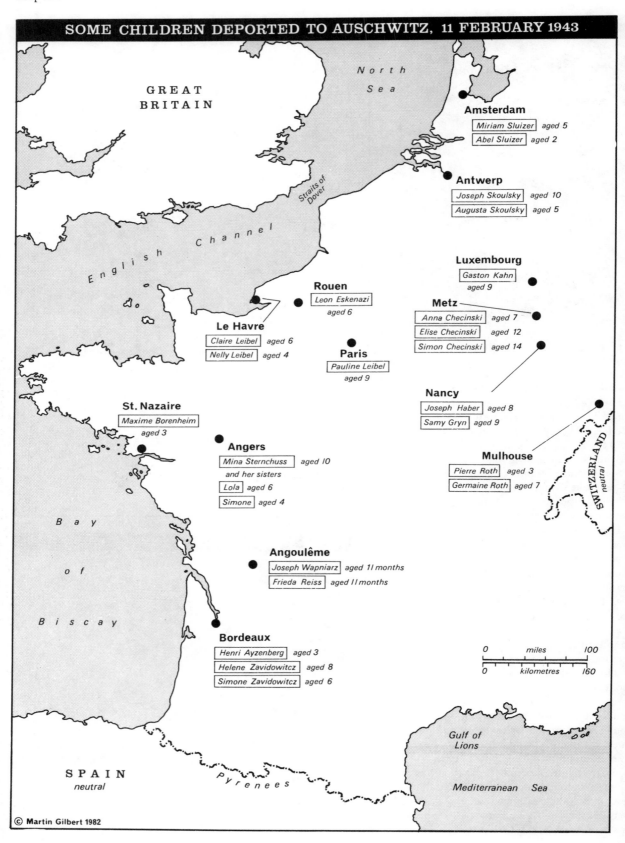

SOME CHILDREN DEPORTED TO AUSCHWITZ, 11 FEBRUARY 1943

North Sea

GREAT BRITAIN

Amsterdam
Miriam Sluizer | *aged 5*
Abel Sluizer | *aged 2*

Antwerp
Joseph Skoulsky | *aged 10*
Augusta Skoulsky | *aged 5*

Straits of Dover

English Channel

Luxembourg
Gaston Kahn | *aged 9*

Rouen
Leon Eskenazi | *aged 6*

Metz
Anna Checinski | *aged 7*
Elise Checinski | *aged 12*
Simon Checinski | *aged 14*

Le Havre
Claire Leibel | *aged 6*
Nelly Leibel | *aged 4*

Paris
Pauline Leibel | *aged 9*

Nancy
Joseph Haber | *aged 8*
Samy Gryn | *aged 9*

St. Nazaire
Maxime Borenheim | *aged 3*

Angers
Mina Sternchuss | *aged 10*
and her sisters
Lola | *aged 6*
Simone | *aged 4*

Mulhouse
Pierre Roth | *aged 3*
Germaine Roth | *aged 7*

SWITZERLAND neutral

Bay of Biscay

Angoulême
Joseph Wapniarz | *aged 11 months*
Frieda Reiss | *aged 11 months*

Bordeaux
Henri Ayzenberg | *aged 3*
Helene Zavidowitcz | *aged 8*
Simone Zavidowitcz | *aged 6*

0 ——— *miles* ——— 100
0 ——— *kilometres* ——— 160

Gulf of Lions

SPAIN
neutral

Pyrenees

Mediterranean Sea

© **Martin Gilbert** 1982

Map 191

OLD PEOPLE DEPORTED TO AUSCHWITZ, 11 FEBRUARY 1943

Suwalki
Théodore Baera
aged 82

Sosnowiec
Berta Schmulevitz
aged 84

Piotrkow
Leja Granek
aged 85

Novomoskovsk
Kiva Makline
aged 80

Cracow
Gitla Wajslfisz
aged 83

Drancy

Paris

Kuppenheim
Marie Dreifuss
aged 85

Teschen
Caroline Neumann
aged 82

Auschwitz

Kishinev
Githel Mandelevitch
aged 91

© Martin Gilbert 1982

Odessa
Esther Krimer   aged 84
and
Fania Krinitchevsky   aged 86

As the deportations from France to Auschwitz continued, neither children nor old people were spared. Among 1,000 Jews deported on 11 February 1943, of whom only 10 survived the war, were several hundred children and old people who were gassed immediately the deportation train reached the camp.

The children whose names and birthplaces are shown opposite were deported together with their parents, except for Joseph and Augusta Skoulsky who were deported alone, and the two Leibel sisters who were deported with their sister Pauline, aged 9, who had been born in Paris.

The young Maxime Borenheim was deported with his 19-year-old mother, who had been born in Warsaw. The three Sternchuss sisters were deported with their 74-year-old grandmother, also born in Warsaw. The Zavidowitcz sisters were deported with their father, who had been born in Brest-Litovsk.

In addition to the old people in their eighties and nineties whose birthpalces are given in the above map, a further 15 old people in their seventies were deported in this particular train: all were likewise gassed on arrival at Auschwitz.

On February 12 the Gestapo reported that three Jews had tried to escape from the train at the French frontier. But each had been caught and forced to continue the journey.

The photograph shows a group of Jewish children from Beregszasz and Bilke arriving at Auschwitz in 1944 *(page 197)*.

Map 192

DISTANT DEPORTATIONS AND THE 'FACTORY ACTION', FEBRUARY 1943

890	2 February
1,184	9 February
1,108	16 February
1,101	23 February

also **952** 3 February
1,000 19 February
913 26 February

Baltic Sea

Treblinka

HOLLAND

Hamburg
1,000

Berlin
7,000

G R E A T E R

Sobibor

FRANCE

Essen
Cologne
1,000

Theresienstadt
1,000
1 February

Frankfurt

Majdanek

Bedzin
Auschwitz

G E R M A N Y

1,000
9 February

998
11 February

1,000
13 February

Munich
1,000

SWITZERLAND
neutral

0   miles   150

0   kilometres   200

© Martin Gilbert 1982

In February 1943 transports reached the eastern death camps from Holland, Berlin, Theresienstadt and Paris *(above)*. Among those deported fom Paris to Auschwitz on February 13 was Gisele Lustiger, who had been born in Bedzin. Her son, Aaron, who had converted to Catholicism before the war, survived the war; in February 1981 he was appointed Archbishop of Paris.

At the beginning of 1943 more than 10,000 Jews were working in factories throughout Germany. On February 27 the SS put into operation the 'Factory Action', deporting these workers to the east *(above),* where few survived. The photograph, taken in 1980, shows some of the fences and watchtowers at Majdanek.

The destruction of slave labour camps also continued, 1,000 labourers being sent from Chrzanow to Auschwitz *(opposite).*

In Eastern Galicia the deportations to Belzec had ceased: those Jews still alive were killed in local cemeteries or nearby woods.

At Bialystok eight SS men were killed

Map 193

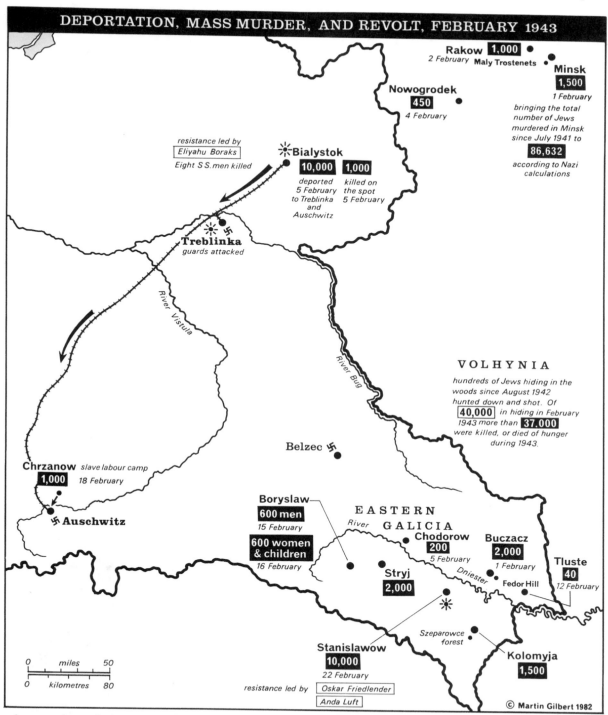

DEPORTATION, MASS MURDER, AND REVOLT, FEBRUARY 1943

Rakow `1,000` •
2 February Maly Trostenets

Minsk
`1,500`
1 February

*bringing the total
number of Jews
murdered in Minsk
since July 1941 to*

`86,632`

*according to Nazi
calculations*

Nowogrodek
`450`
4 February

resistance led by
| Eliyahu Boraks |

Eight S.S. men killed

☀**Bialystok**

`10,000` `1,000`

*deported
5 February
to Treblinka
and
Auschwitz*

*killed on
the spot
5 February*

☀卐
Treblinka
guards attacked

River Vistula

River Bug

VOLHYNIA

*hundreds of Jews hiding in the
woods since August 1942
hunted down and shot. Of*
`40,000` *in hiding in February
1943 more than* `37,000`
*were killed, or died of hunger
during 1943.*

Belzec 卐

Chrzanow *slave labour camp*
`1,000` *18 February*

卐 **Auschwitz**

Boryslaw
`600 men`
15 February

`600 women
& children`
16 February

EASTERN
River
GALICIA
Chodorow
`200`
5 February

Buczacz
`2,000`
1 February

Tluste
`40`
12 February

Dniester
Fedor Hill

Stryj
`2,000`

☀

*Szeparowce
forest*

Kolomyja
`1,500`

Stanislawow
`10,000`
22 February

resistance led by | Oskar Friedlender |
| Anda Luft |

| 0 | miles | 50 |
| 0 | kilometres | 80 |

© Martin Gilbert 1982

when members of a Zionist youth movement
resisted deportation. Captured and deported,
the remnants of the group then attacked the
guards at Treblinka, using one, possibly two,
remaining pistols. But they were quickly
killed: at Treblinka the 700-strong SS and
Ukrainian garrison had a large armoury of
machine-guns and grenades. They also
wielded their whips and clubs without
mercy against men, women and children
staggering from the trains. Even then,
individuals resisted, as when a young
women, stripped naked, snatched a rifle
from a Ukrainian, shot dead two Nazis and
wounded a third, before being overpowered
and viciously tortured until she was dead.

Map 194

THE JEWS OF MACEDONIA AND THRACE DEPORTED, 3-22 MARCH 1943

RUMANIA

River Danube

4 barges

Lom Palanka
left 20-22 March

SERBIA
under German military occupation

Nis

YUGOSLAVIA

Pirot
185

Sofia

BULGARIA

Pristina
249

Radomir *labour camp*

Kriva Palanka
5

Dupnitsa *internment camp 18-19 March*

Kumanova
13

Gorna Dzhumaia *internment camp 18-19 March*

Didimoticon
867

Skopje
3,351

Tobacco factory camp 11-31 March

Stip
551

Drama
589

Paranestion
19

Nea Orestia
194

Veles
18

MACEDONIA

Xanthi
526

EASTERN THRACE

Bitola
3,315

occupied by Bulgaria

Ziliahovo
18

Komotini
878

Souflion
32

Gevgelija
11

Seres
471

THRACE

Kavalla
1,484

Sarzhshaban
12

Dedeagatch
137

Salonica

Thasos
16

Samothrace
3

GREECE

Aegean

Mount Athos

Sea

Dardanelles

TURKEY
neutral

0 miles 40
0 kilometres 60

© Martin Gilbert 1982

After the Bulgarian occupation of the Greek province of Thrace in April 1941, the Germans imposed direct German rule on Eastern Thrace, which lay along the Turkish border (left). In this zone were some 1,250 Jews, most of them in the town of Didimoticon, where the Jewish community could trace its origins back to 1542, to the arrival of refugees from Spain. After 300 years these 'Sephardi' (or Spanish) Jews still spoke a Spanish dialect, Ladino.

On 3 March 1943 the Germans seized the Jews of Eastern Thrace, including the three Jews living on the island of Samothrace. Five days later they were deported by train to Treblinka. Other than 40 who managed to escape the round-up at Nea Orestia, and 33 who evaded deportation from Didimoticon, none of the Jews of Eastern Thrace survived the war.

A day after the round-up in Eastern Thrace, the Jews of Bulgarian-occupied Thrace and Bulgarian-occupied Macedonia were likewise seized, taken to internment camps at Skopje, and inside Bulgaria, and then deported in a total of 20 trains (right), some direct to Treblinka, others to the Danube town of Lom, where they were transferred first by barge through the Iron Gates to Vienna, and then by train.

Within three weeks 23 communities had been destroyed. The Bitola community had been established shortly after the expulsion of the Jews from Spain in 1492.

The photographs were taken on board one of the barges (left) and at a deportation centre.

Map 195

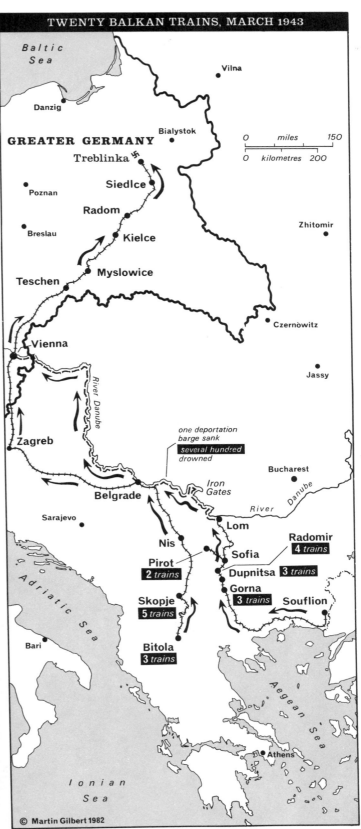

TWENTY BALKAN TRAINS, MARCH 1943

Baltic Sea

Vilna

Danzig

GREATER GERMANY

Bialystok

Treblinka

Siedlce

Poznan

Radom

Zhitomir

Breslau

Kielce

Myslowice

Teschen

Czernowitz

Vienna

River Danube

Jassy

Zagreb

one deportation barge sank
several hundred drowned

Bucharest

Iron Gates

River Danube

Belgrade

Sarajevo

Lom

Nis

Radomir
4 trains

Pirot
2 trains

Sofia

Dupnitsa 3 trains

Adriatic Sea

Gorna
3 trains

Skopje
5 trains

Souflion

Bari

Bitola
3 trains

Aegean Sea

Athens

Ionian Sea

© Martin Gilbert 1982

0   miles   150
0   kilometres   200

Map 196

THE SALONICA DEPORTATIONS, FROM 15 MARCH 1943

GREATER GERMANY

Auschwitz

SLOVAKIA

Vienna

Graz
Maribor

Zidani Most

Trieste

Zagreb

CROATIA

0   miles   150

0   kilometres   200

Belgrade

SERBIA

Adriatic Sea

Nis

Sofia

ITALY

Skopje

BULGARIA

ALBANIA

Salonica
43,850

Kastoria
655

Verroia
424
1 May

GREECE

Aegean Sea

© Martin Gilbert 1982

Within two weeks of the deportation of the Jews of Thrace and Macedonia to Treblinka, the Jews of Salonica were being seized, interned, and deported to Auschwitz (*left*). The photograph shows the preliminary indignities to which they were subjected: compulsory drills until they collapsed.

Jews had lived in Salonica since the time of St Paul. In the twelfth century they had their own mayor. In 1430 their rabbis were placed on the same footing as the spiritual heads of the Greek Church. In the fifteenth and sixteenth centuries, both German and Spanish Jews found in the city a safe haven from persecution. In the nineteenth century the Jews of Salonica were active as artisans, traders, shopkeepers and dock workers. Between the wars many emigrated to Palestine, France and the United States. Others stayed as part of a flourishing community: doctors, lawyers, teachers, and above all stevedores and dock workers.

The first deportation of Salonica Jewry began on 15 March 1943, when 2,800 Jews were forced into 40 cattle trucks and told that they were to be 'resettled' in Poland. Five months later, on 7 August 1943, the last train left Salonica for Auschwitz, where more than 43,000 of Salonica's 56,000 Jews had been killed (*pages 154, 157 and 160 to 162*).

The insanity of the German policy towards the Jews was clearly shown in Salonica, where the Jewish dock workers and port labourers were essential to the efficient operation of the port. But even this practical consideration was of no interest to the Nazis: nothing was to be allowed to stand in the way of the destruction of every

Map 197

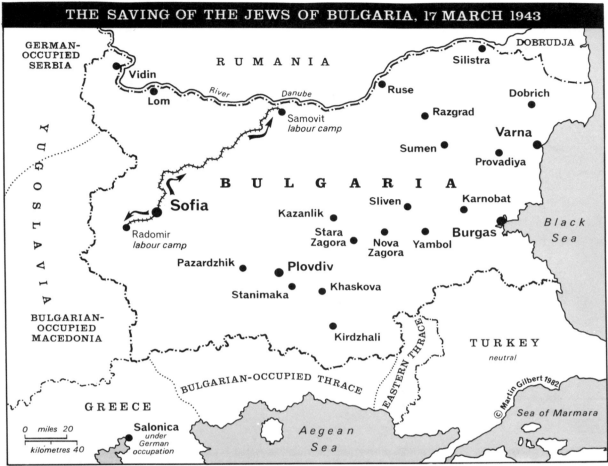

THE SAVING OF THE JEWS OF BULGARIA, 17 MARCH 1943

one of Europe's Jewish communities.

North-east of Salonica, the Jews of Bulgaria (above) were likewise marked out by the Nazis for deportation. In 1934 there were 48,398 Jews in Bulgaria, out of a total Bulgarian population of six million. On 22 January 1941 a 'Law for the Defence of the Nation' gave Jews one month to leave all public posts, and forced almost all Jewish doctors, dentists and lawyers to give up their practices. In addition, a special tax was imposed on all Jewish homes, shops and other property, amounting to a quarter of its value. By the end of 1941, there were some 400 Bulgarian Jews serving in local Bulgarian partisan units.

On 10 March 1943 the SS demanded the deportation of all Bulgarian Jews to Poland, on the same pattern as the deportation from Thrace, Macedonia and Salonica. The Bulgarian Government had already bowed to the demand that 12,000 Jews under Bulgarian occupation in Thrace and Macedonia should be deported. But the demand for the deportation of the 49,000

Jews of Bulgaria proper was resisted by the Bulgarian people: by the King, the Parliament, the intellectuals, and the farmers. The farmers, indeed, were said to be ready to lie down on the railway tracks to prevent any such deportations, and on 17 March 1943 the Bulgarian Parliament voted unanimously against the deportation order.

Not only the King, but the Archimandrite Cyril, and the Papal Nuncio in Turkey, Angelo Roncalli (later Pope John XXIII) protested strongly against the proposed deportations.

As a result of these protests, no Bulgarian Jews were deported to the gas chambers from Bulgaria itself. A few, who were living in Paris at the time of the outbreak of war, has already been deported to Auschwitz (page 121). Others were sent to labour camps at Samovit and Radomir. But these were not punitive camps, as in Germany.

Bulgaria was the only country under German influence or control whose Jewish population actually increased during the war years, from 48,565 in 1934, to 49,172 in 1945.

DISTANT DEPORTATIONS, MASSACRE AND REVOLT, MARCH 1943

resistance

Soviet forces advancing

Braslaw *'thousands'*

Radoszkowicze *the last 300*

Orel

Minsk *'thousands'*

Kursk

fifty escape, and join the 'Revenge' partisan group

Poltava

North Sea

Baltic Sea

Westerbork 5,679 *to Sobibor 5 trains*

Berlin 7,752 *5 trains*

Treblinka

Sobibor

Majdanek

Auschwitz

Khmelnik 1,300 *5 March*

Calais

Luxembourg

Drancy

Prague

Paris

Tours

Mosbach

Munich 113 *13 March*

Lausanne

FRANCE

Montauban

Les Milles 1,400

Zagreb

Belgrade

0 miles 200
0 kilometres 300

Black Sea

Gurs 888 *4 March* 926 *6 March*

Marseilles 997 *23 March* 1,000 *25 March*

Adriatic Sea

Rome

THRACE

Salonica 10,002 *in 4 trains*

© Martin Gilbert 1982

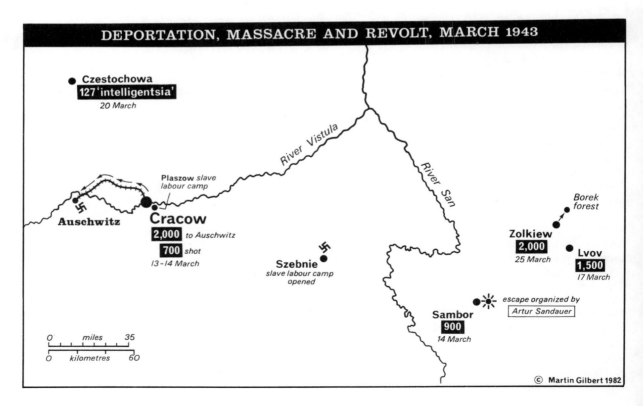

DEPORTATION, MASSACRE AND REVOLT, MARCH 1943

Czestochowa 127 *'intelligentsia'* *20 March*

River Vistula

River San

Plaszow *slave labour camp*

Borek forest

Auschwitz

Cracow 2,000 *to Auschwitz* 700 *shot* *13–14 March*

Zolkiew 2,000 *25 March*

Lvov 1,500 *17 March*

Szebnie *slave labour camp opened*

escape organized by Artur Sandauer

Sambor 900 *14 March*

0 miles 35
0 kilometres 60

© Martin Gilbert 1982

Map 200

During March 1943 five trains left Holland for Sobibor, one train left Paris for Auschwitz and two trains left Paris for Majdanek (*opposite, above*). Among the deportees to Majdanek was the German Jewish painter, Hermann Lismann, who had studied in Lausanne, Rome and Paris. A post-impressionist, he had emigrated to France in 1933. At first he had lived near Tours. Then he escaped to Montauban, from where he was deported.

From Gurs were deported to their deaths all but two of the 51 Jews of Mosbach, who had been deported from Germany to Gurs more than two years before (*page 48*).

Also deported to Majdanek from Paris in March 1943 were Nathan Lewinsztejn, aged 29, and Lajwa Krysztal, aged 40, who had both been born in Lublin, in a suburb of which the Majdanek concentration camp and gas chamber was situated.

From the General Government (*opposite, below*), 10,000 Jews were seized, deported from Cracow to Auschwitz, sent to the slave labour camp in the suburb of Plaszow, or shot in the streets. At Sambor 900 Jews were shot in the town's main square, many mothers being forced to watch their children being shot first. Resistance plans, carefully nurtured, were cut short by the 'liquidation'. At Braslaw (*opposite, above*) the resistance fighters fell at their posts. During the slaughter at Minsk, while thousands were shot, only 50 were able to break out of the armed cordons and reach the partisans.

Among those deported from France in March 1943 were 4,000 Jews from the Marseilles region (*right*), most of whom had been seized two months earlier during 'action Tiger'. Sent to Drancy, they were deported on 23 March 1943 to Sobibor. All the deportees, were gassed on arrival. A second train left Drancy for Sobibor two days later, with 1,000 Jews. All but 15 were gassed. Only five survived the war.

Among the Jews in these two trains were Vidal Farhi and Lea Klauser, both of whom had been born in Jerusalem, Dick and Jacob Prins from the Dutch East Indies (*page 127*) and the 18-year-old twins, Jean and Victor Nerver, who had been born in Calais.

At Les Accates, in the Marseilles region, 16 Jewish children were sheltered, and saved. But the 30 orphans from La Rose, photographed by the author in 1976, were deported to Auschwitz, together with their guardian, Alice Salomon, who insisted on sharing their fate.

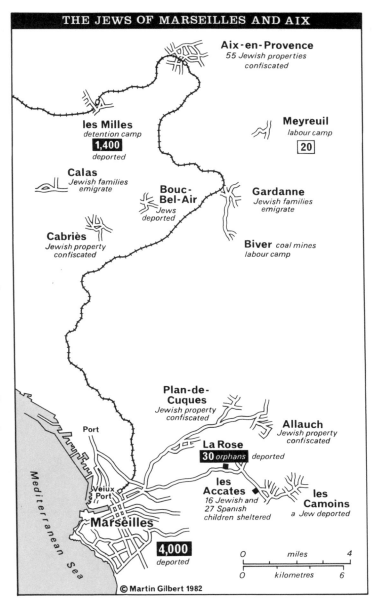

THE JEWS OF MARSEILLES AND AIX

Aix-en-Provence
55 Jewish properties confiscated

les Milles
detention camp
1,400
deported

Meyreuil
labour camp
20

Calas
Jewish families emigrate

Bouc-Bel-Air
Jews deported

Gardanne
Jewish families emigrate

Cabriès
Jewish property confiscated

Biver *coal mines labour camp*

Plan-de-Cuques
Jewish property confiscated

Allauch
Jewish property confiscated

Port

La Rose
30 *orphans* deported

les Accates
16 Jewish and 27 Spanish children sheltered

les Camoins
a Jew deported

Mediterranean Sea

Vieux Port

Marseilles
4,000
deported

© Martin Gilbert 1982

miles 0 — 4
kilometres 0 — 6

Map 201

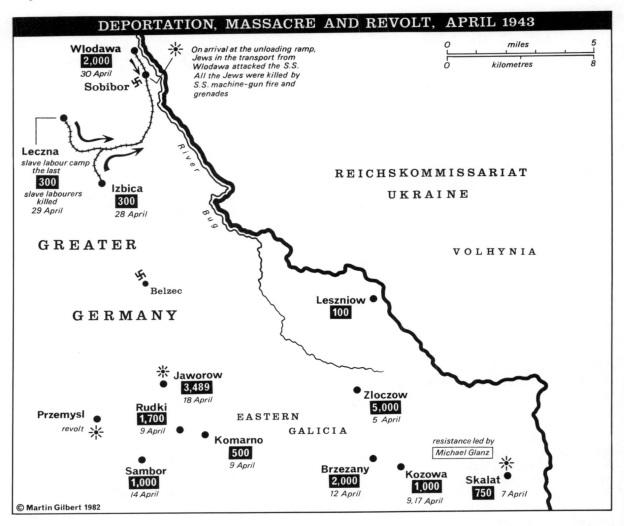

DEPORTATION, MASSACRE AND REVOLT, APRIL 1943

Wlodawa
2,000
30 April

On arrival at the unloading ramp, Jews in the transport from Wlodawa attacked the S.S. All the Jews were killed by S.S. machine-gun fire and grenades

Sobibor

Leczna
slave labour camp the last
300
slave labourers killed
29 April

Izbica
300
28 April

River Bug

REICHSKOMMISSARIAT

UKRAINE

GREATER

Belzec

VOLHYNIA

GERMANY

Leszniow
100

Jaworow
3,489
18 April

Zloczow
5,000
5 April

Rudki
1,700
9 April

Przemysl
revolt

EASTERN

GALICIA

Komarno
500
9 April

resistance led by
Michael Glanz

Sambor
1,000
14 April

Brzezany
2,000
12 April

Kozowa
1,000
9, 17 April

Skalat
750 *7 April*

miles 0 — 5
kilometres 0 — 8

© Martin Gilbert 1982

The killings in Eastern Galicia continued during April 1943 (*above*), as did the distant deportations to Auschwitz and Treblinka (*opposite, above*): nine from Salonica, four from Holland, one from Belgium and one from France.

The 300 Jews of Soly and Smorgonie (*opposite, above*) were brought by train to Vilna, having been told that they were to be resettled in the Kovno ghetto. But instead of going to Kovno, the train stopped at nearby Ponary. A 15-year-old Vilna schoolboy, Yitskhok Rudashevski, noted in his diary the story that reached Vilna within a few hours: 'Like wild animals before dying, the people began in mortal despair to break the railroad cars, they broke the little windows reinforced by strong wire. Hundreds were shot to death while running away. The railroad line over a great distance is covered with corpses.'

All who survived the rail-side massacre of April 5 were shot in the pits at Ponary by the German and Lithuanian SS men. A few hours later 4,000 Jews reached Ponary station from Swieciany, where the ghetto had been virtually unmolested since the Polygon slaughter of September 1941 (*page 77*). They too resisted, with revolvers, knives and fists. A few dozen managed to escape to Vilna. The rest were shot down on the spot.

From Jaworow (*opposite, below*), the Jews already expelled from six nearby village communities, and held in the town, were murdered on 18 April 1943, the Jews of Jaworow itself having already been killed at Belzec the previous November (*page 136*).

From Jaworow, most of those who reached the forests fell in battle against the Germans. There was also resistance in Skalat and Przemysl (*above*), in Belgium (*opposite, above*) and, on a massive scale, in Warsaw (*page 158*).

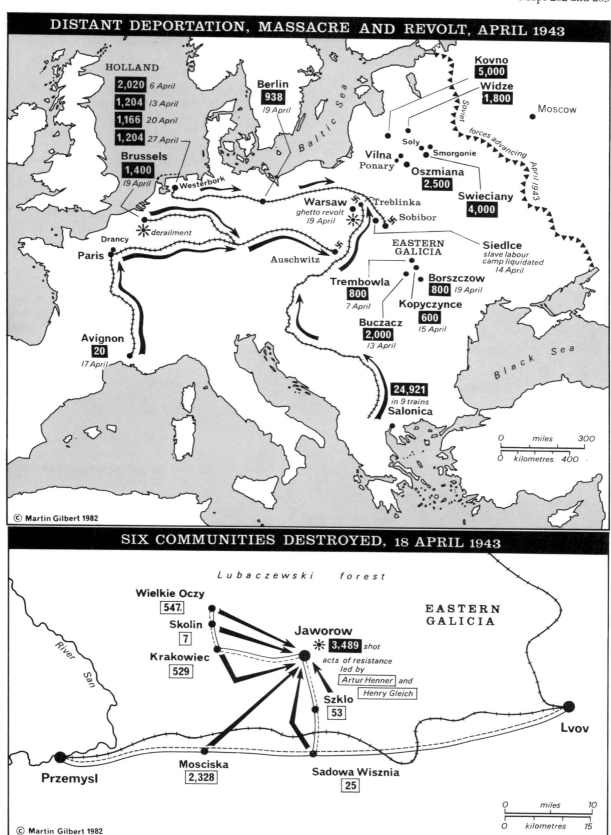

DISTANT DEPORTATION, MASSACRE AND REVOLT, APRIL 1943

SIX COMMUNITIES DESTROYED, 18 APRIL 1943

Map 204

THE WARSAW GHETTO REVOLT, 19 APRIL 1943

River Vistula

Marymont

Zoliborz

Targowek

Powazki

Praga

ghetto

city centre

Grochow

Kolo
Wola

Ujazdowski

W a r s a w

Mokotow

municipal boundary

© Martin Gilbert 1982

0 — miles — 2
0 — kilometres — 3

On 18 January 1943 the Jewish underground in Warsaw had resisted a new wave of deportations. In four days 6,000 Jews had been deported and 1,000 murdered in the streets (page 142). But so fierce was the Jewish resistance and street fighting that the deportations had then been suspended.

The Jewish underground, led by Mordecai Anielewicz, prepared to resist any further attempt to renew the deportations.

On 19 April 1943 a German military force, equipped with tanks and artillery, entered the ghetto in order to resume the death camp deportations. The Jewish units fought back, and the Germans were driven out of the ghetto altogether.

Within a few hours the Germans returned, no longer seeking open conflict with Jewish armed units, but systematically burning down houses in the ghetto street by street, while at the same time killing or driving out with smoke and hand grenades those who were hiding in bunkers or sewers.

On 8 May 1943 the German forces reached the Jewish underground headquarters. In the ensuing battle Anielewicz, and more than 100 of his fighters, were killed. A week later the German commander, General Stroop, reported to his superiors: 'The Warsaw ghetto is no more.'

During the fighting more than 56,000 Jews had been burned alive, shot as they emerged from the burning buildings, or rounded up and deported to Treblinka.

The map shows the municipal boundary of Warsaw, the original extent of the ghetto, and, in solid black, the three much smaller areas to which the ghetto had been reduced following the massive deportations between July and September 1942. The photograph on the left, taken in 1980, shows two of the very few buildings in the ghetto area which survived the otherwise total destruction.

The photographs on the right are both taken from the special album prepared by General Stroop to celebrate his 'victory'. The upper photograph shows a Jewish fighter being brought out of a bunker. The lower photograph shows Stroop himself (facing the camera, clasping his hands, with goggles and gloves), and two captured Jewish fighters, a man and a woman.

As many as 15,000 Jews escaped to the 'Aryan' part of Warsaw. Some were later caught or betrayed. But most, sheltered by the Poles, survived the war, and many were to fight in the Warsaw uprising in August 1944 (pages 206-7).

Map 205

SEVEN DEPORTATIONS, MASSACRE AND RESISTANCE, 4–25 MAY 1943

HOLLAND
1,187 4 May
1,446 11 May
2,511 18 May
2,862 25 May

Baltic Sea

Nowogrodek the last 370 7 May

Bryuchovo 40

The Red Army advances, May 1943

Warsaw 56,000

Germans capture headquarters bunker of Ghetto revolt
The commander of the revolt
Mordechai Anielewicz
killed 8 May

Berlin at least 395 17 May

Sobibor

Brody 2,500 1 May
Jewish resistance against German army and Ukrainian police, 17 May

Auschwitz

GALICIA

Skalat 660 9 May

Sokal 2,500 27 May

Busk 1,000 21 May

Tluste 3,000 27 May

Stryj 1,000 22 May

CROATIA

0 miles 250
0 kilometres 400

Zagreb at least 1,000 7 May
at least 1,000 13 May

from Salonica 10,930 *in four trains*

Black Sea

© Martin Gilbert 1982

At the very moment when the Warsaw ghetto uprising was being crushed, and 56,000 Warsaw Jews were being burned to death, shot, or deported, the deportations continued from outside Greater Germany: four from Holland and two from Croatia.

In the Eastern Galician town of Brody, as well as in Warsaw, Jewish resistance had led to German deaths: but with Soviet forces still more than 300 miles to the east, the Germans were able to devote considerable strength and efforts during May and June 1943 to wiping out the remaining Jewish communities of Eastern Galicia, as seen above and in the map opposite (*below*).

The photograph is of a mother and her three children at the moment of deportation. Most of those marked out to die in Galicia were now taken, not to one of the death camps, but to local forests or gravel pits, or, as at Tluste, to the Jewish cemetery. Here, the executions were carried out with savagery and sadism, a crying child often being seized from its mother's arms and shot in front of her, or having its head crushed by a single blow from a rifle butt. Hundreds of children were thrown alive into pits, and died in fear and agony under the weight of bodies thrown on top of them.

Throughout June the Dutch and French deportations continued (*opposite, above*). On

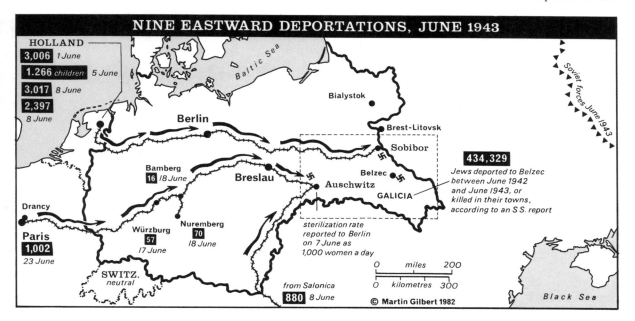

NINE EASTWARD DEPORTATIONS, JUNE 1943

HOLLAND
3,006 *1 June*
1.266 *children* *5 June*
3,017 *8 June*
2,397
8 June

Baltic Sea

Bialystok

Berlin

Brest-Litovsk

Sobibor

Bamberg
16 *18 June*

Breslau

Belzec

Auschwitz

GALICIA

434,329
*Jews deported to Belzec
between June 1942
and June 1943, or
killed in their towns,
according to an S S. report*

Drancy

Würzburg
57

Nuremberg
70

17 June *18 June*

Paris
1,002
23 June

SWITZ.
neutral

*sterilization rate
reported to Berlin
on 7 June as
1,000 women a day*

Soviet forces June 1943

0   miles   200
0   kilometres   300

from Salonica
880 *8 June*

© **Martin Gilbert 1982**

Black Sea

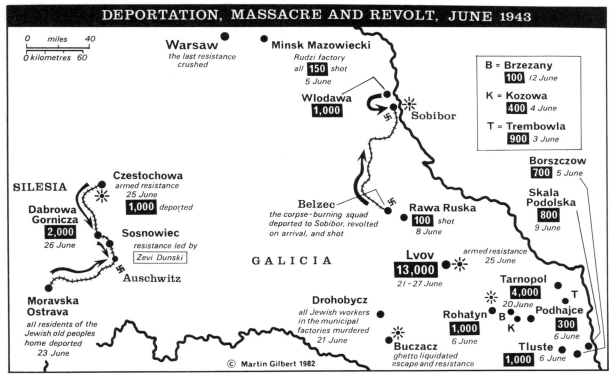

DEPORTATION, MASSACRE AND REVOLT, JUNE 1943

0   miles   40
0 kilometres   60

Warsaw
*the last resistance
crushed*

Minsk Mazowiecki
*Rudzi factory
all* **150** *shot
5 June*

Wlodawa
1,000

Sobibor

B = **Brzezany**
100 *12 June*

K = **Kozowa**
400 *4 June*

T = **Trembowla**
900 *3 June*

Borszczow
700 *5 June*

**Skala
Podolska**
800
9 June

Czestochowa
*armed resistance
25 June*
1,000 *deported*

SILESIA

**Dabrowa
Gornicza**
2,000
26 June

Sosnowiec
resistance led by
Zevi Dunski

Auschwitz

Belzec
*the corpse-burning squad
deported to Sobibor, revolted
on arrival, and shot*

Rawa Ruska
100 *shot
8 June*

GALICIA

Lvov
13,000
21 - 27 June

*armed resistance
25 June*

Tarnopol
4,000
20 June

T

**Moravska
Ostrava**
*all residents of the
Jewish old peoples
home deported
23 June*

Drohobycz
*all Jewish workers
in the municipal
factories murdered
21 June*

Rohatyn
1,000
6 June

B

K

Podhajce
300
6 June

Buczacz
*ghetto liquidated
escape and resistance*

Tluste
1,000 *6 June*

© **Martin Gilbert 1982**

June 5 a total of 1,266 children under the age of 16 were deported from Holland to Sobibor. All were gassed on arrival. Among 1,000 Jews deported from Paris to Auschwitz on June 23, more than 100 were likewise under 16 years. There were also 13 babies and many mothers with young children, all of whom were murdered on arrival, including the eight-months-old Henry

Kaminka deported with his mother Salomée, born in Bialystok, and his father Vital, born in Brest-Litovsk.

In Galicia and Silesia as the killings continued, so too did the resistance (*above*). But with arms almost impossible to obtain, and the local population often unwilling to give shelter, both defence and escape were equally hopeless. But both continued.

Map 208

DEPORTATION, MASSACRE AND REVOLT, JULY 1943

Leningrad

Soviet front line in July 1943

Moscow

Riga • Lida

Shavli • Vitebsk

Kovno • **Vilna**
☀ resistance
24 July

Nowo-Wilejka
*slave labour camp
liquidated
28 July*

• Minsk

North Sea

Baltic Sea

BELGIUM
| 1,553 |
31 July

20 July
☐2 escape
Treblinka ☀

Miedzyrzec
| 200 | *slave labourers*
18 July

Berlin •

Kamionka Strumilowa
| 5,000 | *slave labourers*
10 July

Sobibor •

HOLLAND | 2,209 | *20 July*
| 2,417 | *6 July*
| 1,988 | *13 July*

Malines •

Auschwitz •

Skalat
| 400 | *slave labourers*
28 July

Drancy •

Czestochowa
| 500 | *slave labourers*
20 July

Bolechow
| 300 |
13 July

Paris
| 1,000 |
18 July
| 1,000 |
31 July

Natzweiler • Strasbourg

Black Sea

Jasenovac •
| 800 | *15 July*

Adriatic Sea

Salonica
| 1,800 |
28 July

GREECE

0   *miles*   200
0   *kilometres* 300

Aegean Sea

CRETE   **Heraklion**
| 6 | *Jews shot 6 June 1943*

© Martin Gilbert 1982

As the Red Army began its advance westward in the summer of 1943, the Nazis murdered several thousand Jews who had not been deported to the death camps earlier, but who had been kept alive in order to serve as slave labourers in factories and labour camps. At the same time, the deportations to Auschwitz continued from the furthest extremities of German rule *(above),* including two from Paris, one from Belgium, three from Holland, and the remaining Jews in Salonica *(page 152).*

Six eastern ghettos had escaped 'liquidation' by the Nazis during 1942: Vilna,

Kovno, Shauliai (known to the Jews as Shavli), Riga, Minsk and Lida.

In Vilna *(above and opposite),* where 20,000 Jews lived in the ghetto, a group of 21 young men and women who had been active in the Jewish underground movement decided to try to make contact with the Soviet partisans who were now increasingly active behind the German front line.

The escape of the 21 was successful, but they were ambushed by German soldiers at the Mickun bridge, and nine were killed in the ensuing fighting.

Three days after the ambush at the bridge,

Map 209

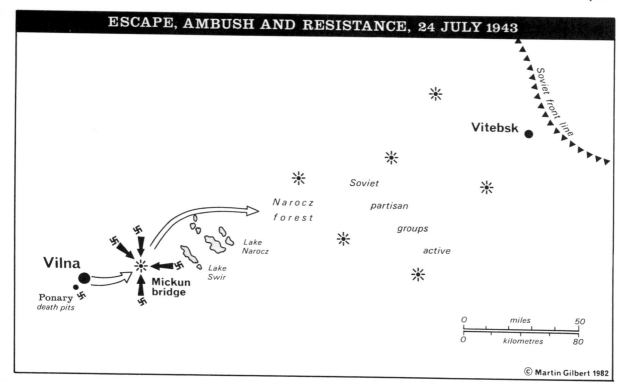

ESCAPE, AMBUSH AND RESISTANCE, 24 JULY 1943

Soviet front line

Vitebsk

Soviet partisan groups active

Narocz forest

Lake Narocz

Lake Swir

Vilna

Mickun bridge

Ponary death pits

| 0 | miles | 50 |
| 0 | kilometres | 80 |

© Martin Gilbert 1982

32 relatives of the nine Jews who had been killed were seized by the Gestapo in Vilna, taken to Ponary, and executed.

Those who survived the ambush continued eastwards to the Narocz forest where they joined the Soviet partisans, and were active in disrupting German military supplies and communications with the front line.

In Vilna itself, the execution of the 32 relatives proved a tragedy for all those who remained in the ghetto. To prevent any further such escapes, the head of the Gestapo in the city, Bruno Kittel, at once made it known that in future the whole family of anyone who escaped to the forest would be killed as a reprisal, while if the man who got away had no family then those who shared his room, or even lived in the same tenement building, would likewise be executed. The Gestapo also decreed that if, from any of the labour gangs of 10 Jews sent out of the ghetto, even a single man failed to return, the remaining nine would be shot. Escapes to the forest ceased. But inside the ghetto the Jewish resistance groups continued to make plans, and to collect arms.

In 1940 the SS had set up a concentration camp at Natzweiler, in Alsace, with 20 satellite labour camps. Between the first executions on 18 September 1942 and the liberation of Natzweiler on 31 August 1944, at least 25,000 prisoners, Jews and non-Jews, died there of starvation and ill-treatment, or were murdered.

Many Jewish and non-Jewish women, active in the French resistance, were executed in Natzweiler, as well as many Russian and Polish prisoners. The meticulous camp records show, for example, eight civilians from Luxembourg shot in the camp on 19 May 1944.

On 6 November 1942 Heinrich Himmler had given his support to a plan to establish a collection of Jewish skulls and skeletons at the Reich Anatomical Institute in Strasbourg, near Natzweiler. On 21 June 1943, 73 Jews and 30 Jewesses were selected in Auschwitz, and sent to Natzweiler, where they were measured, weighed and gassed, and their corpses sent on to the Anatomical Institute in Strasbourg. On 15 October 1944, as Allied forces approached Strasbourg, Himmler ordered the skeleton collection to be destroyed. But all the documents relating to it survived the war.

At Auschwitz itself, medical experiments (*page 107*) continued, and led to the deaths of hundreds of people, especially women. Many hundreds were maimed for life by sterilization and other experiments. Others were deliberately murdered so that the SS doctors could study their bone structure.

Map 210

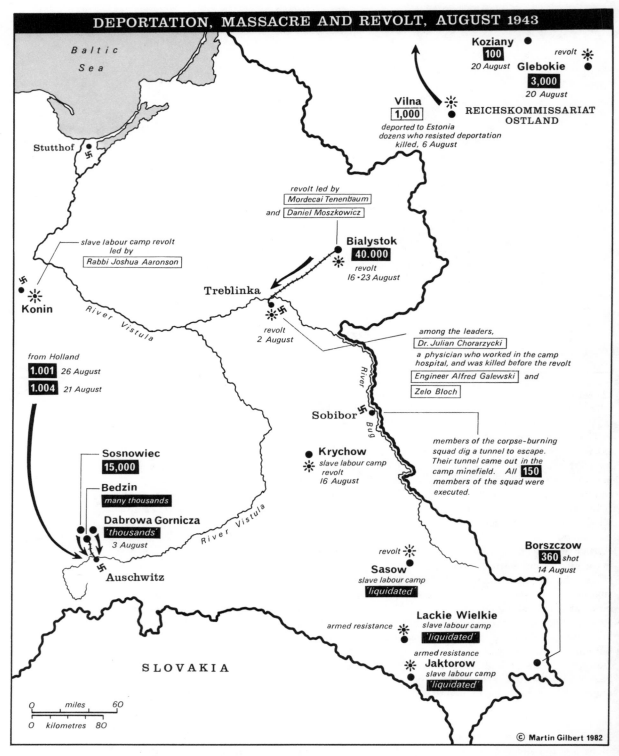

DEPORTATION, MASSACRE AND REVOLT, AUGUST 1943

Baltic Sea

Stutthof

Koziany 100 *20 August*   *revolt*

Glebokie 3,000 *20 August*

Vilna 1,000
deported to Estonia
dozens who resisted deportation
killed, 6 August

REICHSKOMMISSARIAT OSTLAND

revolt led by Mordecai Tenenbaum *and* Daniel Moszkowicz

slave labour camp revolt led by Rabbi Joshua Aaronson

Bialystok 40.000
revolt 16·23 August

Konin

River Vistula

Treblinka
revolt 2 August

among the leaders, Dr. Julian Chorarzycki *a physician who worked in the camp hospital, and was killed before the revolt* Engineer Alfred Galewski *and* Zelo Bloch

from Holland 1.001 *26 August* 1.004 *21 August*

River Bug

Sobibor

Krychow
slave labour camp revolt 16 August

members of the corpse-burning squad dig a tunnel to escape. Their tunnel came out in the camp minefield. All 150 *members of the squad were executed.*

Sosnowiec 15,000

Bedzin *many thousands*

Dabrowa Gornicza 'thousands' *3 August*

River Vistula

Auschwitz

revolt **Sasow** *slave labour camp* 'liquidated'

Borszczow 360 *shot 14 August*

armed resistance **Lackie Wielkie** *slave labour camp* 'liquidated'

armed resistance **Jaktorow** *slave labour camp* 'liquidated'

SLOVAKIA

0   *miles*   60
0   *kilometres*   80

© Martin Gilbert 1982

In August 1943 more than 2,000 Jews were deported from Holland to Auschwitz *(above)*, while several slave labour camps in the General Government were 'liquidated', and their inmates murdered.

The deportation of 40,000 Jews from the Bialystok ghetto to Treblinka led to two major revolts: inside Bialystok itself, when the Germans used artillery and tanks to crush the rebellion, and at Treblinka *(above)*,

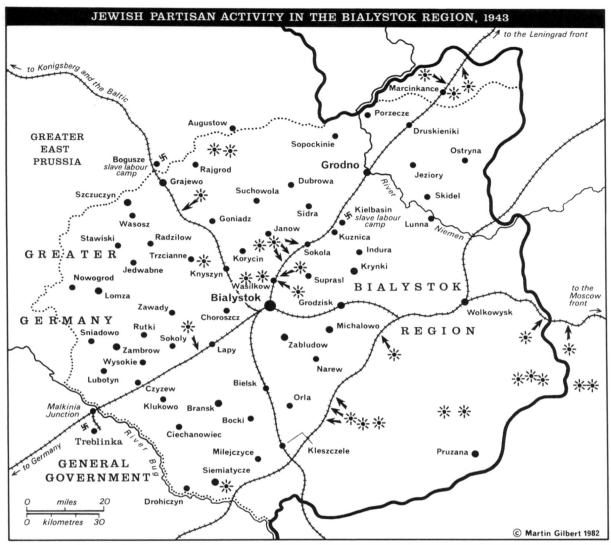

JEWISH PARTISAN ACTIVITY IN THE BIALYSTOK REGION, 1943

where several hundred prisoners battled with guards, and tried to break out across the minefields. But at Treblinka, as elsewhere, all acts of resistance were brutally suppressed. After the Bialystok revolt more than 1,000 Jewish children were seized in the city and deported, first to Theresienstadt, and then to Auschwitz *(right),* while at Glebokie 3,000 Jews who tried to resist being taken out to the nearby woods were massacred in a single day. But those Jews who did manage to escape built up small but active networks of partisan activity. Throughout the Bialystok region *(above)* Jews who had managed to escape from the deportations of 2 November 1942 *(page 133)* did whatever they could to disrupt German rail communication with the Leningrad and Moscow fronts: the arrows show the main partisan attacks.

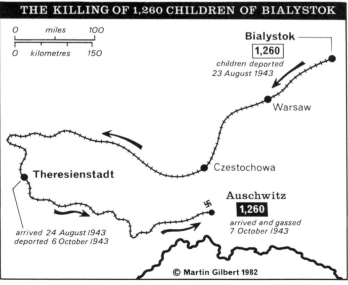

THE KILLING OF 1,260 CHILDREN OF BIALYSTOK

Bialystok — 1,260 children deported 23 August 1943

Warsaw

Czestochowa

Theresienstadt arrived 24 August 1943 deported 6 October 1943

Auschwitz 1,260 arrived and gassed 7 October 1943

© Martin Gilbert 1982

Map 213

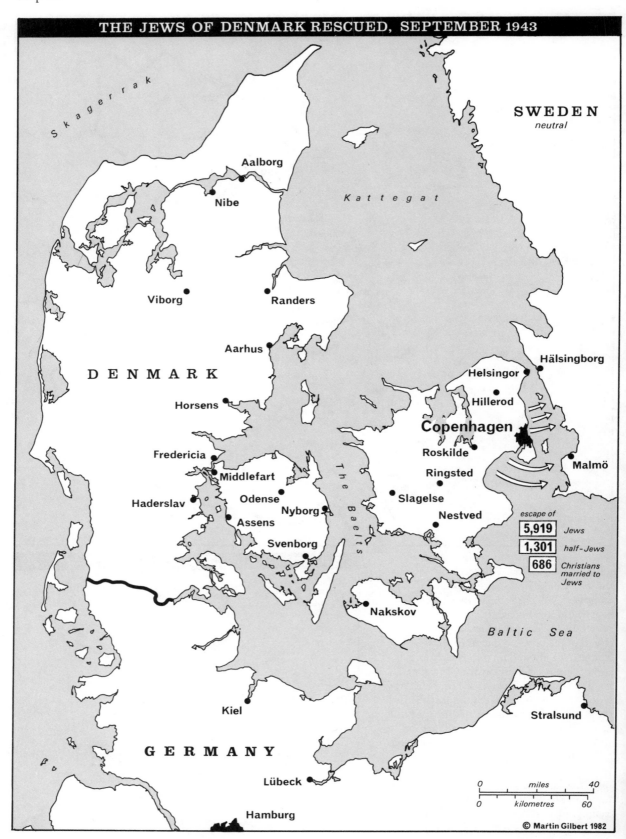

THE JEWS OF DENMARK RESCUED, SEPTEMBER 1943

S k a g e r r a k

SWEDEN
neutral

K a t t e g a t

Aalborg

Nibe

Viborg   Randers

Aarhus

D E N M A R K

Hälsingborg

Helsingor

Hillerod

Horsens

Copenhagen

Roskilde

Malmö

Fredericia

Middlefart

Ringsted

The Baelts

Haderslav

Odense

Nyborg   Slagelse

Assens

Nestved

Svenborg

escape of

5,919	*Jews*
1,301	*half-Jews*
686	*Christians married to Jews*

Nakskov

Baltic Sea

Kiel

Stralsund

G E R M A N Y

Lübeck

0	*miles*	40
0	*kilometres*	60

© **Martin Gilbert** 1982

Hamburg

Map 214

Following the German occupation of Denmark in the spring of 1940, the Germans had embarked on a policy of cooperation and negotiation with the Danish authorities, as embodied in the Danish-German Agreement of 9 April 1940. As a result, the Jews had been left unmolested. But on 28 August 1943, as Danish resistance to the German occupation undermined any chance of continued cooperation, the Germans abolished the Agreement, and declared martial law.

The SS hoped to use this opportunity to deport all Denmark's 7,200 Jews, most of whom lived in Copenhagen, a few hundred in each of the towns and villages shown opposite. Forewarned, however, of the planned deportation, Danes and Jews plotted to ensure that, on the eve of the deportation, Danish sea captains and fishermen ferried 5,919 Jews, 1,301 part Jews (designated Jews by the Nazis), and 686 Christians married to Jews, to safety in Sweden, a country where, between 1933 and 1943, more than three thousand European Jews, including many from Germany itself, had already found refuge (right).

On 1 October 1943 the Germans found only 500 Jews still in Denmark. All were sent to Theresienstadt; 423 survived the war.

The photograph is of Danish Jews waiting in a cellar for the moment of rescue.

SWEDEN AND THE JEWS, 1939-1945

NORWAY

SWEDEN neutral

Stockholm

Goteborg

Nordkopping

North Sea

DENMARK

Malmö

Karlskrona

LITH-UANIA

GERMANY

CZECHO

SLOVAKIA

AUSTRIA

0   miles   200

0   kilometres   300

© Martin Gilbert 1982

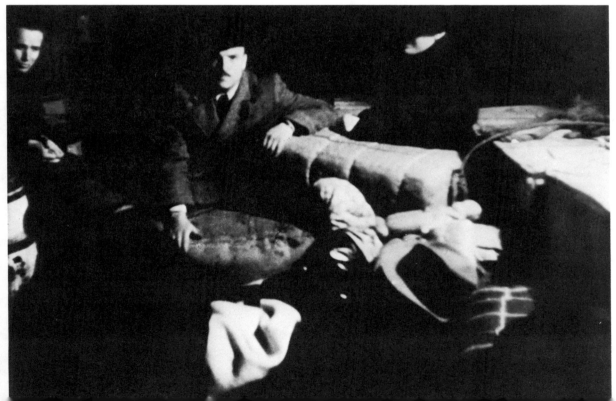

A SLAVE LABOUR CAMP ESTABLISHED, 30 SEPTEMBER 1943

© Martin Gilbert 1982

SLAVE LABOUR CAMPS, 1943–1944

Alderney
deaths include:
Chayim Goldin
7.12.1943
Robert Perlestein
22.12.1943
Seib Becker
30.12.1943
Lucien Worms
7.1.1944
Isaac Stekovsky
8.2.1944
Wilfred Gordeson
26.2.1944
Henry Lippman
2.3.1944
Szmul Kirschenblatt
26.4.1944

© Martin Gilbert 1982

As Soviet forces advanced westwards more and more Jews were taken to slave labour camps in White Russia and Greater Germany. With the disbanding of a Krupp armaments works at Mariupol (*above*), it was relocated at Funfteichen in Silesia. Jews who had just been deported from Sosnowiec to Auschwitz were sent by train to work at Funfteichen, where many died.

In all labour camps, deaths from brutality were a daily occurrence. The map on the left names eight of the 100 Jews who died on Alderney, a British island captured by the Germans in 1940.

One use of slave labour was to obliterate all trace of earlier mass murders. At Himmler's instigation, a series of special units, known collectively as 'Unit 1005', were being forced to dig up the corpses of those slain, to burn them, and to scatter the ashes. This work took nearly two years and involved exhuming more than two million corpses (*opposite, above*).

One such unit was at work at Babi Yar (*opposite*). Others, working at different times at the murder sites shown above, were

Map 217

HIMMLER ORDERS THE EVIDENCE OF MASS MURDER DESTROYED

© Martin Gilbert 1982

themselves murdered once their work was done. The SS wanted no trace to survive either of their crimes, or of the slave labourers who were being forced to hide them. Nevertheless, a few did manage to escape. The Janowska unit, which had begun its grim work in July 1943, revolted four months later *(page 174)*. Even from Borki, where there was an equal number of armed guards as of prisoners, three prisoners survived an attempted break-out.

At Plaszow, in January 1945, a 'unit 1005' was forced to exhume 9,000 bodies from 11 mass graves. At Ponary more than 58,000 bodies were exhumed and cremated between September 1943 and April 1944. The Ponary unit, made up of 70 Jews and 10 Soviet prisoners-of-war who were suspected of being Jewish, was chained while working, and kept at night in a deep pit, access to which was by a wooden ladder which was withdrawn each evening. After digging an escape tunnel for three months with hands and spoons, 40 escaped on the night of 15 April 1944 *(page 181)*. Twenty-five were caught and killed; 15 eluded their pursuers.

The photograph is of a group of prisoners at the slave labour camp at Plaszow.

Map 218

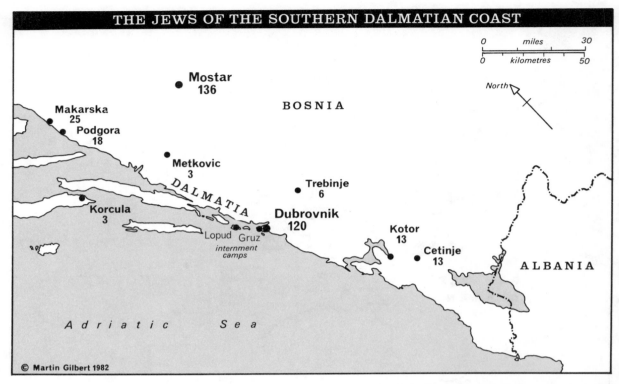

THE JEWS OF THE SOUTHERN DALMATIAN COAST

Mostar
136

BOSNIA

Makarska
25
Podgora
18

Metkovic
3

DALMATIA

Trebinje
6

Dubrovnik
120

Kotor
13

Cetinje
13

ALBANIA

Korcula
3

Lopud Gruz
*internment
camps*

A d r i a t i c   S e a

North

0 _____ miles _____ 30
0 _____ kilometres _____ 50

© Martin Gilbert 1982

In April 1941 the Italian army had occupied Dalmatia, whose small Jewish communities (*above*) dated back to the fourteenth century. The numbers shown are according to the Yugoslav census of 31 March 1931. In November 1942, following German pressure, the Jews of Dalmatia were interned at Gruz and Lopud. In June 1943 they were transferred to the island of Rab (*opposite, above*). With Italy's withdrawal from the war in September 1943, many escaped, and joined the Yugoslav partisans. But the old, the sick, and women with children, were deported to Zemun, and killed.

From France, Belgium, Holland and the north of Italy, newly occupied by Germany, (*opposite, above*) more than 5,000 Jews were deported to Auschwitz, as were Jews from Theresienstadt, Moravia and Galicia. Before the deportation from Tarnow to Auschwitz (*opposite, below*), hundreds of Jews were murdered in the streets, then 5,000 forced into a single train, with an average of 160 in each sealed truck. The train stopped at Bochnia, where more trucks were added, containing a further 3,000 Jews. When it reached Auschwitz, only 400 of the deportees were still alive. The 'survivors' were sent to the gas chambers.

In the east (*opposite, above*), with the deportation of more than 7,000 Vilna Jews to the slave labour camps of Estonia at the end of August and in early September, several hundred Jews managed to escape from Vilna to the forests, and to join the partisans.

Meanwhile, as the Soviet army advanced steadily westward, and the Allied armies were on European soil south of Rome, 2,000 Jews were deported from Minsk to Sobibor.

At Miedzyrzec, and at Sobibor itself, virtually unarmed Jews challenged German troops and SS. At Treblinka, on 2 September 1943, a group of 13 Jewish slave labourers killed their Ukrainian SS guard with a crowbar while working just outside the camp wire. The leader, an 18-year-old Polish Jew, Seweryn Klajnman, put on the dead guard's uniform, took his rifle, and 'marched off' his fellow prisoners as if to a new work detail further off, cursing and bellowing at them as they went, as befitted an SS guard. Guided by one of their number, a carter, who knew the area well, they escaped their pursuers and evaded capture.

Near Kiev, on 30 September 1943, a work unit of 325 Jewish and Soviet prisoners who were being forced, in chains, to dig up and burn victims of the Babi Yar massacre (*page 76*) resisted when they too were about to be killed. The SS overseers opened fire with machine-guns and grenades. Only 14 of the prisoners survived the revolt.

DISTANT DEPORTATIONS, ESCAPE AND REVOLT, SEPTEMBER 1943

NORWAY

SWEDEN
neutral

*North
Sea*

DENMARK

Baltic Sea

Leningrad

Klooga

ESTONIA

Moscow

7,906
escape

Riga

Dvinsk

Soviet front line

HOLLAND

987 *7 September*

1,005 *14 September*

979 *21 September*

7,130
deported

hundreds escape

Minsk
2,000
18 September

Vilna

Treblinka

13 *escape*

GREATER   GERMANY

Sobibor

Auschwitz

MORAVIA

GALICIA

*Jews attack the
S.S. with stones
and bottles.
All attackers
killed.*

Kiev

*revolt of
Jewish & Soviet
prisoners-of-war
29 September*

311 *killed*

14 *escape*

BELGIUM

631 *both
on
20
September*

794

Miedzyrzec
*Jewish youths attack
Germans. 2 Germans
killed,* **5** *Jews shot
10 September*

Paris
1,000

2 September

Vilna
escape organized by

Izik Wittenberg

Joseph Glazman

Abba Kovner

*Black
Sea*

O   miles   200

O   kilometres   300

Merano
24
16–18 September

ITALY

RAB

Adriatic Sea

Zemun

Split **500**

Dubrovnik

Rome

*under
Allied
control*

© Martin Gilbert 1982

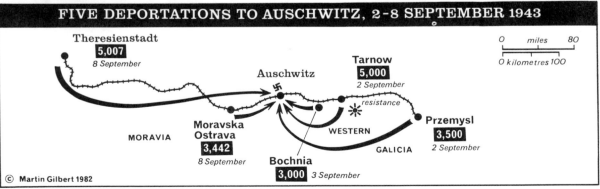

FIVE DEPORTATIONS TO AUSCHWITZ, 2–8 SEPTEMBER 1943

Theresienstadt
5,007
8 September

Auschwitz

Tarnow
5,000
2 September

O   miles   80

O kilometres 100

resistance

Przemysl
3,500
2 September

MORAVIA

**Moravska
Ostrava**
3,442
8 September

WESTERN

GALICIA

Bochnia
3,000 *3 September*

© Martin Gilbert 1982

Map 221

THE JEWS OF ITALY DEPORTED, 9 OCTOBER - 21 NOVEMBER 1943

GREATER

GERMANY

Auschwitz

Moravska Ostrava

SLOVAKIA

Vienna

HUNGARY

SWITZERLAND
neutral

Merano

Bolzano

Villach

Trieste
9 October

Milan
9 November

Vercelli

Verona   Padua

La Risiera di San Sabba

3,000 *Italian prisoners-of-war
murdered by the S.S.
and Ukrainian guards,*

Turin

Asti
Alessandria

Mantua

Parma

Venice
9 November

620 *of Trieste's* **1,920** *Jews
also murdered*

CROATIA

Ferrara
14 September

Modena

Genoa
3 November

La Spezia

Bologna

DALMATIA

San Remo

Pisa

85

Adriatic

Borgo San Dalmazzo

Livorno

Florence
9 November

325

21 November

Sienna

**NORTHERN
ITALY**
*occupied by
Germany
16 September
1943*

Sea

Termoli

Rome
1,015
18 October

Foggia

under

Allied

The front line on 15 November
The front line on 12 October

Naples

control

Salerno

Tyrrhenian

Sea

Ferramonte
di Tarsia

```
O     miles    80
O   kilometres  12O
```

© Martin Gilbert 1982

Map 222

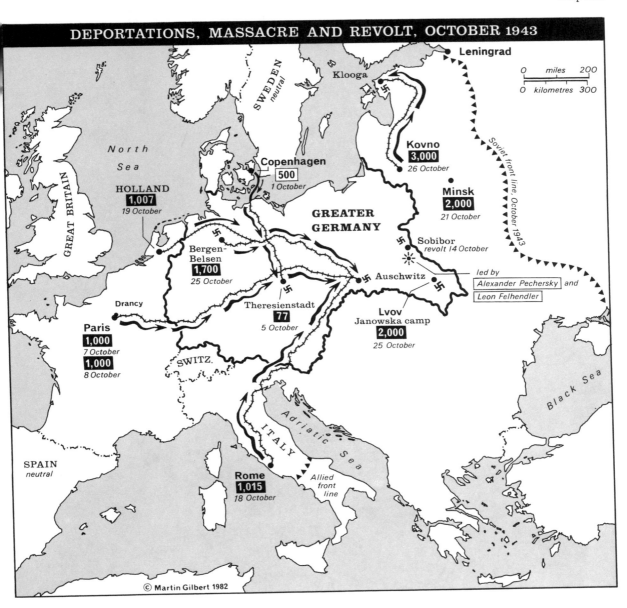

DEPORTATIONS, MASSACRE AND REVOLT, OCTOBER 1943

Leningrad

Klooga

SWEDEN *neutral*

Kovno
3,000
26 October

Soviet front line, October 1943

North Sea

Copenhagen
500
1 October

Minsk
2,000
21 October

GREATER GERMANY

GREAT BRITAIN

HOLLAND
1,007
19 October

Bergen-Belsen
1,700
25 October

Sobibor
revolt 14 October

Auschwitz

led by
Alexander Pechersky and
Leon Felhendler

Drancy

Theresienstadt
77
5 October

Lvov
Janowska camp
2,000
25 October

Paris
1,000
7 October
1,000
8 October

SWITZ.

Black Sea

Adriatic Sea

ITALY

SPAIN
neutral

Rome
1,015
18 October

Allied front line

© Martin Gilbert 1982

On 16 September 1943 more than 37,000 Italian Jews had come under Nazi rule. Some escaped to Switzerland. Several thousand found refuge in Catholic homes. On 16 October 1943, 1,000 Jews were seized in Rome and deported to Auschwitz. Within a month 8,360 Italian Jews, mostly from the towns shown opposite, had been deported to Auschwitz, where 7,749 were murdered.

The deportations from Holland and France to Auschwitz continued. From Kovno 3,000 Jews were sent to the Klooga slave labour camp in Estonia (*above*).

In September (*page 171*) 2,000 Jews and Soviet prisoners-of-war had been deported from Minsk to Sobibor: 80 had been selected

to work as carpenters and joiners. The rest had been gassed. One of the 80, Alexander Pechersky, a Soviet officer and also a Jew, together with other prisoners, planned a break-out. On October 14 the revolt took place: 11 or 12 SS men, and more than a dozen Ukrainian SS guards, were killed. Of the 600 Jews then in the labour camp, 200 were shot while escaping, or were blown up in the camp minefields; 400 escaped, of whom 100 were subsequently captured and killed; others joined Soviet partisan units, and were mostly killed fighting; others died of typhus, or were killed by hostile Polish gangs. Only 30 survived the war, including Pechersky.

Map 223

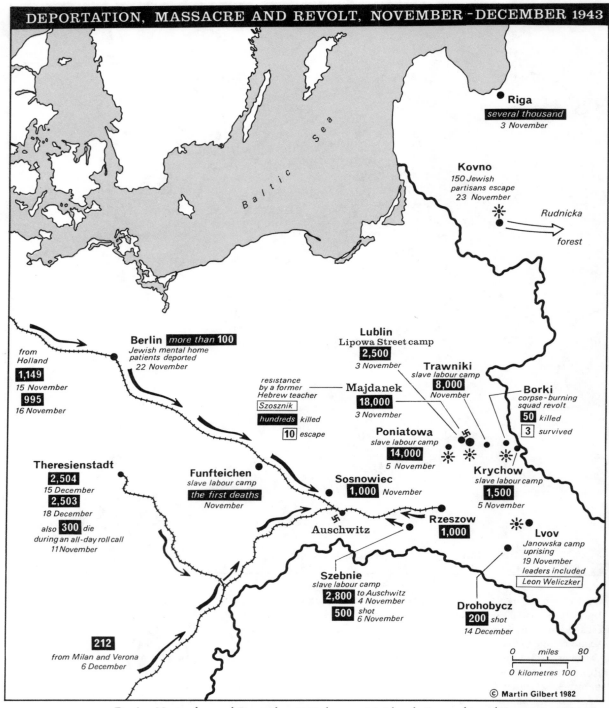

DEPORTATION, MASSACRE AND REVOLT, NOVEMBER-DECEMBER 1943

Baltic Sea

Riga
several thousand
3 November

Kovno
150 Jewish
partisans escape
23 November

Rudnicka

forest

Berlin `more than 100`
Jewish mental home
patients deported
22 November

*from
Holland*
`1,149`
15 November
`995`
16 November

Lublin
Lipowa Street camp
`2,500`
3 November

Trawniki
slave labour camp
`8,000`
November

resistance
by a former
Hebrew teacher
Szosznik
`hundreds` *killed*
`10` *escape*

Majdanek
`18,000`
3 November

Borki
*corpse-burning
squad revolt*
`50` *killed*
`3` *survived*

Poniatowa
slave labour camp
`14,000`
5 November

Krychow
slave labour camp
`1,500`
5 November

Theresienstadt
`2,504`
15 December
`2,503`
18 December
also `300` *die
during an all-day roll call
11 November*

Funfteichen
slave labour camp
the first deaths
November

Sosnowiec
`1,000` November

Rzeszow
`1,000`

Lvov
*Janowska camp
uprising
19 November
leaders included*
Leon Weliczker

Auschwitz

Szebnie
slave labour camp
`2,800` *to Auschwitz
4 November*
`500` *shot
6 November*

Drohobycz
`200` *shot
14 December*

`212`
*from Milan and Verona
6 December*

0   miles   80
0   kilometres   100

© Martin Gilbert 1982

During November and December 1943 the
deportations to Auschwitz continued from
Italy, Holland and Theresienstadt (*above*). At
Majdanek 18,000 prisoners were murdered in
a single day of slaughter, called by the SS the
'harvest festival'. Elsewhere, the SS
continued to destroy slave labour camps.
Jews tried to resist execution, as at

Majdanek, Janowska and Poniatowa (*above*).
Many of the Jews who had managed to
escape the ghettos and camps joined Soviet
partisan groups, or formed small units of
their own. The map opposite shows 35 towns
and villages from which Jews had managed
to escape to the forests. From Kovno almost
all who tried to escape were killed.

Map 224

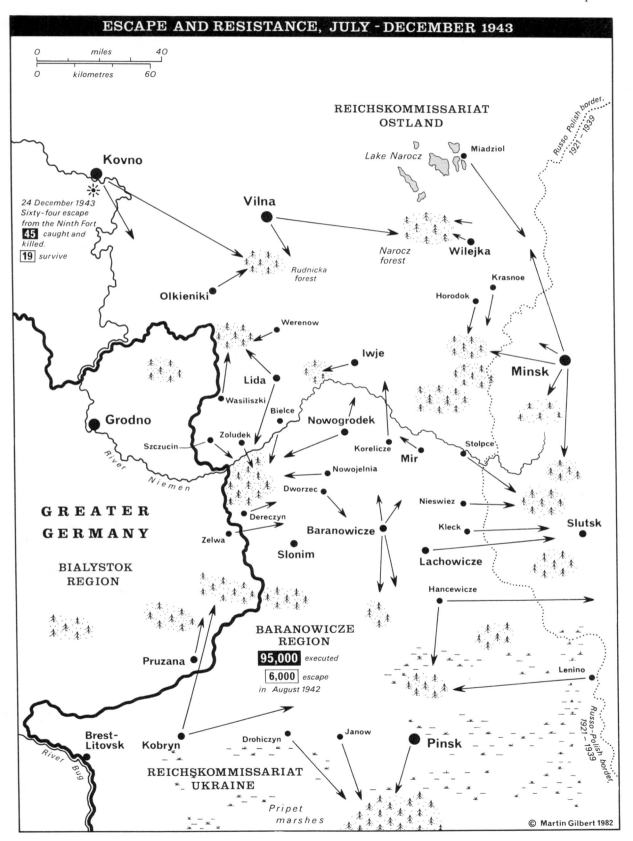

ESCAPE AND RESISTANCE, JULY - DECEMBER 1943

O   miles   40

O   kilometres   60

REICHSKOMMISSARIAT
OSTLAND

Russo-Polish border, 1921-1939

Kovno

Lake Narocz   Miadziol

24 December 1943
Sixty-four escape
from the Ninth Fort.
45 caught and
killed.
19 survive

Vilna

Narocz
forest

Wilejka

Krasnoe

Olkieniki

Rudnicka
forest

Horodok

Werenow

Lida

Iwje

Minsk

Wasiliszki

Bielce

Grodno

Nowogrodek

Szczucin

Zoludek

Korelicze

Mir

Stolpce

River

Nowojelnia

Nieswiez

Niemen

Dworzec

GREATER
GERMANY

Dereczyn

Baranowicze

Kleck

Slutsk

Zelwa

Lachowicze

BIALYSTOK
REGION

Slonim

BARANOWICZE
REGION

Hancewicze

95,000 executed

6,000 escape
in August 1942

Lenino

Pruzana

Russo-Polish border, 1921-1939

Brest-
Litovsk

Kobryn

Drohiczyn

Janow

Pinsk

River Bug

REICHSKOMMISSARIAT
UKRAINE

Pripet
marshes

© Martin Gilbert 1982

175

Map 225

JEWS DEPORTED TO AUSCHWITZ AND GASSED, JANUARY–FEBRUARY 1944

SWEDEN
neutral

North
Sea

Baltic Sea

Narva
86
22 February

Soviet front line

Westerbork
687 27 January
800 10 February

Stutthof
1,000 12 January

Berlin
26 23 February

Malines
417

Drancy

Lodz
95
12 January

Auschwitz

Buczacz
300 Jews in hiding
in the forests for over
six months, surrounded
by German tanks, and
killed, 18 January

Paris
1,068 20 January
985 3 February
1,229 10 February

Bay
of
Biscay

Vienna
37
25 February

Sosnowiec
54 26 February

SWITZ
neutral

Verona

Milan **563**
30 January

Fossoli
462
22 February

Trieste
23 12 January

Adriatic Sea

SPAIN
neutral

Black Sea

0   miles   200
0 kilometres 300

© Martin Gilbert 1982

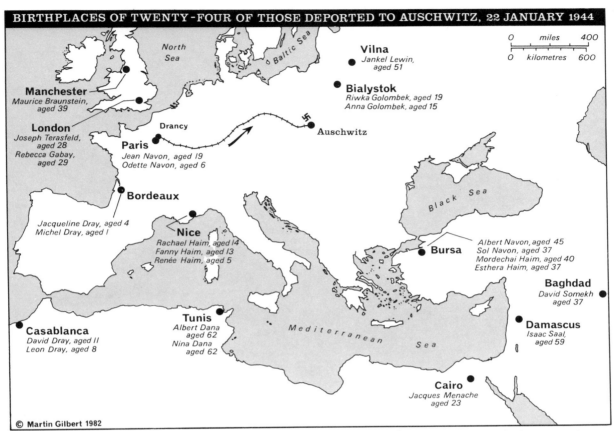

BIRTHPLACES OF TWENTY-FOUR OF THOSE DEPORTED TO AUSCHWITZ, 22 JANUARY 1944

North Sea

Baltic Sea

Vilna
Jankel Lewin, aged 51

Bialystok
Riwka Golombek, aged 19
Anna Golombek, aged 15

Manchester
Maurice Braunstein, aged 39

Drancy

Auschwitz

London
Joseph Terasfeld, aged 28
Rebecca Gabay, aged 29

Paris
Jean Navon, aged 19
Odette Navon, aged 6

Black Sea

Bordeaux
Jacqueline Dray, aged 4
Michel Dray, aged 1

Nice
Rachael Haim, aged 14
Fanny Haim, aged 13
Renée Haim, aged 5

Bursa

Albert Navon, aged 45
Sol Navon, aged 37
Mordechai Haim, aged 40
Esthera Haim, aged 37

Baghdad
David Somekh, aged 37

Tunis
Albert Dana, aged 62
Nina Dana, aged 62

Mediterranean Sea

Damascus
Isaac Saal, aged 59

Casablanca
David Dray, aged 11
Leon Dray, aged 8

Cairo
Jacques Menache, aged 23

0 miles 400
0 kilometres 600

© Martin Gilbert 1982

The map opposite shows the deportations to Auschwitz during January and February 1944. The dates are those of the arrival of each train at Auschwitz; the figures show the actual numbers gassed, according to the records kept by the SS in Auschwitz itself. In all, the SS recorded 13 deportations for these two months, from the Baltic to the Adriatic.

The map above shows the birthplaces, and ages, of 24 of the deportees in one of these 13 deportations, that which reached Auschwitz from Drancy on 22 January 1944. It had left Paris two days earlier, with 632 men, 515 women and 221 children under the age of 18. Of these 1,368 Jews, 749 were gassed on arrival at Auschwitz. As well as those named on the map, the deportees included Jews who had been born in every country in Europe.

Among the Jews deported from Paris to Auschwitz were more than 1,000 who had been born in Turkey, but whose nationality was no protection, despite Turkish neutrality. Some of their birthplaces are shown on the right-hand map.

The photograph is of children in the Dutch deportation centre of Westerbork, on the eve of deportation.

TURKISH-BORN JEWS DEPORTED FROM PARIS

BULGARIA

Black Sea

Edirne

TURKEY-IN-EUROPE

Istanbul

EASTERN THRACE

Silviri

Izmit

Gallipoli

Sea of Marmara

Adapazari

Chanak
(Canakkale)

Bursa

Pazarcik

TURKEY
neutral

Aegean

Bergama

Manisa

Izmir
(Smyrna)

Sea

Aydin

0 miles 60
0 kilometres 80

© Martin Gilbert 1982

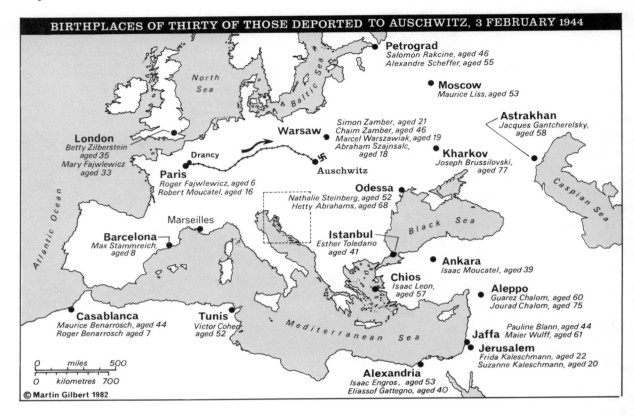

BIRTHPLACES OF THIRTY OF THOSE DEPORTED TO AUSCHWITZ, 3 FEBRUARY 1944

Petrograd
Salomon Rakcine, aged 46
Alexandre Scheffer, aged 55

Moscow
Maurice Liss, aged 53

Astrakhan
Jacques Gantcherelsky, aged 58

Warsaw
Simon Zamber, aged 21
Chaim Zamber, aged 46
Marcel Warszawiak, aged 19
Abraham Szajnsalc, aged 18

London
Betty Zilberstein aged 35
Mary Fajwlewicz aged 33

Drancy

Auschwitz

Kharkov
Joseph Brussilovski, aged 77

Paris
Roger Fajwlewicz, aged 6
Robert Moucatel, aged 16

Odessa
Nathalie Steinberg, aged 52
Hetty Abrahams, aged 68

Marseilles

Barcelona
Max Stammreich, aged 8

Istanbul
Esther Toledano aged 41

Ankara
Isaac Moucatel, aged 39

Chios
Isaac Leon, aged 57

Aleppo
Guarez Chalom, aged 60
Jourad Chalom, aged 75

Casablanca
Maurice Benarrosch, aged 44
Roger Benarrosch aged 7

Tunis
Victor Cohen aged 52

Jaffa *Pauline Blann, aged 44*
Maier Wulff, aged 61

Jerusalem
Frida Kaleschmann, aged 22
Suzanne Kaleschmann, aged 20

Alexandria
Isaac Engros, aged 53
Eliassof Gattegno, aged 40

0 — miles — 500
0 — kilometres — 700

© Martin Gilbert 1982

THE JEWS OF NORTHERN DALMATIA

GREATER GERMANY

AUSTRIA

Lake Balaton

HUNGARY

SLOVENIA

Trieste

ISTRIA

Kraljevica 2
Crikvenica 30

Jasenovac

Senj 6

Rab 4

CROATIA

DALMATIA
Gospic

0 — miles — 60
0 — kilometres — 80

Obrovac 1

Bencovac 1

Knin 1

Drnis 1

BOSNIA

Sibenic 28

Split 210

Dalmatian Coast

Adriatic Sea

ITALY

© Martin Gilbert 1982

On 3 February 1944 yet another train left Paris for Auschwitz. It was the 67th such deportation in nearly two years. The map above shows the names, birthplaces and ages of 30 of the deportees. Also deported, and gassed on arrival at Auschwitz, was the 39-year-old Chief Rabbi of Strasbourg, René Hirschler, who had been born in Marseilles, and his 32-year-old wife Simone. In 1939 Hirschler had been chaplain to those Jewish refugees who had joined the French Foreign Legion in order to fight against Germany. In March 1943 he had become chaplain of all foreign-born Jews in the detention camps in France. He and his wife had been arrested in Marseilles in December 1943.

In all, 1,214 Jews were deported in this one train. Fourteen of the deportees were over 80. More than 100 were under 16 years old. Only 26 survived the war.

The deportees of February 3 included four American-born deportees, the 89-year-old Zadie Abraham, the 81-year-old Clara Kahn, the 81-year-old Pola Modiano, the 57-year-old Michel Feldman *(page 135)*, Murad Gubbay, born in Calcutta *(page 127)*, and the 17-year-old Raymond Strauss, born in the Brazilian city of Sao Paulo.

The Jewish communities, and individual Jews, of northern Dalmatia, according to the Yugoslavia census of 31 March 1931, are shown in the map opposite (*below*). The Jews of Split could trace their Jewish predecessors to the third century AD.

On 11 March 1944, 300 women and children from northern Dalmatia, having been interned at Gospic, were deported to the Croat concentration camp at Jasenovac (*right, below*). Not a single one survived. The men had already been deported to the Sajmiste death camp near Belgrade five months earlier (*page 173*).

In 1941, following the Italian occupation of Dalmatia, the island of Rab which in 1931 had been the home of a single Jewish family, became the centre of a large refugee population, of Jews from Austria, Croatia and Bosnia. Many had been able to join the Yugoslav partisans in September 1943: others mostly women and children, were seized in March 1944, and deported to Auschwitz (*right, below*).

The Jews of Albania had survived unmolested under Italian rule. The first Jews to settle in Albania had been refugees from the Spanish expulsions of 1492. Other refugees had joined them in the sixteenth century from Sicily and southern Italy. By 1927 most of Albania's Jews were living in Koritza (*right, top*). After 1938 several hundred Jewish refugees from Germany and Austria took refuge in Tirana and Durazzo. Following the collapse of Italy in September 1943, they were, at first, unmolested. Then in April 1944, at German insistence, they were interned at Pristina, and consequently deported to Bergen-Belsen. Of 400 Albanian deportees, only 100 survived the war.

These deportations of March and April 1944 took place as the Allied armies in southern Italy were approaching Rome, and after Soviet forces had already crossed the eastern border of Greater Germany and were approaching Lvov.

Meanwhile in Warsaw, on 7 March 1944, the historian Emanuel Ringelblum, who had struggled to collect and preserve as much material as possible about the Warsaw ghetto, and who had managed to hide in 'Aryan' Warsaw after the ghetto revolt, was discovered by the Gestapo, and, together with his family, tortured and killed. Elsewhere in 'Ayran' Warsaw, Polish families, at the risk of their own lives, gave shelter to several thousand Jews, most of whom survived the war.

THE JEWS OF ALBANIA INTERNED

© Martin Gilbert 1982

THREE DEPORTATIONS, MARCH - APRIL 1944

© Martin Gilbert 1982

Map 232

GREEK JEWS DEPORTED TO AUSCHWITZ, 23 MARCH - 2 APRIL 1944

On 15 March 1944 the German authorities assembled trucks and guards throughout mainland Greece, and began a systematic search for more than 10,000 Greek Jews. Half were able to flee into the mountains to find shelter with local peasants, to join Greek partisan units, or to escape across the Aegean to neutral Turkey. Many survived as a result of an instruction issued by Archbishop Damaskinos to all monasteries and convents in Athens and the provincial towns to shelter any Jew who knocked on their doors. But over 5,000 Greek Jews were caught, and deported to Auschwitz. It was an eight-day journey in sealed cattle trucks. Hundreds died during the journey itself.

From the west the French and Dutch deportations continued (*opposite*): there were Jews on these two Paris trains from Hong Kong, Senegal, Liverpool and Samarkand.

In the east there were two rebellions. On 22 March 1944, at Koldyczewo, 10 SS guards were killed, and hundreds of prisoners escaped to join the partisans. Twenty-five escapees were caught, including the leader, who committed suicide. On 15 April 1944

(*see also page 169*) a group of prisoners whose task was to destroy the evidence of mass murder, tried to escape from Ponary. Twenty-five were killed; 15 got away. Five days later, the remaining 40 members of the unit were killed.

Thousands of individual Jews served and fought in the French resistance, and in Yugoslav and Greek partisan units (*above*). More than 300 Jewish soldiers from the Greek Army, and 1,000 other Jews, joined Greek partisan units. A group of 40 Jewish partisans took part in the blowing up of the Gorgopotamo Bridge, breaking German rail communications between Greece and the north. The main Greek national resistance organization in the Trikala, Larisa and Volos region was commanded by Moses Pesah, a Greek rabbi.

Jews also served in Soviet partisan forces which were parachuted behind the German lines in order to disrupt German troop and munition movements. In the Lublin region, by March 1944, were many Jews who had been parachuted into Poland as members of Soviet partisan units. Among these Jews

Map 233

DEPORTATION, MASSACRE AND REVOLT, MARCH - APRIL 1944

Riga

Kovno
ghetto
1,200 *children killed March 1944*

Shauliai (Shavli)
ghetto

Ponary
25 | 15 | *revolt 15 April*
70 | *20 April*

Mogilev

Danzig
Stutthof

Koldyczewo
slave labour camp revolt 22 March
led by Shlomo Kushnir

Berlin

HOLLAND
732 *3 March*
599 *23 March*

Bialystok
region
Jews in Soviet partisan units

Lodz

Lublin
region Chelm

Kiev

Zhitomir
Soviet forces advancing

from Paris
1,501 *7 March*
1,025 *27 March*

Auschwitz

Plaszow   Boryslaw
600
28 March

Czernowitz

SWITZLD.
neutral

Vienna

Jassy

Odessa

Jews in French underground units

Verona

Fossoli   Mantua
559 *5 April*

Jasenovac

Gospic
300
11 March

Jews in Yugoslav partisan units

Jews in Italian underground units

RAB
300

Split

Pristina
300

6,469
deported from Greece to Auschwitz

Rome
57 *Jews among 335 Italians, murdered as a German reprisal, Ardeatine Caves, 24 March*

Allied forces

Jews in Greek partisan units

CORFU

GREECE

TURKEY
neutral

Lamia
1

Patras

Athens

1,500
escape to Turkey by boat

SICILY

Amalias
12

Kalamata
4

Aegion
1   CRETE

RHODES

TUNIS

North Sea

Baltic Sea

Black Sea

Adriatic Sea

Aegean Sea

ITALY

0   *miles*   200
0   *kilometres*   300

© Martin Gilbert 1982

were the commander of the Special Soviet Parachute Battalion, Lieutenant Colonel Henryk Torunczyk, from Lodz; his deputy commander, Joseph Kratko, from Chelm; and the only woman officer in the battalion, Lieutenant Lucyna Herz, who was killed in action while leading a company against a German position on the Vistula. For her bravery she was posthumously awarded the rank of Captain in the Red Army.

Map 234

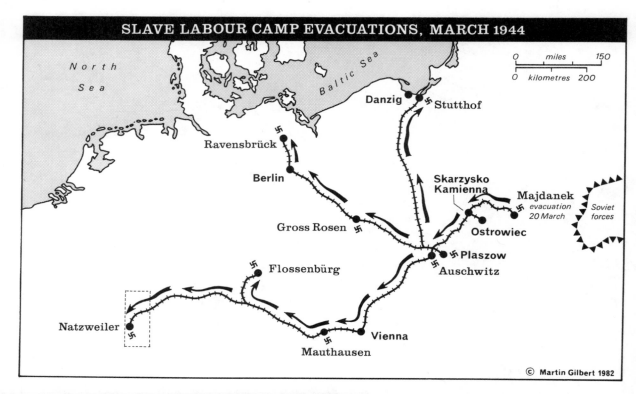

SLAVE LABOUR CAMP EVACUATIONS, MARCH 1944

© Martin Gilbert 1982

As Soviet forces advanced further and further westward, the Germans began the systematic evacuation of the slave labour camps in their path (*above*). From the camp at Plaszow, many hundreds were sent to Auschwitz, others westward to Mauthausen and Flossenbürg, some northward to the concentration camp at Stutthof.

Majdanek itself was evacuated on 20 March 1944, when all sick prisoners were sent direct to Auschwitz to be gassed, while the rest were sent to Gross Rosen, and the women to Ravensbrück and Natzweiler.

The photograph, taken in 1980, shows some of the hundreds of thousands of shoes which the Germans had collected from their victims at Majdanek between 1942 and 1944, hoping to find a technical process which would enable used shoe leather to be turned to some practical or even military purpose. But no such process had been discovered before the camp was evacuated. The shoes remained in their original storehouse.

Even while the first westward evacuations were in progress, the eastward deportations were continuing. Those from Holland, Italy and Paris are shown on the two small maps (*opposite*). More than half of the Dutch Jews sent to Bergen-Belsen and Theresienstadt survived. But most of those sent to Auschwitz perished.

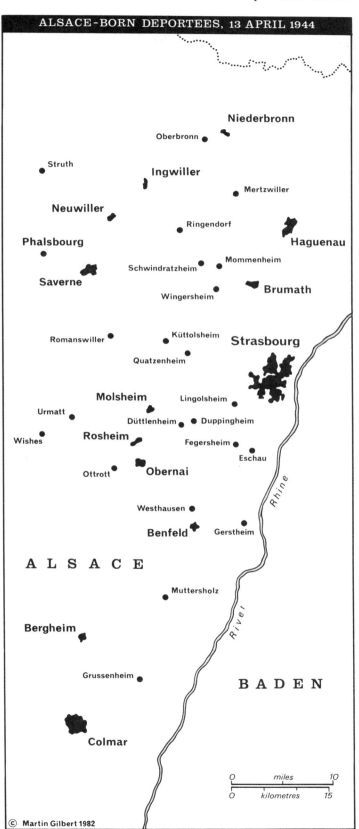

Among those deported from Paris on 13 April 1944 were several hundred Jews who had been born in Alsace, the French province annexed by Germany, first in 1870 and again in 1940. The map on the far right shows some of the towns, villages and hamlets in which these deportees were born, many of them during the period of German rule before the First World War.

In all, 1,500 Jews were deported from Paris to Auschwitz on 13 April 1944, among them 148 children under 12, and a 16-year-old girl, Simone Jacob, who had been born in Nice. Miss Jacob was one of 100 deportees from this particular train who survived Auschwitz. Later, as Simone Veil, she became Minister of Health in the French Government, and, in July 1979, President of the European Parliament at Strasbourg.

From the second Paris deportation that month, on 29 April 1944, those killed included the Yiddish poet from Warsaw, Itzak Katznelson. His wife and most of his family had already been killed at Treblinka.

Map 238

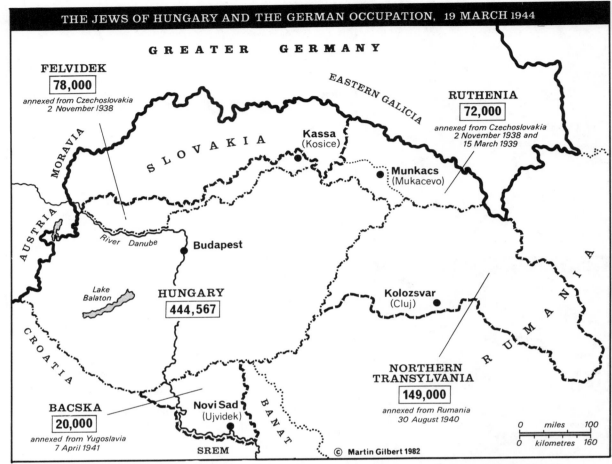

THE JEWS OF HUNGARY AND THE GERMAN OCCUPATION, 19 MARCH 1944

GREATER GERMANY

FELVIDEK
78,000
*annexed from Czechoslovakia
2 November 1938*

EASTERN GALICIA

RUTHENIA
72,000
*annexed from Czechoslovakia
2 November 1938 and
15 March 1939*

MORAVIA

SLOVAKIA

Kassa
(Kosice)

Munkacs
(Mukacevo)

AUSTRIA

River Danube

Budapest

Lake Balaton

HUNGARY
444,567

Kolozsvar
(Cluj)

R U M A N I A

CROATIA

**NORTHERN
TRANSYLVANIA**
149,000
*annexed from Rumania
30 August 1940*

BACSKA
20,000
*annexed from Yugoslavia
7 April 1941*

Novi Sad
(Ujvidek)

BANAT

SREM

0   miles   100
0   kilometres   160

© Martin Gilbert 1982

On 19 March 1944 German control was imposed on Hungary. Suddenly more than three quarters of a million Jews who had hitherto seemed safe from Nazi terror, and in particular from deportation, came under Nazi dominance.

More than a quarter of a million of these Jews lived in areas which Hungary itself had annexed between 1938 and 1941, as shown on the map above. One such area was the Bacska, whose Jewish communities are shown on the map opposite, according to the Yugoslav census of 1931.

In the autumn of 1941 more than 10,000 Jews whose Hungarian citizenship was in doubt had been deported to Kamenets Podolsk, and murdered (*page 68*). A few months later, in January 1942, 1,000 Jews had been massacred in the Bacska (*page 87*).

In January 1943, after more than 50,000 Hungarian Jews had been forced to serve in labour battalions on the eastern front as part of Hungary's war effort against Russia, at least 40,000 had been killed during the fighting or had died after the Soviet army's

victory on the River Don (*page 143*).

Despite the deaths of so many Jews, the Hungarian Government had adamantly rejected two German requests for the deportation of Hungarian Jews to Greater Germany in 1943, and had even begun to institute court proceedings against those responsible for the Bacska killings of 1942.

Hitler himself had protested twice to the Hungarian Government about what he called its 'irresolute and ineffective' handling of the Jewish question, and on 12 March 1944, a week before the German occupation of Hungary, the SS began to plan the complete destruction of Hungarian Jewry.

Within a few weeks of the imposition of German control over Hungary, tens of thousands of Jews were driven from their towns and villages, and forced into ghettos and special camps (*page 186*).

The photograph shows a deportation from a town in the Felvidek region, which Hungary had annexed from Czechoslovakia in November 1938.

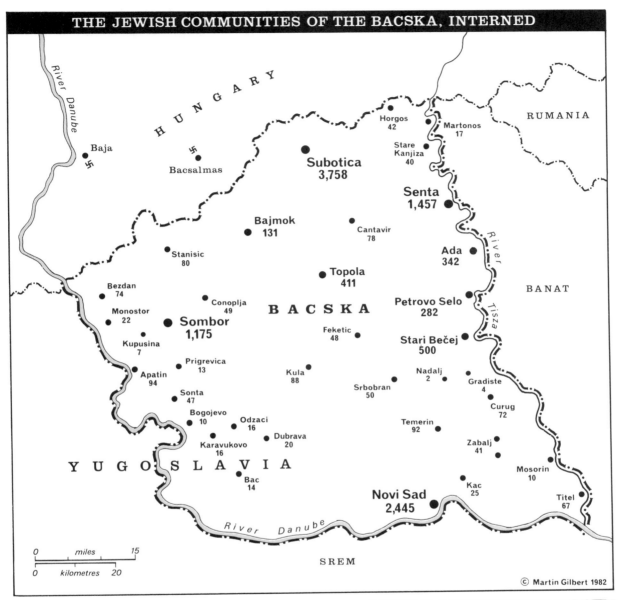

THE JEWISH COMMUNITIES OF THE BACSKA, INTERNED

River Danube

H U N G A R Y

RUMANIA

Baja ⊕

Bacsalmas ⚡

Subotica
3,758

Horgos
42

Martonos
17

Stare
Kanjiza
40

Senta
1,457

Bajmok
131

Cantavir
78

Ada
342

Stanisic
80

Topola
411

B A C S K A

Petrovo Selo
282

BANAT

Bezdan
74

Conoplja
49

Monostor
22

Sombor
1,175

Feketic
48

Stari Bečej
500

River Tisza

Kupusina
7

Prigrevica
13

Kula
88

Nadalj
2

Gradiste
4

Apatin
94

Sonta
47

Srbobran
50

Curug
72

Bogojevo
10

Odzaci
16

Dubrava
20

Temerin
92

Zabalj
41

Karavukovo
16

Mosorin
10

Y U G O S L A V I A

Bac
14

Novi Sad
2,445

Kac
25

Titel
67

River Danube

SREM

0 miles 15

0 kilometres 20

© Martin Gilbert 1982

Map 240

JEWS ASSEMBLED FOR DEPORTATION, 16 APRIL - 23 MAY 1944

GREATER GERMANY

EASTERN GALICIA

SLOVAKIA

Kassa (Kosice)
12,000
11 May

Ungvar
14,000
6 May

Havasko
3 May

Nevicke
3 May

Csap

Munkacs
26,000
15-22 May

Iza 3,000

RUTHENIA

BUKOVINA

Satoraljaujhely
15,000
11 May

Beregszasz
10,000

Huszt
10,000 11 May

Miskolc
21,000
11 May

Kisvarda
2,000 15 May

Nyiregyhaza

Maramarossziget

Vad

Petrova

NORTHERN TRANSYLVANIA

Eger
9,000

Nagykallo
23 May

Szatmarnemeti
24,000

Nagybanya
3,500

Felsoviso
8,000
5 May

HUNGARY

Monostor-Kapolnok
3 May

Bethlen
3 May

Szekelyhid
3 May

Szilagysomlyo
7,000
3 May

Beszterce
8,000 (Bistriza)
3 May

Nagyszollos
8,000 15 May

Des
10,000
3 May

Nagyvarad (Oradea Mare)
36,000
3 May

Kolozsvar (Cluj)
22,000
3 May

Szaszregen
8,000
3 May

Szamosujvar
1,600

Marosvasarhely
6,000
3 May

RUMANIA

Sepsiszentgyorgy
3 May

0 miles 50
0 kilometres 80

© Martin Gilbert 1982

Beginning on 15 April 1944, tens of thousands of Hungarian Jews were forced to leave their homes, and to move into specially designated ghetto areas. The map above shows some of these ghettos, with the approximate numbers held in them.

On entering each Hungarian town or village, one Gestapo method was to seize several leading citizens, and then threaten to kill them unless the community agreed to a punitive ransom. In this way, the Jews of the town were impoverished overnight, without even the money to buy railway tickets. The ransom exercise also made the SS seem plausible: they had said they would release the hostages as soon as the money was paid, and they had kept their word. When the SS then said: 'we have orders to put you in brick factories and timber yards *and no harm will come to you*', it could be believed. 'Quite soon', the SS told those who had been thus confined, 'you will go east to help with the harvest.'

On 15 May 1944 *(opposite, above)* the deportations to Auschwitz began. By mid June a total of 289,357 Jews had been deported to Auschwitz from Ruthenia and northern Transylvania *(see also pages 196-201).*

The map opposite, gives the approximate number of Jews known to have been deported to Auschwitz and then gassed there, from 63 towns and villages in eastern Hungary. The places shown here amount to no more than half of the towns and villages in this region alone from which Jews were deported. At Miskolc and Satoraljaujhely hundreds of Jews were shot as they tried to resist boarding the trains.

An indication of the size of the destruction elsewhere in Hungary during the summer months of 1944 can be seen from the maps on pages 196 to 201.

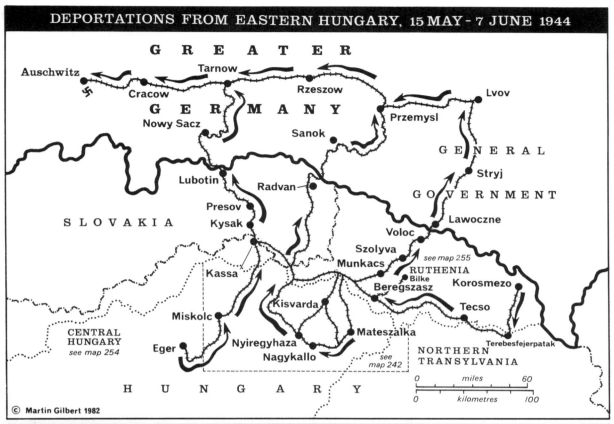

DEPORTATIONS FROM EASTERN HUNGARY, 15 MAY - 7 JUNE 1944

GREATER

GERMANY

Auschwitz

Tarnow

Cracow

Rzeszow

Lvov

Nowy Sacz

Przemysl

Sanok

GENERAL

Lubotin

Radvan

Stryj

Presov

GOVERNMENT

Kysak

Lawoczne

SLOVAKIA

Voloc

Szolyva

see map 255

Kassa

Munkacs

RUTHENIA

Bilke

Korosmezo

Beregszasz

Kisvarda

Tecso

Miskolc

Mateszalka

Terebesfejerpatak

CENTRAL
HUNGARY
see map 254

Eger

Nyiregyhaza

NORTHERN
TRANSYLVANIA

Nagykallo

see
map 242

HUNGARY

| 0 | miles | 60 |
| 0 | kilometres | 100 |

© Martin Gilbert 1982

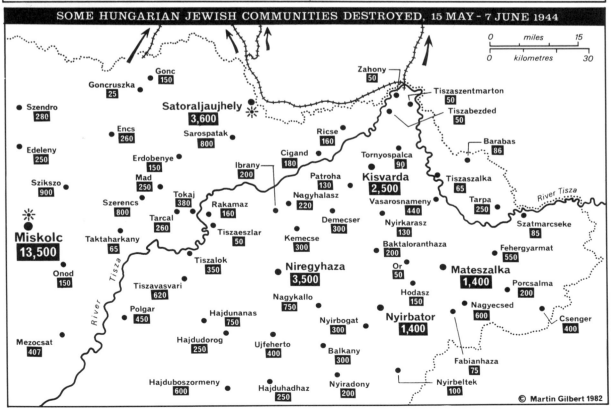

SOME HUNGARIAN JEWISH COMMUNITIES DESTROYED, 15 MAY - 7 JUNE 1944

| 0 | miles | 15 |
| 0 | kilometres | 30 |

Gonc
150

Goncruszka
25

Zahony
50

Tiszaszentmarton
50

Szendro
280

Satoraljaujhely
3,600

Tiszabezded
50

Encs
260

Sarospatak
800

Ricse
160

Barabas
86

Edeleny
250

Erdobenye
150

Cigand
180

Tornyospalca
90

Tiszaszalka
65

Szikszo
900

Mad
250

Ibrany
200

Patroha
130

Kisvarda
2,500

Tarpa
250

River Tisza

Szerencs
800

Tokaj
380

Rakamaz
160

Nagyhalasz
220

Vasarosnameny
440

Szatmarcseke
85

Miskolc
13,500

Tarcal
260

Tiszaeszlar

Demecser
300

Nyirkarasz
130

Taktaharkany
65

Tiszalok
350

Kemecse
50

Baktaloranthaza
200

Fehergyarmat
550

Onod
150

Tiszavasvari
620

Niregyhaza
3,500

Or
50

Mateszalka
1,400

Porcsalma
200

Polgar
450

Nagykallo
750

Hodasz
150

Nagyecsed
600

Csenger
400

Mezocsat
407

Hajdunanas
750

Nyirbogat
300

Nyirbator
1,400

Hajdudorog
250

Ujfeherto
400

Balkany
300

Fabianhaza
75

Hajduboszormeny
600

Hajduhadhaz
250

Nyiradony
200

Nyirbeltek
100

© Martin Gilbert 1982

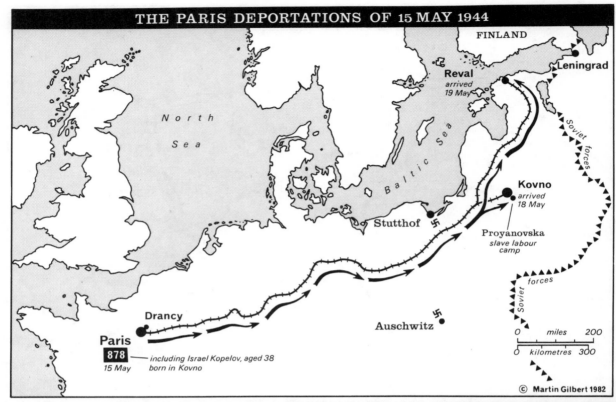

THE PARIS DEPORTATIONS OF 15 MAY 1944

FINLAND

Leningrad

Reval
arrived
19 May

Kovno
arrived
18 May

Soviet forces

North
Sea

Baltic Sea

Stutthof

Proyanovska
slave labour
camp

Soviet
forces

Auschwitz

Drancy

Paris

878
15 May
including Israel Kopelov, aged 38
born in Kovno

| 0 | miles | 200 |
| 0 | kilometres | 300 |

© Martin Gilbert 1982

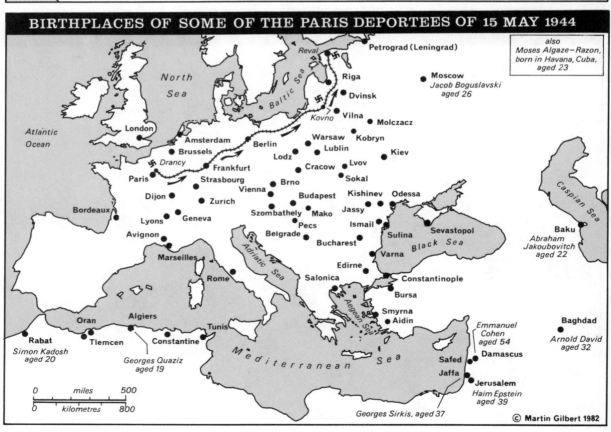

BIRTHPLACES OF SOME OF THE PARIS DEPORTEES OF 15 MAY 1944

also
Moses Algaze–Razon,
born in Havana, Cuba,
aged 23

Reval

Petrograd (Leningrad)

North
Sea

Riga

Baltic Sea

Moscow
Jacob Boguslavski
aged 26

Dvinsk

Kovno

Vilna

Molczacz

Atlantic
Ocean

London

Amsterdam

Berlin

Warsaw

Kobryn

Kiev

Brussels

Lodz

Lublin

Drancy

Paris

Frankfurt

Cracow

Lvov

Strasbourg

Sokal

Dijon

Vienna

Brno

Zurich

Budapest

Kishinev

Odessa

Caspian
Sea

Bordeaux

Szombathely

Mako

Jassy

Lyons

Geneva

Pecs

Ismail

Sulina

Sevastopol

Baku
Abraham
Jakoubovitch
aged 22

Avignon

Belgrade

Bucharest

Varna

Black Sea

Adriatic Sea

Marseilles

Rome

Edirne

Constantinople

Salonica

Bursa

Smyrna
Aidin

Baghdad
Arnold David
aged 32

Aegean Sea

Oran

Algiers

Tunis

Emmanuel
Cohen
aged 54

Damascus

Rabat
Simon Kadosh
aged 20

Tlemcen

Constantine

Georges Quaziz
aged 19

Mediterranean Sea

Safed

Jaffa

Jerusalem
Haim Epstein
aged 39

Georges Sirkis, aged 37

| 0 | miles | 500 |
| 0 | kilometres | 800 |

© Martin Gilbert 1982

Map 245

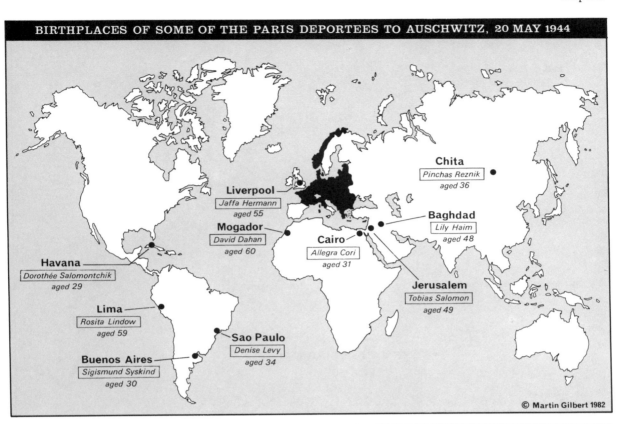

BIRTHPLACES OF SOME OF THE PARIS DEPORTEES TO AUSCHWITZ, 20 MAY 1944

Chita
Pinchas Reznik
aged 36

Liverpool
Jaffa Hermann
aged 55

Baghdad
Lily Haim
aged 48

Mogador
David Dahan
aged 60

Cairo
Allegra Cori
aged 31

Havana
Dorothée Salomontchik
aged 29

Jerusalem
Tobias Salomon
aged 49

Lima
Rosita Lindow
aged 59

Sao Paulo
Denise Levy
aged 34

Buenos Aires
Sigismund Syskind
aged 30

© Martin Gilbert 1982

On the very day that the first deportations took place from Hungary to Auschwitz, a train left Paris with 878 Jews locked into its 15 cattle trucks. All were men. Their destination was not Auschwitz, but Kovno.

After three days and three nights, on 18 May 1944 they reached their destination, and were sent to the Proyanovska slave labour camp. There, 160 of them were shot and the rest evacuated with other Jews from Kovno six weeks later *(page 200)*.

Nearly 260 of the deportees had been sent on to Reval. Six days after their arrival, 60 were taken for work but never seen again. The rest worked on airfield repairs, 60 being taken to a nearby forest and shot on July 14. On August 14 a hundred of the sick were sent to an 'unknown destination'. Four days later the 34 survivors were evacuated to Stutthof *(page 206)*: 15 survived the war.

The lower map *(opposite)* shows some of the birthplaces of the May 15 deportees; the map above shows the birthplaces of 10 of the deportees in the train sent from Paris to Auschwitz five days later. Like several thousand of those murdered at Auschwitz, they had emigrated to western Europe between the wars. The photograph is of a Jew at the moment of departure from Paris.

Map 246

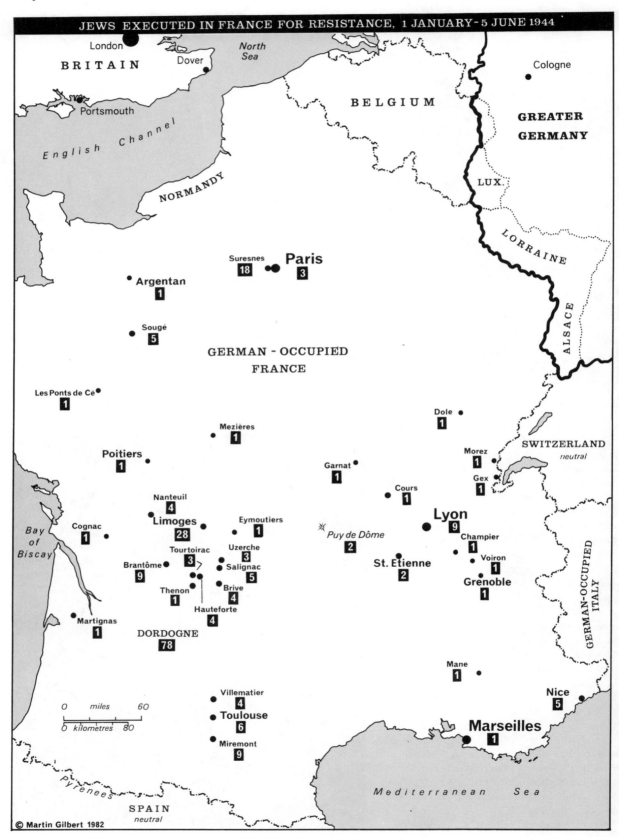

JEWS EXECUTED IN FRANCE FOR RESISTANCE, 1 JANUARY–5 JUNE 1944

London

Dover

North Sea

BRITAIN

Portsmouth

English Channel

NORMANDY

BELGIUM

Cologne

GREATER GERMANY

LUX.

LORRAINE

ALSACE

Suresnes
18

Paris
3

Argentan
1

Sougé
5

GERMAN - OCCUPIED
FRANCE

Les Ponts de Cé
1

Mezières
1

Dole
1

SWITZERLAND
neutral

Poitiers
1

Garnat
1

Morez
1

Gex
1

Nanteuil
4

Limoges
28

Eymoutiers
1

Cours
1

Lyon
9

Champier
1

Cognac
1

Bay of Biscay

Tourtoirac
3

Uzerche
3

Salignac
5

Puy de Dôme
2

St. Etienne
2

Voiron

Grenoble
1

GERMAN-OCCUPIED ITALY

Brantôme
9

Thenon
1

Brive
4

Hauteforte
4

Martignas
1

DORDOGNE
78

Mane
1

Villematier
4

Nice
5

Toulouse
6

Miremont
9

Marseilles
1

Mediterranean Sea

0   miles   60
0   kilometres   80

Pyrenees

SPAIN
neutral

© Martin Gilbert 1982

Map 247

SOME BIRTHPLACES

North Sea · Baltic Sea · Riga · Vilna · London · Hamburg · Schneidemuhl · Berlin · Warsaw · Poznan · Antwerp · Dortmund · Lodz · Lublin · Auschwitz · Saarlouis · Tarnow · Lvov · Paris · Strasbourg · Vienna · Munich · Lyon · Lausanne · Budapest · Grenoble · Trieste · Adriatic Sea · Salonica · Mediterranean Sea · Algiers · Tunis · © Martin Gilbert 1982

In the six months before the Allied landings in Normandy, more than 250 Jews had been executed in France for resistance and acts of sabotage. The place of execution of 229 of them is shown here *(opposite)*. More than half of them had come to France as immigrants, or as refugees, in the decade before the Second World War, when France offered both work and haven.

Among the 28 Jews executed at Limoges was the 67-year-old Victor Rubinstein, who had been born in New York. Nineteen of those executed had been born in Warsaw, eight in Budapest, five in Berlin, five in Vienna and three in Algiers.

One of the six Jews executed in Toulouse, Mandel Langer, had been born in Auschwitz in 1903. Haim Matem had been born in Jerusalem in 1898 when it formed part of the Ottoman Empire.

The map on the left shows some of their other birthplaces.

The photograph shows a Gestapo firing squad in France executing a Jewish member of the Resistance.

Map 248

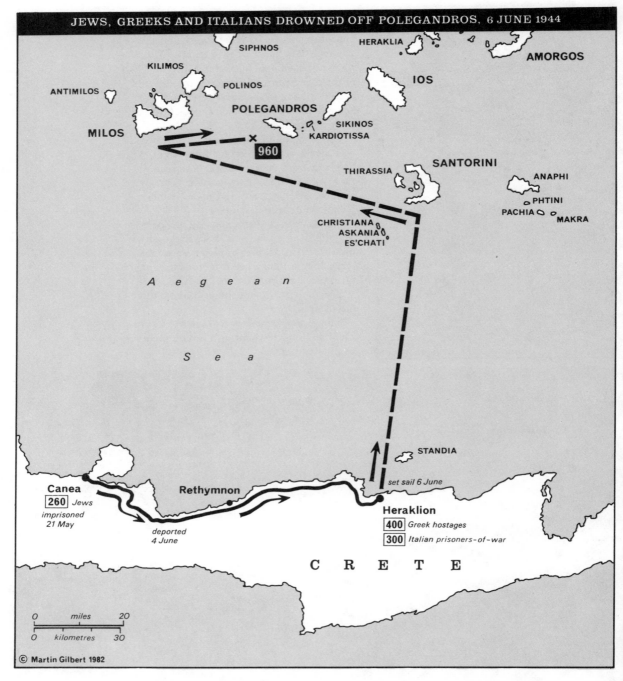

JEWS, GREEKS AND ITALIANS DROWNED OFF POLEGANDROS, 6 JUNE 1944

Jews had lived on Crete since Roman times. Often oppressed, in AD 440 they put their faith in a pseudo-Messiah, who offered to lead them 'dry shod' through the sea to the Promised Land. Hundreds were drowned.

On 21 May 1944 the Gestapo imprisoned all 260 Jews of Canea, and the five families of Rethymnon. On June 4 they were all deported to Heraklion, and two days later, put on board ship and sent across the Aegean Sea towards the island of Santorini.

Deported with the Jews were 400 Greek civilians, who had been seized as hostages, and 300 Italian prisoners-of-war, who for more than four years had been Germany's allies. All were taken 120 miles across the sea, where the ship was deliberately sunk, and all on board were drowned.

Only 7 Cretan Jews managed to survive the war, in hiding.

THE JEWS OF ZANTE SAVED

CEPHALONIA

Cape Skinari

Volimai

Kastastarion

Zante

ZANTE

Mouzaki

Kiliomenon

Kerion

Ionian Sea

Cape Marathia

0   miles   10
0   kms   15

© Martin Gilbert 1982

CORFU JEWS DEPORTED, 14 JUNE 1944

GREATER GERMANY

Auschwitz

Soviet forces

EASTERN GALICIA

Zilina

SLOVAKIA

Budapest

HUNGARY

0   miles   100
0   kilometres   150

Belgrade

SERBIA

Nis

MACEDONIA

Skopje

Adriatic Sea

Allied forces

ITALY

ALBANIA

G R E E C E

Salonica

Aegean Sea

CORFU
1,800

Larissa

ZANTE
257

Athens

Ionian Sea

CRETE

© Martin Gilbert 1982

Despite the presence of Allied forces in southern Italy, and the Soviet advance into Eastern Galicia, the SS still sought out Jews to deport to Auschwitz. One of the areas of their search was the islands of the Ionian Sea, among them Zante, and Corfu, then only 50 miles from the Allied forces in south Italy.

Jews had lived on Corfu (right) since the thirteenth century. During the seige of the island by the Turks in 1716, the Jews had distinguished themselves in defence of the island. During the Italian occupation, from April 1941 to September 1943, there had been no serious hardship, nor did the German occupation on 27 September 1943 lead to any immediate persecution. But on 6 June 1944 all 1,800 Jews were seized by the Gestapo, and eight days later they were deported to what they were told would be 'resettlement' in Poland. The women went overland to Larissa, the men by sea. While at sea they were given nothing to eat or drink and several died. On June 20 all were sent northwards by train, reaching Auschwitz nine days later: 1,600 were sent at once to the gas chamber, and 200 to forced labour.

On Zante (above) both Archbishop Chrysostomos and Lukos Karrer, the mayor, refused to obey the Gestapo order that all 257 Jews on the island should be assembled at the quayside to board the boat from Corfu. 'If the deportation order is carried out', the Archbishop declared, 'I will join the Jews and share their fate.' All 195 able-bodied Jews were sent to safety in remote villages. Sixty old people and children were seized by the Gestapo and taken to the quayside to await the Corfu boat: but the boat was already so overcrowded that it did not stop.

Map 251

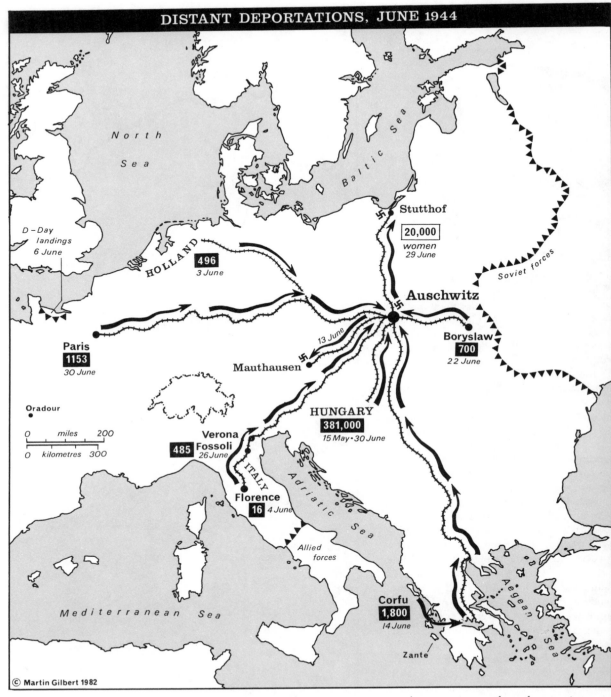

DISTANT DEPORTATIONS, JUNE 1944

As Soviet forces drew nearer and nearer to Auschwitz, and Allied forces landed on the Normandy beaches on 6 June 1944, the deportations to Auschwitz continued. Trains reached Auschwitz throughout June (*above*) from Paris, Italy, Holland, the Eastern Galician town of Boryslaw and from Corfu, as well as from the massive continuing deportations from Hungary (*pages 196-201*).

At the same time as these deportations into Auschwitz, the first evacuation of Jews away from Auschwitz had begun, when prisoners in the slave labour camps drawing their labour force from Birkenau were sent out by train, the men westwards to Mauthausen, the women northwards to Stutthof.

The concentration camp at Stutthof had

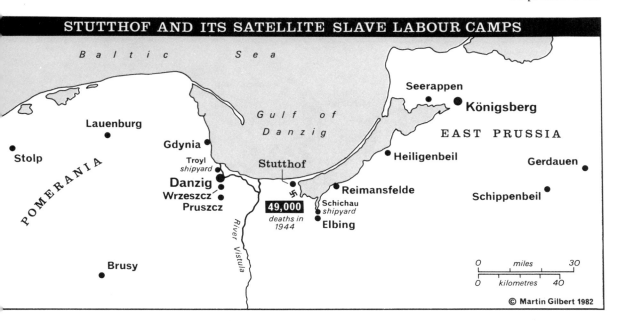

STUTTHOF AND ITS SATELLITE SLAVE LABOUR CAMPS

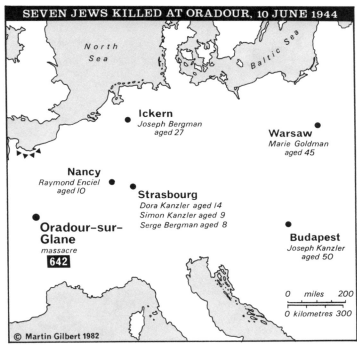

SEVEN JEWS KILLED AT ORADOUR, 10 JUNE 1944

been set up in September 1939 (*page 34*). But it was not until August 1943 that any large number of Jews, several hundred survivors of the Bialystok ghetto revolt, were deported there (*page 164*).

It was in the area around Stutthof that the Germans had begun, in the spring of 1944, to set up more than 60 new labour camps, to replace those which had already been overrun by the Soviet forces. The map above shows the principal towns and camps to which prisoners were sent from Stutthof throughout the summer and autumn of 1944 (*pages 211*).

In the labour camps around Stutthof, conditions were barbaric: of 100 Jewish girls in the slave labour camp at Gerdauen, only three survived the war.

In Stutthof itself, tens of thousands of prisoners died of dysentery, typhus and starvation. Others were brutally clubbed to death while working in the nearby forests, or sadistically drowned in mud. Many were killed by means of phenol injections, and their bodies then burned in the crematorium, in specially designed 'high capacity' ovens.

Altogether more than 52,000 Jews passed through Stutthof, of whom at least 30,000 were women. Only about 3,000 survived the brutal treatment.

In France, four days after the Allied landings, the Germans killed more than 600 French villagers at Oradour-sur-Glane (*right*). The women and children were burned alive in the church, and the men were machine-gunned, as a reprisal against

the killing in another village of an SS army commander by a resistance sniper. Seven of the 642 men, women and children killed at Oradour were Jews: refugees who had earlier been able to escape deportation to Auschwitz by hiding among the friendly villagers. Now they became the victims of another repeated feature of Nazi tyranny, reprisals against civilians. Among the seven were Joseph Kanzler, born in Budapest, and his two children, born in Strasbourg.

Map 254

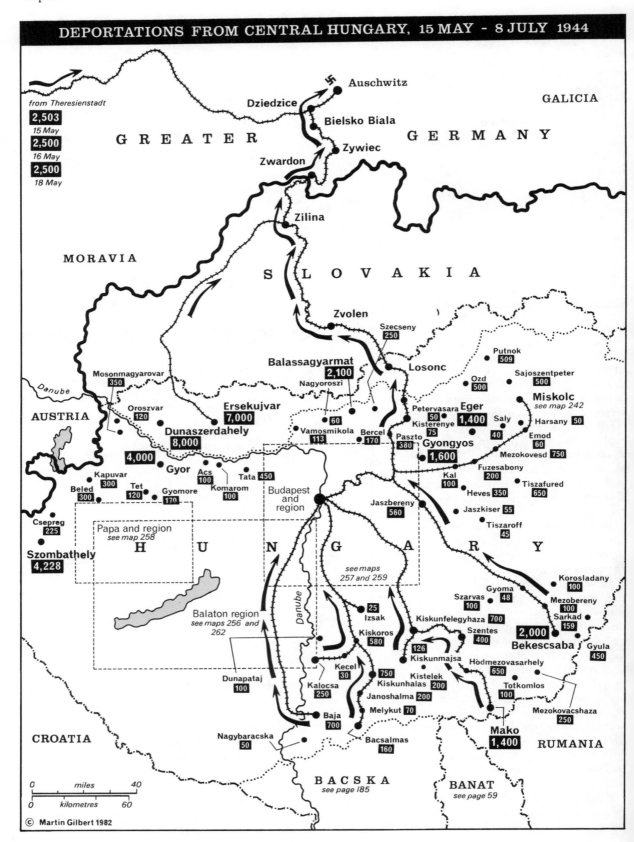

DEPORTATIONS FROM CENTRAL HUNGARY, 15 MAY - 8 JULY 1944

Auschwitz

Dziedzice

Bielsko Biala

Zywiec

Zwardon

GALICIA

GREATER   GERMANY

from Theresienstadt

2,503
15 May
2,500
16 May
2,500
18 May

MORAVIA

Zilina

S L O V A K I A

Zvolen

Szecseny **250**

Balassagyarmat **2,100**

Losonc

Putnok **509**

Sajoszentpeter **500**

Ozd **500**

Miskolc
see map 242

Mosonmagyarovar **350**

Nagyoroszi **60**

Petervasara **50**

Eger **1,400**

Saly **40**

Harsany **50**

Oroszvar **120**

Vamosmikola **113**

Bercel **170**

Kisterenye **75**

Emod **60**

Ersekujvar **7,000**

Paszto **380**

Gyongyos **1,600**

Mezokovesd **750**

AUSTRIA

Danube

Dunaszerdahely **8,000**

4,000   Gyor

 Acs **100**

Tata **450**

Kal **100**

Fuzesabony **200**

Heves **350**

Tiszafured **650**

Kapuvar **300**

Tet **120**

Komarom **100**

Budapest
and
region

Jaszbereny **560**

Jaszkiser **55**

Beled **300**

Gyomore **170**

Tiszaroff **45**

Csepreg **225**

HU

N

G

A

R

Y

Korosladany **100**

Papa and region
see map 258

Szombathely **4,228**

see maps 257 and 259

Gyoma **48**

Mezobereny **100**

Balaton region
see maps 256 and 262

Danube

Izsak **25**

Szarvas **100**

Sarkad **159**

Kiskunfelegyhaza **700**

Bekescsaba **2,000**

Gyula **450**

Kiskoros **580**

Szentes **400**

Kecel **30**

126

Kiskunmajsa

Hodmezovasarhely **650**

Dunapataj **100**

Kalocsa **250**

750

Kiskunhalas

Kistelek **200**

Totkomlos **100**

Janoshalma **200**

Mako **1,400**

Melykut **70**

Baja **700**

Mezokovacshaza **250**

CROATIA

Nagybaracska **50**

Bacsalmas **160**

RUMANIA

B A C S K A
see page 185

B A N A T
see page 59

0   miles   40

0   kilometres   60

© **Martin Gilbert 1982**

Map 255

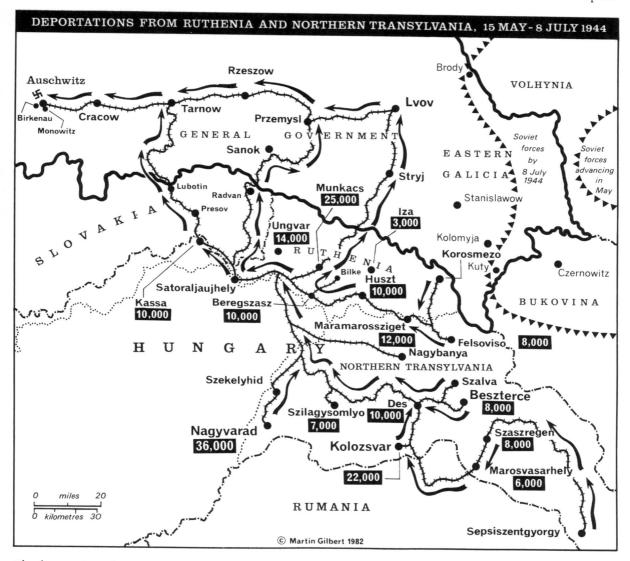

DEPORTATIONS FROM RUTHENIA AND NORTHERN TRANSYLVANIA, 15 MAY-8 JULY 1944

The deportation of Hungarian Jews to Auschwitz had begun on 15 May 1944 from eastern Hungary (*page 187*) and central Hungary (*opposite*). Also starting on May 15, Jews were deported from two of the areas annexed in 1938 and 1940, Ruthenia and northern Transylvania (*above*), where the number of victims exceeded 250,000 in just under eight weeks. The maps show some of these deaths and give an indication of the speed, scale and effectiveness of the Nazi plan; a plan put into operation more than four and a half years after the German invasion of Poland.

Each deportation train bore the deceptive inscription 'German worker-resettlers'. Up to 100 people were forced into each wagon. Like the earlier French, Dutch, Belgian and Greek deportees, they were allowed only a single bucket of water and a single waste bucket to each wagon. Hundreds died during the journey. Many committed suicide or were driven insane by confinement and fear. Others were killed or robbed whenever the train had to stop for traffic control.

The deportations were still in mid course on 'D-Day' when the forces of the Western allies landed on the Normandy beaches (*page 194*). For more than two years the Nazi authorities, and even Hitler himself, had failed to persuade the Hungarian Government, or the Hungarian Regent, Admiral Horthy, to agree to these deportations. Now, in control of Hungary, the Germans hastened to destroy this last unmolested mass of Jewry before Soviet forces, steadily advancing towards Eastern Galicia, entered eastern Hungary.

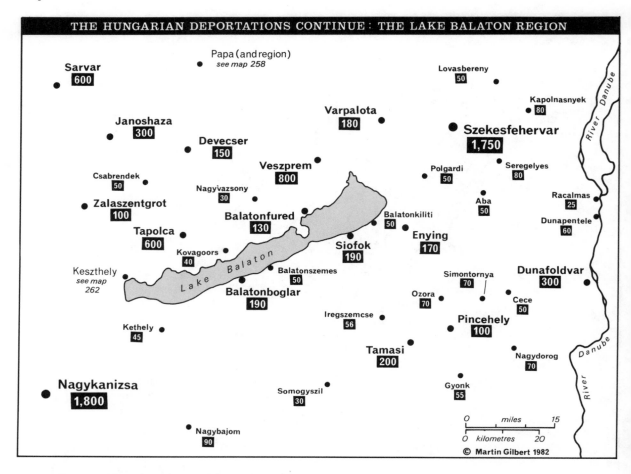

THE HUNGARIAN DEPORTATIONS CONTINUE : THE LAKE BALATON REGION

Sarvar **600**

Papa (and region) *see map 258*

Lovasbereny **50**

Kapolnasnyek **80**

Janoshaza **300**

Varpalota **180**

Szekesfehervar **1,750**

Devecser **150**

Csabrendek **50**

Veszprem **800**

Polgardi **50**

Seregelyes **80**

Nagyvazsony **30**

Racalmas **25**

Zalaszentgrot **100**

Aba **50**

Tapolca **600**

Balatonfured **130**

Dunapentele **60**

Balatonkiliti **50**

Enying **170**

Kovagoors **40**

Siofok **190**

Dunafoldvar **300**

Keszthely *see map 262*

Lake Balaton

Balatonszemes **50**

Balatonboglar **190**

Simontornya **70**

Cece **50**

Ozora **70**

Pincehely **100**

Kethely **45**

Iregszemcse **56**

Tamasi **200**

Nagydorog **70**

Nagykanizsa **1,800**

Somogyszil **30**

Gyonk **55**

Nagybajom **90**

River Danube

Danube River

0 miles 15
0 kilometres 20

© Martin Gilbert 1982

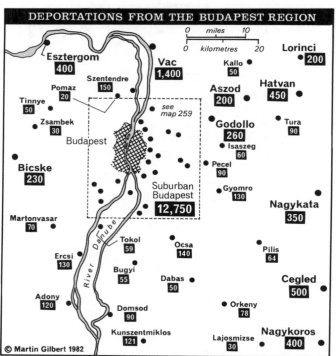

DEPORTATIONS FROM THE BUDAPEST REGION

0 miles 10
0 kilometres 20

Esztergom **400**

Vac **1,400**

Lorinci **200**

Szentendre **150**

Kallo **50**

Hatvan **450**

Pomaz **20**

Aszod **200**

Tinnye **50**

see map 259

Tura **90**

Zsambek **30**

Godollo **260**

Budapest

Isaszeg **60**

Bicske **230**

Pecel **90**

Gyomro **130**

Nagykata **350**

Martonvasar **70**

Suburban Budapest **12,750**

Tokol **59**

Ocsa **140**

Pilis **64**

Ercsi **130**

Bugyi **55**

Dabas **50**

Cegled **500**

Adony **120**

Domsod **90**

Orkeny **78**

Nagykoros **400**

Kunszentmiklos **121**

Lajosmizse **30**

River Danube

© Martin Gilbert 1982

The Hungarian deportations to Auschwitz continued throughout May and June: and were carried out systematically from region to region. Towards the end of June, and in the first week of July, the deportations were focused on the regions of Lake Balaton (*above*), Budapest (*left*), and the outer suburbs of Budapest (*opposite, below*). Jews from even the smallest of communities were seized (*opposite, above*), the Nazi aim being to deport every Hungarian Jew to Auschwitz. To this end, Adolf Eichmann personally supervised the deportations from an office in Budapest.

On reaching Auschwitz, only a few from each train, sometimes only a dozen men out of as many as 4,000 deportees, were kept alive for use as slave labourers; the vast majority was taken straight to the gas chambers, and murdered. The corpses were cremated.

The map opposite (*above*) shows the Jewish communities and families from the Papa region, who were deported to Auschwitz on 4 July 1944 and murdered there. In 1942 many of the young Jews of Papa had been sent to forced labour

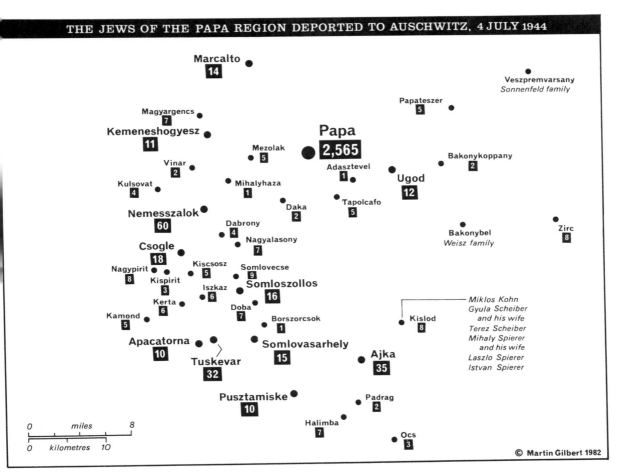

THE JEWS OF THE PAPA REGION DEPORTED TO AUSCHWITZ, 4 JULY 1944

Marcalto 14

Veszpremvarsany
Sonnenfeld family

Magyargencs 7

Papateszer 5

Kemeneshogyesz 11

Papa 2,565

Bakonykoppany 2

Vinar 2

Mezolak 5

Adasztevel 1

Ugod 12

Kulsovat 4

Mihalyhaza 1

Daka 2

Tapolcafo 5

Nemesszalok 60

Dabrony 4

Nagyalasony 7

Bakonybel
Weisz family

Zirc 8

Csogle 18

Kiscsosz 5

Somlovecse 9

Nagypirit 8

Kispirit 3

Iszkaz 6

Somloszollos 16

Kerta 6

Doba 7

Miklos Kohn
Gyula Scheiber
and his wife
Terez Scheiber
Mihaly Spierer
and his wife
Laszlo Spierer
Istvan Spierer

Kamond 5

Borszorcsok 1

Kislod 8

Apacatorna 10

Somlovasarhely 15

Ajka 35

Tuskevar 32

Pusztamiske 10

Padrag 2

Halimba 7

Ocs 3

0 miles 8
0 kilometres 10

© Martin Gilbert 1982

on the Russian front (*page 184*). On 24 May 1944 the remaining 2,565 Jews of the town, and more than 200 Jews from nearby villages, had been confined to a ghetto. A few weeks later they were moved to a concentration camp set up in a factory in the town, in readiness for deportation.

As news of the deportations reached the West, together with the first accounts, by escapees, of the working of the gas chambers at Auschwitz, and of the gassing of Jews from the first trains from Hungary, protests poured in to Budapest: from the Allied leaders, from the King of neutral Sweden, from the President of the International Red Cross, and from the Vatican. These protests reached a climax in the first days of July, as the Papa Jews were about to be deported. Tragically, for them, the protests came too late. Even as the Hungarian Government was deciding to order a halt to the deportations, the 2,800 Jews of Papa were being made ready to be sent to Auschwitz; less than 300 survived. Among those who perished was their rabbi, J. Haberfeld.

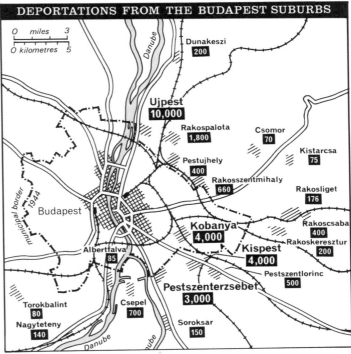

DEPORTATIONS FROM THE BUDAPEST SUBURBS

0 miles 3
0 kilometres 5

Dunakeszi 200

Ujpest 10,000

Rakospalota 1,800

Csomor 70

Pestujhely 400

Kistarcsa 75

Rakosszentmihaly 660

Rakosliget 176

Budapest

Kobanya 4,000

Rakoscsaba 400

Albertfalva 85

Kispest 4,000

Rakoskeresztur 200

Pestszentlorinc 500

Pestszenterzsebet 3,000

Torokbalint 80

Csepel 700

Soroksar 150

Nagyteteny 140

municipal border 1944

Danube

199

Map 260

DEPORTATION, MASS MURDER AND REVOLT, JULY 1944

As Soviet forces approached Shauliai, Kovno, Vilna and Lublin during the first week of July, Jewish partisans were active behind the lines on all these fronts.

On July 2 the SS took the last 3,000 Jews of Vilna, labourers in a factory, and murdered them at Ponary (*above*). Thousands were also killed at Shauliai and Kovno, and thousands more evacuated to Stutthof and Dachau, as the Soviet forces drew near. At Ostrowiec, as the SS sent 2,000 slave labourers towards Auschwitz, some succeeded in breaking out and escaping.

On 4 July 1944 the Jews of Papa (*page 199*) were deported to Auschwitz (*above*). In all, during that first week of July, 50,000 more Hungarian Jews were sent to their deaths (*opposite, above*). Many of these deportees

lived in small communities to the south of Lake Balaton (*opposite, below*). Then, on July 8 the Hungarian Government bowed to the growing international pressure, and ordered the deportations to be stopped. The Germans gave way. More than 437,402 Hungarian Jews had been deported; 300,000 were still alive on July 8, most of them in Budapest, where the deportations had been about to begin, having already reached the suburbs (*page 199*).

Majdanek was entered by Soviet forces on July 23. The SS now accelerated the marches and evacuations away from Auschwitz (*above*), while from France and Belgium (*opposite, above*), as well as from Radom, the last few trains were still being sent into Auschwitz. Not only the final Hungarian

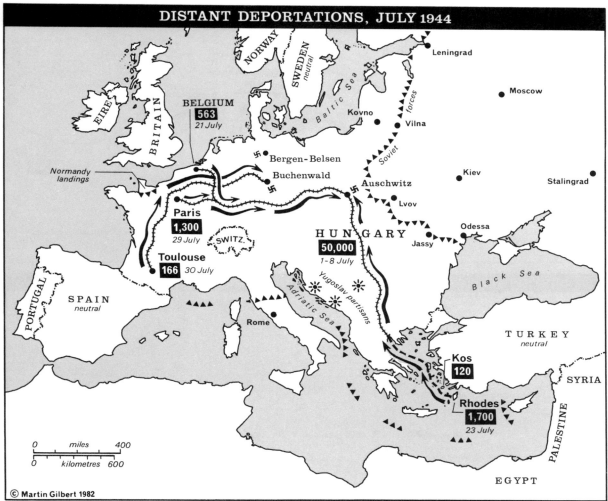

DISTANT DEPORTATIONS, JULY 1944

NORWAY

SWEDEN
neutral

Leningrad

Moscow

Baltic Sea

Kovno

Vilna

EIRE

BRITAIN

BELGIUM
563
21 July

Soviet forces

Bergen-Belsen

Buchenwald

Auschwitz

Kiev

Stalingrad

Normandy landings

Paris
1,300
29 July

SWITZ.

Lvov

Odessa

H U N G A R Y
50,000
1-8 July

Jassy

Black Sea

Toulouse
166
30 July

PORTUGAL

SPAIN
neutral

Adriatic Sea

Yugoslav partisans

Rome

Kos
120

TURKEY
neutral

SYRIA

Rhodes
1,700
23 July

PALESTINE

miles		400
0		
0	kilometres	600

EGYPT

© Martin Gilbert 1982

deportees, but Jews from as far away as the islands of Kos and Rhodes were also still on their way to the gas chambers as more and more 'death marches' away from the camp were ordered, and hundreds of Jews were killed as men and women, weakened by hunger and ill-treatment, were marched westwards towards new labour camps.

In Yugoslavia, Jews fought among partisan units which were liberating larger and larger areas of the Balkans.

It was during these evacuations that Dachau, and soon also Bergen-Belsen, hitherto camps primarily for non-Jewish political prisoners, became camps into which tens of thousands of Jews were evacuated, mostly from the labour camp regions of the east, and in which, while not systematically murdered as in the eastern death camps, they perished in their hundreds from the brutality of the guards, and from starvation and disease.

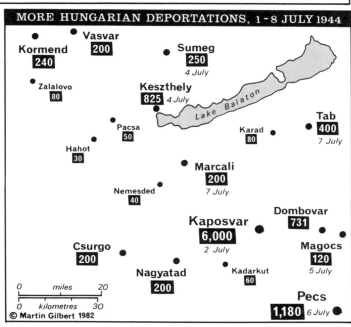

MORE HUNGARIAN DEPORTATIONS, 1-8 JULY 1944

Vasvar
200

Kormend
240

Sumeg
250
4 July

Zalalovo
80

Keszthely
825 *4 July*

Lake Balaton

Tab
400
7 July

Pacsa
50

Karad
80

Hahot
30

Marcali
200
7 July

Nemesded
40

Kaposvar
6,000
2 July

Dombovar
731

Csurgo
200

Nagyatad
200

Kadarkut
60

Magocs
120
5 July

Pecs
1,180 *6 July*

miles		20
0		
0	kilometres	30

© Martin Gilbert 1982

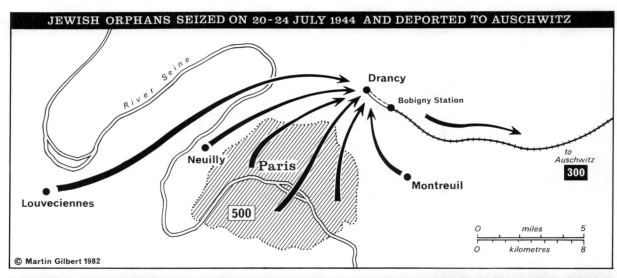

JEWISH ORPHANS SEIZED ON 20-24 JULY 1944 AND DEPORTED TO AUSCHWITZ

River Seine

Drancy

Bobigny Station

Neuilly

Paris

to Auschwitz

300

Louveciennes

Montreuil

500

0   miles   5

0   kilometres   8

© Martin Gilbert 1982

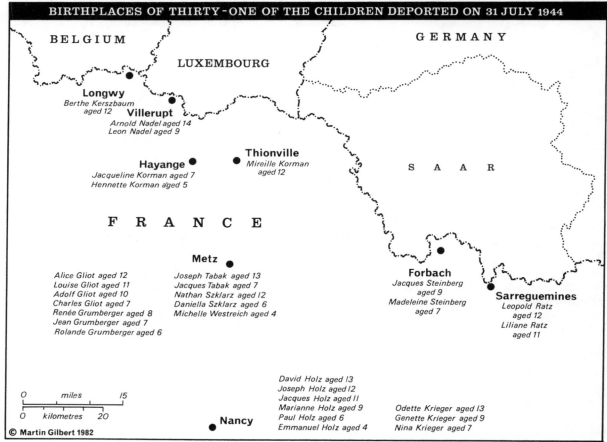

BIRTHPLACES OF THIRTY-ONE OF THE CHILDREN DEPORTED ON 31 JULY 1944

BELGIUM

LUXEMBOURG

GERMANY

Longwy
Berthe Kerszbaum aged 12

Villerupt
Arnold Nadel aged 14
Leon Nadel aged 9

Hayange
Jacqueline Korman aged 7
Hennette Korman aged 5

Thionville
Mireille Korman aged 12

S A A R

F R A N C E

Metz

Alice Gliot aged 12
Louise Gliot aged 11
Adolf Gliot aged 10
Charles Gliot aged 7
Renée Grumberger aged 8
Jean Grumberger aged 7
Rolande Grumberger aged 6

Joseph Tabak aged 13
Jacques Tabak aged 7
Nathan Szklarz aged 12
Daniella Szklarz aged 6
Michelle Westreich aged 4

Forbach
Jacques Steinberg aged 9
Madeleine Steinberg aged 7

Sarreguemines
Leopold Ratz aged 12
Liliane Ratz aged 11

0   miles   15

0   kilometres   20

© Martin Gilbert 1982

Nancy

David Holz aged 13
Joseph Holz aged 12
Jacques Holz aged 11
Marianne Holz aged 9
Paul Holz aged 6
Emmanuel Holz aged 4

Odette Krieger aged 13
Genette Krieger aged 9
Nina Krieger aged 7

On 20 July 1944, while the Allies advanced towards Paris, the SS ordered the arrest of Jewish orphans in the Paris region. Within four days, 500 orphans had been seized, some 300 of whom were among a total of 1,300 Jews deported from Drancy to Auschwitz on 31 July 1944.

The map above, and the maps opposite, show the birthplaces and ages of 67 of these 1,300 deportees. On reaching Auschwitz, 800 of them were gassed, including all the children. Of the 500 adults selected for work in nearby labour camps, 350 survived the last ten months of the war.

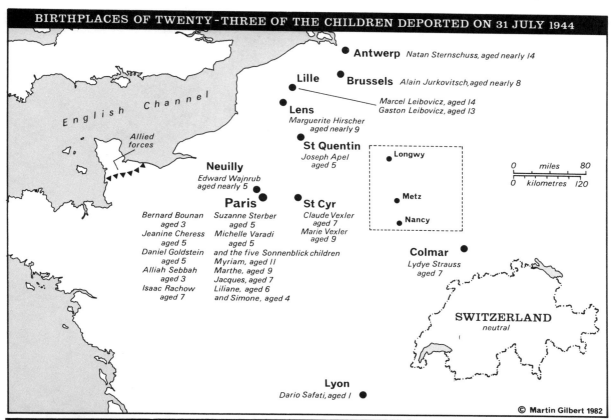

BIRTHPLACES OF TWENTY-THREE OF THE CHILDREN DEPORTED ON 31 JULY 1944

Antwerp Natan Sternschuss, aged nearly 14

Lille

Brussels Alain Jurkovitsch, aged nearly 8

Marcel Leibovicz, aged 14
Gaston Leibovicz, aged 13

Lens
Marguerite Hirscher
aged nearly 9

English Channel

Allied forces

St Quentin
Joseph Apel
aged 5

Longwy

Neuilly
Edward Wajnrub
aged nearly 5

Metz

Paris

St Cyr
Claude Vexler
aged 7
Marie Vexler
aged 9

Nancy

Bernard Bounan
aged 3
Jeanine Cheress
aged 5
Daniel Goldstein
aged 5
Alliah Sebbah
aged 3
Isaac Rachow
aged 7

Suzanne Sterber
aged 5
Michelle Varadi
aged 5
and the five Sonnenblick children
Myriam, aged 11
Marthe, aged 9
Jacques, aged 7
Liliane, aged 6
and Simone, aged 4

Colmar
Lydye Strauss
aged 7

0   miles   80
0   kilometres   120

SWITZERLAND
neutral

Lyon
Dario Safati, aged 1

© Martin Gilbert 1982

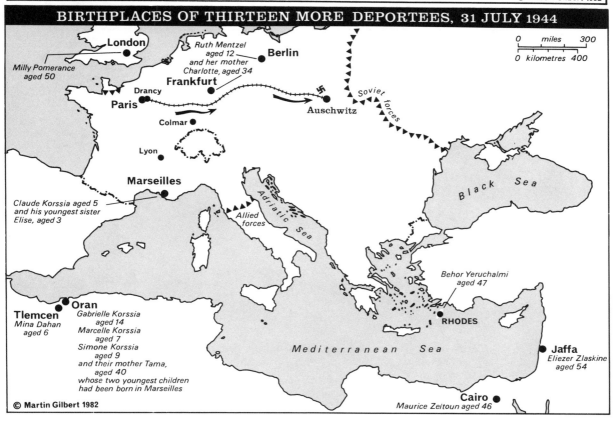

BIRTHPLACES OF THIRTEEN MORE DEPORTEES, 31 JULY 1944

London
Milly Pomerance
aged 50

Ruth Mentzel
aged 12
and her mother
Charlotte, aged 34

Berlin

Frankfurt

Drancy

Paris

Auschwitz

Soviet forces

Colmar

Lyon

0   miles   300
0   kilometres   400

Black   Sea

Marseilles

Claude Korssia aged 5
and his youngest sister
Elise, aged 3

Adriatic Sea

Allied forces

Behor Yeruchalmi
aged 47

Tlemcen
Mina Dahan
aged 6

Oran
Gabrielle Korssia
aged 14
Marcelle Korssia
aged 7
Simone Korssia
aged 9
and their mother Tama,
aged 40
whose two youngest children
had been born in Marseilles

RHODES

Mediterranean   Sea

Jaffa
Eliezer Zlaskine
aged 54

Cairo
Maurice Zeitoun aged 46

© Martin Gilbert 1982

THE ALLIED ADVANCE, 23 JUNE–25 AUGUST 1944

A LABOUR CAMP EVACUATION TO AUSCHWITZ, 22 JULY 1944

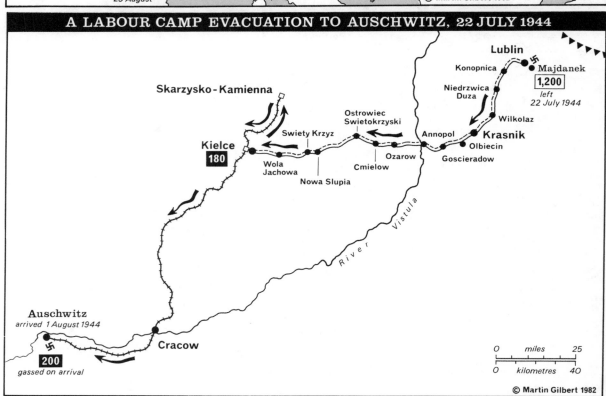

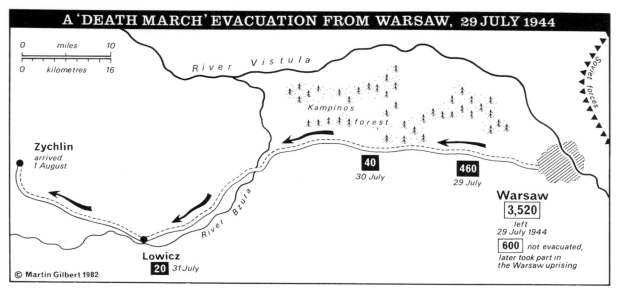

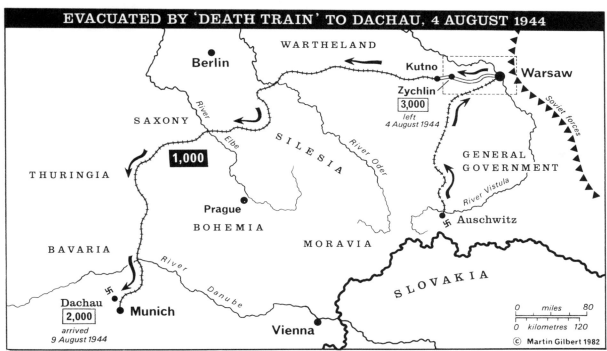

Between 23 June and 25 August 1944 both the Soviet and western Allied forces made considerable advances (*opposite, above*). As Bialystok, Lublin and Lvov were liberated, the Germans accelerated the evacuation of Jews away from the advancing Soviet forces.

As Russian troops approached Lublin, 1,200 Jews, many of them prisoners-of-war who had been captured in September 1939, were marched away on foot, westwards to Kielce, where 180 were killed. The survivors were then sent by train to Auschwitz, where

200 were gassed on arrival.

A similar death march and death train evacuation, during which more than 2,000 Jews died, started from Warsaw a week later (*above*). Those evacuated to Zychlin and then to Dachau were Jews who had been brought from Auschwitz to clear the rubble of the Warsaw ghetto. As this evacuation began, 50 of the slave labourers managed to escape into 'Aryan' Warsaw, and were to fight in the Warsaw uprising later that month (*page 206*).

205

Map 271

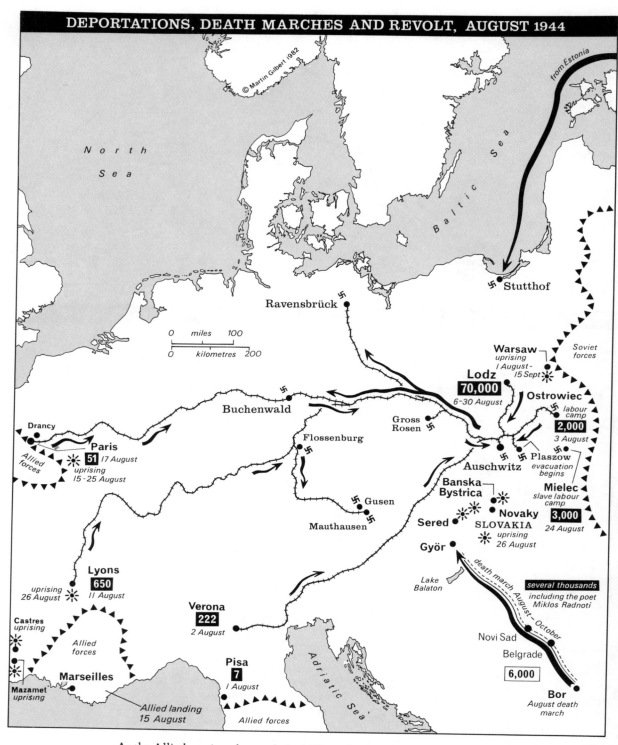

DEPORTATIONS, DEATH MARCHES AND REVOLT, AUGUST 1944

© Martin Gilbert 1982

North Sea

Baltic Sea

from Estonia

Stutthof

Ravensbrück

miles 0 — 100
kilometres 0 — 200

Warsaw
uprising 1 August – 15 Sept

Soviet forces

Lodz
70,000
6–30 August

Ostrowiec
labour camp
2,000
3 August

Drancy

Buchenwald

Gross Rosen

Paris
51 *17 August*
uprising 15–25 August

Allied forces

Flossenburg

Auschwitz

Plaszow
evacuation begins

Banska Bystrica

Mielec
slave labour camp
3,000
24 August

Gusen

Mauthausen

Sered

Novaky
SLOVAKIA
uprising 26 August

Lyons
650
II August
uprising 26 August

Györ

Lake Balaton

several thousands
including the poet Miklos Radnoti

Castres
uprising

Allied forces

Verona
222
2 August

death march August – October

Novi Sad

Belgrade
6,000

Mazamet
uprising

Marseilles

Pisa
7
I August

Adriatic Sea

Allied landing 15 August

Allied forces

Bor
August death march

As the Allied armies advanced, the killing of Jews continued (*above*), with deportations to Auschwitz from Paris, Lyons and Verona, as well as 70,000 sent to Auschwitz from Lodz, the last of the 'working' ghettos.

The evacuations away from Auschwitz

were also gaining in intensity: hundreds died in deportation trains to Ravensbrück and Flossenbürg, Güsen and Mauthausen.

In Pisa the Nazis murdered the Catholic philanthropist Pardo-Roques and six Jews he had sheltered. Hundreds more Jews died

Map 272

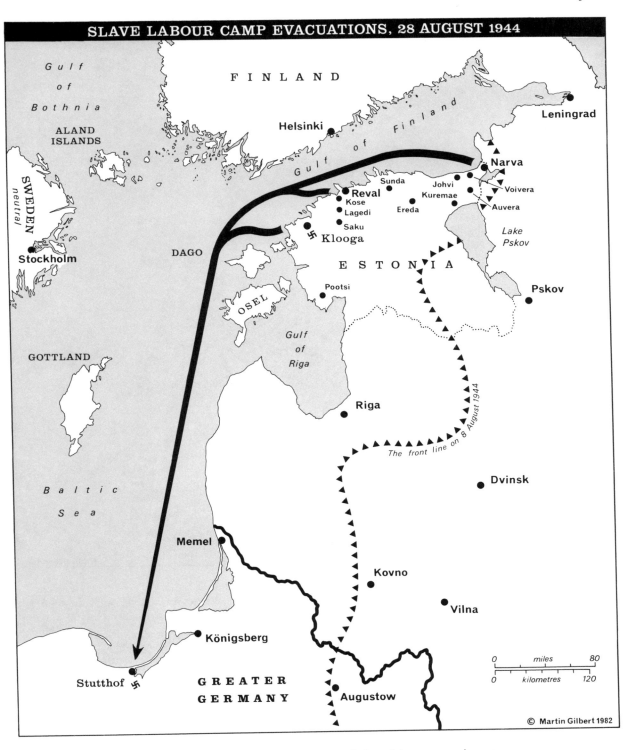

SLAVE LABOUR CAMP EVACUATIONS, 28 AUGUST 1944

Gulf of Bothnia

ALAND ISLANDS

FINLAND

Helsinki

Gulf of Finland

Leningrad

Narva

SWEDEN *neutral*

Sunda

Johvi

Voivera

Reval

Kose

Kuremae

Lagedi

Ereda

Auvera

Stockholm

Saku

Klooga

Lake Pskov

DAGO

E S T O N I A

OSEL

Pootsi

Pskov

Gulf of Riga

Riga

The front line on 8 August 1944

Dvinsk

Baltic Sea

GOTTLAND

Memel

Kovno

Vilna

Königsberg

| 0 | *miles* | 80 |
| 0 | *kilometres* | 120 |

Stutthof

GREATER GERMANY

Augustow

© Martin Gilbert 1982

when the slave labour camps in Estonia (*above*) were evacuated by sea.

During August 1944 Jewish units, and individual Jews, were active in partisan activity in France. In the Warsaw uprising about 1,000 Jews in hiding, and escaped or liberated Jewish slave labourers, took part, including a Jewish battle unit commanded by Shmuel Kenigswein. During the Slovak revolt, a Jewish battalion, as well as hundreds of individual Jews took part in the capture of three major towns.

Map 273

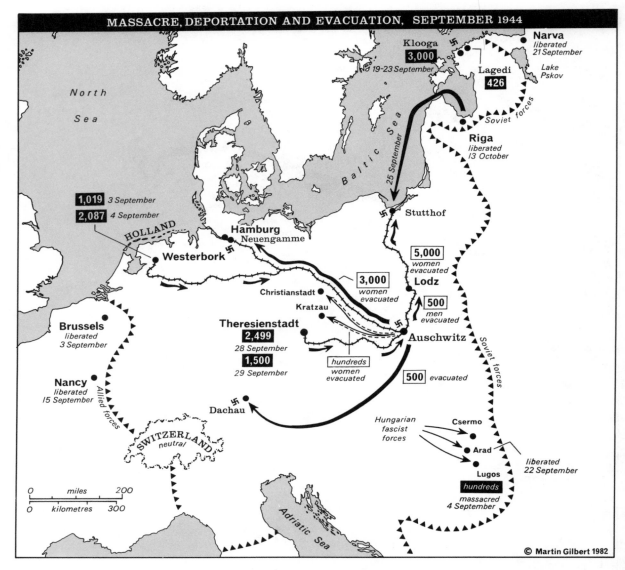

MASSACRE, DEPORTATION AND EVACUATION, SEPTEMBER 1944

Klooga
3,000
19-23 September

Narva
*liberated
21 September*

Lagedi
426

*Lake
Pskov*

Soviet forces

Riga
*liberated
13 October*

North
Sea

Baltic Sea

25 September

Stutthof

1,019 *3 September*
2,087 *4 September*

HOLLAND

Hamburg
Neuengamme

Westerbork

5,000
*women
evacuated*

3,000
*women
evacuated*

Lodz

Christianstadt

Kratzau

500
*men
evacuated*

Theresienstadt
2,499
28 September
1,500
29 September

Brussels
*liberated
3 September*

Auschwitz

*hundreds
women
evacuated*

500 *evacuated*

Soviet forces

Nancy
*liberated
15 September*

Allied forces

Dachau

SWITZERLAND
neutral

*Hungarian
fascist
forces*

Csermo

Arad

*liberated
22 September*

0   miles   200
0 kilometres 300

Lugos
hundreds
*massacred
4 September*

Adriatic Sea

© Martin Gilbert 1982

As Allied forces liberated city after city, the murder of Jews continued. During September 1944 four trains reached Auschwitz from Holland and Theresienstadt *(above)*. Almost all the deportees, including all the old people and children, were gassed.

It was on one of these trains from Holland that Anne Frank, a Jewish girl whose parents had brought her to Holland as a refugee from Germany before the war, was most probably deported to Auschwitz. She later died at Bergen-Belsen.

Also during September 5,000 more women were evacuated out of Auschwitz to Stutthof, and 3,000 to Neuengamme. The photograph shows Himmler at Stutthof.

As Soviet forces approached Klooga, almost all the surviving slave labourers were

slaughtered, among them 1,500 Jews from Vilna, 800 Soviet prisoners-of-war and 700 Estonian political prisoners. Only 85 inmates survived.

In the slave labour camp at Lagedi *(above)* all the Jewish prisoners, including women and babies, were killed only a few hours before the Soviet troops arrived. In northern Transylvania, as Hungarian fascist units seized control, hundreds more Jews were massacred.

Meanwhile, from the many slave labour camps of German-occupied Latvia *(opposite)*, tens of thousands of Jews, many of them already deportees from Vilna and Dvinsk *(page 169)*, were being evacuated by ship to the Stutthof concentration camp region, as Soviet forces cut off the Gulf of Riga.

Map 274

SLAVE LABOUR CAMP EVACUATIONS, 25 SEPTEMBER 1944

© Martin Gilbert 1982

Map 275

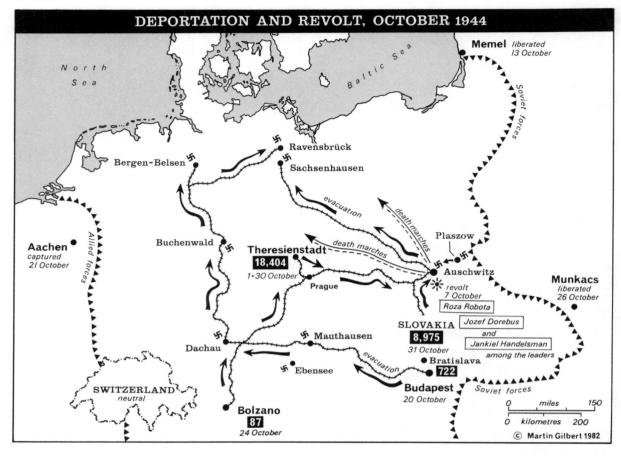

DEPORTATION AND REVOLT, OCTOBER 1944

North Sea

Baltic Sea

Memel *liberated 13 October*

Soviet forces

Ravensbrück
Bergen-Belsen
Sachsenhausen

evacuation

death marches

Plaszow

Aachen *captured 21 October*

Allied forces

Buchenwald

Theresienstadt
18,404
1·30 October

death marches

Auschwitz
☀ *revolt 7 October*

Munkacs *liberated 26 October*

Prague

Roza Robota

SLOVAKIA
8,975
31 October

Jozef Dorebus
and
Jankiel Handelsman
among the leaders

Dachau

Mauthausen

evacuation

Bratislava
722

Ebensee

evacuation

SWITZERLAND
neutral

Budapest
20 October

Soviet forces

0   *miles*   150
0   *kilometres*   200

Bolzano
87
24 October

© Martin Gilbert 1982

Death marches and death train evacuations took place from Auschwitz, and also from Budapest, throughout October 1944. At the same time, Jews from northern Italy and Theresienstadt continued to be sent to Auschwitz, as were more than 8,000 Jews fom Slovakia, deported as a German reprisal against the Slovak revolt *(page 206)*. Among those deported from Slovakia on October 28 was Tobias Jakobovits, author of a history of the Jews of Bohemia and a member of the staff of the Jewish Museum in Prague; he was sent to his death together with the rest of the museum staff.

In Auschwitz, recently arrived Polish, Hungarian and Greek Jews who were being forced to drag the bodies of those gassed from the gas chambers to the crematoria, having secretly managed to gather some explosives from four Jewish girls working in a nearby munitions factory, blew up one of the four crematoria on 7 October 1944. All those who took part in the revolt were subsequently killed, except for a single Jew, Isaac Venezia, from Salonica, who managed to get back into the main camp. In

the final evacuation of Auschwitz *(page 215)*, he was among those sent to Ebensee, where he died of starvation.

Throughout November 1944 every day saw further towns liberated or captured by the Allies. In the west the Americans were on German soil. In the east the Russians had entered East Prussia, and they had captured the two islands at the mouth of the Gulf of Riga *(page 209)*.

In Auschwitz 8,000 more Jews were gassed during November *(opposite)*, before Himmler ordered the gassing to cease. The last gassings took place on November 28. Thousands of Jews were now sent away from Auschwitz by train to concentration camps and labour camps inside Germany. Among those camps were Dachau and Bergen-Belsen, which, while not serving as extermination camps, were nevertheless the scenes of increasing hardship, hunger, disease and brutality. One group of prisoners from Auschwitz was sent to Lieberose, where they were put to work building a special 'city' at Ullersdorf, to serve as a future rest home for German officers.

Map 276

EVACUATIONS AND DEATH MARCHES, NOVEMBER 1944

North Sea

Baltic Sea

Soviet forces

EAST PRUSSIA

Stutthof
12,000

Neuengamme

Ravensbrück

Bergen-Belsen

Luckenwalde

Lieberose

Piotrkow
the last
400

Antwerp
port opened to the allies 26 November

Allied forces

Buchenwald

Auschwitz
8,000

Soviet forces

Saarebourg
liberated 21 November

Flossenburg

400

Kremnicka

Vamosmikola
19 November

Mulhouse
liberated 22 November

Dachau

Enzo Sereni murdered 18 November

Strasshof

Sered
481
3 November

Havivah Reik
killed 20 November

SWITZERLAND
neutral

Mauthausen

Vienna

Budapest
50,000
death march 2-8 November
10,000
perished

Szolnok
liberated 4 November

Allied forces

Enzo Sereni captured

Nagykanizsa
Hanna Szenes captured (murdered in Budapest)

0   miles   100
0   kilometres   150

Ligurian Sea

Allied forces

Adriatic Sea

Yugoslav partisans

© Martin Gilbert 1982

From Stutthof 12,000 Jews, including 4,000 women, were marched south-westward into Germany. Hundreds were killed, or died from exhaustion, on the march. From Piotrkow the last 400 slave labourers were sent to different camps. From Vamosmikola several thousand Jewish prisoners-of-war were sent on a death march across Germany to Luckenwalde. Hundreds died, or were shot, on the march.

On November 2 tens of thousands of Hungarian Jews were driven from Budapest, as Soviet forces approached the city. Whipped and shot by the SS, they were forced westwards towards Vienna: some 4,000 were saved by the intervention of Raoul Wallenberg, a Swedish diplomat, but more than 10,000 died during six days of terror.

Amid these catastrophies, Jewish parachutists, recruited by the British in Palestine and dropped behind the German lines, had tried to make contact with the various Jewish partisan groups. One of these parachutists, a woman called Havivah Reik, took part in the final phases of the Slovak uprising, but was killed at Kremnicka. Another, Enzo Sereni, who had been captured in the German lines in Italy, was taken to Dachau and murdered. A third, Hanna Szenes, captured near Nagykanizsa on the Hungarian-Yugoslav border, was taken to Budapest, tortured, and shot.

Map 277

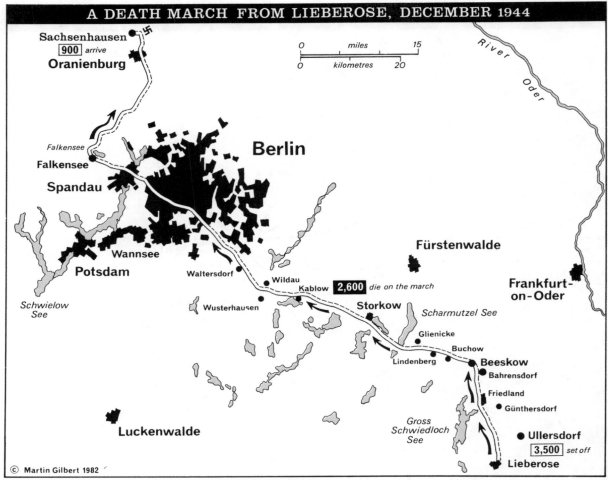

A DEATH MARCH FROM LIEBEROSE, DECEMBER 1944

Sachsenhausen
900 arrive
Oranienburg

Falkensee
Falkensee
Spandau

Berlin

Wannsee
Potsdam

Schwielow See

Waltersdorf

Wusterhausen

Wildau
Kablow **2,600** *die on the march*

Storkow

Scharmutzel See

Fürstenwalde

Frankfurt-on-Oder

River Oder

Glienicke
Buchow
Lindenberg

Beeskow
Bahrensdorf
Friedland
Günthersdorf

Gross Schwiedloch See

● **Ullersdorf**
3,500 *set off*
Lieberose

Luckenwalde

© Martin Gilbert 1982

In December 1944 the Jews who had been sent from Auschwitz to a camp at Lieberose (*page 211*) were evacuated again, forced to march on foot more than 100 miles to the concentration camp at Sachsenhausen (*above*). More than 3,500 set off. Several hundred, too sick to leave the camp infirmary, were shot, and the building set on fire. The march continued in snow and slush, from first light to darkness. Each night the marchers were ordered to make a left turn, march 20 paces, and lie down. At dawn those who could not rise, or could only stumble, were shot. By the time the march reached its destination less than 900 were still alive.

On 6 January 1945 several hundred Jewish women had been taken by train from the Slovak forced labour camp at Sered to Ravensbrück. As the Soviet forces again moved westward, the remaining labour camps on Polish soil were likewise hastily evacuated (*opposite, below*). At Skarzysko Kamienna, where 10,000 Jews had perished in two years, some 5,000 slave labourers

were evacuated by train to new camps. A few were able to run away in the confusion, and to hide until the Soviet forces arrived.

Conditions were no better once the evacuees reached their new camps inside Germany. Brutality, savage beatings, sadistic tortures, hunger, senseless hard labour, and shooting at the whim of the guards, were common to all the remaining camps, where overcrowding reached incredible proportions as the evacuations intensified.

The Allied armies were now ready for their final assault on the German heartland (*opposite, above*). The first to advance, on 12 January 1945, were the Soviet forces. As they did so, the last 47 Jewish slave labourers at the former death camp at Chelmno, knowing that they were about to be shot by the SS as Soviet troops drew nearer, revolted, using a building to hold out in. The SS set fire to the building and then machine-gunned those who fled from it. Only one survived.

THE RED ARMY PREPARES TO ADVANCE, 12 JANUARY 1945

North Sea

Baltic Sea

Danzig • Stutthof

Ravensbrück • Stettin

Hamburg

The Hague

Bergen-Belsen • Berlin • Sachsenhausen • Chelmno • Warsaw

Lodz

Skarzysko

Cologne • Leipzig • Breslau

Brussels

Gross Rosen • Czestochowa • Mielec

Buchenwald • Auschwitz • Plaszow

Frankfurt • Prague

Metz • Zilina

Strasbourg • Tuttlingen • Dachau • Sered

Vienna

Belfort • Munich • Mauthausen • Budapest

Ebensee

SWITZERLAND *neutral*

0 miles 150

0 kilometres 200

© Martin Gilbert 1982

• Jasenovac

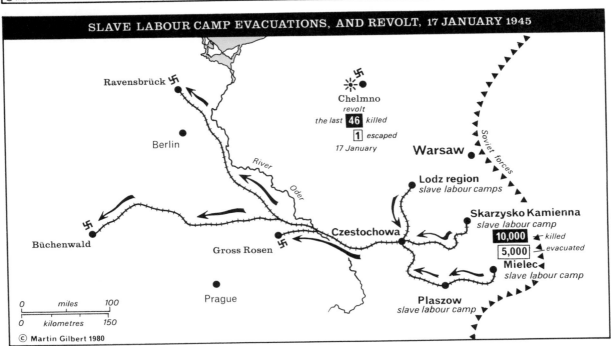

SLAVE LABOUR CAMP EVACUATIONS, AND REVOLT, 17 JANUARY 1945

Ravensbrück

Berlin

River Oder

Büchenwald

Gross Rosen • Czestochowa

Prague

Chelmno

revolt

the last **46** *killed*

1 *escaped*

17 January

Warsaw

Soviet forces

Lodz region
slave labour camps

Skarzysko Kamienna
slave labour camp

10,000 ◄ *killed*

5,000 ◄ *evacuated*

Mielec ◄
slave labour camp

Plaszow
slave labour camp

0 miles 100

0 kilometres 150

© Martin Gilbert 1980

Map 280

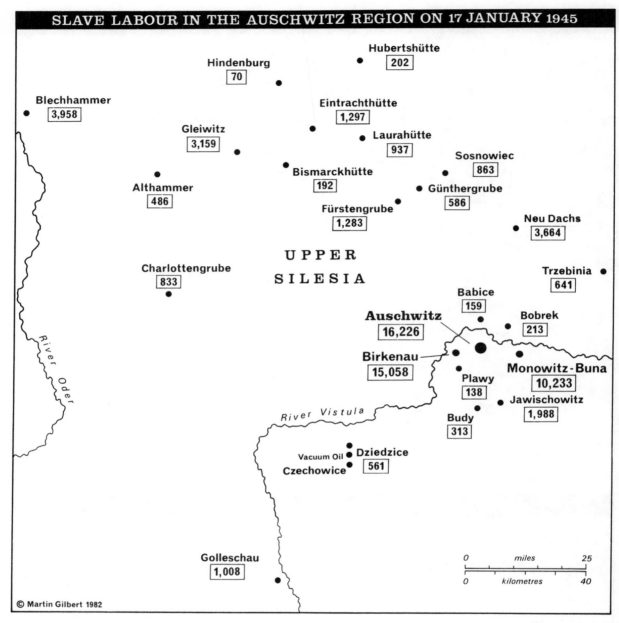

SLAVE LABOUR IN THE AUSCHWITZ REGION ON 17 JANUARY 1945

Hubertshütte
202

Hindenburg
70

Eintrachthütte
1,297

Blechhammer
3,958

Laurahütte
937

Gleiwitz
3,159

Sosnowiec
863

Bismarckhütte
192

Günthergrube
586

Althammer
486

Fürstengrube
1,283

Neu Dachs
3,664

UPPER
SILESIA

Charlottengrube
833

Trzebinia
641

Babice
159

Auschwitz
16,226

Bobrek
213

Birkenau
15,058

Monowitz-Buna
10,233

Plawy
138

Jawischowitz
1,988

River Oder

River Vistula

Budy
313

Vacuum Oil
Czechowice

Dziedzice
561

Golleschau
1,008

0	miles	25
0	kilometres	40

© Martin Gilbert 1982

On 16 January 1945, shortly after the last slave labourers had been evacuated from Czestochowa, Soviet troops entered the city (*opposite, below*). On January 17 the SS recorded (*above*) the number of slave labourers in the Auschwitz region: a total of more than 30,000 men and women. On the following day, January 18, orders were given for the immediate evacuation of all slave labour camps in Upper Silesia. The Jews were to go westward, at first on foot.

Hundreds died on these marches, or were shot as they walked. Many died because, too weak to rise after they had fallen down, they froze to death in the snow. The map opposite (*above*) gives the routes and numbers of only a few of these marches, and of the recorded deaths. Hundreds more died whose deaths were never recorded, or whose graves were never found. Several hundred escaped.

The lower map (*opposite*) shows the general direction of the train evacuations from 18 January 1945, and names 25 of the many dozens of camps to which the evacuees were sent. Many were forced to travel in open railway wagons, exposed to the full fury of winter, and hundreds died of starvation or exposure.

DEATH MARCH EVACUATIONS FROM THE AUSCHWITZ REGION, 18 JANUARY 1945

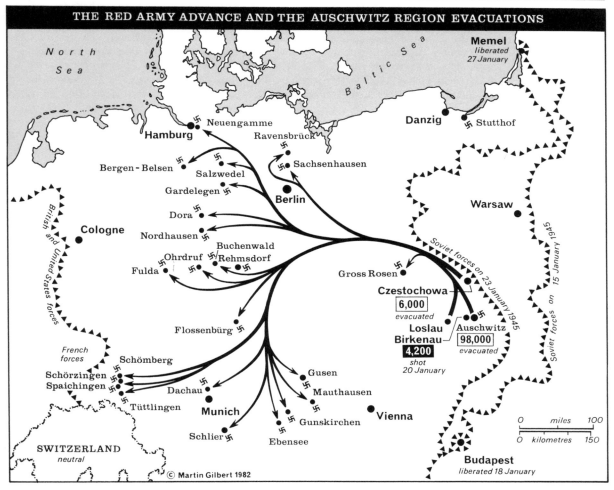

THE RED ARMY ADVANCE AND THE AUSCHWITZ REGION EVACUATIONS

Map 283

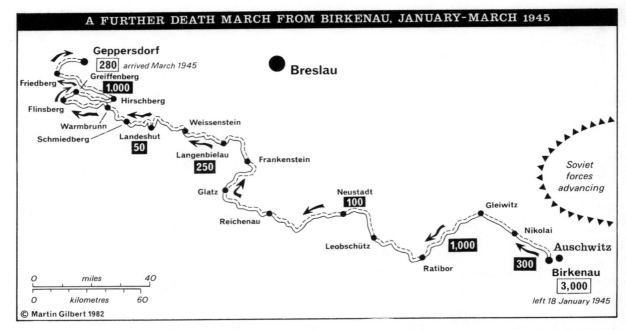

A FURTHER DEATH MARCH FROM BIRKENAU, JANUARY-MARCH 1945

Among the death marches from Birkenau was one which lasted for more than six weeks. Of the 3,000 who set out on foot, only 280 survived. The map above shows their route, and the numbers who died, or were shot, along the way.

The map opposite shows the route both of this march from Birkenau to Geppersdorf, and of five other evacuations which began in the last ten days of January 1945. The shortest was from Königsberg to the Baltic fishing village of Palmnicken. Most of the 3,700 marchers were Jewish women who had been working in one of the branches of Stutthof camp, in Königsberg itself. They were told that they were to be evacuated by sea. On the way, 700 were shot, some at the whim of the guards, others because they stumbled and fell. Then, as the marchers neared the shore, ostensibly to board the boat, the SS opened fire on them with machine-guns. The women were weak and unarmed. But still the will to live was strong in them, and they tried desperately to escape the withering fire. Three thousand were massacred. But about 60 escaped.

From Danzig, and from Stutthof, 29,000 Jews, most of them women, were evacuated by boat and train to camps in Germany. But only 3,000 survived the journey. Three days earlier, from Lamsdorf camp near Breslau, thousands of Jewish prisoners-of-war (*see pages 34-5*) had been sent, on foot, westwards towards Thuringia. Their march, like that of the Jews to Geppersdorf, took

more than six weeks, and hundreds died or were killed during its course.

The fifth evacuation shown here had an equally tragic course, but a less terrible ending. Over 100 Hungarian Jews from Auschwitz had earlier been sent to work in a quarry in Golleschau. On 21 January 1945 they too were evacuated, this time by train, from Golleschau. Sealed in two cattle trucks, the Jews were shunted north, south, and west. No one on the route dared to open the trucks, which were labelled 'Property of the SS', and 20 of the Jews froze to death as the erratic journey continued. After six days the sealed wagons reached Zwittau, where they were detached from another train and left at the railway station. Learning of this, Oscar Schindler, à German Catholic who owned a number of factories, tried to get permission from the SS to shunt the wagons to his munitions factory at Brünnlitz. He was unsuccessful, but then decided to go personally to the railway station, where he found the bill of lading and wrote on the bottom: 'Final destination — Schindler Factory, Brünnlitz.' The wagons were sent on. When they reached his factory Schindler broke open the locks and released the Jews, giving them shelter, food and warmth, at the risk of his own life.

These were not the first Jews whom Schindler had saved. Earlier, he had brought to his factories prisoners from Plaszow, Gross Rosen and other camps, in theory to employ them as slave labour, but in fact to

Map 284

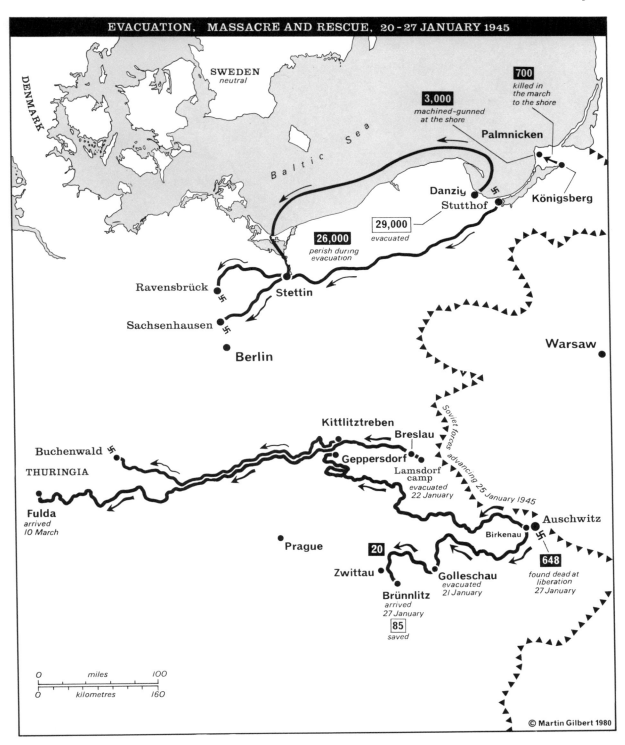

EVACUATION, MASSACRE AND RESCUE, 20-27 JANUARY 1945

SWEDEN *neutral*

DENMARK

Baltic Sea

700 *killed in the march to the shore*

3,000 *machined-gunned at the shore*

Palmnicken

Danzig

Stutthof

Königsberg

29,000 *evacuated*

26,000 *perish during evacuation*

Ravensbrück

Stettin

Sachsenhausen

Berlin

Warsaw

Soviet forces advancing 25 January 1945

Kittlitztreben

Breslau

Buchenwald

THURINGIA

Geppersdorf

Lamsdorf camp *evacuated 22 January*

Auschwitz

Fulda *arrived 10 March*

Birkenau

648 *found dead at liberation 27 January*

Prague

20

Zwittau

Golleschau *evacuated 21 January*

Brünnlitz *arrived 27 January*

85 *saved*

0 miles 100
0 kilometres 160

© Martin Gilbert 1980

protect them. One of these whom Schindler had saved earlier was Moshe Bejski, a young Polish Jew who was to become a Justice of the Supreme Court in Israel 35 years later. When Schindler died in October 1974, his body was taken to Jerusalem; at his funeral many of those whom he had saved walked in final homage to his burial place on the Mount of Olives.

On 27 January 1945, as Soviet troops entered Auschwitz-Birkenau, they found 648 dead inmates: Jews, Poles and Gypsies.

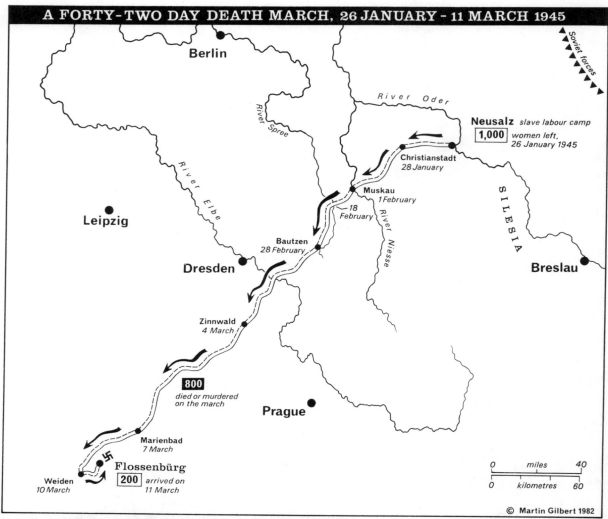

One death march, lasting 42 days, consisted of 1,000 Jewish women who had been working as slave labourers at a camp at Neusalz. On 26 January 1945 they were ordered out of the camp and marched south westwards, accompanied by the beatings and shootings which had become a common-place of death marchers. By the time the marchers reached Flossenbürg *(above)*, all but 200 had been killed. Eight days later the survivors were evacuated again, this time by train *(left)*, and several more had died by the time the train reached Bergen-Belsen.

On 18 February 1945, as the women deportees from Neusalz were crossing the River Spree, more than 500 Jews, hitherto protected because they were married to Christians, were seized throughout Germany and deported to Theresienstadt *(opposite)*. The photograph shows some of the hundreds of children who were sent to Theresienstadt.

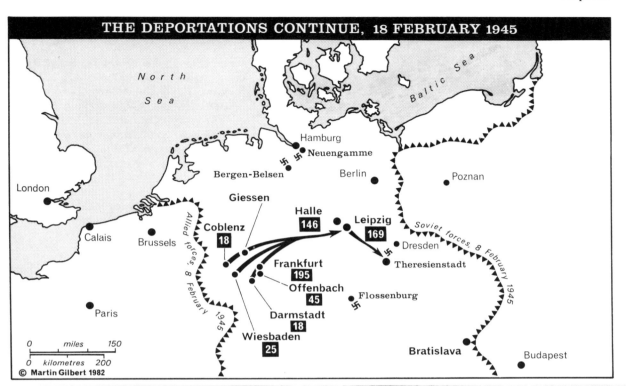

THE DEPORTATIONS CONTINUE, 18 FEBRUARY 1945

Map 288

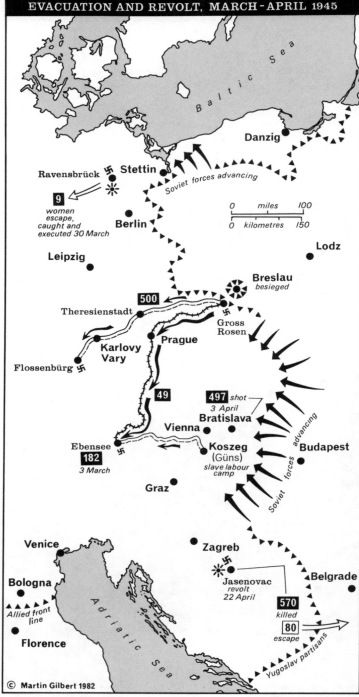

EVACUATION AND REVOLT, MARCH - APRIL 1945

In March and April 1945 Soviet forces drove deep into Germany. But the desire to kill Jews, and to make use of Jewish slave labour, still dominated Nazi policy. In Bratislava, as Soviet troops approached, the Nazis murdered all 497 members of a Jewish slave labour battalion (*above*).

From the concentration camp at Gross Rosen, 3,500 prisoners had been marched west and south, away from the advancing Russians. More than 500 died as they were forced through the rubble of Dresden to the concentration camp at Flossenbürg. A further 2,000 Jews from Gross Rosen were evacuated by train to Ebensee, one of the satellite camps of Mauthausen. In all, 49 died on the journey, and a further 182 during the disinfection procedure at the camp on the day of their arrival, 3 March 1945.

From the slave labour camp at Koszeg, where 3,000 Jews had died of hunger, disease, torture and execution in less than a year, the approach of the Russian army led to yet another death march, also to Ebensee, for the camp's 2,000 survivors (*opposite*). For several weeks they were marched through the hills and mountains of Austria. Anyone who could not get to his feet at the start of the daily march was shot.

Until the summer of 1944 Koszeg had a small Jewish community of 117 people. They had been among the very last Hungarian Jews to be deported to Auschwitz, on 4 July 1944 (*page 200*), two days before the deportations were brought to an end. Only 15 had survived. Among the dead was the rabbi of Koszeg, Isaac Linksz.

Later in 1944 Koszeg had seen the setting up of the slave labour camp which now, in March 1945, was itself being 'liquidated', in the Nazi terminology.

At Ravensbrück, north of Berlin, nine women who escaped were tracked down, and executed.

In the southernmost areas still under German control, less than 1,000 of Bosnia's 14,000 Jews were still alive, in the concentration camp at Jasenovac. There, on 22 April 1945, 600 prisoners, Jews and non-Jews, rose in revolt and attacked their guards. The guards had machine-guns and grenades. The prisoners had knives, sticks and bare hands. In all, 520 of the prisoners were killed: 80 escaped, of whom 20 were Jews.

The photograph is of a prisoner in Mauthausen who had decided to bring an end to his agony by running against the electrified wire. As more and more Jews and other prisoners were being brought into Mauthausen and its satellite camps the deaths there from brutality and starvation rose precipitately: more than 7,000 Jews died at Mauthausen in just over four months, 15,000 Gypsies, and more than 4,000 Soviet prisoners-of-war (*pages 232-3*).

Map 289

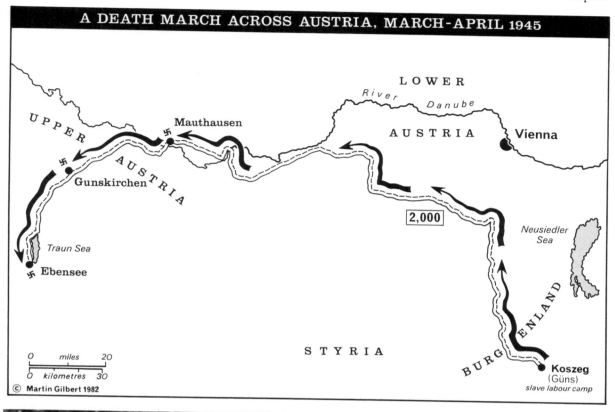

A DEATH MARCH ACROSS AUSTRIA, MARCH-APRIL 1945

LOWER

River Danube

AUSTRIA

Vienna

UPPER

Mauthausen

AUSTRIA

Gunskirchen

2,000

Traun Sea

Neusiedler Sea

Ebensee

BURGENLAND

STYRIA

Koszeg
(Güns)
slave labour camp

0   miles   20

0   kilometres   30

© **Martin Gilbert 1982**

Map 290

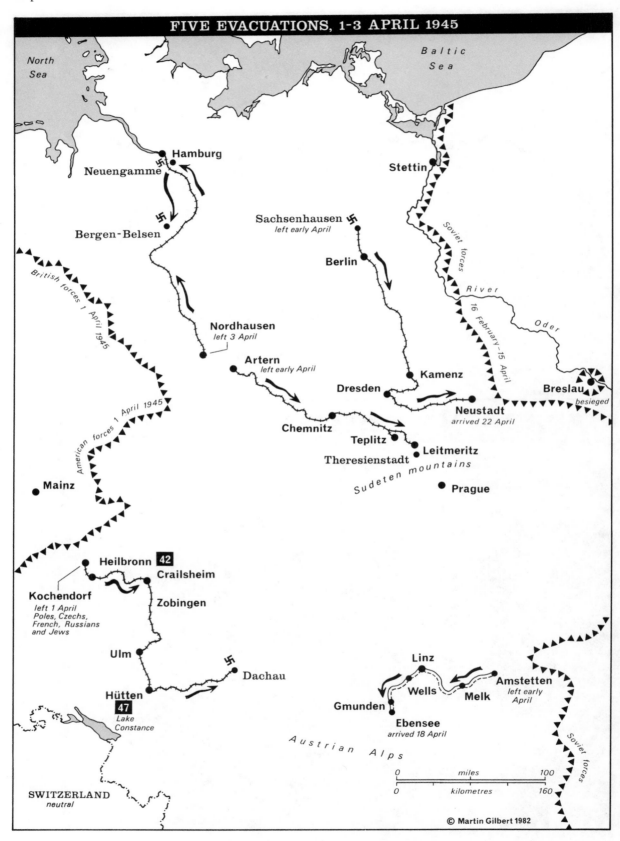

FIVE EVACUATIONS, 1-3 APRIL 1945

North Sea

Baltic Sea

Hamburg

Neuengamme

Stettin

Bergen-Belsen

Sachsenhausen
left early April

Berlin

Soviet forces

River

16 February – 15 April

Oder

Nordhausen
left 3 April

Artern
left early April

Kamenz

Dresden

Breslau
besieged

Neustadt
arrived 22 April

Chemnitz

Teplitz

Theresienstadt

Leitmeritz

Sudeten mountains

Prague

British forces 1 April 1945

American forces 1 April 1945

Mainz

Heilbronn **42**

Crailsheim

Kochendorf
*left 1 April
Poles, Czechs,
French, Russians
and Jews*

Zobingen

Ulm

Hütten **47**
*Lake
Constance*

Dachau

Linz

Amstetten
*left early
April*

Wells

Melk

Gmunden

Ebensee
arrived 18 April

Austrian Alps

Soviet forces

SWITZERLAND
neutral

| 0 | miles | 100 |
| 0 | kilometres | 160 |

© **Martin Gilbert 1982**

Map 291

From the first days of April it became clear that the Russian and western Allies would continue to advance until they met somewhere in the middle of Germany. But still Hitler hoped that the German army would be able to hold out in a mountainous area, either the Sudeten mountains or the Austrian Alps, and continue the war.

Two separate policies now drove the SS to prolong the agony of the death marches: the desire to prevent the Allies from liberating anyone who had been a witness of mass murder, and the wish to preserve for as long as possible a mass of slave labour for all the needs which confronted the disintegrating army: repairing roads and railway tracks, building up railway embankments, repairing bridges, excavating underground bunkers from which the battle could still be directed, preparing tank traps to check the Allied advance, and helping with the incredibly difficult work involved in preparing mountain fortresses deep underground.

Over and above these reasons, however, there remained the ever-present, all-pervading Nazi obsession that Jews were not human beings, that they must be made to suffer, and that it did not matter if they were to die, however cruel the circumstances. The death marches and death trains therefore continued, despite the increasing chaos on the roads and railways following the collapse of both the western and eastern fronts. The map on the left shows five such evacuations; the map on the right, three more, within less than a week.

With the rapid movement of armies, written records are scarce. The number of dead shown on these two maps represents only a fraction of the number of Jews who died from exhaustion, or brutality, in those four days.

Labour camps such as Ohrdruf had only been opened a few months earlier to enable a future army command centre to be built underground by tens of thousands of Jewish slave labourers who had been evacuated from the east. Now these same Jews were being evacuated again as American and British forces pressed in from the west. To go back east was impossible. Only north and south now lay open to traffic. And so thousands of Jews were taken by train to Bergen-Belsen, Dachau, Leitmeritz, Theresienstadt and Ebensee. In each of these camps conditions became so terrible, dominated by starvation and typhus, that hundreds died every day.

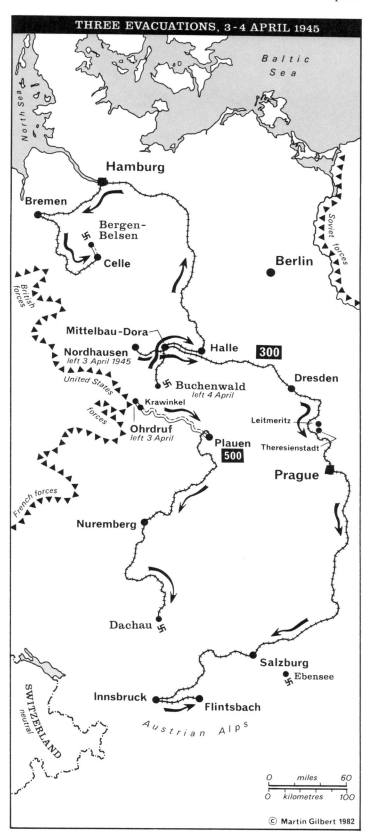

THREE EVACUATIONS, 3-4 APRIL 1945

Baltic Sea

North Sea

Hamburg

Bremen

Bergen-Belsen

Celle

Berlin

British forces

Soviet forces

Mittelbau-Dora

Nordhausen
left 3 April 1945

Halle

300

United States forces

Dresden

Buchenwald
left 4 April

Krawinkel

Leitmeritz

Ohrdruf
left 3 April

Plauen

500

Theresienstadt

Prague

French forces

Nuremberg

Dachau

Salzburg

Ebensee

SWITZERLAND
neutral

Innsbruck

Flintsbach

Austrian Alps

0 miles 60

0 kilometres 100

© Martin Gilbert 1982

Map 292

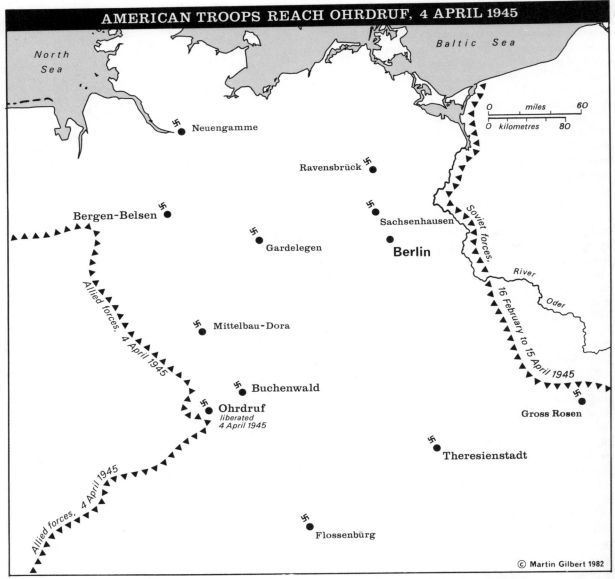

AMERICAN TROOPS REACH OHRDRUF, 4 APRIL 1945

North Sea

Baltic Sea

O miles 60
O kilometres 80

Neuengamme

Ravensbrück

Bergen-Belsen

Sachsenhausen

Berlin

Gardelegen

Soviet forces,

River Oder

Allied forces, 4 April 1945

Mittelbau-Dora

16 February to 15 April 1945

Buchenwald

Ohrdruf
liberated
4 April 1945

Gross Rosen

Theresienstadt

Allied forces, 4 April 1945

Flossenbürg

© Martin Gilbert 1982

On 4 April 1945 United States troops reached the village of Ohrdruf (*above*), where 4,000 camp inmates had died or been murdered in the previous three months, and where hundreds had been shot on the eve of the American arrival. Some of the victims were Jews, others Polish and Russian prisoners-of-war. All had been forced to build a vast underground radio and telephone centre, intended for the German army in the event of a retreat from Berlin.

The sight of the emaciated corpses created a wave of revulsion which spread back to Britain and the United States. General Eisenhower, who visited the camp, was so shocked that he sent photographs of the dead prisoners to Churchill, who at once arranged for several Members of Parliament to visit the camp.

On April 8 all the Jewish inmates at Buchenwald, many of whom had only reached the camp from Auschwitz or Stutthof three months before, were marched out, leaving the non-Jewish prisoners to await the arrival of the Americans. The Jews were driven east, then south, to the concentration camp at Flossenbürg. Others, in camps at Aschersleben and Schönebeck, were driven south, then north again, then back south, first on foot and in trucks, then by train, to Leitmeritz. A third group was sent through the Sudeten mountains to Theresienstadt, 60 being murdered at the village of Buchau.

Map 293

FOUR FURTHER EVACUATIONS, 8–16 APRIL 1945

Magdeburg

Schönebeck
left 12 April

Barby

River Elbe

Aschersleben
left 11 April

Zörbig

Bitterfeld

Torgau

Delitzsch

Leipzig

Colditz

Dresden

River Elbe

Buchenwald
left 8 April

Weimar

Eisenberg

Gera

Freiberg

Jena

Chemnitz

Weida

S A X O N Y

Leitmeritz

Theresienstadt

S U D E T E N L A N D

Johanngeorgenstadt
left 16 April

Plauen

Hof

Karlsbad

Podersam

Buchau
60

B A V A R I A

Eger

S U D E T E N L A N D

Marktredwitz

Bayreuth

Flossenbürg

Weiden

Soviet forces

| 0 | miles | 30 |
| 0 | kilometres | 40 |

© Martin Gilbert 1982

Map 294

BRITISH TROOPS REACH BELSEN, 15 APRIL 1945

North Sea

Baltic Sea

Lübeck
Neuengamme

Hamburg

British forces

Bremen

Putlitz

Ravensbrück

Sachsenhausen

Bergen-Belsen
liberated 15 April

Gardelegen

5,000 deaths
from weakness and exhaustion 15-25 April after liberation

Berlin

front line

18 April

Nordhausen

Mittlebau-Dora

Torgau

Ohrdruf

Buchenwald

Soviet forces

Dresden

15 April

American forces

0 ——— miles ——— 100
0 ——— kilometres ——— 150

liberated 11 April

Theresienstadt

Prague

Nuremberg
liberated 16 April

Flossenburg

Moravska Ostrava

French forces

Stuttgart

Brno

Schömberg
Schörzingen
Spaichingen
Tuttlingen

Dachau

Munich

Mauthausen

Vienna

Günskirchen

liberated by Soviet forces 13 April

Ebensee

SWITZERLAND

© Martin Gilbert 1982

Stutthof

Soviet forces

On 15 April 1945, eleven days after American troops had discovered the mass graves of Ohrdruf, British troops entered Belsen *(above)*. Here the British found evidence of mass murder on an even vaster scale. Of 10,000 unburied bodies, most were victims of starvation. Even after liberation 500 inmates died each day from typhus and starvation; deaths which continued for more than a week after liberation.

Photographs, films and articles about Belsen circulated widely by the end of April, making so great an impact that the word 'Belsen' was to become synonymous with 'inhumanity'. For these were not reports of discoveries by other armies in the distant corners of the Reich, but of horrors as seen by men from London and Manchester, from the Midlands and the North of England, familiar enough with the horrors of war by April 1945, but shocked as they never

thought they could be by the sights that confronted them. 'There had been no food nor water for five days preceding the British entry', a British army review reported. 'Evidence of cannibalism was found. The inmates had lost all self respect, were degraded morally to the level of beasts. Their clothes were in rags, teeming with lice, and both inside and outside the huts was an almost continuous carpet of dead bodies, human excreta, rags and filth.'

Soldiers and nurses set to work to save those who could be saved. But even the arrival of food was too much for hundreds of the inmates, who died as a result of the 'richness' of the British army rations: dried milk-powder, oatmeal, sugar, salt and tinned meat.

On the same day that British troops entered Belsen, American troops entered yet another camp at Nordhausen, where

Map 295

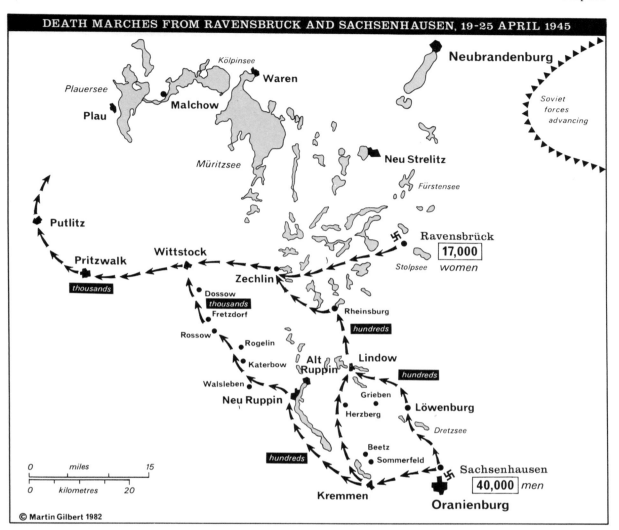

DEATH MARCHES FROM RAVENSBRUCK AND SACHSENHAUSEN, 19-25 APRIL 1945

Neubrandenburg

Soviet forces advancing

Kölpinsee

Waren

Plauersee

Malchow

Plau

Neu Strelitz

Müritzsee

Fürstensee

Putlitz

Ravensbrück

17,000 women

Stolpsee

Pritzwalk

Wittstock

Zechlin

thousands

Dossow

thousands

Fretzdorf

Rheinsburg

hundreds

Rossow

Rogelin

Katerbow

Alt Ruppin

Lindow

hundreds

Walsleben

Grieben

Löwenburg

Neu Ruppin

Herzberg

Dretzsee

Beetz

Sommerfeld

Sachsenhausen

40,000 men

hundreds

0 miles 15

0 kilometres 20

Kremmen

Oranienburg

© Martin Gilbert 1982

hundreds of slave labourers were found, 'in conditions', as the United Stated Signal Corps recorded, 'almost unrecognizable as human. All were little more than skeletons: the dead lay beside the sick and dying in the same beds: filth and human excrement covered the floors. No attempt had been made to alleviate the disease and gangrene that had spread unchecked among the prisoners.'

At yet another camp, Gardelegen, the American troops found, in a huge open pit, the still burning logs on which the bodies of the dead had been cremated.

As the western Allies now had all the evidence they needed of Nazi atrocities, there could be no purpose in further evacuations. Nevertheless, on 15 April 1945, as the western and Soviet armies drew together, 17,000 women and 40,000 men were marched westwards from Ravensbrück and Sachsenhausen (above). A Red Cross official who was present, by chance, as the marchers set off from Ravensbrück wrote in his report: 'As I approached them, I could see that they had sunken cheeks, distended bellies and swollen ankles. Their complexion was sallow. All of a sudden, a whole column of those starving wretches appeared. In each row a sick woman was supported or dragged along by her fellow-detainees. A young SS woman supervisor with a police dog on a leash led the column, followed by two girls who incessantly hurled abuse at the poor women.' Many hundreds died of exhaustion in the effort of the march. Hundreds more were shot by the wayside. The march was quite purposeless, except in the pain and death it caused. For the American and Russian troops had almost come together at Torgau in the centre of the Reich, and were to meet there on April 25.

Map 296

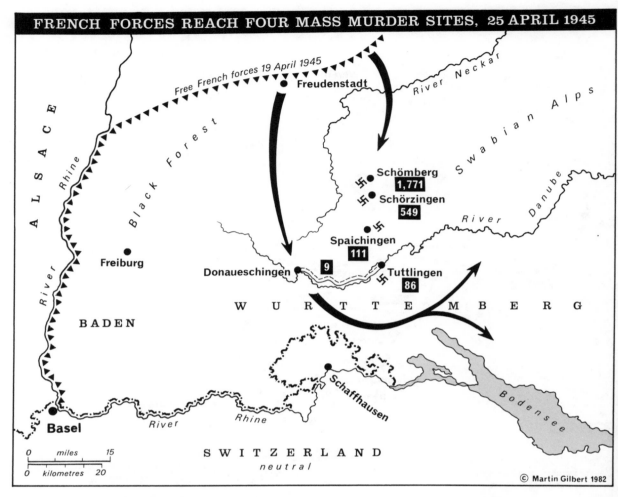

FRENCH FORCES REACH FOUR MASS MURDER SITES, 25 APRIL 1945

In southern Germany it was the turn of French troops to stumble across the evidence of mass murder, and of recent killings. Even amid the beautiful spring fragrance of the Swabian Alps and the upper Danube, it was the stench of death which assailed them.

At four villages mass graves were found of Jews who had earlier been deported from camps and ghettos in the east. With typical Gestapo thoroughness, the names, ages and birthplaces of the victims had all been recorded. The map opposite (above) shows some of these birthplaces. The 39-year-old Peisach Rudnitzki had been born in distant Swieciany, where, in September 1941, nearly 4,000 Jews had been murdered, but where several hundred had managed to escape (page 77), including his own nephew, Yitzhak Rudnitzki, who survived the war as a partisan with the Red Army, and was later to become (as Yitzhak Arad) chairman of Yad Vashem, the holocaust memorial and archive in Jerusalem.

The Second World War was almost over. Yet no corner of the dwindling Reich was free from killing: on 25 April 1945, the day on which French forces reached Tüttlingen, six Jews were taken by the Gestapo at Cuneo, and shot (opposite, above).

Elsewhere, it was a day of historic importance: the meeting at Torgau of Russian and United States forces. Germany had been cut in half. A day later, the Germans evacuated the last survivors of Stutthof by sea to Lübeck (opposite, below). Hundreds died during the voyage. Four days later, while the evacuation ships were still at sea, Soviet troops entered Ravensbrück. In that one camp alone 92,000 Jews and non-Jews, most of them women and children, had been murdered in just over two years. But as the Soviet troops overtook the 'death marchers', several thousand were still alive.

That same day, 30 April 1945, Adolf Hitler committed suicide in Berlin.

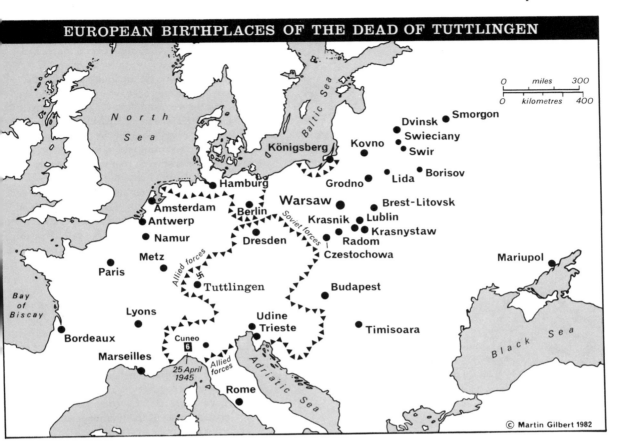

EUROPEAN BIRTHPLACES OF THE DEAD OF TUTTLINGEN

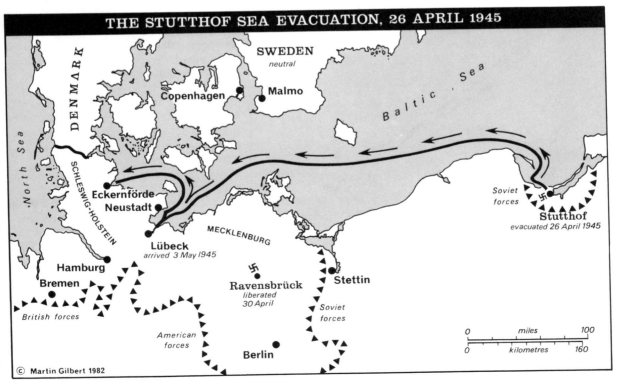

THE STUTTHOF SEA EVACUATION, 26 APRIL 1945

Map 299

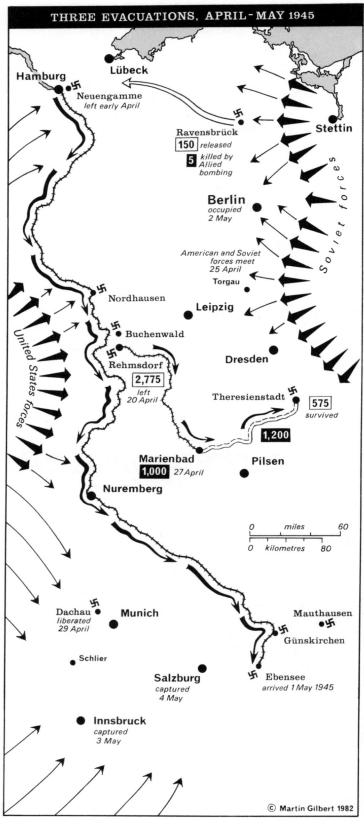

THREE EVACUATIONS, APRIL–MAY 1945

Hamburg

Lübeck

Neuengamme
left early April

Stettin

Ravensbrück
150 *released*
5 *killed by Allied bombing*

Soviet forces

Berlin
occupied 2 May

American and Soviet forces meet 25 April

Torgau

Nordhausen

Leipzig

Buchenwald

Dresden

Rehmsdorf
2,775 *left 20 April*

Theresienstadt
575 *survived*

1,200

United States forces

Marienbad
1,000 *27 April*

Pilsen

Nuremberg

miles 0 — 60
kilometres 0 — 80

Dachau
liberated 29 April

Munich

Mauthausen

Günskirchen

Schlier

Salzburg
captured 4 May

Ebensee
arrived 1 May 1945

Innsbruck
captured 3 May

© Martin Gilbert 1982

Shortly before American troops had liberated Nordhausen on April 15, one last train of concentration camp inmates had been dispatched southwards from Neuengamme, on the long and difficult journey across the war zones, to Ebensee.

At the very moment when the German army itself was made up of those formerly unfit to serve, many of the guards on the deportation trains and in the concentration camps themselves remained the highly trained criminal élite of the totalitarian state. They also remained killers to the end: on 27 April 1945, during a death march in which 2,775 Jewish slave labourers were sent eastward from Rehmsdorf, a satellite camp of Buchenwald, 1,000 marchers were killed by machine-gun fire and grenades at Marienbad station. A further 1,200 were killed as the march continued eastward to Theresienstadt, where 500 were killed on arrival. Only 75 of the marchers survived.

On April 28 the Red Cross arranged with the SS for the transport of 150 Jewesses from Ravensbrück to Sweden, the first of 3,500 Jewish and 3,500 non-Jewish women to be transferred to safety in the last ten days of the war *(page 236)*. On their way through Germany, five of the women were killed during an Allied air-raid.

On April 29 American forces entered Dachau. The photographs opposite are amoung thousands that were taken that day, and in the following week. The top photograph shows the camp as seen from one of the guard towers. Hundreds of bodies still lie in the perimeter ditch and in the open space between the huts and the ditch. The lower photograph, taken by an American serviceman, shows the scene that confronted the Allied troops. Some of the photographs taken after the liberation of Dachau are so terrible that they have never been reproduced, nor have I felt able to reproduce them here.

After the war Dachau was used as a prison for Nazi war criminals, and at a series of war crimes trials in the town of Dachau, 260 SS functionaries were sentenced to death. The principal war criminals were tried at Nuremberg in 1945 and 1946.

In the last year of the war more than 40,000 prisoners had died in Dachau, of whom 80 per cent were Jews. At Buchenwald, which American forces had liberated two weeks earlier, on April 1, 56,549 had died of starvation, disease, or from the deliberate sadism of the guards.

JEWS MURDERED IN MAUTHAUSEN, JANUARY - MAY 1945

NORWAY	1
DENMARK	2
LATVIA	5
ENGLAND	1
HOLLAND	56
SOVIET UNION	25
BELGIUM	70
GERMANY	187
POLAND	3,777
LUXEMBOURG	4
CZECHOSLOVAKIA	135
FRANCE	248
HUNGARY	3,214
RUMANIA	16
ITALY	67
YUGOSLAVIA	13
BULGARIA	1
GREECE	169
STATELESS	37
TURKEY	1

Mauthausen

0 miles 300
0 kilometres 400

© Martin Gilbert 1982

FIFTEEN THOUSAND GYPSIES MURDERED IN MAUTHAUSEN, JANUARY - MAY 1945

HOLLAND	3
POLAND	175
SOVIET UNION	14,876
LUXEMBOURG	14
CZECHOSLOVAKIA	7
FRANCE	28
HUNGARY	1
RUMANIA	6
CROATIA	2
SPAIN	1
ITALY	5
GREECE	3

Mauthausen

0 miles 200
0 kilometres 300

© Martin Gilbert 1982

The last concentration camp to be liberated by the Americans was Mauthausen, together with its satellite camps at Gunskirchen and Ebensee *(pages 234-5)*. In just over four months, more than 30,000 people had been murdered at Mauthausen, or had died from starvation and disease. Jews and Gypsies *(left),* formed the largest groups of those killed. But other groups had also been singled out by the Nazis for cruel deaths: homosexuals, Jehovah's Witnesses, Soviet prisoners-of-war, and tens of thousands of Spanish republicans. These Spaniards had been interned in France in September 1939, deported by the Germans to Mauthausen in 1940, and systematically worked to death in the stone quarry there, or shot at random, until only 3,000 remained alive by January 1945. Of these, 2,163 were killed in the last months *(opposite, below)*. The commandant of Mauthausen, Franz Ziereis, once boasted that he gave his son 50 Jews 'for target practice' as a birthday present.

All inmates at Mauthausen — Jews, Gypsies, homosexuals, religious prisoners, Russians and Spaniards — were subjected to the same vicious cruelties. Among those held in the camp was a British naval officer, Lieutenant Commander Pat O'Leary, GC, DSO. Leary's biographer, Vincent Brome, has recorded in *The Way Back,* published in London in 1968, how Leary 'became familiar with the gas lorries and the sight of prisoners loaded into them who died on the way to nowhere. He saw men kicked, strangled and beaten to death.'

On one occasion, Leary witnessed what happened when another prisoner, who had managed to escape, was recaptured; an SS guard, Leary recalled, 'launched a tremendous blow to the man's jaw. The prisoner's hand went up to ward off a second blow and the guard kicked him savagely in the stomach. As the man doubled up another sledgehammer blow hit his jaw. He fell down. "Up! Up!" The SS man kicked him to attention again. Then alternately he slogged his jaw and kicked his stomach, eight, nine, ten, eleven times, until one tremendous kick in the pit of the stomach brought blood gushing from the man's mouth; he screamed and fell down. The guard continued kicking him in the face, head, groin and legs. The twitching form at last lay quite inert and the pavement was quickly thick with blood.'

Such beatings were commonplace at Mauthausen: hundreds of prisoners being murdered each month by similar savagery.

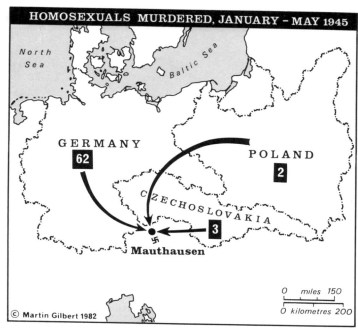

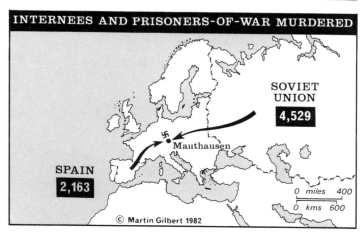

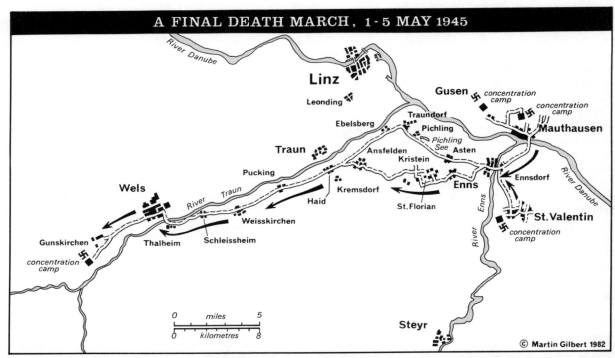

A FINAL DEATH MARCH, 1-5 MAY 1945

River Danube

Linz

Leonding

Traundorf

Ebelsberg

Pichling

Pichling See

Gusen *concentration camp*

concentration camp

Mauthausen

Traun

Ansfelden

Kristein

Asten

Pucking

Kremsdorf

St.Florian

Enns

Ennsdorf

River Danube

Wels

River Traun

Haid

Weisskirchen

St. Valentin
concentration camp

Gunskirchen

Thalheim

Schleissheim

concentration camp

River Enns

Steyr

0 miles 5

0 kilometres 8

© **Martin Gilbert 1982**

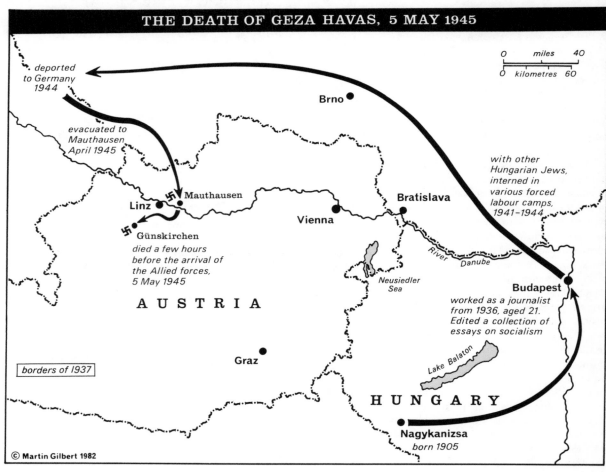

THE DEATH OF GEZA HAVAS, 5 MAY 1945

0 miles 40

0 kilometres 60

deported to Germany 1944

Brno

evacuated to Mauthausen April 1945

with other Hungarian Jews, interned in various forced labour camps, 1941–1944

Bratislava

Linz   Mauthausen

Vienna

River Danube

Günskirchen
died a few hours before the arrival of the Allied forces, 5 May 1945

Neusiedler Sea

Budapest

worked as a journalist from 1936, aged 21. Edited a collection of essays on socialism

A U S T R I A

Lake Balaton

Graz

borders of 1937

H U N G A R Y

© Martin Gilbert 1982

Nagykanizsa
born 1905

Map 307

On 1 May 1945, as the American army approached Mauthausen, the last death marches of the war began, from Mauthausen itself, Gusen and St. Valentin, to Günskirchen (*opposite, above*). Hundreds of marchers fell to the ground as they marched, dying in the mud from sheer exhaustion.

Among those who reached Günskirchen alive was the Hungarian writer and journalist, Geza Havas. But on May 5, only a few hours before the Americans arrived, he died (*opposite, below*).

Starvation, disease and brutality continued to take their toll to the end. From one transport of 4,000 Hungarian Jews, brought earlier to Mauthausen from Auschwitz, and then marched to Günskirchen and Ebensee, only 300 were alive on the day of liberation. Of 1,000 Polish civilian workers, non-Jews, brought to Ebensee from Warsaw in September 1944, only 100 survived. At Ebensee, as the American armies approached, all 30,000 prisoners were ordered into a tunnel packed with explosives. As the historian of Mauthausen, Evelyn Le Chêne, has written: 'The prisoners, to a man, blankly refused. The SS guards were paralysed with indecision. The hordes of humans swayed and murmured. For the first time since their arrest, the prisoners who were not already dying saw the possibility that they might just survive the war. Understandably, they neither wished to be blown up in the tunnel, nor mown down by SS machine-guns for refusing. But they knew that in these last days, many of the SS had left and been replaced by Volksdeutsche. A quick consultation with some of his command made it clear to the Commandant that they too were reluctant either to force the men into the tunnel, or to shoot them down. With the war all but over, they were thinking of the future, and the punishment they would receive for the slaughter of so many human beings was something they still wished — even with their already stained hands — to avoid. And so the prisoners won the day.'

When American troops reached Mauthausen, they found nearly 10,000 bodies in a huge communal grave. Of the 110,000 survivors, of whom 28,000 were Jews, more than 3,000 died after liberation (*right*). Some died because they were too weak or sick to be nursed back to health, others because they left the camp before they were strong enough to begin normal life again.

THE LAST LIBERATIONS, 4–8 MAY 1945

Baltic Sea

Lübeck

Wismar
captured
2 May

Stettin
captured
26 April

Berlin
surrendered
2 May

Breslau
captured 7 May
after a siege of
82 days

Leipzig
captured
19 April

The front line on 7 May 1945

Dresden

Theresienstadt
liberated 9 May

American
forces

Soviet
forces

Prague

American forces

Nuremberg
captured
19 April

Brno
captured
26 April

3,000 died after
liberation

Gusen
Mauthausen

Munich
captured
30 April

Günskirchen

Vienna
captured
13 April

French
forces

Ebensee

Soviet
forces

Graz

British
forces

Trieste

Zagreb

Venice

ITALY
German
armies
surrender
2 May

Yugoslav
partisan forces

Jasenovac
liberated
20 April

Adriatic Sea

0   miles   100

0   kilometres   150

© Martin Gilbert 1982

235

Map 308

WOMEN SURVIVORS OF THE CAMPS DYING IN SWEDEN, MAY-NOVEMBER 1945

Stockholm

SWEDEN
Karlstad
Norrköping

Göteborg

Halmstad

Kalmar

Helsingborg

Malmö

North Sea

Baltic Sea

Vilna
Henia Azulanscha aged 20

Hamburg

Ravensbrück
7,000
evacuated 28 April

Warsaw
Rozika Rosenbaum aged 30

Amsterdam

Lodz *Rachela Galster aged 40*

Dresden
Helena Hausmann aged 20

Sosnowiec
Zofia Alterwein aged 29

Czestochowa *Bronislawa Dorfman aged 16*

Cracow *Cesia Kleiner aged 18*

Lena Veffer aged 21
Anna Watterman aged 24
Eugelina Lissauer aged 14
Rosette Bas aged 20
Fre van Leer aged 28

Prague
Anne Goldschmidt aged 46
Gerda Fischelova aged 23

Uzhgorod *Dina Rothstein aged 22*

Novoselitsa *Helen Abrahamovitsch aged 22*

Lucenec
Sara Ehrenfeld aged 23

Beregszasz
Rozalia Katz aged 20

Györ
Hedwig Gestettner aged 25

Budapest
Ilona Delikat aged 34
Erzsebet Kohn aged 33
Judit Sandor aged 17

Cluj (Kolozsvar)
Sarolta Samu aged 41
Ewa Aron aged 17

ITALY
Regina Cepparo aged 43

Adriatic Sea

Belgrade
Sara Krystik age unknown

Black Sea

© Martin Gilbert 1982

On 8 May 1945 the Allies accepted the unconditional surrender of Germany. More than eleven million civilians had been murdered in cold blood since the German invasion of Poland more than five years before. Among those eleven million were six million Jews *(page 244)*.

Czechs, Frenchmen, Greeks, Italians, Poles, Russians and Serbs had been among the millions of non-Jewish civilians killed in reprisal actions, and in mass executions. But only the Jews had been systematically searched out for death from every region, city, town, village and hamlet of German-dominated Europe. The Nazi aim was to ensure that not one single Jew survived, and 'Jew' was defined as anyone with Jewish parents, a single Jewish parent, or even a single Jewish grandparent.

Despite the Nazi intention, and as a result of the sudden collapse of the German armies, between 250,000 and 300,000 Jews survived the concentration camps and death marches. But the coming of the Allied victory could

not save tens of thousands of these 'survivors', who, as at Dachau, Belsen and Ebensee, were too weak and too sick to live more than a few days, weeks or months, despite all the care and attention lavished upon them, by their liberators. Also, as the historian Evelyn Le Chêne has written: 'Many died from sheer joy. They had lived on hope, on fear and on their nerves for so long that the sudden relaxation of tension, when it came, was too much for them.'

The map above gives the names, ages and birthplaces of 26 out of 3,500 Jewish women who, released from Ravensbrück after Red Cross intervention on April 28 1945 *(page 230)* and sent from there to Sweden, died in the Swedish towns shown here, between May and November 1945. The oldest was 46, the youngest, 14. These women all died after liberation, as had more than 5,000 prisoners at Belsen *(page 226)* and 3,000 at Mauthausen *(page 235)*. Others, amid the confusions and hardships of the immediate post-war world, slowly regained their strength.

Map 309

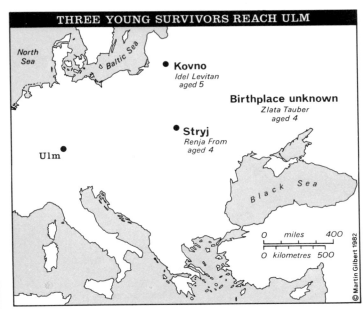

THREE YOUNG SURVIVORS REACH ULM

Among the survivors who reached western Germany after the German surrender in 1945 were several hundred children who were taken to a children's home at Ulm (*above*). There, each child was photographed, and such details as they could recall were set down. Three of those children are shown on the left.

Of Idel Levitan (*top*), born in Lithuania, the son of Micha and Mira Levitan, those who questioned him noted: 'He was with his parents in the Ghetto in Kovno. His parents gave him to Christians. Parents were killed. An aunt took him from the Christians, to Lodz, from where he came with a Kibbutz to Ulm, to the Children's Home.'

Of Renja From (*middle*), born in Eastern Galicia, the interviewer noted: 'She thinks that at the outbreak of the war her mother gave her to Poles. She knew then that she is Jewish, but the Christians with whom she was living forbad her to speak about it. She learned that her mother was murdered by the Germans and thrown into a ditch. She does not remember her father. An acquaintance of her family took her to Germany, to the Children's Home at Ulm.'

Of Zlata Tauber, born in 1941, the person who interviewed her wrote: 'She does not remember her parents, she only knows that she has been in Russia. One brother is in Poland, but he does not want to be Jew because of the persecutions they had to go through. She therefore renounced on him.'

SOME BIRTHPLACES OF DACHAU SURVIVORS

Baltic Sea

0 miles 80
0 kilometres 120

Borders of 1937

Gdynia
Bialystok
Mlawa
River Vistula
Gostynin
Warsaw
Klodawa
Kutno
Lodz
Mszczonow
Kalisz
Sieradz
Pabianice
Radom
Lublin
Belchatow
Piotrkow
Wielun
Szydlowiec
POLAND
Kielce
Sandomierz
Czestochowa
Zawierce
Bedzin
Olkusz
Radomysl
Sosnowiec
Auschwitz
Tarnow
Cracow
Bielsko
Nowy Targ

CZECHOSLOVAKIA

Kosice
Satoraljaujhely
Miskolc
Komarom
Eger
Esztergom
Vac
Hatvan
Jaszbereny
Sopron
Gyor
Tatabanya
Budapest
Papa
Monor
Debrecen
Szombathely
HUNGARY
Lake Balaton
Bekescaba
River Danube
Nagykanizsa
Szeged
Kaposvar
Baja
Mako
Pecs

© Martin Gilbert 1982

MORE DACHAU SURVIVORS

North Sea
Baltic Sea
Riga
Vilna
Oszmiana
Kovno
Rotterdam
Berlin
Warsaw
Amsterdam
Lodz
Przemysl
Kiev
Beregszasz
Dachau
Vienna
Cluj
Budapest

0 miles 400
0 kilometres 500

Rome
Salonica
Corfu
Rhodes
Mediterranean Sea

© Martin Gilbert 1982

The map on the left shows the birthplaces of most of the Jews who had been liberated by the Americans in Dachau. The map above shows some of their other birthplaces. Gradually restored to physical health, many were still distressed. 'It seems to us', Dr Zalman Grinberg told his fellow survivors at the end of 1945, 'that for the time being mankind does not understand what we have gone through and what we have experienced. We fear we will not be understood in future. We unlearned to laugh, we cannot cry any more, we do not understand our freedom yet, all this because we are still with our dead comrades . . . We belong in the mass-graves of those shot in Kharkov, Lublin and Kovno. We belong to the millions gassed and burned in Auschwitz and Birkenau. We belong to those tens of thousands tormented by milliards of lice, living in mud on a starvation diet, with coldness and despair as companions. We are not alive. We are dead!'

The photograph, taken on the day of the liberation of Dachau, shows some of the survivors of death marches and evacuation trains (*pages 205, 208, 210-11 and 223*).

The majority of those who survived the Holocaust sought a new life beyond Europe. The map opposite gives the approximate number who went to the principal havens.

Map 312

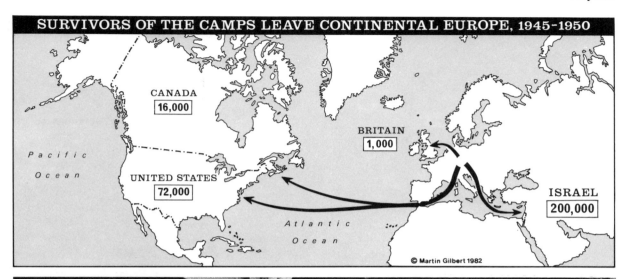

SURVIVORS OF THE CAMPS LEAVE CONTINENTAL EUROPE, 1945-1950

CANADA
16,000

BRITAIN
1,000

Pacific Ocean

UNITED STATES
72,000

ISRAEL
200,000

Atlantic Ocean

© Martin Gilbert 1982

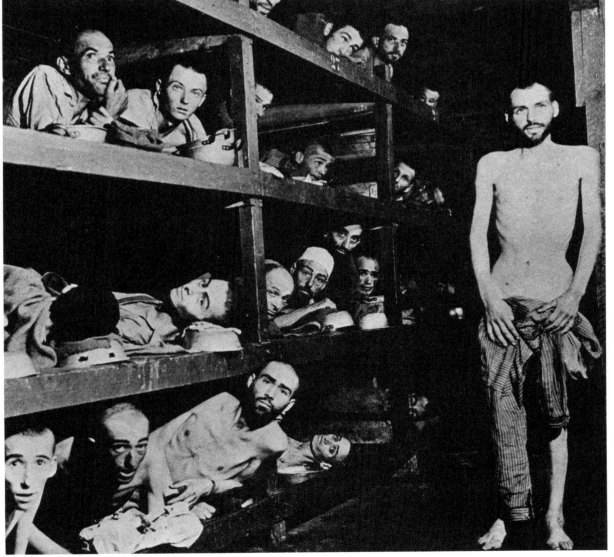

Map 313

ONE MAN'S JOURNEY, 17 JANUARY – 24 OCTOBER 1945

Baltic Sea

Kovno

Vilna
17 January

Minsk
18 January

Baranowicze
19 January

Brest-Litovsk
21 January

Kowel
22 January

0 — miles — 150
0 — kilometres — 250

Przemysl
9 February

Rzeszow
26 February

Lvov
23 January and 31 January

Sanok
2 March

Stanislawow
27 January

Ungvar
5 March

Satu Mare
8 March

Beregszasz
6 March

Oradea Mare
9 March

Szombathely
11 July

Graz
12 July

Budapest
7 July

Cluj
10 March and 2 June

Tarvisio
17 July

Milan
15 August

Arad
5 July

Alba Julia
3 July

Mestre
22 July

Padua
24 August

Bologna
13 September

Adriatic Sea

Bucharest
11 March to 30 June

© Martin Gilbert 1982

Bari
15 September

to Palestine, 24 October

Between 1944 and 1948 some 200,000 survivors left Europe for Palestine, then a British Mandate. Incredibly, the killing of Jews had continued in Poland for more than two years after Germany's surrender *(opposite)*. It was this Polish anti-semitic violence that gave a strong impetus to the 'Bricha', or flight of the Jews to Palestine. Thus, after the killing of two young Jews in Biala Podlaska, all 30 survivors left. In Lublin, Leon Felhendler, one of the leaders of the Sobibor revolt *(page 173)*, was likewise killed; also killed in Lublin, on 19 March

1946, was Chaim Hirschmann, one of only two survivors of Belzec death camp.

The flight to Palestine gained its culminating force with a pogrom in Kielce in which 41 Jews were killed. But the 'Bricha' itself had begun with each region's liberation Thus, shortly after the liberation of Vilna, Dov Levin, a young Jew from Kovno who had fought with the Soviet partisans, embarked on a typical, but nevertheless remarkable journey *(above)*. The war ended while Levin was in Bucharest. But he continued his journey to Palestine.

Map 314

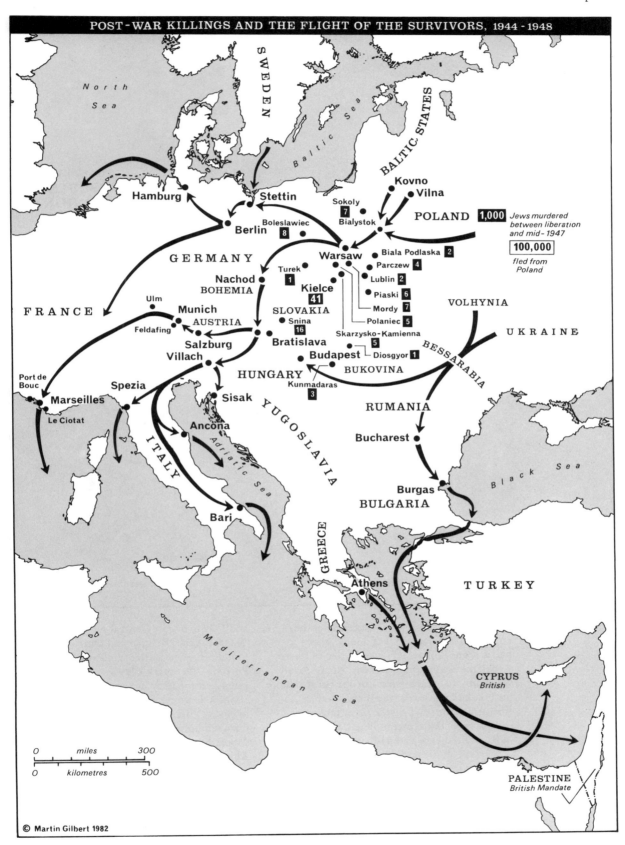

POST-WAR KILLINGS AND THE FLIGHT OF THE SURVIVORS, 1944-1948

North Sea

SWEDEN

Baltic Sea

BALTIC STATES

Kovno
Vilna

Hamburg

Stettin

Sokoly
7 Bialystok

POLAND **1,000** *Jews murdered between liberation and mid-1947*

Berlin

Boleslawiec
8

100,000 *fled from Poland*

GERMANY

Warsaw

Biala Podlaska **2**

Parczew **4**

Turek **1**

Nachod
BOHEMIA

Kielce
41

Lublin **2**

Piaski **6**

SLOVAKIA

Mordy **7**

VOLHYNIA

Ulm
Munich
Feldafing
AUSTRIA

Snina **16**

Polaniec **5**

UKRAINE

FRANCE

Salzburg
Villach

Bratislava

Skarzysko-Kamienna **5**

BESSARABIA

Port de Bouc
Marseilles
Le Ciotat

Spezia

Sisak

Budapest — Diosgyor **1**

BUKOVINA

Kunmadaras **3**

HUNGARY

RUMANIA

Ancona

Adriatic Sea

ITALY

YUGOSLAVIA

Bucharest

Black Sea

Bari

GREECE

Burgas

BULGARIA

TURKEY

Athens

Mediterranean Sea

CYPRUS
British

PALESTINE
British Mandate

0 *miles* 300

0 *kilometres* 500

© Martin Gilbert 1982

241

Map 315

SURVIVORS, AND THOSE WHO RETURNED, 1945

NORWAY
1,000

FINLAND
2,000

SWEDEN

DENMARK
5,500

DANZIG
8,000

Memel

BALTIC STATES
25,000

WESTERN
SOVIET
UNION
300,000

HOLLAND
20,000

BELGIUM
40,000

GERMANY
330,000

POLAND
225,000

LUXEMBOURG
1,000

CZECHOSLOVAKIA
44,000

SWITZ.

AUSTRIA
7,000

HUNGARY
300,000

RUMANIA
430,000

FRANCE
200,000

ITALY
35,000

YUGOSLAVIA
12,000

BULGARIA
50,000

SPAIN

ALBANIA
200

GREECE
12,000

Frontiers
of 1937

0 — miles — 250
0 — kilometres — 400

© Martin Gilbert 1982

CRETE
7

RHODES
161

In addition to the 300,000 survivors of the concentration camps, over a million and a half European Jews survived Hitler's efforts to destroy them. Some were fortunate, as in Germany, to escape from Europe before the outbreak of war or, as in Hungary, that liberation came before the plans for their destruction could be completed. Others, as in Rumania, were saved when their Government, hitherto anti-Jewish, changed its policy in anticipation of an Allied victory. The Jews of Bulgaria were saved by the courage of the Bulgarian people (*page 153*). The majority of the Polish Jews shown here survived because they found refuge in 1939

and 1940 in Soviet Central Asia. More than 20,000 French, Belgian and Dutch Jews had found refuge in Switzerland, Spain and Portugal. Denmark's Jews had been smuggled to safety in Sweden (*pages 166-7*).

Some Jews everywhere, but particularly in France, Belgium, Holland and Italy, survived because the Germans took longer to deport them than time finally allowed: the Allied landings on continental Europe coming while deportations were still in progress. Other Jews all over Europe escaped deportation altogether because they were sheltered by individual non-Jews who risked their own lives to save Jews.

In all, as the map opposite shows, more than 1,600,000 of the Jews who were alive in Europe in September 1939, were still alive in May 1945. The photograph shows one such survivor, in Dachau on the day of the camp's liberation, 29 April 1945.

Map 316

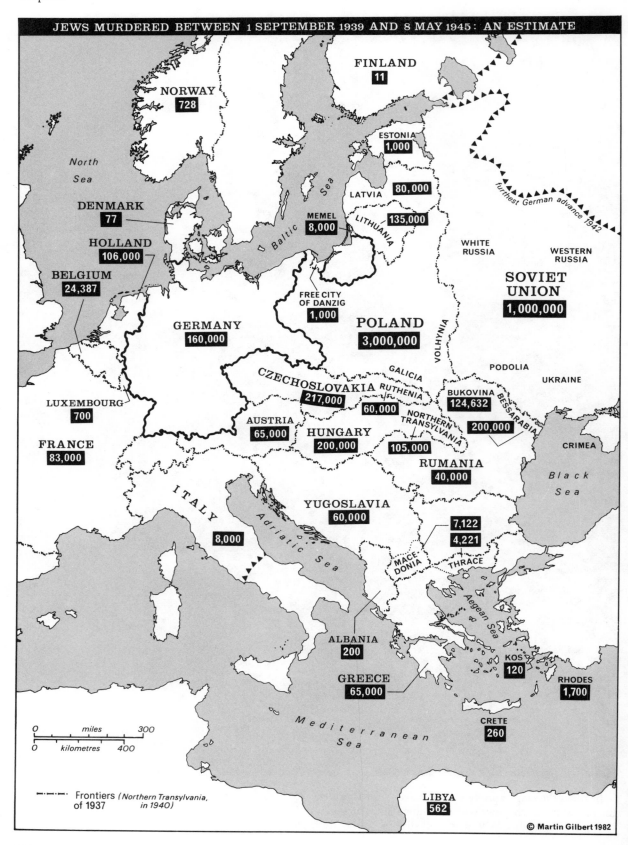

JEWS MURDERED BETWEEN 1 SEPTEMBER 1939 AND 8 MAY 1945: AN ESTIMATE

FINLAND
11

NORWAY
728

ESTONIA
1,000

LATVIA
80,000

MEMEL
8,000

LITHUANIA
135,000

DENMARK
77

HOLLAND
106,000

BELGIUM
24,387

FREE CITY
OF DANZIG
1,000

WHITE
RUSSIA

WESTERN
RUSSIA

SOVIET
UNION
1,000,000

GERMANY
160,000

POLAND
3,000,000

*North
Sea*

*Baltic
Sea*

furthest German advance 1942

LUXEMBOURG
700

GALICIA

RUTHENIA

VOLHYNIA

PODOLIA

UKRAINE

BESSARABIA

CZECHOSLOVAKIA
217,000

60,000

BUKOVINA
124,632

200,000

AUSTRIA
65,000

HUNGARY
200,000

NORTHERN
TRANSYLVANIA
105,000

RUMANIA
40,000

CRIMEA

FRANCE
83,000

*Black
Sea*

I T A L Y

*Adriatic
Sea*

YUGOSLAVIA
60,000

7,122

4,221

MACE-
DONIA

THRACE

*Aegean
Sea*

8,000

ALBANIA
200

KOS
120

RHODES
1,700

GREECE
65,000

CRETE
260

*Mediterranean
Sea*

```
0          miles          300
0        kilometres        400
```

LIBYA
562

Frontiers *(Northern Transylvania,*
of 1937 *in 1940)*

© **Martin Gilbert** 1982

By the most exact estimates of recent research, the number of Jews killed in Europe between September 1939 and May 1945 was nearly six million. This estimate is a minimum; the deaths shown opposite total just over 5,750,000, and are based on such country-by-country and region-by-region records as survive. These records are listed in the bibliography which follows.

Such a total, however, can never be complete. Thousands of infants and babies were murdered, by the Nazi killings squads in the autumn of 1941, for example, before their birth could be recorded for any 'statistical' purpose. Thousands more individuals, especially in the remoter villages of Poland, were 'added' to the deportation trains which left larger localities, without

any numerical register being made of their existence or fate. For several hundred Jewish communities throughout Europe, the most that the historical research of more than 35 years has been able to record is some phrase such as: 'the fate of this community is unknown'. Yet that community, perhaps of 100, or even 1,000 Jews, had existed in 1939, and had been destroyed by 1945.

Throughout Europe, the traveller to this day comes across monuments and gravestones to the victims. Stones mark the mass graves of individuals of whom nothing will ever be known: not their names, their ages, their birthplaces, nor indeed their total number. The photograph shows one such 'war grave', to 11 'unknown' Jews, killed in Austria in the early months of 1945.

Bibliography

I have restricted this bibliography to those works which I have personally consulted in assembling the facts for this Atlas, and have indicated against particular titles those specific maps for which the title was of service. I have also indicated those sources which provided comprehensive material on deportations and other facts incorporated on the maps. To avoid any danger of exaggeration, whenever two sources conflict in the precise number of those murdered in any instance, I have chosen the lower figure. For example, in the case of the Nazi killing squad massacre at Rowne in November 1941, page 81, where contemporary German sources indicate a death toll of at least 18,000, while one recent Jewish source has had reason to estimate that the figure could be as high as 22,000, I have retained the lower figure.

Unpublished sources

The unpublished sources which contained material for individual maps included the following eye-witness testimonies in the archives of Yad Vashem, Jerusalem:

the deportations from Germany to Poland in 1938 (map 19), testimony of Theodor Hatalgy 03/3206;

the Hajerat-M'Guil labour camp in the Sahara (map 59), testimony of Avraham Alfassi, 03/963;

the Jassy death train (map 73), testimony of Binyamin Rabinovitz, 03/897;

the deportation from Norway to Auschwitz (map 164), testimony of Dr L. Eitinger, a German refugee doctor, 01/255;

the deportation from Corfu to Auschwitz (map 250), testimony of Eliahu Uschman, 03/3041;

the deportation from Rhodes to Auschwitz (map 261), testimony of Hanna Zironi, 03/3171;

the deportation of Jews from Albania to Bergen-Belsen (map 230), testimony of Yisrael Teitelbaum, 03/3252;

the Warsaw to Zychlin death march (map 269), testimony of Henech Abramovitch, M I/E, 1605/1489;

the 42-day death march from Neusalz (map 285), testimony of Alisa Besser, 03/3394;

the Stutthof death camp and death marches (map 298), testimony of Pninna Sela, 03/638;

the Palmnicken massacre (map 284), testimony of Celina Moskowitz, 03/1108;

the rescue of Jews by Oskar Schindler (map 284), 01/164;

the post-war murder of Jews in Poland (map 314), at Sokoly near Bialystok, testimony of Icchak Szajder, and at Skarzysko-Kamienna, M 11/B, 244 and M1/PZ;10/632.

For a general guide to all European localities, deportations, slave labour camps, resistance, escape to the partisans, and death marches of the period, I consulted Yehuda Bauer (editor), *Guide to Unpublished Materials of the Holocaust Period,*

volume 3, Jerusalem 1975; volume 4, Jerusalem 1977 and volume 5, Jerusalem 1979.

For the death march from Mauthausen to Gunskirchen (map 305), I found important material on a single-sheet map, 'Weg des Todesmarsches Mauthausen-Gunskirchen', in the Yad Vashem archives, O 15/23-1-4.

For many of the other death marches between June 1944 and May 1945 (maps 290, 291, 292 and 299), I drew on material in 'Vol. 2, Death Marches (Marches de la Mort), Routes and Distances', issued on 28 May 1946 by the Intelligence Section of the UNRRA Central Tracing Bureau.

For the location of mass murder sites, revolts and slave labour camps in eastern Poland, now western White Russia (including maps 88, 98 and 216), I was fortunate to be able to consult 'The Jewish Underground in the Ghettos of Western Byelorussia during the Holocaust', a doctoral thesis submitted by Dr Shalom Cholawski to the Senate of the Hebrew University of Jerusalem in December 1977.

The fate of the Jews of Bessarabia (map 78) is described in 'The Rumanian Jewry between 23.8.1944 and 31.12.1947', a doctoral thesis submitted by Dr Jean Ancel to the Senate of the Hebrew University of Jerusalem in September 1979.

For further details of the slave labour camps in the Sahara (map 59), I consulted the letter and documents submitted by Dr E. Schaefer to the Wiener Library, London, 16 April 1958.

Other unpublished materials from which I have drawn material include:

'Treatment of Jews in Upper Silesia', 6 May 1938, a report by R. F. O'N Bashford, the British Vice-Consul in Breslau, copy in Foreign Office papers 371/21635 (map 8);

'Concentration, Work and Punishment Camps in the British Zone, I Germany, II Austria', Foreign Office papers 371/57528 (map 278): lists camps known to have existed between 1939 and 1945 in the British Zones of Germany and Austria, with notes on location, type of camp, and conditions inside the camps;

'Jews in Nazi Europe, February 1933 to November 1941', memorandum submitted to the Inter-American Jewish Conference, Balitmore, Maryland, 23 November 1941, by the Institute of Jewish Affairs (including maps 43, 44 and 52): includes a list of 27 towns and villages from which Jews were expelled in German-occupied Poland, 19 localities to which the Jews of Cracow were expelled, and 21 cities and towns in which ghettos had been established, with the number of Jews in each;

'List of Persons Imprisoned in Terezin/Theresienstadt', Czechoslovak Relief Action, London, March 1945 (alphabetical list of names, ages and last domicile);

'Tableaux Recapitulatif des Israelites et Tziganes deportés du camp de rassemblement de Malines vers les camps d'Extermination de Haute

'Silesie', Brussels 28 November 1977 (lists 25 deportations from Belgium to Auschwitz, with dates and details, and 4 deportations elsewhere: also 11 attempts at escape, with dates);

'Overzicht van de uit Nederland Gedeporteerde Joden', Rijksinstituut voor Oorlogsdocumentatie (Netherlands State Institute for War Documentation), Amsterdam n.d. (lists 68 deportations from Holland to Auschwitz, 19 to Sobibor, 7 to Theresienstadt and 8 to Bergen-Belsen, with dates and numbers of those deported).

'German Extermination Camps — Auschwitz and Birkenau', issued by the Executive Office of the President, War Refugee Board, Washington D.C., 26 November 1944 (includes the report of four escapees from Birkenau, Rudolf Vrba and Alfred Wetzler, 33 pages, and Czeslaw Mordowicz and Arnost Rosin, 6 pages).

The Palestine High Commissioner's comment at the time of the 'Struma' disaster (map 103) is in his telegram No. 257, Most Secret, in the Colonial Office papers, London, reference 733/446/76021.

I based the map on page 240 (map 313) on Dov Levin's diary of his journey from Vilna to Palestine, and on his letter to me of 3 July 1980.

I obtained further information used in this Atlas in conversation in Jerusalem on 23 December 1980 with:

Shmuel Krakowski, recollections of the evacuation of Dziedzice (map 281), and of the Rehmsdorf to Theresienstadt evacuation (map 299).

Judge Moshe Bejski, recollections of the Schindler Jews (map 284).

Hadassa Modlinger, recollections of the evacuation from Ravensbrück to Sweden (map 299).

I received further spoken testimony from:

Hugo Gryn, the Ruthenian deportations (map 255) and the Lieberose death march (map 277), in conversation in London, 11 January 1979, and from

Leon Pommers, the escape of Jews across the Trans-Siberian railway, (map 69) in conversation in Jerusalem, 14 May 1979.

I am also grateful to Alexander Pechersky, the leader of the revolt at Sobibor (map 222), for his letter of recollections, sent from Rostov-on-Don, on 16 December 1980.

I have based two maps (maps 310 and 311), on 'Sharit Ha-Platah', 5 volumes, Dachau 26 June 1945 (names, birthplaces and dates of birth of survivors in the former concentration camps). Volume 1, revised Munich 1946, covers Dachau; volume 2, Buchenwald and others; volume 3, Bergen-Belsen, Salzwedel, Gardelegen and Theresienstadt; volume 4, Linz, Buchenwald (children aged 16-17), Dachau, Braunschweig, Mannheim, Mauthausen, Innsbruck, Celle, Regensburg; volume 5, Feldafing, Dachau, Allauch and others.

The map on page 224 (map 292) was based in part on 'Atrocities and other conditions in Concentration Camps in Germany', Report of the Committee Request by Gen. Dwight D. Eisenhower through the Chief of Staff, Gen. George C. Marshall, to the Congress of the United States, 79th Congress, 1st Session, Document No. 40, Washington 15 May 1945.

Published documents

Two principal published sources from the point of view of German policy and practice are the *Trial of the Major War Criminals before the International Military Tribunal: Official Text,* 42 volumes, Nuremberg 1947-1949 and the *Trial of War Criminals Before the Nuremberg Military Tribunals under Control Council Law No. 10,* 15 volumes, Washington D.C., 1949-1953.

There is also a comprehensive guide to more than 3,000 of the documents submitted at the Nuremberg Trials in Jacob Robinson and Henry Sachs (editors), *The Holocaust, The Nuremberg Evidence, Part One: Documents,* Jerusalem 1976. I have plotted details on the maps from many of these documents, reference L, NG, NO, NOKW, PS, RF and D, and in particular from the documents dated:

26 October 1938, expulsion of Polish Jews from Germany, reference NG 2014 (map 19);

8 November 1938, report of expulsion of Polish Jews from Germany, NG 2010 (map 19);

27 February 1940, statistics of Warthegau expulsions, NO 5348 (map 43);

29 February 1940, further statistics of Warthegau expulsions, NO 5402 (map 43);

28 March 1940, Stettin and Schneidemühl deportations to Lublin region, NG 2490 (map 37);

31 October 1940, report of 6,504 German Jews deported to the Pyrenees, NG 4934 (map 49);

3 July 1941, only 2,000 Jews left in Siauliai, NO 4537 (map 73);

7 July 1941, 400 Jews killed in Riga, NO 2935 (map 73);

13 July 1941, 500 Jews being shot every day in Vilna, NO 2937 (map 73);

27 August 1941, murder of 11,000 Hungarian Jews at Kamenets Podolsk, PS 197 (map 74);

27 August 1941, 4,000 Jews killed in Jassy, NG 4962 (map 74);

3 September 1941, 300 Jews shot at Ananayev, NOKW 1702 (map 86);

19 September 1941, *Einsatzkommando A,* reports 46,692 Jews killed in Lithuania in less than three months, NO 3149 (map 87);

19 September 1941, 1,303 Jews killed at Berdichev, NO 3149 (map 86);

2 October 1941, report of 33,771 Jews killed at Babi Yar on 29 and 30 September 1941, NO 3137 (map 86);

11 October 1941, 449 shot in Belgrade area in three days, NOKW 497 (map 86);

13 October 1941, death of Dutch Jews in Mauthausen NG 2710 (map 90);

15 October 1941, *Einsatzgruppe A,* reports having killed 125,000 Jews and 5,000 non-Jews, L 180;

24 October 1941, deportation of 50,000 Reich

Jews to Riga and Minsk, PS 3921 (map 92);

26 October 1941, Jews shot in Odessa, NO 3403 (map 86);

29 October 1941, 8,000 Jews shot at Mariupol, NOKW 1529 (map 86);

1 November 1941, 7,000 Jews murdered at Borisov, NOKW 3146 (map 94);

3 November 1941, *Einsatzgruppe C,* reports on killing of 75,000 Jews, NO 3157;

14 November 1941, *Einsatzgruppe B,* reports on killing of 45,000 Jews, NO 2825;

19 November 1941, 10,000 Jews killed in Dnepropetrovsk, NO 2832 (map 94);

25 November 1941, 1,200 Buchenwald inmates deported to Bernberg, NO 907 (map 94);

30 November 1941, 14 Jews killed at Armyansk, NOKW 1532 (map 94);

8 December 1941, report of 15,000 Jews killed in Rovno (Rowne) a month earlier, NO 2827 (map 94);

12 December 1941 'shooting on the spot' a solution in Serbia, NG 3354 (map 96);

12 December 1941, *Einsatzgruppe D,* reports killing 55,000 Jews, NO 2828;

14 December 1941, killing of 76 Jews at Karasubazar, NOKW 2029 (map 96);

end 1941-early 1942, the 'Jaeger report' on *Einsatzgruppe A* killings in Lithuania and Latvia, totalling 137,346 deaths, listed under men, women and children, between July 4 and 25 November 1941, PS 2273;

1 January 1942, killings at Simferopol on previous day, NOKW 2231;

14 January 1942, Estonia 'cleared of Jews' and 26,900 Jews killed in Riga, NO 3279 (map 98);

17 January 1942, 22 Jewish partisans shot at Evpatoria, NOKW 1524 (map 102);

20 January 1942, minutes of Wannsee Conference, NG 2586 G(7) (maps 99 and 100);

28 February 1942, 36 Jews executed at Feodosiya, NOKW 1862 (map 102);

8 April 1942, murder of 91,678 Jews in the Crimea, NO 3338 and NO 3359 (map 102);

1 May 1942, 22 Jews executed at Feodosiya, NOKW 1717 (map 102);

1 May 1942, Warthegau extermination 'in progress', NO 246 (map 117);

30 May 1942, Dr Clauberg proposes medical experiments at Auschwitz, NO 211 (map 122);

9 June 1942, despatch of a gas van from Belgrade to Riga, PS 501 (map 127);

30 June 1942, report of 52,000 Slovak Jews already deported, NG 4553 (map 126);

9 July 1942, deportations from Belgium, NG 002 (map 134);

6 August 1942, Dr Clauberg requests second sterilization unit for Auschwitz, NO 210 (map 122);

11 August 1942, Hungarian protests against anti-Jewish measures, NG 1856 (map 238);

20 August 1942, Italian refusal to deport Croat Jews, NG 2368 (map 89);

27 August 1942, 95,000 Jews executed in Baranowicze district, and 6,000 escape to partisans, NG 1315 (map 224);

3 September 1942, 27,069 French Jews already deported, RF 1227;

11 September 1942, reports of 17,000 Dutch Jews already deported, NG 2631;

18 September 1942, Jews to receive no meat, meat products or eggs in Greater Germany, NG 1651;

24 September 1942, further Italian refusal to deport Croat Jews, NG 3165;

25 September 1942, Rumanian Jews deported from France, NG 1971 (map 155);

3 October 1942, Jewish resistance groups in Germany reported to the Ministry of Justice in Berlin, NG 683;

20 November 1942, third Italian refusal to deport Croat Jews, NG 2345;

6 December 1942, forced labour in Tunisia, NG 2099 and NG 3150 (map 188);

18 February 1943, report of 86,632 Jews murdered in Minsk, NO 3339 (map 193);

4 March 1943, planned deportation of Croat Jews, NG 2348 (map 205);

16 May 1943, the Stroop report on the destruction of the Warsaw ghetto, PS 1061 (map 204);

7 June 1943, Dr Clauberg reports sterilization rate at Auschwitz of 1,000 women a day, by a single physician with assistants, NO 212 (map 206);

7 June 1943, pro-Jewish demonstrations in Sofia, NG 2357 (map 197);

21 June 1943, Jewish skeleton collection plans for Strasbourg, NO 091 (map 208);

30 June 1943, total of 434,329 Jews deported from Galicia by 27 June 1943, L 018 (map 206);

5 July 1943, six Jews shot earlier at Heraklion, NOKW 2907 (map 208);

15 July 1943, order to deport all 800 Jews still alive in Croat concentration camps, NG 2413 (map 208);

4 October 1943, Danish resistance to deportation of Jews, NG 3920 (map 213);

17 October 1943, Jews arrested in Rome, NO 315 (map 221);

2 November 1943, 73 Jews and 30 Jewesses from Auschwitz to Natzweiler, for a collection of Jewish skeletons, NO 086 (map 208);

6 April 1944, arrest of Jewish children in children's homes, and deportation to Drancy, RF 1235;

14 April 1944, report of deportation of Greek Jews on 23-25 March 1944, NOKW 2520 (map 232);

23 April 1944, deportation of Hungarian Jews to start on 15 May 1944, NG 2233 (map 240);

28 April 1944, Corfu deportation plans, NOKW 1985 (map 250);

4 May 1944, progress of ghettoization and deportation plans for Ruthenia (200,000 ghettoized) and Transylvania (110,000 to be ghettoized), NG 2262 (map 240);

8 June 1944, statistics of Hungarian deportations, NG 5620 (map 241);

16 June 1944, renewal of Slovak deportations, NG 2261 (map 251);

3 July 1944, deportations from Rhodes, NOKW 1795 and NOKW 1802 (map 261);

10 September 1944, Jewish forced labourers, 6,000 in all, at Bor, NOKW 981 (map 273);

15 October 1944, order for destruction of Jewish skeleton collection at Strasbourg, NO 807 (map 208);

27 October 1944, deportation of total of 437,402 Jews from Hungary reported, NG 5573 (map 260);

22 January 1945, Stutthof death march orders, NO 3796 (map 284);

25 January 1945, Stutthof death march schedule, NO 3792 (map 284);

23 May 1945, testimony of Franz Zeireis, Commandant at Mauthausen, NO 1973 (map 300);

18 March 1946, affidavit by Baron van Lamsweerde on the Rehmsdorf to Theresienstadt death march, D924 (map 299);

6 June 1947, affidavit by Paul Blobel on Unit 1005 to obliterate traces of mass graves, NO 3829 (map 217);

23 October 1947, eye-witness account of gas vans used in Riga, NO 5511 (map 127).

Single sheet maps
Among the historical atlases and maps consulted were several single-sheet maps on specific themes, including:

Jean Ancel, *Transnistria Inclusiv Provinciile Afectate De Deportari Masive*, Jerusalem, n.d. (the Transnistrian camps and death marches) maps 78 and 80;

Dokumentačná Akcia, *Deportácia Židov zo Slovenska*, Bratislava, June 1948 (deportation routes and numbers from Slovak towns and villages) maps 126 and 128;

Herbert Froboess, *Deutschland 1945*, Munich n.d. (location of concentration camps and sub-camps in Greater Germany, including the Natzweiler and Mauthausen sub-camps) map 278;

Dr Gollert, *Die Territoriale Verteilung der Juden in Warschau nach Polizeikommissariaten, Volkszahlung vom 24 Februar 1940* (gives percentage of Jews throughout Warsaw, before the expulsions into the ghetto) map 55;

C. Jablonski, *Podzialy Administracyjne Wojewodztwa Lodzkeigo i Obszarow Przyleglych 1939-1945r.*, Lodz 1972 (wartime administrative boundaries of the Lodz region) map 42;

Edward Kossoy, *Judenvernichtung im Donauraum*, Munich, n.d. (deportation routes with dates and numbers, from Austria, Slovakia, Bukovina, Ruthenia, Transylvania, Banat, Bacska and Serbia, with inset of concentration, labour and internment camps in Italy);

Edward Kossoy, *Polen*, Munich, n.d. (concentration camps and labour camps throughout Poland, with insets on France, Transnistria, North Africa, Upper Silesia, and Warsaw region);

Edward Kossoy, *Polen und Balticum am Ende des sweiten Weltkrieges*, Munich, n.d. (death camps, concentration camps, slave labour camps, deportation routes with dates and number, from the General Government, the Baltic States, Upper Silesia, Danzig-West Prussia, East Prussia and the Warthegau);

League of Nations, *Territory of Saar Basin*, scale 1:100,000, 3 May 1919 (map provided as annex 2 to the Treaty of Versailles), London 1919, map 7;

Militärgeographischen Institut in Wien, single sheet maps of western Russia (borders of 1914), reprinted Vienna 1940, scale 1:200,000;

Mitteleuropa in der ersten Hälfte des Jahres 1945 n.d. (concentration camps and their satellite camps, with front lines on 1 April, 14 April and 6 May 1945, and the dates on the liberation of the camps maps 290 to 294 and map 307;

Lieutenant Popescu, *Transnistria*, 1.43, maps 78 and 80.

Zidovske Pracovne Tabory A Strediska Na Slovensku, Bratislava, 5 July 1943 (locates Jewish labour camps in Slovakia) map 216.

Atlases
Several Atlases provided historical as well as geographical information not obtainable elsewhere, among them:

O. A. Beloglazova (editor) *Atlas S.S.S.R.*, Moscow 1954;

Wladyslaw Czaplinski and Tadeusz Ladogorski, *Atlas Historyczny Polski*, Warsaw 1968;

Deutscher Generalatlas, 1:200,000, Stuttgart 1967-1968;

George Goodall (editor), *Philips' International Atlas*, 5th edition, Liverpool 1945 (includes the boundaries of German-occupied Poland, plates 53-54, of German-occupied Czechoslovakia, plates 59-60, and of Hungarian-occupied Transylvania, plates 63-64);

Dimitri Kosev and others, *Atlas po Bulgarska Istoria*, Sofia 1963;

Janusz Lopatto (editor), *Samochodowy Atlas Polski 1:500,000*, Warsaw 1979 (road Atlas of Poland, 34 map spreads, town plans and gazetteer);

Dr Oswald Muris, *Hansa Weltatlas*, Leipzig 1943 (includes the European frontiers of September 1943, and the internal administrative divisions of Greater Germany);

T. Dodson Stamps and Vincent J. Esposito, *A Military History of World War II: Atlas*, West Point 1953 (168 campaign maps, including 7 maps on the Polish campaign, 5 maps on the Balkan campaign, 22 maps on the war in eastern Europe, 26 maps on the war in western Europe, 15 maps on the war in North Africa and 16 maps on the operations in Italy).

Books and articles
There are now nearly five hundred 'memorial' books on the destroyed Jewish communities of Europe; including more than 400 for Poland, 20 for Rumania, 13 for Russia, 5 for Lithuania, 4 for Czechoslovakia, 4 for Germany, 1 for Yugoslavia (Sombor), 1 for Greece (Salonica) and 1 for

Latvia. I have tried to make the fullest possible use of these books, some of which are listed in the bibliography, and to which there is, up to 1973, a comprehensive guide in David Bass, 'Bibliographical List of Memorial Books Published in the years 1943-1972', in *Yad Vashem Studies,* ix, Jerusalem 1973, pages 273-321.

The Bulletin of the Jewish Historical Institute in Warsaw, founded in 1951, contains many important articles on the fate of Polish Jewry. Of particular value are the tables of deportations from towns, villages and hamlets throughout Poland, prepared by Tatiana Berenstein (Berensztyn), Danuta Dabrowska, Adam Rutkowski and Szymon Datner, and which I have listed in the bibliography of published works.

For the basic historical facts of more than a thousand separate communities overtaken by the Holocaust, as well as for the country-by-country entries, and a specific Holocaust section, each with its own bibliography, I have used Cecil Roth (editor in chief), *Encyclopaedia Judaica,* Jerusalem 1972, 16 volumes. The individual community entries in these sixteen volumes are being substantially supplemented by the Yad Vashem project, *Pinkas Hakehillot Encyclopaedia of Jewish Communities,* of which the following six volumes have already been published and which provide detailed information on the life and destruction of several hundred of the communities plotted in this Atlas:

Rumania, volume 1, Jerusalem 1969;
Germany-Bavaria, Jerusalem 1972 (including maps 108 and 109);
Hungary, Jerusalem 1976;
Poland: the Communities of Lodz and its Region, Jerusalem 1976;
Poland: Eastern Galicia, Jerusalem 1980;
Rumania, volume 2, Jerusalem 1980.

Other published works which proved indispensable in the preparation of this Atlas were:

Activité des Organisations Juives en France sous L'Occupation, Paris 1947.

S. Adler-Rudel, 'The Evian Conference on the Refugee Question', in *Leo Baeck Institute Year Book* xiii, 1968, pages 235-73.

Reuben Ainsztein, *Jewish Resistance in Nazi-Occupied Eastern Europe,* London 1974.

Henry Allainmet, *Auschwitz en France: La Vérité sur le seul camp d'Extermination en France, Le Struthof,* Paris 1974 (about Natzweiler).

American Jewish Committee, *The Jews in Nazi Germany: A Handbook of Facts Regarding the Present Situation,* New York 1935 (documents on anti-Jewish measures and the text of laws affecting the Jews).

Jacob Apenszlak (editor), *The Black Book of Polish Jewry,* New York 1943.

Jacob Apenszlak and Moshe Polakiewicz, *Armed Resistance of the Jews in Poland,* New York 1944.

Yitzhak Arad, *Ghetto in Flames: the Struggle and Destruction of the Jews in Vilna in the Holocaust,* Jerusalem 1980 (lists all murder 'actions' in Vilna between 1941 and 1944).

Yitzhak Arad, *The Partisan,* New York 1979 (the story of Swieciany, Vilna, and Jewish partisan activity).

Schlomo Aronson, *Beginnings of the Gestapo System: the Bavarian model in 1933,* New Brunswick, New Jersey 1969.

Z. Asaria, *Zur Geschichte der Juden in Osnabrueck,* Osnabrück 1969.

K. J. Ball-Kaduri, 'Berlin is "Purged" of Jews: The Jews in Berlin in 1943', in *Yad Vashem Studies,* v, Jerusalem 1963, pages 271-316 (includes lists of 11 deportations from Berlin to Auschwitz between 12 January and 12 March 1943, and 8 to Theresienstadt between 12 January and 17 March 1943).

Yehuda Bauer *Flight and Rescue: Brichah,* New York 1970 (map 314).

Yehuda Bauer, 'Rescue Operations Through Vilna', in *Yad Vashem Studies,* ix, Jerusalem 1973, pages 215-223 (map 69).

Arieh L. Bauminger, *Roll of Honour,* 2nd edition, Tel Aviv 1971 (non-Jews who saved Jews).

Norman H. Baynes (editor) *Hitler's Speeches,* 2 volumes, London 1941.

Wladyslaw Bednarz, *Das Vernichtungslager zu Chelmno am Ner,* Warsaw 1946.

Tatiana Berenstein, 'Eksterminacja Zydow w Galicji 1941-1943' *Biuletyn Zydowskiego Instytutu Historycznego,* number 61, Warsaw, 1967 (12 statistical tables of the ghettoization, deportation and destruction in 139 Jewish communities in Eastern Galicia between 1941 and 1943).

Tatiana Berenstein, 'Martyrologia, opór i zaglada ludnosci zydowskiej', in *Biuletyn Zydowskiego Instytutu Historycznego,* number 21, pages 56-83, Warsaw 1957 (10 statistical tables listing the size, deportation and destruction of Jewish communities in the Lublin district between 1939 and 1944).

Adolf Berman, 'The Fate of Jewish Children in the Warsaw Ghetto', in Yisrael Gutman and Livia Rothkirchen (editors), *The Catastrophe of European Jewry,* Jerusalem 1976, pages 400-421.

Blackbook of Localities whose Jewish Population was Exterminated by the Nazis, Yad Vashem, Martyrs' and Heroes' Remembrance Authority, Jerusalem 1965 (lists the number of Jews town by town and village by village, according to the pre-war census returns, in Poland, Germany, Yugosalvia, Austria, Hungary, Rumania, Greece, Czechoslovakia, Holland, Norway, Luxembourg, Estonia, Latvia, Lithuania and the Soviet Union).

Nachman Blumenthal (editor), *Yizkor Baranow: A Memorial to the Jewish Community of Baranow,* Jerusalem 1964.

Joseph Borkin, *The Crime and Punishment of I. G. Farben,* New York 1978 (slave labour at Auschwitz-Monowitz, based on the published Nuremberg War Crimes Trials records).

Randolph L. Braham, *The Destruction of*

Hungarian Jewry: A Documentary Account, 2 volumes, New York 1963 (documents on German deportation policy, with facsimiles).

Randolph L. Braham, *The Politics of Genocide: the Holocaust in Hungary,* 2 volumes, New York 1981.

Randolph L. Braham, *Hungarian-Jewish Studies,* 3 volumes, New York 1966, 1969, 1973.

Randolph L. Braham, 'The Kamenets Podolsk and Delvidek Massacres: Prelude to the Holocaust in Hungary', in *Yad Vashem Studies,* ix, Jerusalem 1973, pages 133-156.

B. Brilling (editor), *Westfalia Judaica.*

Zvie A. Brown and Dov Levin, *The Story of an Underground: the resistance of the Jews of Kovno (Lithuania) in the Second World War,* Jerusalem 1962.

T. Brustin-Berenstein, 'Deportacje i Zaglada Skupisk Zydowskich w Dystrykcie Warszawskim' in *Biuletyn Zydowskiego Instytutu Historycznego,* number 3, Warsaw 1952 (11 statistical tables of the ghettoization, deportation and destruction of Jews in Warsaw, and of Jewish communities throughout the Warsaw region).

Tadeusz Bystrycki (general editor) *Skorowidz Miejscowsci Rzeczpospolitej Polskiej,* 4 volumes, Warsaw and Przemysl, 1934 (lists the location of all towns, villages and hamlets in inter-war Poland).

Frederick B. Chary, *The Bulgarian Jews and the Final Solution, 1940-1944,* Pittsburgh 1972 (map 197).

Marta Cohen (editor and translator), *Hanna Senesh: Her Life and Diary,* London 1971 (map 276).

Congrès Juif Mondial, Section de Roumanie, Commission d'Etudes, *Le Massacre des Juifs de Jassy,* Bucharest 1946 (photographs and documents of the town and train massacres, June-July 1941) (map 73).

Danuta Czech, 'Deportation und Vernichtung der griechischen Juden', in *Hefte von Auschwitz,* II, 1970 (lists 19 train deportations to Auschwitz from Salonica between 20 March and 18 August 1943 and two from Athens and Corfu on 11 April and 30 June 1944).

Danuta Czech, 'Kalendarium der Ereignisse im Konzentrationslager Auschwitz-Birkenau', in *Hefte von Auschwitz,* numbers 2-9, Oswiecim, 1959-64 (records all deportation trains reaching Auschwitz between March 1942 and November 1944, with dates, and the fate of those on them).

D. Dabrowska, 'Zaglada Skupisk Zydowskich w "Kraju Warty" w okresie Okupacji Hitlerowskiej' in *Biuletyn Zydowskiego Instytutu Historycznego,* number 13, Warsaw 1955 (16 statistical tables of the ghettoization, deportation and destruction in the city of Lodz and other towns and villages of the Warthegau).

Szymon Datner, 'Eksterminacja Zydow w Okregu Bialostockim', in *Biuletyn Zydowskiego Instytutu Historycznego,* number 60, Warsaw 1966 (8 statistical tables of the ghettoization, deportation and destruction in Bialystok and the Bialystok region), see in particular map 168.

Szymon Datner, *Las Sprawiedliwych* (the forest of the righteous), Warsaw 1968 (the story of non-Jewish Poles who helped Jews in Poland).

Szymon Datner, *Walka i zaglada bialostockiego ghetta,* Lodz 1946 (the Bialystok ghetto revolt) (map 210).

Szymon Datner, *55 Dni (i.ix-15. x 1939) Wehrmachtu w Polsce,* Warsaw 1967 (map 29).

A. de Cocatrix, *The Number of Victims of the National Socialist Persecution,* International Tracing Service, Arolsen, 12 April 1977.

Louis de Jong, 'The Netherlands and Auschwitz' in *Yad Vashem Studies,* vii, Jerusalem 1968, pages 39-55.

Lucjan Dobroszycki, 'Restoring Jewish Life in Post-War Poland', in *Soviet Jewish Affairs,* volume 3, number 2, London 1973 (details of Jews killed by Poles after liberation) (map 316).

Giuliana Donati, *Deportazione Degli Ebrei Dall' Italia,* Milan, March 1975 (lists 14 deportations from Italy to Auschwitz, and 7 other deportations, between 16 September 1943 and 14 December 1944, with the fate of the deportees).

Giuliana Donati, *Ebrei in Italia: Deportazione, Resistenza,* Florence 1975.

S. M. Dubnow, *History of the Jews in Russia and Poland from the earliest times until the present day,* 3 volumes, Jewish Publication Society of America reprint, Philadelphia 1946 (map 3).

Krzysztof Dunin-Wasowicz, 'Zydowscy wiezniowie KL Stutthof', *Biuletyn Zydowskiego Instytutu Historycznego,* number 63, Warsaw 1967 (lists 26 deportations of Jews into Stutthof between 29 June 1944 and 14 October 1944; and 14 deportations of Jewish men, women and children out of Stutthof between 21 July 1944 and 12 December 1944).

Dr Max Freiherr du Prel, *Das General-Gouvernement,* Würzburg 1942 (preface dated Vienna, 10 March 1942: a 404-page German survey of the General Government, with maps and photographs).

Georges Dunand, *Ne perdez pas leur trace!,* Neuchatel 1951 (the fate of the Jews of Bratislava, by an eye-witness between September and December 1944).

Ralph Durand, *Guernsey under German Rule,* London 1946.

Stanislaw Duszak, *Majdanek,* Lublin 1980.

Helmut Eschwege, 'Resistance of German Jews against the Nazi Regime', *Leo Baeck Institute Year Book* xv, 1970, pages 143-180.

Liliana Picciotto Fargion, *L'occupazione tedesca e gli ebrei di Roma: documenti e fatti,* Milan 1979.

Benjamin B. Ferencz, *Less Than Slaves: Jewish Forced Labor and the Quest for Compensation,* Cambridge Massachusetts, 1979.

M. R. D. Foot, *S.O.E. in France: An Account of the British Special Operations in France 1940-1944,* London 1966.

Josef Fraenkel (editor), *The Jews of Austria, Essays on their Life, History and Destruction,* London 1967.

Philip Friedman, *Roads to Extinction: Essays on the Holocaust,* New York and Philadelphia 1980 (includes essays on the destruction of the Jews of

Lvov, the Gypsies, and Jewish resistance).

Główna Komisja Badania Zbrodni Hitlerowskich w Polsce, *Obozy hitlerowskie na ziemiach polskich 1939-1945: Informator encyklopedyczny,* Warsaw 1979 (lists 5,877 labour camps, ghettos, concentration camps and other mass murder and atrocity sites with a comprehensive bibliography for each of these localities).

Dr Branko Gostl (and others), editors, Federation of Jewish Communities in Yugoslavia *Spomenica 1919-1969,* Belgrade 1969.

Günter Grass (and others), *Danzig 1939: Treasures of a Destroyed Community,* New York 1980.

Yisrael Gutman, 'The Genesis of Resistance in the Warsaw Ghetto', in *Yad Vashem Studies,* ix, Jerusalem 1973, pages 29-70.

Yisrael Gutman, *The Jews of Warsaw 1939-1943 Ghetto-Underground-Uprising,* Jerusalem 1977 (in Hebrew) (lists the monthly deaths from starvation in Warsaw in 1941 and 1942).

Yisrael Gutman and Efraim Zuroff (editors), *Rescue Attemps During the Holocaust,* Jerusalem 1977 (proceedings of the second Yad Vashem International Historical Conference, Jerusalem, 8-11 April 1974).

Gideon Hausner, *Justice in Jerusalem,* New York 1966 (the Eichmann Trial, narrative and extracts from evidence).

Heinz Heger, *The Men with the Pink Triangle,* London 1980 (memoirs of a homosexual at Sachsenhausen and Flossenbürg, with an historical introduction by David Fernbach).

Celia S. Heller, *On the Edge of Destruction: Jews of Poland Between the Two World Wars,* New York 1977 (map 12).

I. Heller and Z. Vajda, *The Synagogues in Hungary,* New York 1968.

Raul Hilberg, *The Destruction of the European Jews,* Chicago 1961 (New Viewpoints edition, New York 1973).

Raul Hilberg (editor), *Documents of Destruction, Germany and Jewry 1933-1945,* London 1972.

Sir John Hope-Simpson, *The Refugee Problem: Report of a Survey,* London 1939.

International Committee of the Red Cross, *Documents relating to the work of the International Committee of the Red Cross for the benefit of civilian detainees in German Concentration Camps between 1939 and 1945,* Geneva 1965 (contains an eye-witness account of the evacuations from Ravensbrück and Sachsenhausen in April 1945) (map 295).

Jewish Black Book Committe, *The Black Book: the Nazi Crime Against the Jewish People,* New York, 1946 (a Soviet source for German war crimes against Jews and others).

Albert Kalme, *Total Terror: An Exposé of Genocide in the Baltics,* New York 1951.

Abraham I. Katsh (editor and translator), *The Warsaw Diary of Chaim A. Kaplan,* New York 1965.

Robert Katz, *Death in Rome,* London 1967 (the Ardeatine caves massacre of 24 March 1944) (map 233).

Yitzhak Katznelson, *Vittel Diary (22.5.43-16.9.43),* Kibbutz Lohamei Haghettaot, Israel 1972 (map 231).

Donald Kenrick and Gratton Puxon, *The Destiny of Europe's Gypsies,* London 1972 (map 182).

Joseph Kermish, 'The Warsaw Ghetto Uprising in the Light of a hitherto Unpublished Official German Report', in *Yad Vashem Studies,* ix, Jerusalem 1973, pages 7-27.

Serge Klarsfeld, *Additif au Mémorial de la Déportation des Juifs de France,* Paris 1981.

Serge Klarsfeld, *Le Mémorial de la Déportation des Juifs de France,* Paris 1978 (lists dates of each deportation from France, executions in France, and the names of all deportees and others killed) (see in particular maps 51, 113, 114, 136, 148 to 150, 155, 159, 169 to 172, 243 to 147, 153 and 263 to 266).

David Knout, *Contribution à l'histoire de la Résistance Juive en France 1940-1944,* Paris 1947.

Edward Kossoy, *Handbuch zum Entschädigungsverfahren,* Munich 1958 (details of camp numbers and regional origin of deportees at Auschwitz, Dachau and elsewhere; a note of Jewish names in all European languages, and the date of all Jewish holy days during the war; also Displaced Persons camps, reparations, and emigrant ships to Palestine).

Yehezkiel Korn, *Jewish Agricultural Settlement in the Crimea, 1922-1947,* Jerusalem 1973 (in Hebrew) (map 102).

Shmuel Krakowski, 'The Fate of Jewish Prisoners of War in the September 1939 Campaign' in *Yad Vashem Studies,* volume xii, Jerusalem 1977 (maps 32 and 35).

Shmuel Krakowski, *Jewish Armed Resistance in Poland 1942-1944,* Jerusalem 1977 (in Hebrew).

David Kranzler, *Japanese, Nazis and Jews: the Jewish Refugee Community of Shanghai, 1938-1945,* New York 1976 (map 16).

Kriegstagebuch des Oberkommandos der Wehrmacht, 4 volumes, Frankfurt-am-Main, 1965 (dates on which the German army captured, and then lost, towns and territory: volume 1, 1 August 1940 to 31 December 1941; volume 2, 1942; volume 3, 1943; volume 4, 1944-45, edited respectively by Hans-Adolf Jacobsen, Andreas Hillgruber, Walther Hubatsch and Percy Ernest Schramm).

Gedalia Lachman, 'The Destruction of Skala', in Max Mermelstein-Weidenfeld (chairman, editorial committee), *Skala,* Tel Aviv 1978.

Isaac Landman (editor), *The Universal Jewish Encyclopaedia,* 10 volumes, New York 1939 (contains details of anti-Jewish violence through eastern Europe during the 1930s) (maps 10 to 12).

Jehuda-Gyula Lang, *A Pápai Zsidóság Emlékkönyve,* Tel Aviv 1973 (lists the villages and names the deportees from Papa and the Papa region) (map 258).

I. M. Lask (editor), *The Kalish Book,* Tel Aviv 1968 (maps 44 and 54).

Evelyn Le Chêne, *Mauthausen: The History of a Death Camp,* London 1971 (maps 300 to 304).

Eugene Levai, *Black Book on the Martyrdom of Hungarian Jewry*, Zurich 1948.

Liberated Jews Arrived in Sweden in 1945, 2 volumes, Malmö 1946 (includes list of Jewish refugees dying in Sweden in 1945, part 1 Czechoslovakians, part 2 Dutchmen, part 3 Hungarians, part 4 Italians, part 5 Poles, part 6 Rumanians, part 7 Stateless formerly Germans, and part 8 Yugoslavs) (map 308).

Liste Alphabetique des Personnes, en majorité Israelites, Deportées Par Les Convois Partis du Camp de Rassemblement de Malines entre le 4 Aout 1942 et le 31 Juillet 1944, 3 volumes, Brussels, 1 July 1954.

Dora Litani, 'The Destruction of the Jews of Odessa in the Light of Rumanian Documents', *Yad Vashem Studies*, vi, Jerusalem 1967, pages 135-154.

Czeslaw Madajczyk (editor), *Zamojszczyzna-Sonderlaboratorium SS*, 2 volumes, Warsaw 1979 (documents on the expulsion and massacre of Poles in the Zamosc province) (map 179).

Ber Mark, *Uprising in the Warsaw Ghetto*, New York 1975 (map 204).

Albert Menasche, *Birkenau (Auschwitz II), Memoirs of an eye-witness, how 72,000 Greek Jews Perished*, New York, 1947.

Sybil Milton (translator and editor), *The Stroop Report: The Jewish Quarter of Warsaw Is No More!* facsimile edition, New York 1979 (map 204).

S. Moldawer, *The Road to Lublin*, New York 1940 (map 37).

Michael Molho, *In Memoriam: Hommage aux Victimes Juives des Nazis en Grèce*, Salonica 1973 (lists numbers of Greek Jews murdered, community by community) (maps 196 and 232).

Werner Nachman and Heinrich Freund, *Sie Sind Nicht Vergessen*, Mannheim, n.d. (the deportation of Jews from the Saar, Baden and the Palantinate to Gurs, in October 1940) (maps 49 and 50).

Donald L. Niewyk, *The Jews in Weimar Germany*, Baton Rouge, Louisiana 1980.

Albert Nirenstein, *A Tower from the Enemy: Contributions to a History of Jewish Resistance in Poland*, New York 1959.

Miram Novitch, *Le Passage des Barbares: Contribution à l'Histoire de la Déportation et de la Résistance des Juifs Grècs*, Nice, n.d.

Miriam Novitch (editor), *Sobibor: Martyrdom and Revolt, Documents and Testimonies*, New York 1980 (map 222).

Miklos Nyiszli, *Auschwitz: A Doctor's Eye-witness Account*, New York 1960.

Opinia, Warsaw, 25 July 1946, page 7 (lists those killed in the Kielce pogrom).

Wila Orbach, 'The Destruction of the Jews in the Nazi-Occupied Territories of the USSR', in *Soviet Jewish Affairs*, volume 6, no. 2, 1976 (lists localities with Jewish death tolls).

Nissan Oren, 'The Bulgarian Exception: a Reassessment of the Salvation of the Jewish Community', in *Yad Vashem Studies*, vii, Jerusalem 1968, pages 83-106 (map 197).

Papers Concerning the Treatment of German Nationals in Germany, Command Paper 6120 of 1939, Germany No. 2 of 1939, London 1939 (treatment of German Jews in German concentration camps, 1933-1939).

Edmond Paris, *Genocide in Satellite Croatia: A Record of Racial and Religious Persecution*, Chicago 1961.

Robert O. Paxton, *Vichy France: Old guard and New Order, 1940-1944*, London 1972.

Stanislaw Piotrowski, *Hans Frank's Diary*, Warsaw 1961.

Republic of Poland, Ministry of Foreign Affairs *The German Occupation of Poland, Extract of Note addressed to the Governments of the Allied and Neutral Powers on May 3, 1941*, London 1941.

Polish Ministry of Information, *The German New Order In Poland*, London 1942.

Walter Poller, *Medical Block, Buchenwald: the Personal Testimony of Inmate 996, Block 36*, London 1961.

Bernard Postal and Samuel H. Abramson, *The Traveler's Guide to Jewish Landmarks of Europe*, New York 1971.

Werner Präg and Wolfgang Jacobmeyer (editors), *Das Diensttagebuch des deutschen Generalgouverneurs in Polen, 1939-1945*, Stuttgart 1975 (contains Hans Frank's speeches to his officials on ridding the General Government of Jews).

Miklós Radnóti, *The Witness* (selected poems, translated from the Hungarian by Thomas Orszag-Land), London 1977 (map 271).

Leyzer Ran (editor), *Jerusalem of Lithuania Illustrated and Documented*, 3 volumes, New York 1974 (the story of the Jews of Vilna through photographs).

Jacques Ravine, *La Résistance Organisée des Juifs en France 1940-1944*, Paris 1973.

Gerald Reitlinger, *The Final Solution: The Attempt to Exterminate the Jews of Europe 1939-1945*, London 1953.

Eugen Rosenfeldt, *Tuttlingen*, Tuttlingen 1947 (maps 296 and 297).

Herbert Rosenkranz, *Verfolgung und Selbstbehauptung Die Juden in Österreich 1938-1945*, Vienna 1978 (details of all emigration and deportations from Austria).

Ryszard Rosin (editor), *Zbrodnie Hitlerowskie w Lodzi i Województwie Lódzkim*, Lodz 1942 (Nazi crimes in Lodz and the Lodz region).

Henryk Ross, *The Last Journey of the Jews of Lodz Litzmannstadt*, Tel Aviv 1950.

Livia Rothkirchen, *The Destruction of Slovak Jewry: A Documentary History*, Jerusalem 1961.

Royal Institute of International Affairs, *Chronology of the Second World War*, London 1947.

Yitskhok Rudashevski, *The Diary of the Vilna Ghetto, June 1941-April 1943*, Tel Aviv 1973 (map 202).

A. Rutkowski, 'Zaglada Zydow w dystrykcie radomskim', *Biuletyn Zydowskiego Instytutu Historycznego*, number 15, Warsaw 1955 (13 statistical tables of the ghettoization, deportation and destruction in the Radom district, including the cities of Radom and Kielce, between 1939 and 1945).

Ernst Schäfer (editor), *Ravensbrück,* Berlin 1960

Rabbi Israel Schepansky, *Holocaust Calendar of Polish Jewry,* New York, July 1974 (in Hebrew).

Gertrude Schneider, *Journey Into Terror: Story of the Riga Ghetto,* New York 1979.

A. J. Sherman, *Island Refuge: Britain and Refugees from the Third Reich 1933-1939,* London 1973 (map 15).

Dušan Sindik (editor), *Secanja Jevreja na Logor Jasenovac,* Belgrade 1972 (memoirs of Jews in the Jasenovac camp).

Derrick Sington, *Belsen Uncovered,* London 1946 (map 294).

Tadeusz Skutnik, *Stutthof: Informator historyczny,* Gdansk 1979

George H. Stein, *The Waffen S.S., Hitler's Elite Guard at War 1939-1945,* London 1966

Zosa Szajkowski, *Analytical Franco-Jewish Gazetteer 1939-1945,* New York 1966.

Zosa Szajkowski, *Jews, Wars and Communism,* 2 volumes, New York 1972 and 1974.

Zvi Szner (editor) *Extermination and Resistance: Historical Records and Source Material,* volume 1, Kibbutz Lohamei Haghettaot, Israel 1958.

Arieh Tartakower and Kurt R. Grossman, *The Jewish Refugee,* New York 1944 (maps 15 and 16).

Totenbuch Theresienstadt, Vienna 1971, volume 1, 'Deportierte Aus Osterreich' (lists 50 deportations into Theresienstadt between 21 June 1942 and 15 April 1945, and 66 deportations out of Theresienstadt, with numbers and destinations between 9 January 1942 and 28 October 1944).

Michael Tregenza, 'Belzec Death Camp', in *The Wiener Library Bulletin,* 1977, volume xxx,

pages 8-25.

Germaine Tillion, *Ravensbrück,* Garden City, New York, 1975.

Max Ungar (printer), *Mauthausen 8.8.1939-5.5.1945,* Vienna n.d.

Dr A. Ungerer (editor), *Verzeichnis von Ghettos, Zwangsarbeitslagern, und Konzentrationslagern,* Munich 1953 (lists date of establishment of ghettos in Poland and also expulsions, labour camps and concentration camps).

Zorach Warhaftig, *Uprooted: Jewish Refugees and Displaced Persons After Liberation,* New York, November 1946 (maps 312 and 315).

Leon Weliczker Wells, *The Janowska Road,* New York 1963 (maps 222 and 223).

Janusz Wieczorek (editor), *Scenes of Fighting and Martyrdom Guide: War Years in Poland, 1939-1945,* Warsaw 1968 (town-by-town and locality-by-locality notes of monuments to Nazi atrocities in Poland, post-1945 boundaries).

Mary H. Williams (editor), *Chronology 1941-1945,* United States Army in World War II, Special Studies, Washington 1960.

Leni Yahil, *The Rescue of Danish Jewry,* Philadelphia 1969 (map 213).

The Yellow Spot, the outlawing of half a million human beings, London 1936 (documents on anti-Jewish measures in Germany between 1933 and 1935, introduction by the Bishop of Durham dated 12 February 1936) (map 6).

Yitzhak Zuckerman, 'The Jewish Fighting Organization — Z.O.B. — its Establishment and Activites', written in Warsaw in March 1944, published in Yisrael Gutman and Livia Rothkirchen (editors), *The Catastrophe of European Jewry,* Jerusalem 1976, pages 518-548 (map 131).

Index